ABOUT THE AUTHOR

Mike Swinson is an Australian who grew up on a mixed sheep, wheat, wool and cattle farm in central west New South Wales (NSW). That old saying, 'You can take the boy out of the bush, but you can't take the bush out of the boy' applies to Mike. He left the bush life that he loved and moved into radio and television broadcasting, joining first the Australian Broadcasting's Corporations (ABC) Rural Department, then moving into television current affairs, TV documentaries, TV gardening and TV news.

His work has been recognised with a number of state, national and international awards, including winning the 'Golden Ear' award at the 12th annual International Agricultural Film Festival in Berlin in 1982, then with journalisms highest level of recognition, a Walkley Award in 1996 for 'Best Coverage of a Current Event,' with 'Lynn's Story,' a harrowing account of the aftermath of the Port Arthur Massacre. This was followed by an ATOM (Australian Teachers of Media) award in 2011 for a power industry documentary, 'Back to Basics.'

Living in Hobart since 1978, home has always been a large 'bush block,' a throwback to Mike's early days growing up in the western districts of NSW and not wanting to feel 'hemmed in' by suburbia. Mike has run his business, Corporate Image Matters since leaving the secure folds of the ABC in 2001. He is a magazine editor, a crisis management consultant to the aged care industry and still dabbles in an old fashioned way in the art of video production. He can now add fully fledged author to this list.

Opposite: Painting of Muir's Boatyard by Paul Hurd.

BLOOD, SWEAT & THE SEA

PREFACE

You may well ask the question, "How did you come to write this book?" I have asked myself that same question many times over. I was approached by John Muir, who I knew from my days as a TV news and current affairs reporter and presenter with the Australian Broadcasting Corporation (ABC). He'd spoken to someone who knew me and said, "Try Mike."

I knew John's reputation as a 'hard driving man,' someone who I had heard on my grapevine was, focussed and successful. As a current affairs journalist one doesn't often get to produce TV stories about people like John, more usually it's the flotsam and jetsam of our society that attract our attention. The 'have-nots' or the 'have-too-much and got it illegally or unethically,' or those who have not been treated fairly by our political or economic system.

Now my time as the author of this remarkable story is coming to a close, I can reflect on the John Muir I now know. He is undoubtedly a 'hard man.' He has driven himself and others relentlessly over the decades, with a remarkable level of commitment from his employees and a team of people scattered all over the globe to achieve the goals he has set, sometimes with what seem impossible deadlines attached. Yet as you will discover as you read on he can be as soft as a kitten.

He can be what Australians call 'a tough bugger,' (in Australian slang it is a term of endearment) but that's not surprising given that he grew up in the rough and tumble streets of Battery Point in Hobart, learning to look after himself as he fought and played hard.

John kept playing it hard throughout his amazing career, as he built Muir Engineering from a small business in a steel shed next to his Dad's Battery Point boatyard to the internationally successful marine export business it is today.

It is a remarkable story and one that I have loved writing, even though at times I have been heard to curse the name John Muir because he has changed something again, or set another deadline. Like those who have stood the test of John Muir's relentless drive before me, I have worked like the blazes to meet his demands, hopefully with success.

I want to take this opportunity to thank and acknowledge a few people.

John for his patience, eye for detail, support and for his extraordinary capacity to remember technical details and specifications, dates, times, events and people from decades past. John's wife Wendy, for talking openly to me in our first interview, giving me a deep insight into the way her husband works and into the way she thinks.

Georgie Pajak for her frankness, support, encouragement and for being a great sounding board when I needed one. It is Georgie who, more than anyone, is responsible for the book concept and its design layout. Over an eighteen month period she compiled more than seven hundred pages of information, including almost one hundred interviews, some short, many long. She spent many hours on the phone, nationally and internationally, and has not only sorted and catalogued hundreds of family and archival images, but has taken many of those herself.

It is Georgie who can take the credit for this unique publication's wonderful 'look and feel.'

Phil Muir, John's first cousin, for his eagle eye, his Muir passion, his tireless search for historical family details and his IT skills. Phil spent several months scanning and documenting over a thousand images, and has made himself available, often at short notice, as a part of the production team, always there with a smile, a word of encouragement and the offer of a helping hand.

In the hectic weeks prior to the book going to the printers, Phil undertook the thankless task of another proof reading before Georgie inserted images and finalised design and layout.

I also want to acknowledge the dozens and dozens of people who have provided endless anecdotes, stories and images that give this book a heart and soul. Without their openness, frankness and willingness to share it would have been an uphill journey.

Finally I want to thank fellow author Nicole Mays (a former Tasmanian) for her unique role as the editorial consultant. It was Nicole who kept me on track, picking up missing facts, identifying sections that needed more detailed historical background or suggesting where my sentence construction, rough at the best of times, could be improved. I cannot believe how productive Nicole is. We would email a draft chapter to her and within a few hours it was back, with dozens of amendments or suggested improvements. She is a marvel and an historical researcher extraordinaire. I look forward to reading her next book, part two of the story of the Boat Builders of Battery Point.

Phil, Nicole and Georgie, I could not have managed to complete this book without you. Thank you from the bottom of my heart.

This book is chock a block with stories of courage, of determination and of survival against the odds. I think it's a 'good read,' but I'm biased. I hope you enjoy reading it as much as I have enjoyed writing it.

MIKE SWINSON

October 2016

FOREWORD

by

ROBERT CLIFFORD, AO

Battery Point boys don't cry.

When the bailiffs knocked on our Battery Point door one day in 1979, Kerry was not amused to say the least when the burly gentlemen wanted to know who owned the fridge.

John Muir, or at least his bookkeeper, had sent the bailiffs in to collect. Did we owe Muirs money? Yes, but I was not a happy customer. The shaft and stern bearings of my second catamaran were not up to my exacting standards, the bearing was so tight that the shaft would not revolve, even with the help of a long lever… and besides I was skint. My international customer George Galanopolis had let me down, his deposit cheque had bounced, and times were tough.

I made sure that John's invoice never even got into the payment hat for a month or two because of that but eventually we settled. We still do business with one another. The marine business is a tough one. It is little wonder that Battery Point boys over the centuries have prospered in good times and bad. John and Wendy have built up a strong business over the years, and produced products of high quality for the global market. They are a hell of a lot better now than those original shaft and stern bearings were, in fact I know Muir Engineering have gone on to establish a global reputation as one of, if not the, best in the business.

Like John I was born in Hampden Road, Battery Point and lived in King Street. King Street on the southern side of the Sandy Bay/Battery Point Rivulet is strictly speaking not Battery Point, those of us on the southern side: the Onns, the Randalls and Cliffords, were always slightly at odds with the Battery Point clique and that included the Muirs.

I had my first job in the school holidays rigging cradles to slip boats for "Sharky" Taylor next door to Muir's. I was privileged to meet and work with many of the characters of Battery Point. Perc Coverdale, "Chooky" Newman, the Purdons, the Burnetts, the Creeses and of course the Muirs. How fortunate us lads were to have such splendid teachers. We learned our marine trades, but more importantly we learned how to conduct our businesses on an international level. It was a school of hard knocks, where you learnt to pick yourself up after being knocked down and get on with life, learning hard lessons on the way.

How was this achieved from the isolation of Battery Point Tasmania? What is it about Battery Point that allowed the local lads to take on the maritime world? I suggest the Sydney to Hobart race has a lot to do with it. This iconic race has made it possible for many a local sailor to travel the world visiting and working in the global marine industry. They have done it well too. The reputation of Hobart sailors is second to none. This in turn has given the general marine industry of Tasmania a huge leg up. Everyone in the marine industry knows where Tasmania is, where Hobart is, and of course where Battery Point is.

John and Wendy are to be congratulated on their endeavours. Wendy and the other girls of Battery Point have more than played their part. Kerry tells me that as a small girl, she and her friends and sisters often baited Ma Dwyer, who chased them up the road. Battery Point has some stories to tell.

The quality of Tasmanian marine products is second to none. There are a lot, as you will discover as you follow the fascinating journey of John Muir, his family, employees, and the vast range of individuals he got to know and work with from around Tasmania, mainland Australia and the world.

I still (despite the visit of the burly gentleman enquiring after the ownership of our fridge) have great pleasure in specifying Muir winches on Incat new builds.

If I may be so bold to use an appropriate quote from one of my favourite authors, a much admired Australian author and poet, CJ Dennis, from his poem 'Work, a Reflection':

> **"** *For it's – Graft – Toil – It's work,*
> *It's performance that is needed in the land,*
> *Recognition by the student,*
> *Of the principle is prudent,*
> *But it never yet has shifted any sand.*
> *And hell is full of futile folk who scorned the verb 'to do,'*
> *Who 'recognised the principle,' but failed to follow through.* **"**

Not John Muir, not on yer nelly mate!

BOB CLIFFORD, AO.

ABBREVIATIONS, ACRONYMS

and

SYMBOLS

%	Percent
ABC	Australian Broadcasting Corporation
AC	Alternating Current
AIMEX	Australian International Marine Export Group
AUD	Australian Dollar
BBC	British Broadcasting Corporation
BOM	Bureau of Meteorology
CAD	Computer Aided Design
katabatic	A wind produced by the flow of cold dense air down a slope
cc	Cubic centimetre
CEO	Chief Executive Officer
CIMA	Compagnia Italiana Magneti Accessori
CSIRO	Commonwealth Scientific and Industrial Research Organisation
CNC	Computer Numeric Control (computer-controlled manufacturing machines)
DC	Direct Current
ft	Foot
GDP	Gross Domestic Product
GFC	Global Financial Crisis
GRP	Glass Reinforced Plastic (fibreglass)
GRT	Gross Register Tonnage (a meure of a ship's total internal volume)
hp	Horsepower

IMO	International Maritime Organisation
IMTEC	International Marine Trades Exhibit and Conference
Incat	International Catamarans
kg	Kilogram
km	Kilometres
km/hr	Kilometres per hour
kt	Knot
kW	Kilowatt
lb	Pound
m	Metre
METS	Marine Equipment Trade Show
mm	Millimetre
OECD	Organisation for Economic Co-operation and Development
QC	Queen's Counsel
RDM	Richardson Devine Marine
SCFC	Sullivans Cove Ferry Company
t	Metric tonne
TAHO	Tasmanian Archive and Heritage Office
UK	United Kingdom
US	United States
USA	United States of America
USSR	Union of Soviet Socialist Republics

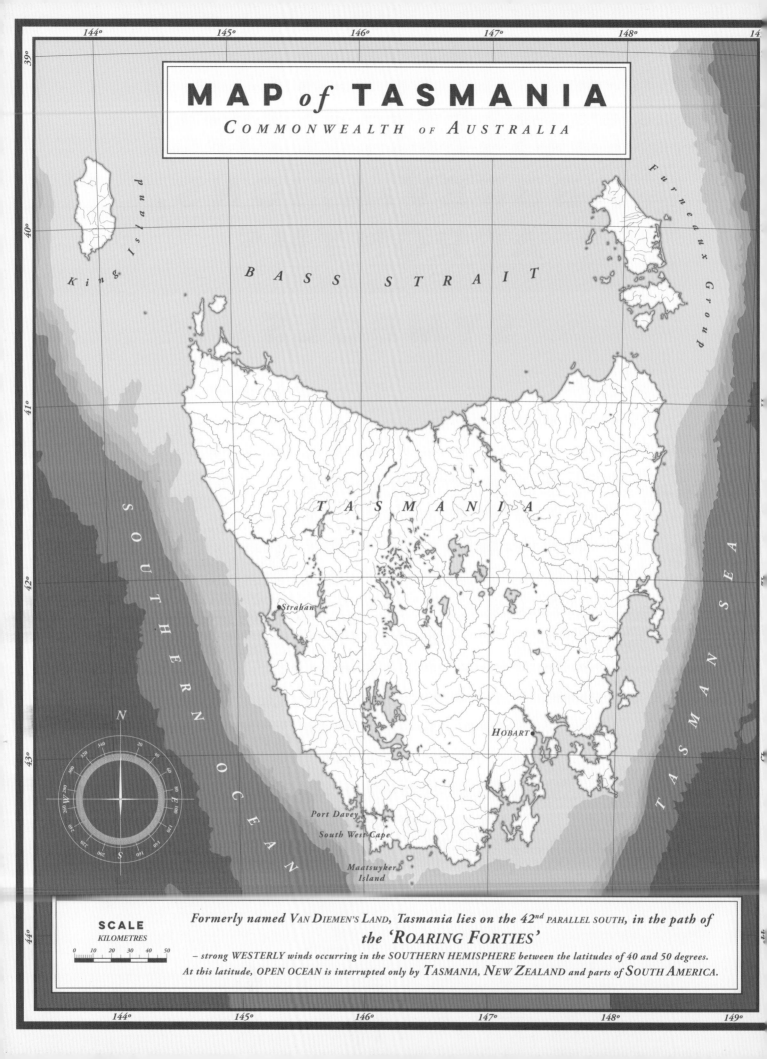

MAP *of* TASMANIA

COMMONWEALTH OF AUSTRALIA

King Island

Furneaux Group

BASS STRAIT

SOUTHERN OCEAN

T A S M A N I A

TASMAN SEA

•Strahan

HOBART •

N

Port Davey

South West Cape

Maatsuyker
Island

Formerly named VAN DIEMEN'S LAND, *Tasmania lies on the* 42ND PARALLEL SOUTH, *in the path of*
the 'ROARING FORTIES'
– strong WESTERLY *winds occurring in the* SOUTHERN HEMISPHERE *between the latitudes of 40 and 50 degrees.*
At this latitude, OPEN OCEAN *is interrupted only by* TASMANIA, NEW ZEALAND *and parts of* SOUTH AMERICA.

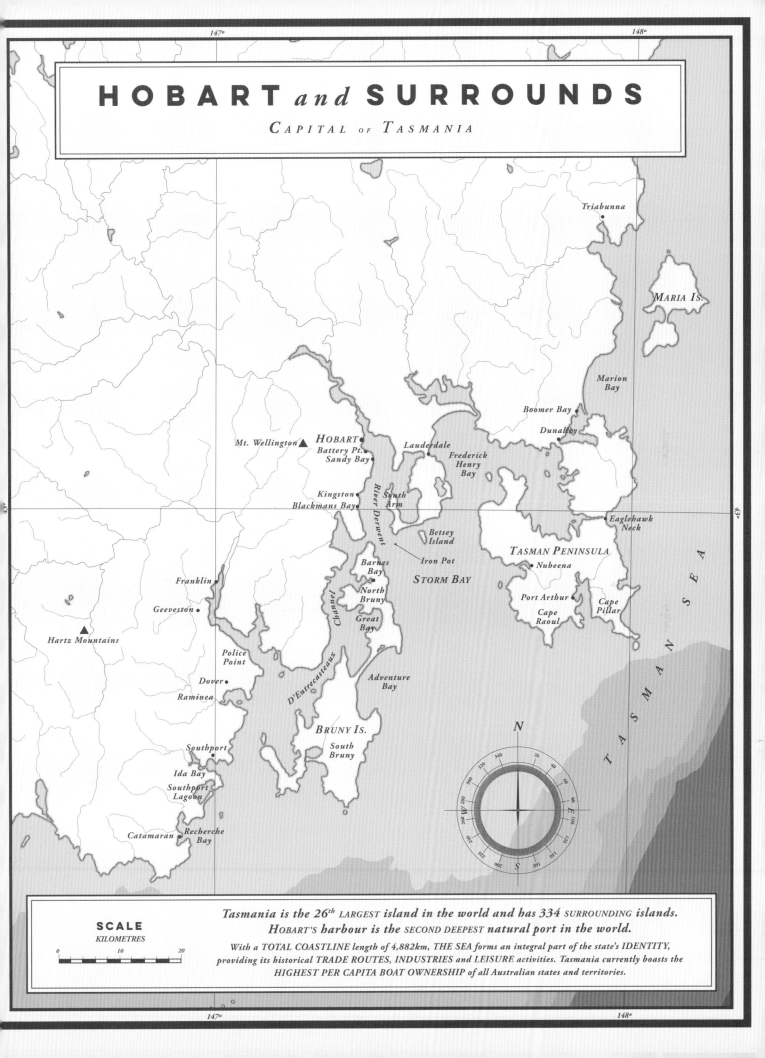

HOBART *and* SURROUNDS

CAPITAL OF TASMANIA

Triabunna

MARIA IS:

Marion Bay

Boomer Bay

Dunalley

Mt. Wellington ▲ HOBART
Battery Pt.
Sandy Bay

Lauderdale

Frederick
Henry
Bay

Kingston
Blackmans Bay

South
Arm

River Derwent

Betsey
Island

Iron Pot

Eaglehawk
Neck

TASMAN PENINSULA

Barnes
Bay

Nubeena

Franklin

Channel

North
Bruny

STORM BAY

Port Arthur

Cape
Pillar

Geeveston

Great
Bay

Cape
Raoul

Hartz Mountains ▲

Police
Point

D'Entrecasteaux

Adventure
Bay

Dover

Raminea

BRUNY IS.

South
Bruny

N

Southport

Ida Bay
Southport
Lagoon

Catamaran

Recherche
Bay

TASMAN SEA

SCALE
KILOMETRES

0   10   20

Tasmania is the 26th LARGEST island in the world and has 334 SURROUNDING islands.
HOBART'S *harbour is the* SECOND DEEPEST *natural port in the world.*

With a TOTAL COASTLINE *length of 4,882km,* THE SEA *forms an integral part of the state's* IDENTITY,
providing its historical TRADE ROUTES, INDUSTRIES *and* LEISURE *activities. Tasmania currently boasts the*
HIGHEST PER CAPITA BOAT OWNERSHIP *of all Australian states and territories.*

CONTENTS

13   INTRODUCTION

19   THE MUIR MARITIME LEGACY

41   RITES OF PASSAGE

73   INTO THE WORKFORCE

83   THE BUSINESS BEGINS

91   THE START OF SOMETHING NEW

107   BOAT SHOWS AND THE MOVE TO KINGSTON

135   THE WORLD IS OUR OYSTER IN THE EIGHTIES

165   STORM GATHERS AND BREAKS

193   SURFING INTO THE NINETIES

229   THE NINETIES ROLL ON

253   TASMANIA THE POWERHOUSE

279   THE MEGAYACHT MILLENNIUM

309   SURVIVING THE GLOBAL SUPERSTORM

337   THE MODERN MUIR FAMILY

375   HERE FOR THE LONG HAUL

APPENDIX

399   THE MUIR FAMILY TREE

401   MAX MUIR AND FAMILY

407   ARNOLD AND MICHAEL WHITE

411   **INDEX**

INTRODUCTION

This is the biography of a remarkable man, a Tasmanian. A man who started from scratch, defied the odds and built an internationally successful business in spite of the obstacles. He is a former diesel fitter who turned his hand to designing and manufacturing some of the world's best anchoring and mooring systems. To achieve this success, given he was already experienced with boat building and propulsion, he studied the marine engineering trade, employed the best tradesmen and sourced material locally.

Robert John Muir (known by all as John) wasn't destined to be just another small time Australian manufacturer, he was destined for greatness in this globally competitive world. He learnt his trade, started small and slowly built to take on the world's best. He took them on in their own backyards, in the United Kingdom (UK), Europe, the United States of America (USA) and Asia, and slowly, year by year, he beat them at their own game.

Even more remarkably, he did it from the bottom of a little known island called Tasmania, its gale lashed shores lying in the midst of the Roaring Forties. An island that sits on the southern extremity of the Australian continent.

David McQueen, a megayacht boat builder who has been in the industry since he was 16 years old, described John's business location and achievements this way:

> *"This remarkable equipment has come out of a little place called Tasmania, which half the world doesn't even know exists; out of a place called Kingston, which people definitely don't know of; and it's sold by these funny Tasmanians who are dogmatic, passionate, and brilliant at what they do. They're the ultimate product."*

For those men and women who choose to go to sea, winches, anchor systems and the right ground tackle are the difference between life and death. John Muir had the foresight, a dream to build the perfect winch. He did, and as the business grew so did the size and capacity of his winches. Today many seafarers across the globe owe their lives to John's commitment to creating perfection.

It was in December 1996 and the 56 metre (m) three masted schooner *Adix*, one of the largest sailing yachts in the world, fitted with Muir windlasses and capstans (anchor equipment) was cruising in the Chilean Archipelago at latitude 54 degrees south. The schooner had been on an extensive cruise throughout the Pacific, up towards Alaska, south to San Francisco, then south again, as the plan was to cruise down to the Antarctic Peninsula. So far the weather had been relatively kind, storms for sure but in the open ocean that's what this schooner was designed to handle with ease.

What the skipper, Tasmanian-born Paul Goss, didn't know was that ahead lay the greatest test the yacht's design and its anchoring gear had ever faced. Thankfully it passed the test, because otherwise many of those on board could have perished.

Paul Goss: "Around Christmas Day we found ourselves anchored in a picturesque bay somewhere at the eastern end of Cockburn Strait at around 54 degrees south. In relative terms, that's about 960 kilometres south of Hobart.

Paul Goss: "The anchorage was virtually land-locked with a narrow entrance, outside of which was a tight and complicated waterway where every stony wall has the potential to be a lee shore. (A lee shore lies on the leeward, or downwind side of a ship and onto which a ship could be wrecked in foul weather.) This is typical of the area, and although conventional wisdom says 'cut and run' for sea room if the anchorage becomes threatening, that logic did not really apply to the situation we found ourselves in. In any case, this particular night we decided to swing to the anchor as the weather looked settled and quiet.

"However, by nightfall, the wind banged in quickly, and by midnight it came out of the darkness with great force. It is always a katabatic wind with no settled direction due to the rocky, mountainous terrain, and although we anchored with a lot of scope, we were now at its mercy with no room to escape.

"It would be imprudent to cast two anchors without at least a stern line, as the possibility of twisted chains doesn't bear thinking about, so in this case

> *This is isolated terrain, no-one lives anywhere near here. There are no Coast Guard boats to rescue you if it all goes belly up, they were on their own.*

"Although we had heard all the stories about the weather, it is hard to be prepared for the ferocity of it until you are actually there. Common practice for smaller boats is to tuck into a corner and run long lines ashore from each corner of the vessel, but this is not always practical for a 400 tonne schooner with a lot of windage, when exposed beam-to. Either way, the key is to be prepared.

"Although summer time is the right time to be there, the weather is more volatile because the depressions moving through are compressed by the summer highs to the north. Consequently, it can change very quickly. What is a still, attractive bay on arrival, can very quickly transform into a spume blown cauldron."

The anchorage they chose was beautiful, the water was calm, the scenery stunning and you think that "God's in his heaven and all's right with the world," but not so. God, or someone, had a surprise in store for them all!

we dropped the port anchor and gave her plenty of chain. By the early hours, we had 380 kilograms of anchor on the bottom, and had veered six shackles (165 metres) of 26mm stud-link chain, weighing 2,475kg, with virtually nothing left in the locker."

All this in the dead of night with no idea of whether or not they were being blown closer and closer to the rocky shore. This is isolated terrain, no-one lives anywhere near here. There are no Coast Guard boats to rescue you if it all goes belly up, they were on their own.

Paul Goss: "We will never know if the anchor was in sand or not, but it was a very rocky bottom, and it was probably a combination of this and the right ground tackle that kept us secure that wild night. With no constant wind strength and direction, the heavy moisture-laden gusts were coming from different quarters, and the boat would accelerate away until the chain took up and arrested her motion. We stood watch all night of course, but there was really nothing

SAILING YACHT *ADIX*

*Top: SY **Adix** on the River Derwent, during its 1997 visit to Hobart. Above left: The VRC15000 anchor winches produced by Muir from aluminium-bronze, designed to develop a patina with age in keeping with the style of the yacht. Above right: The **Adix** logo, designed by Paul Goss (formerly a graphic designer) used on the capstans.*

we could do except hang on and bear it. When the chain came up hard, it would pull you off your feet if you weren't prepared for the sudden snatch of the cable. All night she yawed, juddered and snatched at her anchor, while the noise of the chain over the rocks meant no rest for the off-watch.

"By 0830 hours the next morning there was not a breath of wind in the cove. We set about hauling the chain and, miraculously, it came aboard in one piece and undamaged. We marveled at the bright spots of raw metal covering the chain where it had been scoured by the rocks, stark evidence of the torture the cable endured all night long.

"In thirty five years at sea as a professional, the experience of that night remains as the greatest endorsement of good gear. Our Muir capstans and windlasses have served us well over the years, and will continue to do so for a long time to come. Give me plenty of good chain and the right gear to handle it, every time."

Those windlasses and chain stoppers that quite possibly saved Paul Goss's life, and the lives of his passengers and crew, came from the engineering business of John Muir, a business that started in a steel shed next door to his father's boatyard and slipway at Battery Point in Hobart, Tasmania.

The standard of perfection that John set, from the very beginning was driven by sage advice from his internationally famous boat builder and designer father, Jock Muir.

"When you design and build an anchor winch, make sure that it's over engineered and no part of it can fail, even under the most

66 *In thirty five years at sea as a professional, the experience of that night remains as the greatest endorsement of good gear. Our Muir capstans and windlasses have served us well over the years, and will continue to do so for a long time to come. Give me plenty of good chain and the right gear to handle it, every time.* 99

– PAUL GOSS, CAPTAIN, SY *ADIX*

JOCK MUIR

Above: John's father, Ernest Jack 'Jock' Muir, was a legendary Tasmanian boat designer and builder, having designed, built and raced many Sydney to Hobart Yacht Race winners.

OLD ACQUAINTANCES

*Paul Goss and Max Muir onboard John's yacht **Shonandra** in 1991.*

arduous of sea conditions. Make sure the winch cannot fail. Build the winch stronger than the foredeck on which it sits, so if anything fails it is the foredeck, not the winch."

John's focus, drive and sheer bloody minded determination built the business from that steel shed into one of the world's best, exporting its maritime gear to boat and yacht builders around the world. He succeeded against all the odds, Muir's anchor and mooring winches continue to be sought after by the makers of super yachts, pleasure cruisers, commercial and fast ferries, defence and patrol boats and other work boats from around the world.

That 'bloody minded determination' and 'never say die till you get the order' attitude came at a cost to John's health, when he nearly died on a sales trip to North America. There was also a cost to his family

and some close work associates. It is this remarkable personal journey that we explore in this biography. The events and the people that influenced John as he grew up, began and built the business, travelled endlessly across the globe, mostly on his own, refusing to accept defeat when confronted by European boat builders who wondered who was this bloke from an island most had never heard of. Why should they buy his anchor and mooring winches for their rich and privileged clients who demanded the best of everything? Eventually they did, and most still do.

This biography is a mix of anecdotes and insights into the remarkable and unique personal life journey of John Muir, his family, friends and business associates, as well as the amazing success story and business history of Muir Engineering which he began in 1968. It is a fascinating journey.

I admire John Muir's business acumen, have ever since I first met him when working for the ABC's news and current affairs programs. Yet while I admire John and his achievements, I don't envy him at all. However I am intrigued to discover why he drove himself the way he did and still does. Why he behaves the way he does. How he does business and mixes with the owners and managers of large and small shipyards, building sailing yachts and power boats, work boats and fast ferries, to the people who design and build megayachts and motor yachts and takes it all in his stride.

Singer and songwriter Bob Dylan once said, "A man is a success if he gets up in the morning and goes to bed at night and in between does what he wants to do." By Bob Dylan's definition, John Muir is a roaring success!

horseback on large and small pastoral stations in the Australian outback. A dog that is courageous, tireless, robust, compact, agile, well-muscled, powerful and determined! All adjectives that also describe John. These are not dogs to lie around the living room all day or live happily in the backyard with only a 15 minute walk to keep them happy. These are dogs that never give up, never let go, are fearless, loyal, and full of energy and punch, just like John Muir.

I'm not sure just how in touch with their inner self people like John Muir are, it's not a criticism, it's just an observation. To meet him socially you would not notice anything unusual, but there are strong external forces at work that have moulded this man. John is from a seafaring and boat building family, growing up on an island that according to experts can seriously influence who you

> *Singer and songwriter Bob Dylan once said, "A man is a success if he gets up in the morning and goes to bed at night and in between does what he wants to do." By Bob Dylan's definition, John Muir is a roaring success!*

The key to this story is not only 'the why' but also 'the how' and 'who else'; these were pivotal in the journey of John Muir. Georgie Pajak, the book's tireless researcher and talented graphic artist, and I have both discovered that getting some people to open up, to share emotions and the intricacies of life's remarkable journey is difficult. Nigh on impossible with some. It has been made all the more fascinating however by our slow process of discovering how to deal with John, his demands, day and night. His passion for the business, his obstinance, his ego, his drive, his need for control, of knowing what is or isn't going on and if it isn't, why not! When will it be fixed? When will the project meet its timelines? This is the real John Muir at work, this is how he got to where he did, a driven man, with a desperate need to know what is going on, at every stage of the process. It is an insight into a man who Australians describe as 'like a bloody Blue Heeler.'

For those who have never heard of this unique Australian working dog, a Blue Heeler is a breed of cattle dog, renowned for its ability to control mobs of cattle, to nip the heels of wild bullocks and bring them back to the mob, working closely with men and women on

are, who you become in this world. As a boy, growing up near the rough and tumble boatyards of Battery Point John Muir learnt 'the law of the jungle' from an early age, battling his younger brothers, the bigger and older boys of his suburb, and school, the elements of wind and water and eventually the shipyards of the world. The man became the business and the business is certainly the man.

John Muir built his global business from scratch. For 44 years Muir Engineering was at the very core of who he was as a human being, who he was as a man and a businessman. Then in 2012 he stepped down as Managing Director and sold a controlling share of the business to a private equity company. Today, John is still that same man who built the business even though he is now moving onto other things.

THE MUIR
MARITIME LEGACY

The Muirs are of Scottish descent and have links to family members scattered across the globe. The Scots themselves are a socially defined ethnic group of people, drawn mainly from the Picts and the Gaels. Fiercely independent, they were regarded as true warriors in their day. There is undoubtedly some of that warrior mentality embedded in the genes of John Muir.

In the 1800s thousands of Scots left their homes, most migrating to Canada, the USA and Australia. The story of the Muir family's journey across the world to Australia is twofold: one by choice, free settlers searching for a new and better life. The other involuntary, a journey in convict shackles, chains, mainly confined to the ships' holds for the duration of the voyage, coping with the most extraordinary hardships.

The first Muir to arrive as a free settler was John's great grandfather, William Jenkins Muir. He arrived in Sydney onboard the 1,524 tonne (t) Aberdeen clipper *Samuel Plimsoll* on 19 August 1876. The vessel had made the journey from Plymouth in just 78 days, a stark contrast to the slow crawl of the convict ships first sent to Australia in the decades before. William Jenkins Muir was one of 405 immigrants on board, the manifest mostly made up of single men in their early 20s who had spent their teenage years learning trades. They were a welcome addition to the settlers in this new and isolated country.

On the other side of the family, Elizabeth Duncan, William Jenkins Muir's future wife, was born in Hobart on 25 October 1857, the daughter of two Scottish convicts. A native of Greenock, her father James was a shipwright by trade who had arrived in Hobart on 21 May 1842 as one of 266 male convicts on board the *Isabella*. He had been sentenced to 10 years transportation at the Liverpool Assizes, having been found guilty of stealing a portmanteau while employed as acting mate of the vessel *Albatross*. (A portmanteau is a leather bag or suitcase with two sections. We don't know if the stolen bag contained valuables and was worth the trouble, or not!) By the mid-to-late 1840s James Duncan was assigned to Peter Degraves at his Battery Point shipyard, where he was more than likely involved in construction of the largest vessel yet built in Australia at the time, the 562t *Tasman*.

Also a native of Greenock, Elizabeth Duncan's mother, Elizabeth Campbell McBride, had arrived in Hobart on 4 January 1847, as one of 168 convicts on board the *Elizabeth & Henry*, having been sentenced to seven years transportation for stealing a bed, shawl and clothes. It was the fourth time she had been caught stealing. (This was a girl who would do whatever it took to survive. She wasn't about to give up and chuck life in simply because things got tough. These are qualities we see surfacing in the Muir family in later generations.)

These days it's called guts, grit and determination and as with the female side of the Muir family that same will to survive has been passed down through the generations. Is it a part of the Muir genetic makeup?

Scottish-born free immigrant, and John's great grandfather, William Jenkins Muir was born at 64 Constable Street, Dundee, on 4 February 1857, the third of four children born to William and Agnes Muir, nee Jenkins. His father, born in Kirriemuir, a small agricultural town located 30 kilometres (km) inland of Dundee, had moved to Dundee as a teenager to take up work as a starcher in one of the jute mills. By the time of his marriage in 1850 William Muir was working as a seaman, involved in the UK coastal trade, transporting coal to Dundee from Newcastle. Yet the death of his wife, the mother of 7 year old William Jenkins Muir, meant that William was forced to return to the mills to support his family. Unfortunately, he too died five years later in 1869 from typhoid fever. He was 40 years of age. His son William Jenkins Muir, aged 12, had lost his mother and father and the family were left to survive as best they could.

With both parents deceased and only just entering his teenage years, William Jenkins Muir was forced into work, finding employment at one of the nearby jute mills. He would soon leave Scotland bound for the other side of the world. Without a mother to tend the family and home, then losing his father, and work at the jute mills the only source of employment, it's no wonder he opted to set sail for Australia. These days it's called guts, grit and determination and as with the female side of the Muir family that same will to survive has been passed down through the generations. Is it a part of the Muir genetic makeup?

In the mid-to-late 19th century there was a thriving fishing industry based on the Scottish east coast, employing tens of thousands of people, catching and processing the resource. In the cities the industrial revolution was in full swing. In Dundee, jute factories were in full production, using low paid workers, young and old, male and female. But those same workers were hearing stories from returning seamen and reading letters from those who had left for new wealth and opportunities in Canada, the USA and Australia. They left in

droves. The gold rush in Australia had begun in 1851, and within two years hundreds of thousands of new settlers had arrived. In 1852 alone, 370,000 immigrants arrived in Australia and the economy of the nation boomed.

Upon arrival in Australia, William Jenkins Muir found work as a seaman, following in the tentative maritime path forged by his father. In 1878 he was employed as an able seaman on board the 162t intercolonial schooner *Malcolm*, operating out of the port of Hobart. It plied between Sydney, Hobart, other interstate and New Zealand ports. Later that year he met and then married Elizabeth Duncan at St Georges Church, Battery Point.

Leaving his seafaring days behind, William Jenkins Muir was appointed second assistant keeper of the Derwent Lighthouse in September 1889. Six months later he was appointed second assistant keeper of Goose Island Lighthouse, part of the Badger Island group in Bass Strait, where he remained for several years. Between 1894 and 1902 William Jenkins Muir was keeper at the Low Head lighthouse. Following that, he was transferred to Cape Wickham Lighthouse on King Island where he remained, as senior assistant, until May 1904. He next spent three years as superintendent of the Maatsuyker Island Lighthouse.

In mid-1907, William Jenkins Muir was appointed head keeper of Cape Sorell Lighthouse at Macquarie Heads, on Tasmania's west coast, where he remained until April 1913. His final appointment was head keeper of the Mersey Bluff Lighthouse in Devonport, where he stayed until the light was automated in the early 1920s.

All told, William Jenkins Muir spent more than 30 years with the Lighthouse Service, living and working at desolate, isolated pockets of the state, in regions plagued by treacherous waters and compounded by remorseless weather. The sites were tough, arduous places to live and work and the men and their families who kept them, like the Muirs, were of a strong resolve, enduring conditions far beyond their culpability and likely expectations.

Several stories highlight this sense of isolation and deprivation. Shortly after William Jenkins Muir and his family arrived at Maatsuyker Island in mid-1904, he witnessed a ship in trouble as it battled large seas and strong winds, trying desperately to sail northwest. It was the barque *Acacia* that had departed Port Esperance (south of Hobart) on 20 June 1904 with a cargo of timber destined for Port Adelaide. He saw it struggling past the lighthouse and told his son Ernie, "I saw the ship go past and thought, it's not going to make it!"

Shortly after William Jenkins Muir and his family arrived at Maatsuyker Island in mid-1904, he witnessed a ship in trouble as it battled large seas and strong winds, trying desperately to sail northwest. It was the barque Acacia that had departed Port Esperance (south of Hobart) on 20 June 1904 with a cargo of timber destined for Port Adelaide. He saw it struggling past the lighthouse and told his son Ernie, "I saw the ship go past and thought, it's not going to make it!"

MAATSUYKER ISLAND LIGHTHOUSE

Maatsuyker Island Lighthouse, where John's paternal great-grandfather worked as superintendent in the early 20th Century. Photo: National Library of Australia (1956). Lighthouses and Beacons - Maatsuyker Island lighthouse, Tasmania [photographic image]. 1 photographic negative: b&w, acetate.

**MAATSUYKER ISLAND LIGHTHOUSE,
LATITUDE 43° 39.5' S; LONGITUDE: 145° 16.2' E**

*Likely taken on its opening day in 1891 and dcorated with International Code of
Signals (flags). The lighthouse stands 15m tall and sits 107m above sea level, atop the
cliffs at the south side of Maatsuyker Island. It is Australia's most southerly lighthouse.
Shown in the background are the island group's rocky outcrops, Needle Rocks.
Photo: TAHO*

It didn't and was wrecked with the loss of all nine hands on the rocky coastline near Mainwaring Inlet, just north of Maatsuyker Island on an isolated stretch of Tasmania's west coast. It took nearly five months of search efforts to locate any sign of the wreckage.

Lighthouse stories abound, but another in particular is worth sharing: An early, maybe even the first, lighthouse keeper thought he and his family would enjoy fresh eggs, so they took with them to their new home chooks (another unique Australian expression, meaning a laying hen.) Within a few days the birds were nowhere to be found, until it was discovered that gale force winds had blown them all off the rock and into the surrounding ocean where, one assumes, they drowned.

This story is also worth sharing. In September 1912, while William Jenkins Muir was tending the Cape Sorell light, the tower was struck by lightning. The tower shook and William later relayed that he thought it about to collapse. Upon examination he found that the lightning had struck the wind vane and travelled right through the house, blowing off a door from its metal hinges. The Muir family were lucky to escape unharmed that night.

William Jenkins Muir died in Hobart in 1929 in his early 70s, survived by at least half of the 10 children born to his first wife, Elizabeth Duncan and another four children born to his second wife, Florence Holmes. One of those 14 children was John's grandfather, Ernest Jenkins Muir, or Ernie as he was affectionately known. Ernie was a true seafarer and early in his career worked as a seaman.

"Ernie worked on coastal boats, plying interstate runs for several years. In his late teens he was deckhand on a three masted schooner, *Handa Isle*. Under a tough skipper Ernie learnt basic navigation and seamanship skills. Finally he signed on for the runs to and from Adelaide carrying loads of timber and general cargo."*

It was a tough life, sailing in all kinds of weather, surviving gales and mountainous seas in the waters of Bass Strait and beyond. Ernie was one of 12 crew on board the *Natal Queen* (another three masted schooner) when she was wrecked on the rocky shores of Adventure Bay, Bruny Island, in June 1909. Seafarers risk life and limb every time their vessel puts to sea. Virtually every male member of the Muir family has survived life threatening moments at sea, yet nearly all members of the family share an unequivocal passion for the sea. Ernie Muir, John's grandfather, was no exception. He had fond memories of climbing the lighthouse tower on Maatsuyker Island as a teenager, gazing out to sea, watching sailing vessels struggle around the far Southwest Cape of Tasmania on their way to and from Hobart. It is a wild part of the world.

ABOVE AND BELOW: ERNIE MUIR
Taken around 1972, Muir's Boatyard Battery Point. Ernie, a regular visitor at the boatyard, always had a handkerchief with him.

OPPOSITE PAGE:
THE *NATAL QUEEN*
*The three-masted barque **Natal Queen** wreck at Adventure Bay, Bruny Island in 1909. John's grandfather Ernie Muir was one of the crew on the vessel when it was wrecked.*
Photo: Maritime Museum of Tasmania

* Source: Maritime Reflections. Jock Muir, Chris Hudson and Jocelyn Fogagnolo

Jock says his father (Ernie Muir) instilled a love of the sea in all five of his children: "We were all encouraged to sail and race small boats as kids. From the time Max and I began cadet dinghy racing in the late 1920s, Dad was a constant observer and critic from his Battery Point home based 'lookout.' I remember it benefited our performance immensely."

Ernie Muir sailed in local yacht races, as well as in the 1947 Sydney to Hobart alongside three of his sons, Jock, Don and Wallace. The boat was *Westward*, built by Jock and several shipwrights in a paddock off Queen Street in Sandy Bay and launched only a few months prior. It proved to be a successful family venture; *Westward* was second across the line and won the race on handicap.

The seafaring side of the Muir family is as strong, if not stronger today than it was generations ago. To this day there are sailing champions in the family in small racing boats and also winners of the world renowned Sydney to Hobart Yacht Race.

"As islanders, Tasmanians identify strongly with their maritime heritage. Barques and brigantines, whaling, Antarctic exploration and memories of the many trading ketches, small craft and steamers that sailed in and out of the harbours and coves and of a vigorous interstate passenger and interstate and international freight trade, live in the romantic imagination of almost the entire population."*

It's easy to understand why John Muir, and his father before him, took on the trades they did and began the businesses they built. A close look at the Muir ancestral lineage suggests an inextricable link between Muirs, wind and water, carried down from generation to generation. John's father Jock and his three brothers worked in the boatbuilding industry. Jock's grandfather was the seaman who became the lighthouse keeper. The generation before, back in Scotland, were the first to propagate the Muir maritime seed.

Alistair Mant, the author of the unauthorised biography of John Muir's mate and business associate Robert Clifford, grappled to come to an understanding of what made Robert Clifford the man he is today. John Muir is born of the same background influences, from a seafaring family, with tradition and history at work on him and his brothers from the day they were born.

"You can't understand Robert Clifford (read: John Muir) and the extended family without an understanding of Tasmanian culture in particular and island cultures in general. Tasmanians are a maritime people who have traded successfully with their own kind on a global basis since not long after first white settlement. So, to an extent, this is also a biography of Tasmania – and of a quintessentially Tasmanian yachtsman."

* Source: The Companion to Tasmanian History. Audrey Hudspeth, Centre for Tasmanian Historical Studies.

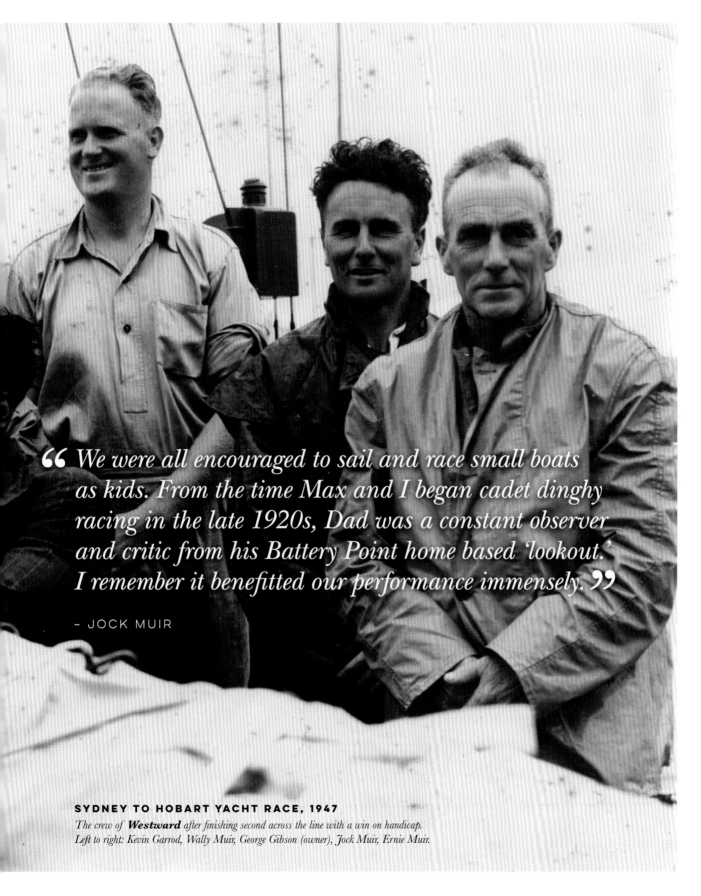

> **_We were all encouraged to sail and race small boats as kids. From the time Max and I began cadet dinghy racing in the late 1920s, Dad was a constant observer and critic from his Battery Point home based 'lookout.' I remember it benefitted our performance immensely._**

– JOCK MUIR

SYDNEY TO HOBART YACHT RACE, 1947

*The crew of **Westward** after finishing second across the line with a win on handicap.*
Left to right: Kevin Garrod, Wally Muir, George Gibson (owner), Jock Muir, Ernie Muir.

This is also a biography of a quintessentially Tasmanian yachtsman and businessman who like Robert Clifford saw an opportunity and grabbed it with gusto!

Dr Gail Goss, Ph.D., Pd.D., M.Ed., speaker, author and a specialist in Human Behavior, Parenting and an Education Expert, says parental role models have a huge impact on boys.

"Boys will model themselves after their fathers. They will look for their father's approval in everything they do and copy those behaviours that they recognize as both successful and familiar. Thus, if dad was abusive, controlling and dominating, those will be the patterns that their sons will imitate and emulate. However, if father is loving, kind, supportive, and protective, boys will want to be that.

"Human beings are social animals and we learn by modeling behavior. In fact, all primates learn how to survive and function successfully in the world through social imitation. Those early patterns of interaction are all children know and it is those patterns that affect how they feel about themselves, and how they develop. Well-bonded boys develop securely with a stable and sustained sense of self. Who we are and who we are to be, we are becoming, and fathers are central to that outcome."

Professor Fiona Wood AM, a world renowned Plastic and Reconstructive Surgeon in the area of burns and scar management, says her father was critical to her success in life.

"Having a dad that inspired me to work and live to my potential; to make choices so that you get up in the morning and enjoy what you do is a gift that is constantly with me."

John Muir is openly affectionate when he talks about his father Jock. Not only was Jock his adored Dad, he was also John's mentor, just as Jock's father, Ernie, was for him. It was Ernie who paid 20 quid (pounds) for Jock's first cadet dinghy *Mayfly*. Then followed the ground breaking *Kittiwake* which Ernie commissioned W. P. "Skipper" Batt (of the Forster Cup fame) to build at Battery Point from red cedar timber in 1930. It was one of only a dozen or so cadet dinghies in Tasmania at the time. Jock and his brother Max proved their skill at the helm of *Kittiwake*, both representing Tasmania in the Stonehaven Cup in the early 1930s. Jock won the national title in 1933, Max won it in 1935. Decades later, John's brothers Ross and Greg would repeat this success.

Jock and his three brothers began in the trades, with Jock in metal working. They went onto become boat builders and successful yachtsmen. Jock served an apprenticeship in sheet metal work at Charles Davis in Hobart, however he yearned to be designing and building boats. He had managed to get that job against 80 other desperate applicants during The Depression. Work was unbelievably scarce and he was openly thankful for the rest of his life about what that opportunity meant to him.

During his time at school and later when working at Charles Davis, Jock spent his spare time mucking about and helping out at the boat building operations of yachting legends like Percy Coverdale. He lived just up the road a bit in Battery Point and that proximity certainly helped. Percy was the first really strong influence that inspired Jock to dream of becoming a boat builder. Jock and his lifelong sailing mate Neall Batt used to offside for Percy, passing up gear, holding planks and 'generally just getting in the way.'

> *John Muir is openly affectionate when he talks about his father Jock. Not only was Jock his adored Dad, he was also John's mentor, just as Jock's father, Ernie was for him. It was Ernie who paid 20 quid (pounds) for Jock's first cadet dinghy* **Mayfly**.

OPPOSITE: FATHER AND SON
Jock and John on **Lady Nelson***, 1967, during a sea trial around Bruny Island.*

One of the sparks that ignited his imagination and set Jock on his boatbuilding course in life was when his maternal grandfather William Haigh gave him his first carved boat. "It was made out of Huon Pine and I will never forget that smell as long as I live." Soon after, his father and Jock got together and carved another model boat, again in Huon Pine. This was a serious model, with sails, rudder, rigging and ballast, designed to race. Jock soon won the Sandy Bay Regatta for model boats. He was hooked.*

Jock Muir: "There's no question, these model boats taught a generation of us how to sail at an early age. They were marvelous little boats, built of timber and about 120cm long… the skippers of the little craft rigged them onshore then set them on their way. They followed closely in small dinghies, rowing flat out to keep up. If they couldn't steer a straight course they were useless."

Jock remembers one race that started at Sandy Bay, took all day to complete and saw the boats sail way down the river to the Iron Pot and back. The boys also rowed the entire distance, resetting sails and directions as they followed the small yachts. On another occasion Jock and his future brother-in-law, Dave McAllister, sailed their model yachts (rowing behind them in small dinghies) from Sandy Bay to the Iron Pot, then to the eastern side of Lauderdale Beach, carted their dinghies and yachts across the narrow spit and sailed and rowed back to Sandy Bay.

* Source: Maritime Reflections. Jock Muir, Chris Hudson and Jocelyn Fogagnolo)

ABOVE: *MAYFLY*
Jock's first cadet dinghy. Photo: Maritime Museum of Tasmania

LEFT: *KITTIWAKE*, C. 1930S
*Built by Skipper Batt at Battery Point in 1930.
Photo: TAHO*

BELOW: *KITTIWAKE 3 (K3)* 2016
Built by Jock Muir in 1976, and recently purchased from the Royal Yacht Club of Tasmania by Greg Muir and Kenn Batt.

Jock and his wife Mollie (John's mum) set high standards in both family and business life and encouraged all of their children to do their best.

LEFT: JOCK MUIR

Jock was named as one of Tasmania's Top Ten Sailors in local Hobart newspaper, The Mercury, in 2004. Earlier in the 1990s, Jock had been named as one of the 'Ten Tasmanians of the Century' by the same publication. Article: The Mercury

Current research shows that fathers with trade qualifications are not as good at the fathering business as dads with university degrees. Well, the Muir family are an amazing exception to those findings. There are no signs of professional qualifications in the family until John's brother Greg breaks the mould.

Yet Jock has been acknowledged in the Hobart Mercury newspaper in the 1990s as one of the ten Tasmanians of the 20th century. The others included Premier Eric Reece, Lieutenant Colonel Henry Murray (a winner of the Victoria Cross during World War I), Tasmania's first Olympic athlete Bill Barwick, aviation pioneer Harold Gatty, William Leitch (of Aussie Rules fame), internationally acclaimed actor Errol Flynn, journalist and author Roy Bridges, Australia's first female member of federal parliament, and subsequently of cabinet, Dame Enid Lyons and naturalist and conservationist Gustav Weindorfer. For Jock it was an amazingly eminent bunch to be associated with. He has also been acknowledged as one of the ten Tasmanian yachtsmen of the century.

Jock and his wife Mollie (John's mum) set high standards in both family and business life and encouraged all of their children to do their best. At a relatively young age John and his two younger brothers established their own businesses within the Tasmanian boating and fishing industries. The Muir name at that time was well known and certainly gave all the boys a head start. Yet, hard work and determination saw them became successful businessmen in their own right. Greg and Ross later went on to establish Yacht Distributors and Ross his own ship chandlery.

As a great island continent, Australia is heavily dependent on overseas shipping, but Tasmania has additional disadvantages. Isolated from the mainland, its dependence on interstate shipping is two and a half times greater than that of any other Australian state.

In the early days of European settlement, Hobart was on the favoured route to Sydney and ships could sail down on the westerlies. Second only in importance to Sydney, Hobart became a pre-eminent whaling port in the southern seas. Merchant captains brought convicts and cargo and then went whaling and trading. The export of whale oil to Britain underpinned the colony's economy, while it also supplied wheat, timber, sheep and produce to the burgeoning settlements of Port Phillip and South Australia. An important wooden shipbuilding industry was established, aided by the rush to send vessels to the goldfields.*

Nicole Mays, our historical researcher and author in her own right, writing in her book, 'The Boat and Shipbuilders of Battery Point,' says, "The 1870s was by far the most active period for Hobart's boat and ship builders. During this decade, Tasmania's economy was booming, fuelled primarily by the newly developed mining industry. There was greater confidence in the state and the standard of living rose.

"This prosperity resonated to all sectors of the economy and Hobart's ship and boat building industries were stimulated by an increased demand for new vessels, particularly ketches and passage boats to ply the developing river trade, as well as whaleboats to compete in local regattas and private races.

"In contrast, demand for new vessels was low during the 1880s and 1890s. Tasmania entered into a recession, unemployment rose and people fled the state for greener pastures on the mainland. There were sharp decreases in the number of new vessels commissioned. The use of steam power also greatly affected the demand for new passage boats to furnish the river trade, as well as waterman and pleasure boats for use in the local tourist trade.

"The 1890s saw the Tasmanian economy continue to decline, fuelled primarily by a downturn in world mineral prices. The recession of the previous decade evolved into a full-blown depression. The Van Diemen's Land Bank collapsed, wages fell and unemployment rose. Yet, the recreational sport of yachting began to emerge during the middle of this decade and the local ship and boat builders were thankfully a part of its popularity."

> **66** *Business and life is all about getting a break and if you get a break you don't screw it up.* **99**

– JOHN MUIR

It's easy to see that Tasmania and Tasmanians are inextricably linked to the oceans that surround them. They, like John Muir, don't see the distances and isolation as a great problem, simply something that has to be dealt with as best you can.

According to John Muir, success in life is about getting 'breaks,' as he calls them.

ABOVE: JOCK MUIR, BATTERY POINT
C. 1930s, at what is now Taylor Brothers' boatyard.

OPPOSITE, TOP: COVERDALE'S SLIP
Westwind *om Coverdale's Slip in 1939, adding extra lead to the keel. Left to right: Ernie, Colin Snook, Jock.*

OPPOSITE, BOTTOM: MAX MUIR
Jock's brother Max was a regular visitor at the Battery Point boatyard, and did his best to keep John and his brother Ross in order.

* Source: 'The Companion to Tasmanian History.' Audrey Hudspeth
Centre for Tasmanian Historical Studies

"Business and life is all about getting a break and if you get a break you don't screw it up. Fisherman gave our family many breaks. My first break was working with Jock and his brothers, then with uncle Don McAllister, then at Webster Woolgrowers, then again with Dad and with his support, I set up on my own. Someone gives you a break. You just don't bloody get it, you can't just sit there on your backside and hope for it to happen. Somebody has to say, 'I reckon you can do it' and gives you a go, you know."

John vividly remembers, to this day, standing outside the Battery Point Boatyard, on a cold winters day, when his uncle, Jock's brother, Max said, 'take your hands out of your pockets John.' I asked why? He said 'so you can pick up a broom and sweep up,' adding, 'if you trip over, you won't fall on your face and break your nose.' He used to say to me, 'you've got two ears and one mouth, so make sure you listen twice as much as you speak.'

There are rare moments when John can reflect on his success and who supported him, allowing him the time and space to make it happen.

"If you persevere, stay at school, do your trade, get through that, get married and start a business, then a family, you need a break and people behind you. You're married to a lady for 45 years. Wendy said, 'I need the medal, not you John.' You stick with it because you're cautious about what would happen if you stopped

your business or your relationship. I'm being honest here. I was lucky. I could travel anytime, anywhere I wanted to, and from that point of view I guess I got out of Wendy's hair. She did a lot of stuff with the kids and my stuff and helped me run the business, so the gate's been pretty well open for me all the time."

Through The Depression of the 1930s Jock Muir had begrudgingly completed an apprenticeship with Charles Davis, a metal fabrication firm in Hobart, earning just enough to support himself and the building of a 36 foot (ft) cruising yacht in the backyard of his parents' home in Colville Street, Battery Point. (Jock was just 21 years old.) Launched in late 1937, Jock sailed *Westwind* for several years in the local cruiser class and used her for local and interstate fishing and pleasure trips. Family folklore says that Jock built *Westwind* with the intention of sailing around the Pacific. However, by the time he was ready to embark on this journey, he had fallen in love with the daughter of a neighbour, Mollie McAllister. A month before the couple's wedding Jock sailed *Westwind* to Sydney where the vessel was sold, the proceeds used to finance the newlywed couple's relocation to the mainland.

*As the 45 ft vessel, **Wake**, neared completion in mid-1945, Jock was struck down with polio… Jock later told John that it was the heavy physical work of boat building, constantly up and down ladders that helped him to free up his limbs and got him going again.*

By the time their second child, John Muir, came along in mid-1944, Jock had achieved his career goal and was operating a boat building and brokerage business out of Mosman Bay, New South Wales. Joined by his brother Don Muir, as well as Tim Chambers, the trio spent much of World War II building lifeboats for the United States Army. Jock, Mollie and their growing family set up residence in nearby Rose Crescent, Mosman.

In early 1945 Jock began supervising the building of his own fishing trawler at Narooma on the New South Wales south coast. Unfortunately the shipwright tasked with the vessel's construction did not carry out the work within the expected timeframe. Jock, Mollie and their two kids (Lynette and John), were forced to move to Narooma during the latter stages of construction to oversee the process and

ABOVE: HALCCYON DAYS

Mollie at the Rose Crescent, Mosman, residence Jock bought with the intention of raising his family in Sydney.

LEFT: EARLY BUSINESS

Jock's Castlecrag boat hiring based in Middle Harbour, Sydney, 1942. The yacht moored out front is Bingle.

BELOW, CLOCKWISE FROM LEFT: MUM, DAD AND BABY

Mollie McAllister, c. 1938; Jock Muir, 1941; John in 1946, aged around 2 years.

complete the vessel. As the 45ft vessel, *Wake*, neared completion in mid-1945, Jock was struck down with polio, a debilitating disease that saw him spend several months in hospital and dramatically limited his capacity to work.

Though Jock and Mollie had left Tasmania with the intention of permanently settling in New South Wales, Jock's illness forced the family to return to Hobart, where they arrived in early 1946.

Jock later told John that it was the heavy physical work of boat building, constantly up and down ladders that helped him to free up his limbs and got him going again.

Determination, guts, grit, a never give in attitude were all qualities that would surface in his children, particularly John. The puppy Blue Heeler of Battery Point was watching and learning from his father. In fact all three Muir boys acknowledge that they are driven men, desperate to work hard and succeed at what they take on. Not driven by the desire to become rich, not at all, it's a case of 'you have to work hard in life in order to do well.'

Initially, on their return from Sydney, with Jock partly crippled from polio, the growing Muir family moved in with Mollie's parents at 14 St Georges Terrace, Battery Point. While Jock convalesced, the couple prepared for the birth of their third child, Ross, in April 1946. Slowly Jock's strength returned and he began reconditioning marine engines and advertising them for sale in the local press. By December 1946 his health had recovered enough to enable him to crew on Colin Philp's 20t welded steel sloop *Southern Maid* in that year's Sydney to Hobart Yacht Race.

By 1947 Jock's star continued to rise with an order received from an interstate buyer for a large fishing cruiser. However, with the hull only partially complete, the sale of the vessel fell through. Thankfully George Gibson, Jock's long-time friend and former mainsheet hand from his cadet dinghy sailing days, was able to take over the order. Built in a paddock off Queen Street in Sandy Bay, the 42ft Bermuda-rigged cutter *Westward* was launched in September 1947.

Despite that setback from polio, Jock navigated and co-skippered *Westward* in the 1947 and 1948 Sydney to Hobart yacht races, winning both races on handicap. No wonder he was subsequently named one of the ten Tasmanians of the Century. *Westward* is still the only Tasmanian yacht to win two Sydney to Hobart yacht races on handicap.

Back in Hobart, in 1948 Jock set about establishing a boatyard at Battery Point. John's cousin, Bill Foster, relays the story that the frames for *Lass O'Luss*, the first yacht launched from Jock's Battery Point boatyard, were steamed and the keel adzed in the same paddock where *Westward* was built. The frames and keel were then transported to Jock's Battery Point yard, along with a demountable shed containing a large saw. The following day the keel was set up and the frames

the day after that. The story continues that when Percy Coverdale arrived at his boatyard on the following morning and looked over at Jock's yard, he couldn't believe his eyes. There stood a small saw shed, along with the keel and frames of a 47ft racing sloop!

Built to the order of John Colquhoun, a yachtsman of Sydney, *Lass O'Luss* was launched from Jock's boatyard on 4 December 1948. It would have been an extremely hectic, though extremely monumental week for both Jock and Mollie, as only the day prior their fourth child, Greg, had been born.

The following decades saw Jock build racing and cruising yachts and fishing boats of all shapes and sizes. His design and craftsmanship qualities earned him a well-deserved reputation as one of Australia's best boat designers, builders and ocean-going yachtsmen.

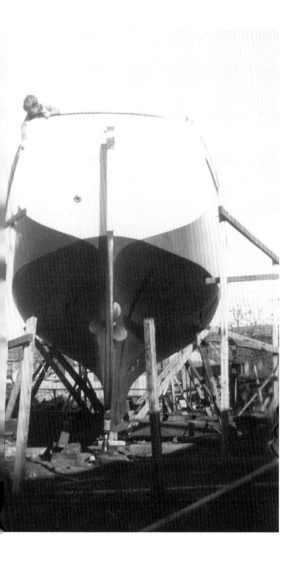

FAR LEFT: JOCK'S FIRST YACHT BUILD

Westwind under construction in the backyard of Ernie and Minnie Muir's (Jock's parents) house at 42 Colville Street, Battery Point, in 1937.

LEFT: SYNDEY-HOBART WINNER IN THE MAKING

Westward under construction in a backyard at Queen Street, Sandy Bay, in 1947. *Westward* remains the only Tasmanian yacht to win two Sydney to Hobart yacht races on handicap. A young John is seen here atop the stern.

ABOVE: *WESTWARD, NORTHWARD*

Cruising to Sydney for the beginning of the Sydney to Hobart Yacht Race, 1947.

He was virtually never home for Christmas with the family and was working hard at the boatyard and racing locally. John Muir was to emulate this pattern of behavior, spending many Christmases away and many months travelling the globe every year as his business grew. It was what you did because it was what was needed to build an internationally successful business. After all, it's what his father did wasn't it? Like father, like son, role models at work.

The Muir family ran an open house. Friends and relatives came and went, visiting boat owners likewise. Everyone was welcome and Mollie's hospitality was memorable. But for one lad, Nikolaus Zak aged 13, of Greek descent, who had just arrived in Battery Point from Queenstown on the Tasmanian west coast, the Muirs and particularly Mollie became a second family. A safe haven when things at Niko's home started to fall apart.

Nikolaus Zak: "I first met Ross Muir at New Town High School and we discovered we were virtually neighbours. I started sailing with him when I was 13. The really nice thing about my association with the Muir family was that I was so easily accepted as part of the family.

"When my Mum got really sick and had to go to hospital in Melbourne she went and saw Mollie and asked her if she could look after me. My stepfather was working in the mines away from Hobart, so I actually lived with the Muir's for about two weeks. I spent as much time there as I would at home. It didn't matter to them that I was what some called then a 'wog.' They didn't care, I was another kid who needed help and support and they willingly provided that to me. I have never forgotten their kindness."

With business prospects improving, in the early 1950s Jock, Mollie and their four children moved to 16a St Georges Terrace, next door to the house previously inhabited by Mollie's mother and brother. It was here that the Muir family lived for about a decade. Jock established a successful boat building business close by on the shores of the Derwent, ultimately becoming one of Australia's finest boat builders and designers. An uncle, Don McAllister (colloquially known as Don Mac), also lived with the Muir family during the 1950s.

Due mainly to its geographic isolation, over the years Hobart's growth has been slow. The city has experienced extreme economic boom and bust periods throughout its history. In its early years the city grew from being a defensive outpost and penal colony to become a world centre of whaling and ship building, only to suffer a major economic and population decline in the late 19th century.

The early 20th century saw another period of growth on the back of mining, agriculture and other primary industries, but the world wars had a very negative effect on Hobart, with a severe loss of working age men. Like most of Australia, the post-war years saw an influx of new migrants from Eastern and Southern Europe, such as Italy, Greece, Yugoslavia and Poland. Many went to work on the new hydro-electric dam construction projects.

In the later years of the 20th century, migrants increasingly arrived to settle in Hobart from Asia. Despite the rise in migration from parts of the world other than the UK and Ireland, the population of Hobart remains predominantly ethnically Anglo-Celtic and to this day has the highest percentage per capita of Australian born residents of all the Australian capital cities.*

* Source: The Companion to Tasmanian History. Audrey Hudspeth Centre for Tasmanian Historical Studies

ABOVE: MR WATSON'S COTTAGES
Built in 1858 for local shipyard workers, this row housing is a great example of working man's housing of the shipbuilding era.

BELOW: REMINISCING
John, Niko Zak and Ross Muir outside the Muir's old family house at 16 St Georges Terrace, Battery Point, 2016.

RITES
of
PASSAGE

Growing up, moving from boyhood to manhood, particularly in the modern world, is a difficult journey for many boys. Not so in almost every indigenous community around the world. For tens of thousands of years, the journey of a boy through to manhood has involved facing one's fears, passing a series of physical and mental 'exams' or 'tests,' followed by feasting and a tribal celebration! Modern young men no longer go through the 'rites of initiation' ceremony.

According to one of the world's leading educators and psychologists, Tasmanian, Dr Steve Biddulph, whose books have sold over 4 million copies worldwide: "People's lives have always depended on men being nurturing and life-protecting and men themselves only thrive if they have a sense of purpose and an ethos for life. Becoming a man is both a slow and a rapid process. It happens slowly, but it also comes to a climactic moment when a boy has to snap out of childishness and take hold of his life, that moment needs lots of help."

I'm not sure how much help John Muir had when he snapped out of his childhood.

For him growing up was a mix of hard work, hard play, competition between siblings and competition to survive in the tough local neighbourhood of Battery Point in Hobart.

When Battery Point was first populated in the 1830s it was soon a mix of the well to do and not so well to do. Officers of the penal colony and local merchants built grand houses close to the port and their businesses. Lower class labourers and a motley collection of those involved in the nearby maritime industry, mostly seafaring folks, rented smaller cottages.

Historical records show that Battery Point was pretty much farmland for the first few decades of Hobart's history. It wasn't until the 1830s and 1840s when streets were built, subdivision commenced and the mix of the 'haves' (i.e. ship merchants like Captain Andrew Haig who wanted to be close to the New Wharf, built the sandstone Georgian mansion Narryna) and the 'have nots' (i.e., small cottages like Mr Watson's cottages along Napoleon

Street were built for the shipyard workers) moved in. Formal shipbuilding at Battery Point didn't begin until 1835. Prior to that, shipbuilding mostly occurred at Hobart's Old Wharf along Hunter Street.

During the last decade of the 19th century and the early decades of the 20th century, many local industries went into decline and things were made much worse when The Depression hit in the 1930s. Battery Point's smaller cottages were mostly rented, a few were owned by those who worked nearby in the boat and shipyards. Work was scarce and money hard to come by. The suburb became quite run down and was not regarded as one of the more prestigious suburbs of Hobart.

During the latter part of the 20th century, the area was 'discovered' by real estate agents and investors began to realise what a gem it was.

One of John's childhood friends, Niko Zac said "If you'd told anyone you lived at Battery Point back then, people just wouldn't want to know you. It was a really working class place. Now it's some of the most expensive real estate in Tasmania!"

As Niko so rightly points out, these days Battery Point is a 'silvertail' suburb. A mixture of large waterfront million dollar mansions, reconstructed historically significant workers cottages and substantial homes for the new suburban elite and wealthy middle class.

For John Muir, growing up in and around Battery Point was a blend of freedom and survival.

"Certainly living in Battery Point when I was young, there were some hard heads around who thought they were pretty good. They would have a go at you if there was someone else around to support them, but they'd turn away rather than do something on their own. It was a bit of a rough place. Unlike my brother Ross sometimes, I would never go and provoke a fight. I wasn't a tall bloke and I wore glasses and on occasions I was called 'four eyes' or worse.

ABOVE LEFT: SALAMANCA PLACE LOOKING ACROSS TO BATTERY POINT, C. 1950S

At the middle of last Century, the now salubrious Salamanca Place was a rough and dirty industrial area, featuring the legendary 'Blue House,' The Esplanade Hotel, so named for the frequent fighting and police attendances. Photo: TAHO.

ABOVE RIGHT: WHARF AREA LOOKING OUT TO THE RIVER DERWENT, C. 1950S

Elevated view of the Sullivans Cove wharf area, from Watermans Dock on the right to Hunter Street and Macquarie Wharf on the left. Photo: TAHO.

OPPOSITE PAGE: NEW TOWN TECHNICAL HIGH SCHOOL, C. 1950S

John's high school provided the technical building blocks for a career in manufacturing. Photo: TAHO.

BELOW: WOODWORKING CLASS

New Town Technical High School woodworking class, 1950s. Photo: TAHO.

"I wouldn't cop it sweet from anyone at my schools, even though someone was always trying to make sure you knew your place in the school pecking order. It wasn't my intention to be at the top, although on occasions I was pushed there and held my ground! Generally it's not people your own size who want to have a crack at you, it's someone bigger.

"On my first day at New Town Tech School, I remember standing around chatting to some of my mates when this big foreign boy, a fair bit taller than me, had a go at me. You can tell when it's coming, the hair stands up on the back of your neck and you have to get prepared as best you can. He had a couple of his mates with him and he said;

'Hey four eyes I hear you can look after yourself!'

'Who's askin?' I said, cause he was a big bloke.

'Me' he replied.

"There followed a bit of scrapping inside the school yard until it was agreed to go off school grounds and have a fair dinkum round or two! We had a good following of his supporters and mine.

"As soon as we were outside the school fence, he just put his head down and rushed straight at me. In a matter of seconds I had him in a headlock and I charged him head first into a nearby telegraph pole. It knocked him out flat and shut him up.

"A few others had a go at me after that and they soon realised I could look after myself when I had to."

There was obviously nothing wrong with John's 'fight or flight' reaction. He remembers thinking in that instant of acute self-awareness when trouble like this strikes, that if he didn't do something and do it quickly, he would be in ongoing trouble from this bully and his mates. Is that thinking part of his sailing background? Having to make decisions in an instant then be prepared to change that decision again soon after?

> **❝ Generally it's not people your own size who want to have a crack at you, it's someone bigger. ❞**
>
> – JOHN MUIR

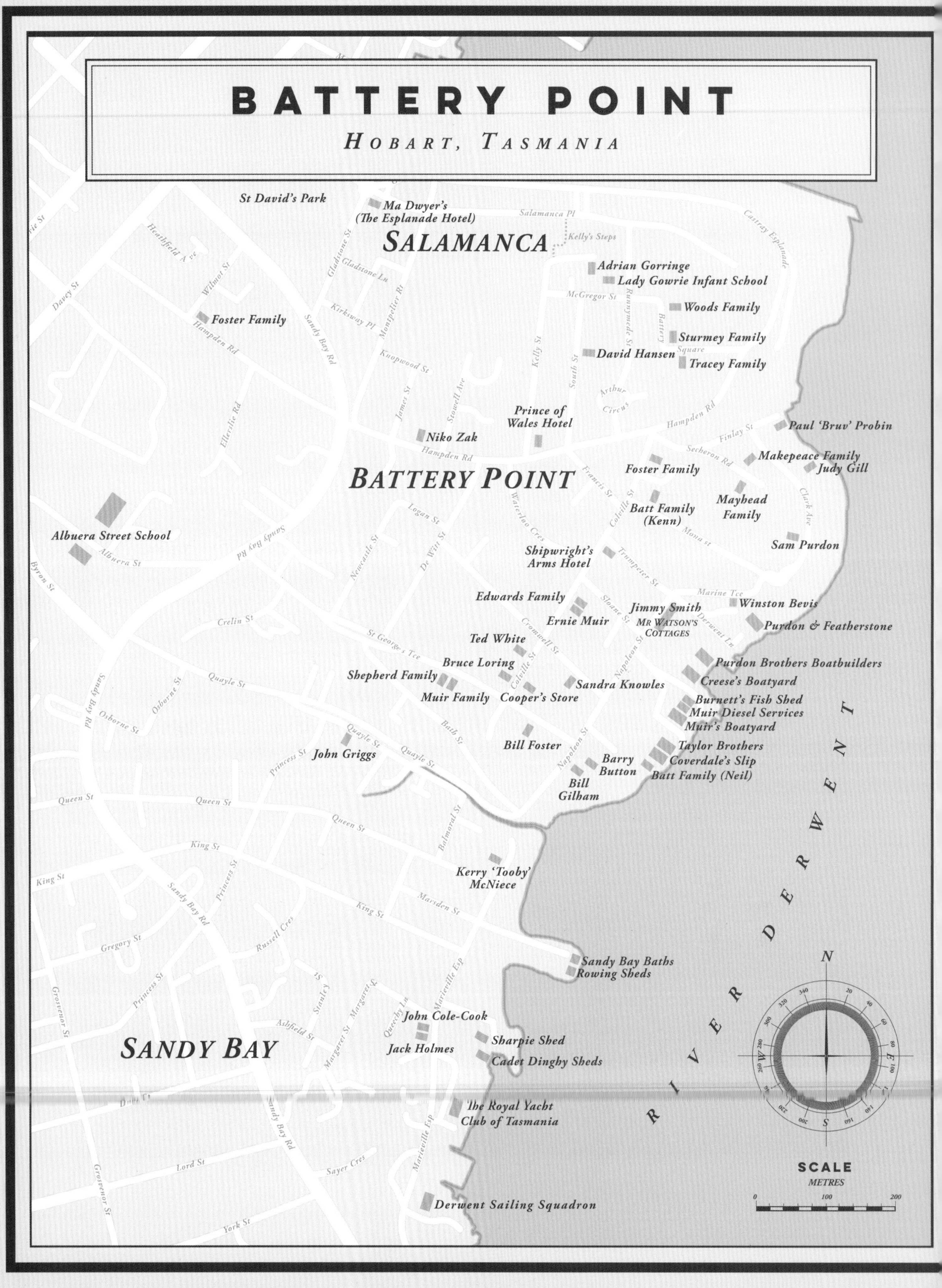

BATTERY POINT
HOBART, TASMANIA
St David's Park
Ma Dwyer's
(The Esplanade Hotel)
Salamanca Pl
SALAMANCA
Kelly's Steps
Castray Esplanade
Gladstone St
Gladstone Ln
Heathfield Ave
Wilmot St
Davey St
Adrian Gorringe
Lady Gowrie Infant School
McGregor St
Runnymede St
Woods Family
Battery Square
Sturmey Family
David Hansen
Tracey Family
Foster Family
Hampden Rd
Kirksway Pl
Montpelier Rt
Sandy Bay Rd
Knopwood St
Kelly St
South St
Arthur Circus
James St
Stowell Ave
Ellerslie Rd
Prince of
Wales Hotel
Niko Zak
Hampden Rd
Finlay St
Paul 'Bruv' Probin
Secheron Rd
Makepeace Family
Judy Gill
BATTERY POINT
Foster Family
Francis St
Waterloo Cres
Colville St
Batt Family
(Kenn)
Mayhead
Family
Clark Ave
Logan St
De Witt St
Newcastle St
Albuera Street School
Albuera St
Sandy Bay Rd
Mona St
Sam Purdon
Shipwright's
Arms Hotel
Trumpeter St
Byron St
Marine Tce
Edwards Family
Winston Bevis
Sloane St
Jimmy Smith
Mr Watson's
Cottages
Ernie Muir
Derwent Ln
Purdon & Featherstone
Crelin St
Cromwell St
Ted White
St George's Tce
Napoleon St
Purdon Brothers Boatbuilders
Bruce Loring
Colville St
Creese's Boatyard
Shepherd Family
Sandra Knowles
Quayle St
Muir Family
Cooper's Store
Burnett's Fish Shed
Muir Diesel Services
Muir's Boatyard
Osborne St
Bath St
Taylor Brothers
Quayle St
Bill Foster
John Griggs
Princess St
Quayle St
Napoleon St
Barry
Button
Coverdale's Slip
Batt Family (Neil)
Bill
Gilham
Queen St
Queen St
Queen St
Balmoral St
King St
King St
Princess St
Kerry 'Tooby'
McNiece
Marsden St
King St
Sandy Bay Rd
RIVER DERWENT
Russell Cres
Gregory St
Sandy Bay Baths
Rowing Sheds
Princess St
Stanley St
Margaret St
Marieville Esp
Grosvenor St
Ashfield St
Queechy Ln
John Cole-Cook
Sharpie Shed
SANDY BAY
Jack Holmes
Cadet Dinghy Sheds
The Royal Yacht
Club of Tasmania
Sandy Bay Rd
Marieville Esp
Lord St
Sayer Cres
Grosvenor St
SCALE
METRES
0
100
200
Derwent Sailing Squadron
York St
N
S
E
W

The Blue Heeler of Battery Point was out and about, wagging his tail, watching closely what was going on around him with an eagle eye and learning fast from life's experiences. John Muir is an individual who doesn't easily forget lessons learnt from life's school of hard knocks.

"My Mum's brother, Uncle Don Mac or Spike as he was called, was a physically capable bloke. He was a wrestler and a boxer and trained young people including us boys in self-defence. He set up and sponsored the Hobart Police Boys Club. Back in those days if somebody put their arm out to me and I felt threatened, I'd just get it and put them straight on the floor. You can twist it until you break it if you have to. We were fit and as tough as we had to be to survive. Our Dad used to take us to the boxing and wrestling at the City Hall where we gleaned some more defensive moves for our own well-being. On several occasions we entered the boxing ring at the Royal Hobart Regatta just for the experience. "

Uncle Don McAllister (Don Mac) and his brother Dave operated a well-equipped mechanical services workshop where they manufactured Demac oil heaters, central heating and ventilation systems and had a sheet metal works. He generously gave the Muir boys work in their spare time and during holidays.

"As a teenager I worked with Uncle Don, his younger brother Dave McAllister and their nephew, my cousin, Ted White. The projects included installation and commissioning of mechanical services in the new Commonwealth Bank building, Risdon Prison, New Norfolk Hospital and the New Norfolk Pulp and Paper Mill."

From the McAllister side John picked up a variety of technical skills that served him well as he grew slowly towards manhood.

John, his brothers Ross and Greg and sister Lyn were always encouraged by their parents to be independent, play sport and be competitive, to sail and to keep fit.

OUTDOOR CHILDHOOD

Left: Ross (front), John (back, middle) and Lyn boating with Aunty Ida (Jock's brother Don Muir's wife), far left, and grandfather Ernie, far right.
Centre: Lyn enjoying summertime boating with friends.
Right: John (left), Greg (front, centre) and Mollie (right) picnicking with family and and friends.
Top: John's cousin Ted White in 2016.

HOBART WATERFRONT, C. 1960

An aerial view from the middle of last century shows the thriving Sullivans Cove port precinct.

The port is a hive of activity as dozens of ships load with 8 to 9 million boxes of apples destined for the UK and Europe. The first apple tree in Tasmania was planted by Captain Bligh in the 1700s and by the 1950s and 1960s the apple industry was booming. Tasmania was known as 'The Apple Isle.' When Britain joined the Common Market in 1973 it was seen as the beginning of the end. The industry was decimated and even though today it has bounced back and is a strong export industry, levels of production are still well below those boom times.

Battery Point in the far left of the frame, was a rowdy place with a rough mix of boatyards, slipways and rowdy pubs.

Photo: TAHO

Uncle Don Mac built a nice home near the entrance to the Huon River, at Police Point. It became known to the Muir family as 'the farm' and was a favourite place to visit.

It was to Uncle Don Mac that John's mother, Mollie, turned for help when John and his younger brother Ross were constantly roughing each other up and she was at her wits end about how to change their behaviour. She asked Don to 'help sort them out.' One such encounter that is worth recalling was when John and Ross had been wrestling and fighting, as they did regularly on the back lawn. John recalls he hurt Ross. Not long after an obviously grumpy Ross ambushed John and broke his nose with a milk bottle!

"I remember Ross got a good hiding when Dad came home."

Even now sibling rivalry and the competitive spirit still flourishes in the Muir family although not at that same physical level anymore.

It was a rough and tumble school of life for John Muir and his younger brothers. Loved and supported by their parents, they were encouraged to work and play hard, to become independent and be able to look after themselves when the going got rough. John grew up in an era when there was freedom to roam the streets, on occasions to get into mischief and be adventurous. He, his brothers and mates took every opportunity to do just that.

There were a number of key family members who also played integral roles in the moulding of the modern day John Muir, particularly his father, boat builder, designer and ocean-going yachtsman, Jock and to a lesser degree, Jock's brothers Max and Wally Muir.

John, his brothers Ross and Greg and sister Lynette were always encouraged by their parents to be independent, play sport and be competitive, to sail and to keep fit. Wind and water were destined to play a large part in John's journey from boyhood to manhood and were to continue to play a large part for the rest of his life.

Clinging tenaciously to one area of foreshore in the modern Battery Point, looking south down the huge Derwent Estuary, is a remnant industry. An envelope of foreshore where for more than 180 years ship and boat builders, including the Muir Boatyard business owned by John's father Jock, who designed and built some of Australia's finest racing and cruising yachts, have operated. Today it's still a motley collection of old and new tin sheds, surrounded by boats of every shape,

size and condition, in varied states of repair. Old and new timber jetties jut into the Derwent, all just down the road from the famous local watering hole, 'Shippy's of Battery Point,' the 170 year old local pub.

This is the playground where John passed through his rites of passage into manhood. Here and on the waters of the Derwent and beyond, sailing with and without his parents. With and without their permission.

In the early days there were billycart races down Napoleon Street, a rough gravel road and a deadly drop, with a fence and creek at the bottom. If you managed to successfully negotiate the corner at the bottom, there was a narrow timber bridge to tear across then slowly come to a stop along Marieville Esplanade. The competition was fierce between John and his brothers, Ross and Greg and other local boys intent on winning at any cost.

"We had no fear. I can't ever remember being scared. If we needed to stop you had to jam the heels of your boots onto the gravel, these billycarts didn't have any brakes. Generally, we shot straight down, down the road, left across the bridge. I suppose I was about fourteen then. One of the younger boys would always be stationed at the bottom of Napoleon Street to hold back the cars while the race was on."

One of John's closest mates, both then and now, Adrian Gorringe remembers it well. One of his billycarts was a bit flash, it had four lightweight aluminium wheels, weighed less and was one of the fastest on the track. Everyone's billycarts were home-made.

These kids, spending time in and around thriving boatyards quickly became adept at working metal and wood, more often than not with a nearby adult to ask for help or advice.

John Muir: "Ross and I were down on the ground floor in the woodworking shop. I'm not clear on how it happened but I switched on the wood buzzer. I didn't realise that Ross had two of his fingers resting on the sharp spiralled cutter. All hell broke out when Dad heard Ross screaming. He rushed down the stairs to see the finger nail side of Ross's two fingers shaved off! There was blood everywhere!

I'm sure I heard Ross mumble, 'now you've got me back for smashing your nose.'

I tried to explain to Dad that I didn't know Ross had his fingers near the buzzer, but he wasn't having any of that and he picked up a board and hit me fair across my backside as someone rushed Ross off to hospital."

CHANGING SCENERY

Battery Point has changed dramatically over the course of a century. In the early 20th Century, it was largely rural land, developing toward the middle of the century into a working class, semi-industrial neighbourhood. Finally, toward the end of the last century its proximity to the beautiful waterfront was realised, along with its heritage and cultural value, and real estate prices boomed.

*Opposite, top: **Patsy** under construction in the beginnings of Jock Muir's boatyard shed, 1950.*

Opposite, bottom: The Shipwright's Arms (Shippy's), a popular pub in Battery Point, early last century. The pub still operates today.

Above: A painting of the Muir's boatyard commissioned by Lyn Denehey (née Muir) by V Saska.

Adrian Gorringe also has clear memories of those years. "My early billycart was built from old tea chests I got from my Mum and Dad's grocery shop on the corner of Dunn and Macquarie Street, right opposite the City Hall. They also had a firewood business selling wood, coal and coke. They had the farm on Bruny Island, where they cut the wood, then shipped it up to Hobart on river ketches like the *May Queen*."

John and Adrian both advanced from billycarts to share driving their first go-cart driven by a lawn mower engine. John made his go-cart when he was 14 with the help of Adrian and his father Trevor Gorringe and stored it at Adrian's Battery Point home. They would drive the contraption around the streets in the evenings when the police weren't about to catch them.

The boys knew their parents were happy for them to be out and about because Adrian's father was regarded as 'one of the boys' and was the unofficial crew and pit stop manager. He was always ready to attend to repairs to the carts' lawn mower engines and running errands here and there for the boys who were concentrating on the serious business of racing.

Adrian's father Trevor and his Uncle Reg owned the business known as Gorringe Bros. Wood and Coal Merchants which was passed down to them by their father.

TREACHEROUS

Overlooking Marieville Esplanade, Napoleon Street is one of Hobart's steepest streets and provides a serious challenge for cyclists and pedestrians. The street overlooks Marieville Esplanade, the Royal Yacht Club of Tasmania, the Derwent Sailing Squadron and Sandy Bay. Photos: TAHO

ABOVE: OLD MATES

John's long time friend Adrian Gorringe. From a childhood together in Battery Point racing billycarts, to sailing mates as adults, as on **Trevassa***, above, in the 2014 Bruny Island race.*

BELOW: 'THEORY 1', 1958

A sketch of a two-stroke street kart similar to the one John and his friends drove around the streets of Battery Point as kids. John's versatile uncle Wally Muir helped John form and weld the chassis, and John either made or scavenged the rest of the components. Adrian Gorringe painted it. Illustration: Cathy McAuliffe.

They would drive the contraption around the streets in the evenings when the police weren't about to catch them.

Adrian has fond memories of visits to the farm, known as Kirbly Lodge on Bruny Island, with his father in an old Dodge truck on the first Bruny Island vehicular ferry, the *Melba*. The truck would load 7t of super-phosphate from the Zinc Works to fertilise the farm and then bring 7t of firewood back to Hobart on the return trip.

Upon arrival back at the wood yard, the wood would be docked into lengths for domestic use by a circular saw driven by a steam engine, then it was delivered around Hobart and suburbs by Reg, accompanied by Adrian in school holidays. The delivery trucks were not modern or flash, they were two 1929 'A' model Ford trucks, no roof and no doors. Pay for the day was an 'Uncle Fatty' pie, two shillings and eyes full of sawdust and aching shoulders from tossing the wood off the truck.

Everyone in the family was expected to pitch in and assist with numerous chores in the boatyard, at the wood yard or on the farm. Wherever and whenever help was needed.

Adrian continued to run the wood yard for his father and uncle after leaving school at the end of 1962 until April 1966, when he was conscripted into the army and later that year sent to the Vietnam Conflict. He was one of the lucky ones who came home.

For John, his brother Ross and Adrian Gorringe, the weekends were not all free time. On Saturday evenings they delivered the Saturday Evening Mercury newspaper to the homes and businesses of Battery Point and beyond, even to ships tied up around the Hobart waterfront. It was John's first venture into the world of business. Lessons were learned about the benefits of customer service with a smile, doing whatever it took to get a sale. A good sale meant a good tip, more pocket money for the week ahead.

One of his most fondly remembered customers was 'Ma' Dwyer, the owner of the Esplanade Hotel, or 'The Blue House' as it was known. It was down in Salamanca and John clearly remembers Ma, with her long gold burnished or smokey hair, fondly rubbing his head with her hand as he gave her the paper and received a good tip in return if he was lucky.

Hobart-based journalist and author Mike Tatlow produced a revealing series on the ABC called 'Shady Characters of Hobart Waterfront.'

"Salamanca brothel madam and loveable larrikin 'Ma' Dwyer was one of Hobart's shady characters in the mid-1900s. The old taverns and grog shops of Salamanca attracted the shadier-than-grey characters in Hobart's early days, from convicts to whalers to villains."

THE BLUE HOUSE

The old Esplanade Hotel, Salamanca, is now the site of an Irish Murphy's pub.

> ❝ *They weren't just men…In the mid-1900s Ma Dwyer's pub and brothel, the Esplanade Hotel, was a notorious haunt for some of Hobart's underbelly. It was better known as the Blue House because of the rampant fights that broke loose there.* ❞

– MIKE TATLOW; 'SHADY CHARACTERS OF HOBART WATERFRONT'

"They weren't just men," he said, "In the mid-1900s Ma Dwyer's pub and brothel, the Esplanade Hotel, was a notorious haunt for some of Hobart's underbelly. It was better known as the Blue House because of the rampant fights that broke loose there."

Yet in keeping with John's memories, Mike Tatlow's research revealed a warm hearted publican.

"The brothel madam is said to have had a heart of gold. She was generous with free drinks for a hard-luck story. But she also had some quirky management skills," said Mike. "Apparently she rigged up a system of strings tied to the beds in the brothel above the pub. The strings ran through the floor and were attached to bells near the bar so that Ma, who worked the bar below, would know that the girls were working."

John's father Jock used to joke with the boys about Ma, asking, "Would you run if she chased you?" John reckons his response was "Depends, Jock." Clearly thinking but not telling his Dad at the time that the truth was much closer to "Don't worry, if Ma Dwyer chased me I'd run like the blazes!"

An alternative historical investigation from the Tasmanian Archive and Heritage Office (TAHO) suggests that Ma didn't run a brothel, but didn't bother to check too closely on who or what the rooms were used by or for. If John remembers seeing anyone he knew going in or out of Ma Dwyer's he doesn't talk about it, even now! He has learnt that it pays to hold your tongue sometimes.

"We boys always had to earn our money, especially if we wanted to buy something."

In his later years as John built his business, he seemed to know instinctively that to ensure he won an order for a new winch or anchor system he had to do whatever it took to keep the potential customer happy. John would often travel halfway round the globe if that's what it took to get a new customer or keep an existing one. Many's the time, after he was married and with two children, the kids would come home and ask their Mum Wendy, "Where is Dad, I haven't seen him for a few days?" The answer was more often than not, "He's in the US, or Europe and he will be back when he's finished over there."

Delivering newspapers, working to earn money to build billycarts or later racing boats or tinkering with engines kept John on the streets and at the same time, off the streets.

He was becoming a keen observer of human nature, learning fast, watching how other people behaved and reacted. He stood close by his mates and siblings. Mateship, that defining Australian character is important to John Muir.

"We had really great parents (Jock and Mollie Muir). They were really like best friends. We'd all go cruising together. The first motor cruiser we bought was named *Hintok*, a Hartley 28 footer with a 10ft beam and a 6 cylinder Ford turbocharged diesel. As Mum often commented *Hintok* was noisy when she was at full speed, all of 15 knots. From our perspective she was like a floating caravan. Well built by the original owner from marine plywood, fully fibreglassed all over. There was plenty of room, the large engine box was a table. If there was a full crew I slept on the ready-made double bunk in the cockpit. Others slept in the double bunk up forward."

Jock once said to both John and Wendy when they were away on the boat together, with their eldest daughter Alex, who was just a few months old, "Spend as much time as you can with your children and always take them with you on the boat, because 16 years will go like that. After that they will want to stay home and go places with their mates and do their own thing."

Not a truer word said, for at around 16 years of age both Alex then Shona did just that! But that sage fatherly advice did not stop John from endlessly travelling the globe during the years he was building and maintaining the business.

One of the lessons you learn quickly when you are on the water is that there is one person in charge, the skipper. He or she is the boss and you can expect to get yelled at, screamed at sometimes to do something really quickly. It can be a 'win or lose' reaction, even a life or death situation if you are not fast enough. It's one of the hard lessons John learnt and learnt well. In his business John was 'the skipper' and everyone who worked for him knew it.

John first went to sea with his father as a teenager, doing more than a dozen yacht delivery trips. For centuries before, boys of this age or younger were inducted into the British Navy as midshipmen and quickly graduated to manhood once at sea. In 1959, at the age of

GORRINGE BROS. BUSINESSES
Top: Gorringe Brothers Groceries, where Adrian's father Trevor was born, c. 1930s.
Middle and bottom: Gorringe Bros wood cart and wood yard, early 20th Century.

15, John was invited to crew on board *Lass O'Luss* in the Sydney to Hobart Yacht Race and for many years he was the youngest crew member to take part in the annual event. Skippered by owner John Colquhoun of Sydney, *Lass O'Luss* was a 41ft sloop, designed for ocean cruising by Englishman Robert Clark and built in 1948 by Jock Muir and his staff at Battery Point. She first raced in the 1948 Sydney to Hobart Yacht Race. By the time John was on board 11 years later, she was competing in her fifth race.

"John Colquhoun had the starboard saloon lower bunk and I had the bunk above. We slept with our feet facing forward. Above the skippers head on the bulkhead was a small wooden barrel with a tap on it and I was curious to know what it contained.

The skipper would have a small glass of whatever was in the barrel before he went on deck and when he came off watch. I did ask him when he came off watch, 'What was in the barrel?' and it's a long time ago now but it was either rum or whisky."

FAR RIGHT: SHARPIE RACING
*John sailing **Stratus** on the River Derwent in the 1970s. John, Bob Laing and Chris Fuglsang.*

BELOW RIGHT: CRUSADER
*With friends and family at Battery Point, John launches his first sharpie, **Crusader** in the mid-1960s. John skippered, Adrian Gorringe was mainsheet.*

BELOW: STRATUS
*John's long time friend Chris Fuglsang racing **Stratus** on the River Derwent, 1971. Same race as above.*

RIGHT: SHILO
John's lightweight sharpie, c. 1970.

> " *Our Dad told us boys more than once, 'Cars cost you money, you'll never make any money out of cars.'* "

John started sailing lightweight Sharpies when he was 19 and represented Tasmania in the national titles three times and won his share of state titles. He first competed in *Crusader* (1964 to 1967), a Sharpie which John built himself with the help of Adrian Gorringe, John Griggs, Wayne Denehey and Paul Hurd. Next came *Rebel* (1967 to 1969), built by John with the help of John Griggs and father Bruce and Paul Hurd. She was followed by *Stratus* (1970 to 1974), built by Bruce Darcey with assistance from Paul Hurd and finally, *Shilo* (1975 to 1976), built by John, his brother Ross and Paul Hurd.

John's brothers Ross and Greg were both Australian champions in cadet dinghies, following in their father's footsteps. Jock and his brother Max had each won the national championship series, known as the Stonehaven Cup, in 1933 and 1935 respectively.

John Muir: "My brother Greg was the only cadet dinghy skipper to win all his races and invitation races in the Stonehaven Cup, held in Hobart in January 1967. He was the Australian champion that year. I had a lot of good friends who sailed in cadet dinghies and Sharpies."

While John's brothers were sailing he was tinkering with motor cars, working at the boatyard, or in Jock's engineering shop making or fixing something.

"Our Dad told us boys more than once, 'Cars cost you money, you'll never make any money out of cars.'"

Ocean cruising and yacht deliveries were also part of John's young and ongoing life, often with his father. It included the delivery voyage from Hobart to Sydney of the 48ft *Trevassa*, a cruiser/racing yacht designed and built by Jock, his brother Max and employees

TREVASSA THEN AND NOW

*Left, in 1970 nearing completion at Battery Point. Right and below, in 2016, restored to all her former glory. The three Muir brothers completed most of the restoration on **Trevassa**, including the anti-fouling (Ross, right), most of the brightwork and the beautiful custom steering wheel and table, both also handmade by Ross.*

TREVASSA RETURNS

*In 2012 **Trevassa** was returned to the Muir family, in accordance with her former owner Russell Duffield's wishes.*

ABOVE: LEAVING ROYAL SYDNEY YACHT SQUADRON

*The crew of Peter Creese, Greg Muir, Robert Featherstone, Tim Greene, John Griggs, John Muir and Stewart Griggs sailed **Trevassa** back to Hobart.*

LEFT: SAILING OUT OF SYDNEY HARBOUR

Left: Peter Creese, John Griggs and Robert Featherstone.

BELOW: *TREVASSA* ENTHUSIASTS

From left: Dave Wardrop, Rodney Jackman, Greg Muir, John Muir.
Front row from left: Bill Foster, Ted White, Ross Muir.

LEFT: ONBOARD *HINTOK*

Mollie with granddaughter, Shona, at 15 months, 1979.

BELOW: PLAY TOGETHER, STAY TOGETHER

*One of the family trips onboard **Shonandra**, 1990. Left to right: Wendy Muir, Shona Muir, Sue Cowle, Tammy Cowle, Alex Muir, Natasha Cowle, Anne Roule.*

OPPOSITE PAGE LEFT: TOGETHER AGAIN

*The Muir siblings onboard **Trevassa** after its return to Hobart, 2016.*

OPPOSITE PAGE RIGHT: FATHER AND SON

*John and Jock on **Lahara**, Newport NSW, 1991.*

at the Battery Point boatyard. *Trevassa* has a special part in the hearts of the Muir family. After 41 years of ownership, Russell Duffield mentioned to both Jock and John that when he could no longer use the boat that he wanted it to go back to Hobart to the Muirs and it did.

Since 2012, *Trevassa* has been owned by John and his brothers Greg and Ross. She is moored at the Royal Yacht Club of Tasmania's marina alongside John and Wendy's 48ft pilot house cruising yacht *Westward II*.

On *Trevassa*'s delivery voyage to Sydney in July 1971 the crew included the owner Russell Duffield, Jock and John Muir, Dave Wardrop (a well-known Muir boatyard shipwright), Tim Bailey (a fisherman) and Ken Ryman (the navigator/doctor). Despite their collective sailing experience, they were to survive a life threatening moment, unlike anything any of the crew and John's father had experienced before.

"We were well abeam of Green Cape on the Australian south coast, running with a tri-sail and storm jib before a waning south westerly gale. The seas were big and lumpy. I was below with Dad, Dave Wardrop and Ken Ryman. Suddenly I felt the stern lift and looking skywards over the scupper boards I saw a humongous sea breaking behind us.

"*Trevassa* was standing almost vertical with her mast virtually horizontal to the water as she plunged downwards on what must have been a huge rogue wave. The wave, we estimated later was at least 60 feet high. That's the height of a six to seven story building. Jock said in a dry way, 'Looks like we are going down to Davey Jones Locker.'

"He later mentioned the huge wave was caused by two big following seas colliding and breaking together. The next huge wave washed the boat flat. Down below a knife flew from its scabbard across the cabin and nicked Ken Ryman's nose. (Our doctor/navigator.) Incredibly that was the only injury to anyone.

"I was first on deck and surprised to see the mast and the two storm sails intact. Jock was next on deck and Russell handed over the wheel to him. Tim Bailey, a Bicheno cray fisherman yelled to Jock, 'Jock I've never been as scared at sea like this. I will pay you $1,000 if you can get me off the boat soon.' Jock responded that there was no way to do that as it was too rough and they were a long way from the coast.

"When *Trevassa* was within sight of Tathra Heads on the south coast of New South Wales, and the wind and sea had abated, Jock asked Tim if he still wanted to get off. The answer was, 'No thanks, I'll stay on till we get to Sydney.'"

John's memory of the incident includes this revealing comment, "You don't have time to be scared, you just cope with things as best you can, there is little else you can do. You are at the mercy of the elements."

Both his brothers have experienced similar, if not worse life threatening moments at sea. In the 1960s, for example, Ross (with no life jacket or safety harness attached) was sailing off the Tasmanian east coast with his father Jock, his brother Greg and others on a vessel's delivery trip to Victoria when a big sea hit the yacht.

John Muir: "The boat was thrown around like a cork and Ross was flicked into the water. As he went over Greg yelled out 'Man overboard' but wondered deep inside if Ross was gone. It was dark and in very rough seas. Jock and Adam Brinton scrambled up from below and heard Ross yelling 'I'm back out here.' Feeble light coming from a porthole had enabled Ross to see a rope trailing nearby as he was flicked into the rough water. Miraculously he had grabbed hold of the mainsheet (the rope) and was hanging on for grim life in the turbulent water behind the yacht. He was soon pulled back on board. We were all physically strong and determined, so that's probably how Ross survived in that instance. He was just 18."

Over 50 years later that incident remains indelibly etched into Greg Muir's memory. He will never forget the moment where one second his brother is sitting beside him, both jammed in the boat's cockpit and in an instant, his brother is gone, washed overboard into the black stormy waters.

Greg Muir: "It was in 1964 on the delivery voyage of a boat called the *Trilby 2*. I was 16 and my brother Ross was 18, we were aboard a boat that was built for inshore racing. It was a 30 footer, a Sparkman & Stephens Gulfstream 30 design, built by Athol Walter from down the Huon for a Melbourne client. She was fairly lightly constructed and was not set up with safety gear since she was built as an inshore crusier. Jock had the delivery job and his crew included Ross, Adam Brinton, Andy Van Niewenhuisen and me.

"We were sailing north just off Bicheno (on the east coast of Tasmania) in a big southerly. It was around midnight and I was helming with Ross sitting next to me braced in the cockpit. There were no lifelines fitted and we did not have safety harnesses or life jackets on.

"We were knocked flat by a big following sea and somehow I managed to let the yacht broach. When we righted I found Ross was gone, he had been washed overboard. I heard him yell and we realised he was dragging along in the water to leeward and was hanging onto the mainsheet.

"Had he let go we had no way of finding him in those conditions.

"Adam and Jock raced up on deck and dragged him aboard. I happily passed the tiller to Jock who then enjoyed surfing down the ever increasing sized waves while Ross and I took a breather below.

"We both still talk about the incident and how lucky Ross was to survive."

> ❝ *Trevassa was standing almost vertical with her mast virtually horizontal to the water as she plunged downwards…* ❞

DAVY JONES' LOCKER
Russell Duffield's sketch of **Trevassa**
plunging down a huge, rogue wave.

These are the moments when boys become men in an instant. There's no time for counselling, no time to sit and de-brief with dad or mum. Ross and Greg just 'go below for a break' after a terrifying and death defying incident. The boys are left to themselves to sort out feelings, fears and emotions, because Dad is at the helm of the yacht trying to make sure that worse things don't happen in the pitch dark and stormy conditions. Ross was a split second from certain death. As luck would have it, as he was thrown into the water he saw a rope (mainsheet) hanging over the side and in an amazing act of desperation grabbed it and held onto it for dear life, yelling loudly that he was 'out here in the water.'

Reality in that moment for Ross, having been tossed into the water is terrifying. It's dark, stormy and waves are breaking around him, as he hopes someone will hear him and pull him back on board before he is knocked down and drowned by another big wave. Hoping he will be pulled to safety before cold and exhaustion take over and he feels the rope slowly slipping from his numbed fingers and disappears into the inky darkness around him.

ABOVE: ROSS MUIR
Ross Muir steering **Trevassa** *in August 2012, in fairer weather.*

BELOW: RELIVING THE DRAMA
John in 2016, sitting in the exact seat on **Trevassa** *where he was when she capsized on her delivery trip.*

Both John's brothers have experienced similar, if not worse, life threatening moments at sea.

Coping with wild seas and storms is part and parcel of life as an ocean going sailor and the Muir family has been doing it for decades if not centuries. Greg was also to undergo a life threatening moment himself when competing in the Sydney to Hobart Yacht Race in 1977. It's a moment that to this day he still has nightmares about.

"I almost drowned and thought at the time that there were other and better ways I could spend my Christmas holidays."

Greg and his mate Phil Chugg were co-owners of the Bruce Farr designed *Farr Fetched*. They were running down the New South Wales coast, about 145km off Gabo Island, into a building storm. Dark clouds approached and the storm hit with winds around 40 knots (kt), then the wind speed increased even further.

"We did not have a very experienced seagoing crew aboard, so we sheeted in and sailed into the building storm under a storm jib and tri-sail, nurturing the boat over the building waves.

In hindsight, and if we had more experience aboard, we would have eased sheets and surfed the yacht and run a course out towards the east of Tasmania. That would have been a hairy ride, but a true blast of adrenalin!

Conditions deteriorated through the night and the waves increased in height. The result was we were getting blown about at the top of each wave, and were underpowered in the troughs because we didn't have enough sail area.

It was just on dawn when a huge wave broke over us and we were picked up like a toy boat and turned upside down. The result was that our port side cabin windows were smashed and we half filled with water."

Where was Greg? He was, like Ross, overboard.

"I was thrown overboard and luckily was attached by my safety harness and line and was being dragged along half underwater on the leeward side and was finding it hard to breathe. Water was everywhere. I recall looking up at our 12 foot wide yacht and wondering if it was going to right itself and what would happen to me when it did. After a short time she righted and some of crew came on deck and dragged me aboard."

Repairs were completed, the smashed windows covered, water bailed and the motor started. They tacked and headed back to

> ## *I almost drowned and thought at the time that there were other and better ways I could spend my Christmas holidays.*
>
> – GREG MUIR

ABOVE AND BELOW: *FARR FETCHED*
Owned by Greg Muir and Phil Chugg in the 1980s. Later sold to Don Calvert.

the safety of the harbour at Eden. Some of the crew flew home. Next morning the storm had abated, Greg and Phil were refreshed after a good night's sleep and the yacht had an easy cruise home to Hobart in the days that followed.

What saved the boat from sinking that day was the speedy action of the crew and having access to storm boards. (These are carried on board in case of emergencies like this.) The boards were hastily held and screwed in place over the shattered cabin windows with a couple of hand drills.

In case you were thinking these life threatening moments are simply a case of being in the wrong place at the wrong time, think again. The stretch of water (Bass Strait and the nearby waters off Tasmania's east coast and the south coast of New South Wales) where Greg and Phil were sailing, where Ross almost drowned, has a fearsome reputation for sea going conditions that test yachts and crews to the limit and beyond.

In 1998 the Sydney to Hobart fleet of 115 yachts left Sydney Harbour bound for Hobart. They did not know that a deep low pressure system was forming to their south. The resulting storm force winds (70kt and stronger, similar to a tropical cyclone) and huge 30m seas would decimate the fleet.

There were reports of a huge waterspout near one yacht. Five boats sank, six sailors died, 66 yachts withdrew, 55 sailors had to be airlifted to safety by rescue helicopters. The resulting rescue efforts involved

35 military and civilian aircraft and 27 Royal Australian Navy vessels and proved to be Australia's largest ever peacetime rescue operation.

From the start, the Sydney to Hobart has endured a fearsome reputation. That did not stop John's father Jock from competing in a total of 19 races. His first was in 1946, the second year the event was held, and his final attempt to take the coveted title was in 1971. During the process Jock had sailed his way into yachting history, having won on handicap in 1947 and 1948 in *Westward*, a boat he built in a paddock in Sandy Bay. Jock also finished first across the line in the 1949 and 1953 Sydney to Hobart races, the former in *Waltzing Matilda*, a vessel that he built and the latter in *Wild Wave*, a locally built cutter he designed and supervised the building of. However the 1953 win was short lived as Wild Wave was subsequently disqualified on protest, following a breach of the rules at the start of the race. Not giving up, Jock went on to win the race on line honours in 1955 (as co-skipper on board *Even*) and in 1960 (as sailing master on board *Kurrewa IV*).

There is a revealing quote from a crew member, Kevin Jarrod, of the Jock Muir built boat *Westward* when it was competing in the 1948 race with Jock at the helm in very rough conditions.

"Jock was quite happy to take the tiller and would be calmly whistling a tune while all around him the sea was particularly ugly and yet Jock was obviously loving every minute of it."*

As anyone who has a family that includes boys knows, boys love being boys and doing things where the consequences have not always been well thought through. In this case it was 'when the cat's away!' It was Christmas of 1960, John was 16 years old and his Dad was away as sailing master on *Kurrewa IV*, the yacht that was destined to win line honours in that year's Sydney to Hobart Race. John and a mate Roger Martin, decided on the spur of the moment to 'borrow' one of Jock's motor boats from the slipway in Battery Point. It was early on a Saturday morning, the weather looked ok and they were heading down the river into the channel. The plan was to go to Uncle Don Mac's farm at Police Point, a journey of about 60km.

John Muir: "It's a fair way, the boat's motor only pushed us along at 6 knots in calm water, so we were in for a long trip. It turned out to be a rough day and the weather got worse as the day went on. From memory it was blowing fresh sou-west more or less straight on the nose. The boat had a forward cabin and two bunks and a fishing well. She was about 24 foot long and eight foot wide. The Lister air cooled engine was outside of the well and there was a lot of water around. We were bailing like blazes to keep her going until the water got into the air intake and she died.

"Our Uncle Max (Muir) heard that we were in trouble from one of his mates and he came and helped us out. He was really yelling and mad, because at the time we were on the east side of the channel abeam of Barnes Bay not far from Alexanders Bay lighthouse.

"Fortunately for us Uncle Max towed us into the nearby North Simmonds Bay and we tied up to the ferry terminal adjacent to the Gorringe's holiday place. Here we dried the boat out and Uncle Max bought us life jackets and told us to head home in the morning.

There were reports of a huge waterspout near one yacht. Five boats sank, six sailors died, 66 yachts withdrew, 55 sailors had to be airlifted to safety by rescue helicopters. The resulting rescue efforts involved 35 military and civilian aircraft and 27 Royal Australian Navy vessels and proved to be Australia's largest ever peacetime rescue operation.

* Source: Maritime Reflections. Jock Muir, Chris Hudson and Jocelyn Fogagnolo.

CALM BEFORE THE STORM
Shonandra in 1998, during the eventful 50th Sydney to Hobart Yacht Race with Duncan Wood steering. John swore and declared after this that he'd never compete in the Sydney-Hobart in another cruising boat, it was "too bloody hard."

"We decided the following morning not to go back and we continued south to Police Point at the entrance to the Huon River. When we arrived late that afternoon Uncle Don Mac gave us another blast for being out in the bad conditions. After a warm dinner we bunked overnight in the house and headed back up the river early on the Monday morning.

"Dad was not impressed when he found out about our adventure and gave us both a good talking to. We hadn't asked to borrow the boat and secondly we were out in bad weather with no lifejackets. Unhappy was an understatement!"

"Looking back John says they should have got a good hiding. "We boys got the stick from Dad from time to time and sometimes he might ground us for a night or two. But as I got bigger, and if I was going to get a real hiding back in those days I might have resisted it pretty hard!"

John also recalls another delivery voyage with his father that could have gone terribly wrong, one that he was happy to remind Jock about if his Dad was having a go at him for doing something 'adventurous or stupid.'

"Jock undertook the delivery of a 19 foot Chris-Craft speed boat from Battery Point to Port Arthur. So we had Dad, in his late 40s, our cousin Bill Foster in his late 20s, my sister Lyn in her late teens, my brother Ross, 13, and myself at 15. A fairly large crew for a small boat. When we left Battery Point there was a light breeze, the weather was good and in flat water we would have made it to Port Arthur in just over two hours.

"By the time we got to Storm Bay the wind had changed to an increasingly strong nor-wester. None of us were wearing life jackets. Everyone but Jock was aghast at the terrible conditions. We were taking on a lot of water from the big waves and wild sea spray. Ross says he still recalls the sea coming on board even though he was only 13 at the time. Luckily she had a windscreen for when we were surfing. If there weren't energetic young hands onboard we would have sunk."

To get what I call 'a realistic' view of this escapade, you need, not just the memories of men or as it was in that case, boys, but also the perspective a young female teenager, John's sister Lyn aged 17. It's an acknowledged fact that young women reach emotional maturity long before most young men do. They have a more mature outlook on life at a much younger age and are mostly free of bravado and traditional male behaviour.

Lyn Denehey (nee Muir): "We left early, five o'clock in the morning to get round to Port Arthur. No life jackets or anything like that and no phones in those days or emergency beacons. I'm not sure that we even had flares in a locker somewhere.

"It was just this little open boat going out to sea. We got to Cape Raoul and it was just horrendous. Dad was at the wheel and we'd go up and bounce back down and I was screaming. John was trying to comfort me."

ABOVE: UNCLE 'DON MAC'
John's uncle Don McAllister (Mollie's brother) was a best mate of the three Muir boys and sister Lyn while they were growing up.

OPPOSITE: REMINISCING
Bill Foster, left, and Dave Wardrop, who both worked at Muir's boatyard under Jock.

> **❝** *None of us were wearing life jackets. Everyone but Jock was aghast at the terrible conditions.* **❞**

– JOHN MUIR

There is a soft and caring side to John Muir, you have to dig deep to find it, but it's there none the less.

"As for Billy (Bill Foster), I have asked him about it and he admitted he was terrified too. He didn't think we'd make it and Dad probably didn't either. No wet weather gear, no life saving gear or anything. We finally made it to Port Arthur to the jetty and there were people on the jetty and they said, 'Where have you come from?' and we said, 'Hobart' and they just wouldn't believe us."

John Muir: "When Dad was battling the rough sea we pulled back to seven or eight knots, keeping just in front of the breaking waves and surfing them because we couldn't go any slower or we would have been awash. Five or six miserable hours later we limped into Port Arthur and were met by the boat's new owner Harold Groom. I heard him say to Dad how dangerous he thought it was to be out in that kind of weather and that we were lucky we weren't drowned.

We were hungry and cold, so we had something to eat, dried out and warmed up. In the evening Mr Groom drove us all home. I dare not repeat what Mum said to Dad when she found out what had happened."

According to Jock's oldest child, his daughter Lyn, her husband, Wayne Denehey, describes the Muir family as 'without any fear of the water and the dangers it can bring.' That sentiment may have been seriously re-inforced after another ocean sailing escapade that involved, Jock and Mollie, Lynn and Wayne and their three quite small children.

Jock always managed to beg or borrow a boat from a friend whenever he needed one for the family to go for a sail.

Lyn Denehey: "I remember growing up Dad would always be able to get his hands on somebody's boat for us to use. I felt sorry for Mum, at least I do now when I look back, because it was usually a boat with a sail. They probably didn't have motors in those days and there we'd be, all these kids- us four on board, and Dad with no fear of the water and what might happen.

"I know my husband Wayne says 'you Muirs, you've just got no fear with the water like out there,' but he's not been brought up with boats the way I have, so I used to make him really nervous when we had our boat, but I was always quite happy if Dad was there and we were not on our own.

"About 40 years ago we got caught one day sailing down the east coast on the *Iola*. It was the little boat's maiden voyage. She was a small 32ft motor sailer, built I think by Wilsons down the Huon, and she was a really lively boat. There was Mum and Dad, Wayne and I and our three small children on board.

"We called into Riedle Bay on the eastern side of Maria Island, it was Christmas Eve and a local fisherman gave us some crayfish. A few days later on the way home, I remember Dad asked me which way we should go, should it be through the Dunalley canal or should we stay out to sea and head south round Tasman Island?

"I said, 'let's go around Tasman.' The kids were only young and unfortunately we copped it on the way home. The yachts competing in the Sydney to Hobart were coming past us and quickly disappearing into the squalls and rain. It was so rough that Dad was literally thrown off the wheel a few times. We didn't have any sails up and needed to put up a storm jib.

> 66 *It was just this little open boat going out to sea. We got to Cape Raoul and it was just horrendous. Dad was at the wheel and we'd go up and bounce back down and I was screaming. John was trying to comfort me.* 99

– LYN DENEHEY

Jock said to Wayne, 'go out and put that sail up.'

Wayne wasn't having a bar of that, he said 'I'm not getting out there.'

So I said 'I'll go out and do that.'

Quick as a flash Wayne said 'you're not going out there.'

"So we just had to lock the cabin tight with all of us below decks and hope for the best. The kids were screaming. Mum's in the stern cabin trying to comfort our three. I'm terrified. Wayne was absolutely terrified and that was probably his maiden voyage I reckon. We finally managed to pull in to Port Arthur and Mum got straight off the boat, took the three kids and went to find where she could get on a bus to go back to Hobart.

"We sat there in the calm waters beside the Port Arthur Settlement and it was all wonderfully quiet. After, I don't know, an hour or so, Dad said, 'what are we going to do?' Wayne just said, 'it's bloody now or never, we'll go,' I was amazed because he was terrified. So we go out into Storm Bay and it was like a mill pond so we sailed slowly and safely home. It just goes to prove that predicting the weather is really difficult."

LEFT: THE DENEHEY FAMILY, C. 1978

From left: Wayne Denehey, Mollie Muir, Louise Denehey (in front), Michael Denehey, Lisa Denehey, Lynette Denehey (née Muir) and Jock.

BELOW: EVERYONE WELCOME

The Muirs were very inclusive of friends and family in sailing adventures. Adam Brinton, shown here with Jock who treated him like another son, was well regarded by the family.

OPPOSITE PAGE

TOP: LYNETTE DENEHEY (NÉE MUIR)

*Jock and Lynette onboard **Shonandra** in 1984.*

BOTTOM: NEARING THE FINISH LINE

*Jock and others, 1953 Sydney to Hobart Yacht Race on **Wild Wave** where they were first across.*

Over the years many hundreds of sailors, including the Muir family, have put their faith and lives in the hands of skipper extraordinaire Jock Muir; he never let them down. He was also a father who didn't wield a strap or belt to keep the kids in line. While he was the sort of man who 'spared the rod,' his younger brother, Uncle Max was not. He was Jock's right hand man at the boatyard and he didn't take any nonsense from his nephews or anyone else. He ran the boatyard hard and no-one was game to cross him. Well, not until the boys got a bit older and gamer.

John Muir: "He used to give us a boot up the backside or a strap across your bum. That's if he could catch us when we played up. One time he chased me up the stairs and gave me a hard whack across the backside that really hurt. So I waited till he went outside and had his lunch. When he wasn't looking I let down the tyres on his bike and he had to push it home that night. Somehow Dad found out and gave me a really good talking to and didn't want to hear anything about what Max did.

After a few years I got on really well with Max as we understood each other better and by then he and Auntie Phyllis had two boys of their own, Philip and Stephen.

You know, when you're growing up and you look back, your parents are pretty well always right and there was always some reason why they may say 'No' or 'You will not go out tonight.' That didn't necessarily mean we always did as we were told!"

The lessons of life were being learnt the hard way. One lesson in particular has stuck in John's memory like glue.

"We all live under the law of the jungle. You only get out of life what you can negotiate. Don't expect much to be free!"

In his early years at Albuera Street Primary School John had trouble concentrating and taking things on board. No-one understood why until in grade six his teacher asked him to read out what was on the blackboard.

"It was probably the first time I'd ever been asked to do that. I said, 'No I can't.' 'Come up here' she said 'Can you read it now?' I would have said, 'Yes' but still not be able to read it. Within a few weeks I had glasses and everything became clear."

John was 13 and from that moment on his schoolwork improved dramatically. In his third year of high school he passed with flying colours, topping the school in English, maths and woodwork.

One of the most remarkable insights into the way John Muir behaves in business, neither giving nor receiving any quarter, how determined he was and still is and his sense of right and wrong, is this story.

It was a day like many others. John and his younger brother Ross were at their Dad's boatyard when they overheard an argument between Jock and a customer.

John Muir: "I was about 16 at the time and still at New Town Tech. Ross was 18 months younger. I overheard a customer getting angry and telling Dad he didn't have the money or couldn't get the money to pay for the work that had been completed on his charter boat. I don't remember how much it was but it would have been in the thousands of pounds as he had a lot of new work done.

I think he swore at us. I said, 'Yes mate and there's two of us, so make sure you fix Jock up or that'll be it. You'll not get your boat out of the shed till you pay what's owed.' Understandably he wasn't very happy with that. We were tough teenagers, kids with a reputation. People knew well we could be buggers at times and no doubt he probably was very nervous after this. Low and behold, the next day he went and saw Jock and fixed the account up, paid the lot. We never said anything to Dad about it and let it rest. I was curious, wondering if he had told Dad about it. If he had, then Dad might have just said, 'You'd better pay up then!'"

The Battery Point Blue Heeler had learnt another lesson in business, one that he would never forget. Sometimes you have to stand up for yourself because no-one else is going to do it for you. Even though in this instance the boys were trying to protect their father, for John, the kid with the gumption to take on a grown man, it was all about stopping people from walking all over his Dad. As much as John loved and admired his father, Jock normally was not of such an aggressive nature and he would have known in the end the customer had to have his boat back to go to work. Most likely he wasn't going to get his boat until he paid up.

> **We all live under the law of the jungle. You only get out of life what you can negotiate. Don't expect much to be free!**
>
> – JOHN MUIR

I said to Ross, we need to have a talk to this bloke because he's not paying Dad his money. When we saw he was on his own I said to Ross, 'Just hang on here ('here' was on Muir's jetty that ran out into quite deep water) and I'll go and get him and we'll just go down the jetty a bit further and talk to him.'

So, we're out the end of the jetty with this bloke with about ten feet of water below us at high tide, and I said, 'I heard you and Jock arguing and you saying that you are not going to pay him.' He said, 'That's right.' I said, 'Well, you need to pay him, fix him up and if you don't quick smart you'll be down there (in the water) with concrete shoes on.'

Did John think at the time that there may have been another outcome, one where this bloke tells the boys to 'Buzz off' or worse still, shove them both in the water? What would he have done then?

John Muir: "Rest assured if he tried we would have retaliated, we wouldn't have backed away. Never. He had to come into our shed to get his stuff and his boat, but you've got to be careful."

Muir folklore has it that there were occasions in later years when John and one of his employees would climb over a high fence to get to a boat that had one of their winches installed, but not paid for. Armed with spanners and wrenches and under cover of darkness,

ALBUERA STREET SCHOOL, C. 1957

An archival photo shows John as a student, on the left with hands clasped. John discovered he needed glasses after a teacher recognised he couldn't read the blackboard properly. His studies subsequently improved in leaps and bounds.
Photo: TAHO

they would remove the winch gear and cart it home. No-one ever seemed to complain. Is John a larrikin? Or just the product of a family and local culture with a strong sense of right and wrong? Either way, John's justification for that action is that what he did is no different to a repossession agent coming to collect money or goods that hasn't been paid for.

A lot of suppliers may not go so far for various reasons. However when an invoice says the goods remain the seller's property until paid, then as John sees it that customer hasn't a leg to stand on.

During his formative years John had learnt to be competitive. He already had a history of never shirking a fight. The Blue Heeler was out and about and growing up fast from a pup to an adult male.

BELOW: FIRST STEPS TOWARD SUCCESS
John attended primary school at the local Albuera Street School, shown here c. 1950s. Photo: TAHO

INTO
the
WORKFORCE

It's now 1961 and John Muir has left high school after exceeding himself academically, particularly in English, maths, wood and metal work, skills that would stand him in good stead for the rest of his working life. While at school he hadn't been idle, his life consisted of a mix of hard play, football and cricket and hard work, working for his father in the boatyard, with his Uncle Don Mac on various large building projects around greater Hobart and in workshops whenever the opportunity arose.

The Tasmanian economy was thriving, heavy industry was at the centre of Hobart's working world. At the heart of the local economy was the Electrolytic Zinc Company (Nyrstar) on the banks of the River Derwent, a huge industrial complex employing thousands of people, mostly men, in its zinc production complex. Like every other mining based industry the world over, there were good times and bad times and those times were reflected in the city's economic life.

Further upriver was Australia's biggest pulp and paper mill at Boyer, drawing on Tasmania's rich forest resource. It was churning out thousands of tons of newsprint every year to feed the newspaper printers in Sydney and Melbourne. These newspapers had an insatiable demand for newsprint and were described at the time as having 'Rivers of Gold' flooding in from the huge numbers of advertisements that were published daily. These industries and others like them in northern Tasmania were all built on the promise of cheap hydro-electric power from the rivers that were dammed on the state's west coast.

Agriculture was another booming industry sector, even though storm clouds were gathering, Tasmania was internationally famous as 'The Apple Isle.' During the export season of January to June, dozens of ships would be lined up in the River Derwent waiting their turn to dock and load the tens of thousands of cartons of apples and pears that were destined for the markets of the UK, Europe and southeast Asia.

The waterfront and the nearby boatbuilding yards of Battery Point were hives of industry, as were the nearby pubs and watering holes that relied on waterside workers, seamen and others to fill the tills every day. Ma Dwyer's hotel was one such establishment relishing the money generated from a bustling port.

JOHN AS A YOUNG LAD
In his early twenties, c. late 1960s.

A.G. WEBSTER WOOLGROWERS
Above, the old building in Melville Street, Hobart, where John worked as an apprentice. These original buildings are being surrounded by new developments.

A young man from northern Tasmania, in his early twenties, travelled to Hobart for the first time and was taken to the hotel to 'see the seedy side of life.' He said he will never forget the sight of drunken women brawling on the floor near the bar, scattering tables and chairs, clawing at one another, screaming obscenities and being egged on by the men at the bar. Behind the bar was Ma Dywer herself, complete with cigarette dangling from her bottom lip, watching everything but doing nothing to stop the brawling. He wondered at the time why the police didn't close the pub down, but was told at a later date that they thought it was better left open, so that when they needed to find a particular criminal on the run from the law, they would always visit Ma's establishment first. It was home for the underbelly elements of Hobart!

Hobart was unashamedly a working man's city. Politically it was and had been for decades a Labor stronghold. At the time John entered the workforce the Premier was 'Electric Eric Reece.' A man with a tough reputation, a man convinced that future prosperity would be built on more hydro-electric power schemes and more heavy industry if it could be enticed to the state. These were traditional heavy industries that employed hundreds of apprentices every year.

John Muir: "Before I had the apprenticeship with Webster's, I was talking to my father about what I would like to do and I told him I would like to pursue a trade in engineering. My father, being the sort of bloke he was, contacted Jim Robinson (who he knew) and enquired about the possibility of a job or an apprenticeship for me. He showed us both around the Webster's workshop a few days later and then offered me the job."

John's first job with A. G. Webster Woolgrowers was as an apprentice diesel fitter, one of the biggest agricultural service businesses in the state. Here, in the Melville Street workshop, John fell under the watchful eyes of three immigrants, who brought with them their European work ethic and commitment to quality. There was to be none of the traditional Australian attitude of 'She'll be right mate,' no way.

APPRENTICING

John, aged 18, as a second year apprentice for A.G. Webster Woolgrowers, where he went on to complete a diesel fitting trade.

John spent his time doing the sort of things he had done as a kid, but at a much higher level, working on trucks, tractors and other heavy machinery, like Allis Chalmers tractors and bulldozers, Mack trucks, Lister and Gardner marine and stationary diesel engines. He also was involved in chainsaw sales and service.

John Muir: "Webster's was a great place to work with a variety of people from Europe combining many skills and trades. We had mechanics, welders, fabricators and spray painters. We did engine repairs and rebuilds, diesel injector servicing and there was a large spare parts division.

"I loved it, every minute of it. Even though you were covered in grease and dirt, your hands were soaked in diesel and oil, it didn't matter. I was immersed in something I had loved since I was young. I didn't earn much as an apprentice (my first pay was five pounds, seven shillings and six pence) but my pay went up each year and after four years, I scored a full time job with Webster's. I went onto managing the diesel fuel pump and injector servicing section for two years prior to

leaving. I spent a total of six years of service, retaining no end of experience, knowledge and many friends."

The Webster's workshop was managed by a well-respected fellow, Jim (Robbie) Robinson. Jim had spent a long time at Webster's and understood all the products, the spare parts, and all facets of the engineering and service side of the business.

That's how Hobart life worked then, it was all about who you knew and your family's reputation. John's father Jock would have happily vouched for his son's work ethic, his capacity to learn and the broad range of mechanical skills, some of which he already possessed.

Nothing much has changed over the years; it's still much like that now.

However, John was also fortunate that working at Webster's were several senior staff members and other first class tradesmen who were to play no small part in his future life. They provided insights into how people think in Europe and were great role models.

John Muir: "There were two foremen running the large workshops, one was Hans Kramer, a large and strong German nicknamed 'The Bull.' He had the run of the workshop with another smaller fellow, Dick Starke, also a German, who managed and serviced all the transmissions, drive, gearboxes and some diesel work for the Webster agencies.

"I soon became aware of the European approach to getting things done – neither bloke would take no for an answer. Both were scrupulous operators and made sure all work under their supervision was thoroughly checked and delivered on time.

"I spent a good part of my apprenticeship as a diesel fitter, re-building and servicing engines with a good friend and mentor, Dutchman Ben Pastoor. Ben had served his trade at DAF Trucks in Holland and worked hands-on and managed the majority of engine rebuilds.

John Muir : "I can vividly remember the first time I noticed Wendy Harwood. It was when she came up to the counter of the diesel service workshop, where I was working in Melville Street, to enquire about the costing of a repair. To be honest, I was awe-struck by this beautiful girl, and within two weeks I approached Wendy to ask her out."

This was to be another turning point in John's early life. Wendy would eventually become John's wife, after heading off on a trip to Europe for 18 months at age 22. While Wendy was away travelling, John was in the early throes of setting up his own business. John and Wendy would go on to have two daughters, Alexandra and Shona. She would also become the pillar of support he needed to build his business locally, on the mainland and later, internationally. Their relationship has been buffeted over the years because of John's dogged determination to build

While Wendy was away travelling, John was in the early throes of setting up his own business. John and Wendy would go on to have two daughters, Alexandra and Shona. She would also become the pillar of support he needed to build his business locally, on the mainland and later, internationally.

At that time I was particularly interested in the British built Gardner marine engines, which without doubt were one of the most popular marine and locomotive diesel engines sold throughout Australia and across the world."

Coincidentally, Germany and Holland share a border, have a very similar ethos and world-wide reputation of doing things once and doing them right. Later in life John Muir would go courting business from some of the world's most respected megayacht builders in Germany and Holland.

One day when working in the injector room, John was suddenly struck by a lightning like bolt from the blue. A girl, not just any girl, but in John's eyes, 'the most beautiful girl I had ever seen,' walked into the service desk area where he was working. It turned out she was 17 year old Wendy Harwood who worked in the accounts section nearby. John was 20 and he was smitten. For him it was all over, a done deal, this was the girl of his dreams, now he had to summon up the courage to ask her out!

and maintain the business. Travelling overseas for long periods, often at a moment's notice can put strains and stresses on any relationship. Despite the odd storm or two this one has endured for 46 years.

It's quite evident John's father's work ethic and commitment had a strong influence on his children as all three boys excelled in the world of competitive sailing and all went on to establish successful businesses, connected in some way to wind and water. It's certainly in their blood, it may well be in their genes. Their collective success also owes a considerable debt to an understanding mother and subsequently, understanding and supportive wives.

In the time before the courtship with Wendy developed and while it was in its infancy, John was out and about with his mates, doing what most normal young men do the world over. Exploring his world, testing his limits, doing things that were risky to life and limb. He is lucky to still be alive and not just from harrowing experiences when at sea with his father.

LOVE AT FIRST SIGHT

John was struck by Wendy Harwood the moment he laid eyes on her. Six years later, in 1970, they were married.

Experts like Steve Biddulph suggest that research tells us you have to try and keep boys safe until they are at least 25 years old. That's how long it takes for them to learn that risky behavior can be life threatening and sometimes leads to an early demise or serious accident from which they may never recover. Girls on the other hand, have a much better developed sense of survival and develop a higher level of emotional intelligence at an earlier age. Boys are slow learners with some things, but quick on the uptake with others.

John Muir: "Back then I had a Morris 840 in British Racing Green with a soft top. Ross had an identical car with a black paint job, we used to spray them ourselves. I can recall a couple of incidents which still make me chuckle. One Sunday morning after a wet night, my mate Bruv and I were humming around in the Morris, on wet grass, going a bit fast, and I found myself needing to brake in a hurry. There was a wire

rope fence straight in front of me. I locked the wheels up and we skidded under the thick metal cable fence. The cable was at bonnet height and virtually decapitated the car. We had the good sense to throw ourselves onto the floor otherwise what happened to the car could have happened to us!"

A couple of months earlier, after another mishap, Bruv (Paul Probin) had helped John straighten up a bump on a mudguard of his precious Morris. Both boys were the mothers of invention. That's the way they grew up, if something breaks or goes wrong, you fix it yourselves or get help to do so. They headed to the boatyard, rigged up a block and tackle to overhead gear and started to straighten the car up.

John Muir: "Bruv was quite handy at car repairs and I heard him telling someone just recently about when he'd applied for his first job as an apprentice panel beater with a panel beating business Cramp

SAILING BUDDIES, 2013
*Jim Lockhard, left, and Paul Probin, right,
are childhood friends of the Muir boys.*

1948 MORRIS 8/40
*Johns Morris was dubbed 'Theory' as it was a guinea pig for a whole
lot of engineering and panel beating. Illustration: Cathy McAuliffe.*

Brothers. The manager had asked him what previous experience he had. He mentioned two or three repairs he'd done with me and the manager thought he sounded like that was some good experience, so he offered Bruv the job."

Bruv ran the business, Bruv's Bodyworks in Mornington on Hobart's eastern shore until the early 2000s and sold it around 2005. He looked older than his years, so when it came time to go to the pub, where the legal drinking age was 21, Bruv always managed to easily get inside, the others tagging along behind trying to be inconspicuous.

John Muir: "After a prize night at the yacht club, we all turned up at the Shipwright's Arms in Bruv's dad's car, a Plymouth – either inside it or standing on the running boards. We drank at the back bar in Shippies, as it was affectionately known. The licensee, Mrs Batchelor didn't seem to mind that we were underage. On another occasion Bruv was drinking in the bar with older friends Frizzle and Walchy, when the police licensing boys came in and dragged Frizzle and Walchy outside and booked them for underage drinking, but left Bruv in there assuming he was of legal age.

"Around this time our folks bought a house in Nelson Road in nearby Sandy Bay and I used the garage as a

workshop, where I did my first major independent job on an engine rebuild on Doug Nichols's Fordson tractor."

That little Morris Eight convertible was treated by John with the utmost respect, despite the odd run in with a cable fence, stump or bumper bar of another car.

According to another mate, China (Paul Hurd), while John was working at Webster's he was in the habit of removing the engine of his Morris on Saturday, including all the major engine components, alternator, starter motor, pistons, gear box, head, any other moving parts and would have it all back together by late Sunday evening, running like a charm. Amazingly, said China, there were never any leftover nuts, bolts or washers.

A deeper understanding of what makes John the man he is comes from a former employee Richard Fader, who went on to buy a ship chandlery business from the Muir family.

Richard Fader: "John's passionate about what he does, he's extremely passionate, bordering on the irrational sometimes. I think it comes from him deciding he's going to do something and he'll just get on and do it. Sometimes his people management skills play second fiddle to his drive to design and build the perfect winch or windlass, but his heart is always in the right place.

"" *John's passionate about what he does, he's extremely passionate...* ""

– RICHARD FADER

RICHARD FADER

Former Muir's Chandlery employee and later owner, Richard and his brother Edward have gone on to own and operate several marine businesses, including Purdon and Featherstone (a division of Tasmanian Shipping Supplies), and Offshore Unlimited.

"I think John's big thing is, and I've spoken to him about this a number of times, that he wants to make something. He's likes making things and then says, 'I made that.' Where I came from a retail background, our family owned Fitzgerald's the department store in Hobart, they used to buy and sell stuff. It was a retailing background, and John could never quite grasp that. He just wanted to make something. He'd look at things and say, 'I could build that' or 'I could build that better. I'll buy it, pull it apart, get the basis of it and make a better one.'

"So it was always about physically making something, and that probably came from Jock's days where he took a bit of timber and turned it into a boat. Whereas his younger brother Ross was more, 'I'll buy it, put a bit of margin on it and I'll resell it.' I don't think that was ever of any real interest to John. Sometimes the money didn't matter as much as the drive to have the Muir name on the winch, anchor system or windlass."

Meanwhile John's father's boatyard and slipway were one of the busiest in Battery Point. One time John remembers Jock told him they had performed over 250 slippings in one year. Boats were brought up for a quick scrub, antifoul, hull repair, general maintenance and rejuvenation, engines changed over or underwater gear serviced, repainted and then back in the water.

In those days slipping plans were hand drawn in the yard's slipping book then duplicated on a piece of plywood approximately A5 size, detailing the respective dimensions. This was generally done once the boat was on the slip and out of the water. Amongst some of the memorabilia at the boatyard today are hundreds of these slipping plans.

Working conditions in and around the various boatyards were hardly the best or the brightest. Sometimes you had to make do with what was there when it came time for the 'essentials' of life, that singular call of nature, well, basic doesn't even begin to describe the 'dunny.'

John Muir: "Along the Battery Point waterfront, as far as I can remember, all the shipyards had a long-drop style toilet (dunny) on the end of the jetty, which we used to refer to as the 'country toilet.' (These structures are all long gone now!)

"One cold winter's night, I was working late finishing a job, when nature called, so I made my way down to the end of the jetty, no torch to hand. It was a wet, windy, cold night with some swell boiling underneath the jetty, hardly a nice place to be. I felt my way around to the front of the toilet that faced the water, keeping close to its side, as the walkway was narrow and tricky to negotiate, especially when it's dark. It was always wise to step carefully down the three steps to the toilet, in much the same way as you'd use a ladder.

"The last step was supposed to be the toilet floor, which to my surprise, had washed out, or some bugger had pulled it out before they went home. Next thing I know I'm floundering in the water with crap all over my arms, trying desperately not to get it in my mouth, wondering what the hell had happened.

On every sea going voyage, John's father, Jock, religiously kept a log of the trip. One of the more quirky entries were the 'yodelling' incidents. Yodelling is one of those odd Australian slang words for 'vomiting' or 'seasickness' in polite terms.

"I swam ashore, cleaned up as best I could, went home and promptly had a long hot shower. I laid in bed that night, bemused, reflecting on the night's events. Needless to say, the very next morning the floor was replaced and thoroughly nailed in!"

There are an almost endless series of stories and escapades involving John, his brothers and his young mates, sailing competitively, drinking the same way, driving here and there before the days of breathalyser units were even thought of.

Adrian Gorringe said he remembers in 1964 when Ross was competing in the sailing races for the Stonehaven Cup, being held in Hobart, Mollie and Jock billeted a couple of boys from Western Australia.

Adrian Gorringe: "One of them got a bit inebriated one night and heaved up (vomited) out of the bedroom window which was directly above the kitchen window. Vomit splashed onto the outside of the kitchen window. Next morning Mollie was seen busily trying to wipe the evidence off the outside of the window, wondering out loud if it was the seagulls at fault. Meanwhile the boys were blissfully ignorant, asleep, trying to get over the effects of a hangover."

TOP: JOCK MUIR
December 1953, after completion of the Sydney to Hobart Yacht Race onboard **Wild Wave**.

ABOVE: JOCK AND MOLLIE
John's much loved parents, c. mid-1980s.

OPPOSITE: LEARNING THE ROPES
John, aged 14, crewing on **Renene** *during its delivery trip to Melbourne in 1958. This trip saw John win the 'yodelling' prize. John always looked forward to these trips with his dad, as he learned so much and there was plenty of time to talk about life and the world.*

The sailing families of Hobart used to billet entrants from other states who were competing in the national races. Adrian said he also remembers his mother having to cope with the after effects of 'too much booze' from young sailors who were billeted with them.

On every sea going voyage, John's father, Jock, religiously kept a log of the trip. One of the more quirky entries were the 'yodelling' incidents. Yodelling is one of those odd Australian slang words for 'vomiting' or 'seasickness' in polite terms. On one delivery voyage from Hobart to Melbourne of a newly completed yacht, John won the 'yodelling' prize. There were some other times that he was crook (unwell, seasick) at sea, but he like many others has learnt to overcome that problem.

Once John had finished his time with Webster's, he started working with his father at the Battery Point boatyard. The germ of an idea was growing in his subconscious, that of starting his own business. Like father, like son, wind and water at work again.

John was slowly realising the best way he could continue to work and do what he wanted to do was start his own business and he knew then what he wanted to do and where. It may not have been the dream of the internationally successful winch business that evolved but it was the idea from whence the amazing Muir winches reality began.

You can wonder where this drive, this determination to succeed began. It was in all three Muir boys, the urge to win, the work ethic, the dedication, focus and a degree of sheer bloody mindedness. Is it learned behavior, or is it genetic? Experts will tell you it's learned and they were getting lessons from a father and grandfather with all those characteristics. The capacity for financial success is, however, one trait that is certainly not genetic. John's business was destined to be hit with economic storms but survived every battering.

The Muir boatyard had a small engineering workshop that was to be the first home for John's new business venture. With the help and support of his father, grandfather, uncles and friends, John was to set sail on the most amazing journey of his life.

The Muir maritime legend was growing. Jock built his first boat in the backyard of his parents' house. Following several years spent in Sydney, he established his boatyard and slipway at Battery Point in 1948 and was now about to support and mentor his eldest son on his first foray into the world of business.

BELOW: SIBLING RIVALRY
Greg, left, and John en route to the Brisbane Sharpie Nationals in 1969 in John's EH Holden station wagon. Ross also competed on **Venom II**. *All three boys raced against each other.*

THE BUSINESS BEGINS

The years have flown by for John Muir, working firstly for his father in school holidays and on weekends and for his Dad's brother, Uncle Don Mac, on large building sites around Hobart. For four years he was apprenticed as a diesel fitter, then another two years on full pay, still at Webster Woolgrowers, rising quickly to team leader, working in the fuel pump and injection workshop.

These years were to provide vital background experience for young John. Working hard, he watched how others behaved or didn't, listening to his immigrant workplace mentors, two Germans and a Dutchman. He realised more and more that quality of service, meeting deadlines, treating customers well, knowing what you were doing could make or break you in any line of business.

John's mentors at Webster's imbued him with an understanding of how important a European work ethic was. A total commitment to quality and workmanship.

Muir's Boatyard and slipway was John's next job, working alongside his father and other family members. There was Uncle Max, Jock's younger brother, a working foreman and without doubt a stalwart in the overall operations of the boatyard including new builds, repairs and maintenance. There was Uncle Wally, Jock's other younger brother who could turn his hand to anything mechanical, electrical or that needed fabricating. He had served his mechanical fitters apprenticeship with John's Uncle Don Mac. This is the way it was for the broader Muir family.

In 1968 the Muir boatyard was slipping and servicing large and small vessels, designing and building fishing boats, commercial vessels and sailing yachts up towards 60ft in length. The yard also operated two slipways, one capable of handling vessels up to 80t and the other up to 30t.

Life for the Muir family was busier than ever, as the boys got older and matured into young men, the fisticuffs and wrestling matches gave way to competitive sailing, girlfriends and business adventures.

ROSS'S COMPETITIVE SAILING

*Left: On Ross's sharpie **Venom**, from left, John Wilkinson, forward hand, Bob Laing, mainsheet, Ross Muir, skipper, in the mid 1960s. Right: Ross's cadet dinghy, also named **Venom**, sailing on the Derwent, c. 1962. Aft Ross, centre John Griggs, forward hand Adrian Gorringe.*

All the family generally got together on a Sunday morning over breakfast. There would be Jock (if he wasn't off sailing in a Sydney to Hobart race), Mollie, the boys, sister Lynette and sometimes a boyfriend or girlfriends. Some Sundays were brighter and noisier than others. The ones where one of the brothers had won at sailing the day before were chirpy, particularly if they had beaten a brother or two. For the vanquished, it was a case of grin and swallow one's pride, secretly gritting your teeth, determined to reverse the situation when next on the water.

The three Muir boys all knew that sailing wasn't just a joyful pastime, sure you had some fun and in John's case the wilder the weather the better. But at the back of their minds, embedded in their subconscious was the Muir ethic, 'You are out there to win!'

When the boys were racing their smaller boats, Jock was sometimes on the water in a pick-up or support boat, following the Sharpies and cadet dinghies and conveying his thoughts and racing suggestions on

tactics to the boys. Back in the 1920s and early 1930s while Jock's father, Ernie, didn't follow the young sailors in a support boat, he was watching the races from his house at Battery Point and would make suggestions about tactics once Jock and Max were back home.

John, his two brothers and their crew mates also had their own way of communicating with each other.

"Our group of yachties developed an unusual competitive strategy. We could speak in code and we all had peculiar code names. When we were yelling to one another, suggesting tactics or strategies we would talk backwards. Our conversations were secret and it used to frustrate our competitors. We did it in front of girlfriends and even our parents.

"I was Nhoj, Ross was Ssor or Horsc, Greg was Gerg, sister Lyn was Nyl. We spoke of Mollie as Yllom and Jock as Kcoj. Sometimes I'd call Jock Kay-Cee-Oh-Jay. I don't think they ever worked out what we were saying or if they did they didn't let on at all!"

MUIR'S BOATYARD, 1968

Oil painting by Paul Hurd showing, left to right, the original Muir's Boatyard shed, **Anaconda II** *(the white boat, owned by Guy Ellis), a steel boat for sale at the time, Muir Diesel Services workshop, and Burnetts's fish shed.*

All three of the Muir boys built and sailed small racing boats. Ross and Greg sailed international cadets, then cadet dinghies, then lightweight Sharpies that were racing boats with a planing hull. The Sharpies could really fly and boasted a substantial sail area as well as a spinnaker and three crew.

In 1968, leasehold land became available next to the Muir's Boatyard and slipway at Battery Point and it meant suddenly there was space available for a new workshop. Being adjacent to the slipways was an ideal location for engine and general boat servicing work.

Keen to start his own business and what better spot than right next to his Dad's thriving boat building and repair operation, meant John could expand the business offering to Jock's existing clients. John's years as a diesel fitter meant he was ideally placed to rebuild and repair boat engines, provide new ones for new builds and generally be a wonderful addition to his father's boat construction and repair business.

As he began setting up, preparing plans for the new shed, he could call on advice from his extended family, starting with grandfather Ernie Muir.

Ernie was another Muir with a strong work ethic, more than happy to share his knowledge and wisdom with his grandson. He was always pottering about the boatyard, helping where he could and even cleaning up if he saw the need. Don't forget, Ernie was a determined old codger who even in his eighties, walked from Battery Point, across the Tasman Bridge and on to his daughter's house in Howrah, then back again in the afternoon, a simple jaunt of twenty-odd km, three times a week. In summer, Ernie often swam from the boatyard to Wrest Point and back.

"Some good advice Ernie gave me early on was to eat three regular meals every day, get lots of regular exercise and keep the stress to a minimum! I'm not sure I always remembered to do that as the business grew, particularly when it expanded overseas."

It was business stress, the physical and mental toll of many long overseas trips from Tasmania to markets in Asia, Europe, USA and Canada, and his dogged determination to do what had to be done when he was travelling, that some years later almost cost John his life.

> **❝** *Some good advice Ernie gave me early on was to eat three regular meals every day, get lots of regular exercise and keep the stress to a minimum!* **❞**
>
> – JOHN MUIR

In these early days the fact that Hobart was 12,000km from New York, London and Stockholm didn't enter the subconscious of John Muir's brain. It didn't need to. These were times when he was focused on doing what he had learnt to do at his uncle's business and at Webster's, installing, rebuilding and repairing diesel engines, working until the job was done.

Hobart in the latter part of the 1960s was facing tough economic times. In February 1967, many of the city's outlying suburbs and surrounding areas of southeast Tasmania had been ravaged by huge bushfires that claimed the lives of 62 people in a single day of heat and horror.

Over 100 separate fire fronts raged out of control, destroying more than 1,200 homes. About 60,000 livestock also died in the inferno. It proved to be and remains as one of the worst natural disasters in Australia's history.

On the world scene trouble was brewing. Britain was soon to vote on joining the Common Market (European Union) and the consequences for the huge export apple industry in Tasmania were predicted as dire, if it happened.

The decision when it came led to the decimation of the once thriving apple and pear industry and left production areas like the Huon Valley as economic disaster zones, destined to remain poverty stricken for decades.

Despite that, Jock Muir's boatbuilding business was in full swing and John's new venture was to blossom and grow.

Hobart's population in the late 1960s was around 110,000, just over the required number of people for a city to become self-sustaining. Nightclubs were opening as the baby boomer generation got into full swing. Girls' hemlines were rising, blokes' trousers were stovepipes and shoes were long and pointy toed. Pubs and clubs were discovering the delights of pop music, folk and jazz. To the older generation, those who had survived The Depression and World War II, it looked like the world was spinning out of control.

FLYING HIGH

John's grandfather Ernie Muir was a go-getter and his advice set the tone for many of John's successes in life and business. Shown here at Cambridge Airport near Hobart in the mid-1940s, Ernie went flying, sailed, and – up until the time he died – walked and swam regularly.

Author Jim Marwood in 'Notes from Sweetbreads out of Season' provides a fascinating glimpse into Hobart and the state of Tasmania.

"In the early sixties, Pat's 'Bistro' opened, with Pat Collins (a refugee from Melbourne) as genial host and social catalyst. It was Tasmania's first independent restaurant with the use of a full liquor licence. The venue became the centre for a generation of artists, young professionals and 'lefty' politicians. The owners of nearby pubs had fought its licence application tooth and nail, and lost.

"Pat was convinced the state was run by a dark oligarchy involving the Tasmanian Club, the Legislative Council and of course The Mercury (then still the private domain of the conservative Davies Brothers). When Pat was interviewed for commercial radio by a young woman, who showed little knowledge of food and wine, Pat was delighted to be asked his opinion of Tasmania. His response quickly ended the session. Beaming his most benign smile, he replied, 'There's a worm in the… apple!' (Meaning Tasmania the 'Apple Isle.')

"All through the 1960s, Pat Collins' Bistro was a freewheeling centre for argument and dissent. The long-running, conservative Reece Government was losing its grip on power, opposition was growing to our Vietnam intervention and fledgling conservationists were opposing the destruction of Lake Pedder. Social complacency was further shattered when bushfires burned through southern Tasmania in 1967, but for the younger generation, it was a small green pill that brought greater change by disconnecting sex from pregnancy, changing lives forever."*

New freeways ran north through the growing suburbs, linking north and south. The Tasman Bridge had been built, linking east and west. Cadbury's chocolate factory was expanding into not just a factory but also a burgeoning tourist destination. The blight of our convict past at Port Arthur was also attracting increasing numbers of Australians, keen to see and hear the reality of Tasmania's brutal past. Other industries like Silk and Textiles and Blundstone Boots were thriving. Eventually both of these companies would either close or leave Tasmania for cheaper production countries in Southeast Asia.

John Muir wasn't oblivious to all of this, but he was focussed on doing what he wanted to do: starting his own business. The idea had been festering in his head for a while. He could see an opportunity and he took it with both hands.

John Muir: "Muir's boatyard had a small engineering workshop that helped me take my next step. We were digging the shed's foundations by hand when a bloke called Trevor Brown, one of Dad's good customers, offered to help. He owned one of Jock's earlier pilot boats (the *Captain McKenzie*) that he plied on the Maatsuyker Island run to service the island's lighthouse and provide supplies to the lighthouse keeper and his family.

"One day when Dad was helping to load supplies onto his boat, Trevor saw us working on the site, without hesitation he offered to lend us his backhoe to help dig foundations and level the slab area. We used this as a 'contra deal,' which was very helpful in the early days of trying to get established with little cash flow available."

Jock became John's closest mentor as he built the shed, installed workshops and machinery, took on new employees and built the business.

"Dad helped me with various aspects of setting up a small business and passed on great advice about metal work, engineering, boat building and invoicing. One of many things I recall was him telling me was not to do what he had done and to spread my customer base, so not to be caught out with one or two main customers at any time. He also said to always keep clear of anyone who might offer me a bribe."

> 66 *One of many things I recall was him telling me was not to do what he had done and to spread my customer base, so not to be caught out with one or two main customers at any time. He also said to always keep clear of anyone who might offer me a bribe.* 99

* See more at: http://www.tasmaniantimes.com.au/index.php/article/sweetbreads-a-tale-of-protests-polaroids-and-the-pill-in-1960s-hobart#sthash.e1JLXiea.dp

DEVASTATION

The 1967 Hobart bushfires were the most deadly bushfires that Tasmania has ever experienced, leaving 62 people dead, 900 injured and over seven thousand homeless.
Photos: TAHO

Financial stress can take a terrible toll on many people and Jock was hit and hit hard when in September 1951 Federal Treasurer Sir Arthur Fadden introduced a budget that called for large increases in income, sales and other taxes. In particular, the budget increased the sales tax on pleasure boats from 10 to 33% effective immediately, then backdated it. Just what was a luxury boat and what was a working boat was left to bureaucrats who knew little or nothing about the industry. Jock was at the time, halfway through building two new boats, both classed as 'luxury' builds. The contracts were already signed and the extra cost was going to fall entirely on Jock's shoulders.

John Muir: "As I understand, at the time of signing both these customers, there was a 10% sales tax on pleasure craft. Both yachts were well advanced when the government of the day brought in retrospective 33.3% sales tax. This all but crippled the boatyard because the tax had to be paid on the boat at the time of sale, but couldn't reasonably be passed onto the customer when they'd already signed a contract for a fixed amount.

only too well one or other of those sides of John Muir. "Life and work's a jungle and you don't take no for an answer. You have to work out who you can work with and who you can't and how you can get around it."

It transpired that some twenty years after the two vessels had been built, the owner of the larger vessel, who had refused to pay the sales tax that was owing, passed away. His widow contacted Jock and made an arrangement to pay a reasonable proportion of the tax component. Obviously Jock wasn't expecting this, so it must have been a very pleasant surprise after such a long wait. 'All good things come to those who wait!'

Once the small shed, 12m by 6m, was built, within three months John was up and operating. The first registered business name was Muir Diesel Services. As the name suggests that's what the business was all about.

John Muir: "As diesel fitting was my trade, I started off servicing and overhauling engines, propeller drives and shafts. The Muir Boatyard was always busy, building new boats, slipping and repairing older ones. When

Jock was hit and hit hard when in September 1951 Federal Treasurer Sir Arthur Fadden introduced a budget that called for large increases in income, sales and other taxes. In particular, the budget increased the sales tax on pleasure boats from 10 to 33% effective immediately, then backdated it.

"Of the larger of these two vessels, the owner certainly could afford it, however he refused to pay any additional cost. The owner of the smaller vessel, being a thorough gentleman, came to an arrangement with Jock in making sure the extra cost was covered fairly.

"The larger vessel had shown a significant loss at the time of launching and the smaller vessel was closer to breaking even."

The Muirs are strong willed. John, the Battery Point Blue Heeler, is seemingly indestructible. Lick you to death when he likes you, look out if he doesn't. Variously described as a 'streetfighter,' or a 'hard man,' he plays it tough when he has to, gives no quarter and expects none in return.

As John says, in a moment of quiet reflection: "I can be hard and fierce and I can be soft and gentle." There are a number of individuals who know

I started working with Jock he was building a yacht called *Trevassa*. The project took three years and money was really tight. At the same time he owned and operated two abalone boats and spent time away abalone fishing. He was one of the very first involved in the business. In that third year (1971) I was cashed up enough to be able to buy into the boatyard."

As time progressed and John's business grew, he broadened his capacity to include repairs to fishing boats including propeller shafts, stern gear, hydraulics, steel shoes under wooden boats and engine overhauls.

John Muir: "We were by now selling and servicing a range of marine diesel engines as well as distillate and attracting some new customers. Plenty of new work came our way from the boatyard and within two years I had hired boiler maker/welders and machinists, including my first apprentice.

MUIR'S BOATYARD, 1977.

Showing the signage for John's first business, Muir Diesel Services. Photograph by Margaret Bryant, courtesy of TAHO.

"Within the extremities of the smallish workshop we had installed three lathes, a universal milling machine with many attachments for multi-purpose machining and boring operations, grinders, pedestal and bench drills and several welding machines. We managed to finance all this with cash flow, so it meant I wasn't taking much money out of the business for us to live on.

"Older fishing vessels were being pulled up on the slipways and required extensive repairs and maintenance, so we pushed on, designing and manufacturing winching and hauling equipment."

This proved to be the turning point for the business, although at that time John had no idea of the future opportunities that the global megayacht and boat market held. John had simply seen an opportunity to build something. That's what drives his excitement, that's what he loved to do as a kid, make stuff!

By the end of 1974 the business was thriving and had changed its name to 'Muir Engineering Pty Ltd.' It had more than doubled its original workshop floor space, expanded engineering operations and sales. The number of employees had increased, with just over

20 full time people on the payroll. A range of pleasure and workboat "manual" anchor winches, all designed by John and his staff were also in production.

John was also building business relationships that continue to this day. One of the first was with a local Hobart based foundry, Skeels and Perkins.

Andrew Perkins: "When my brother Alan and I first started producing castings for Muir's (about 1969), we were both quite young and relatively inexperienced in business. I looked up to John and would often ask myself, 'What would John do in this situation?'"

Andrew and Alan were working with their father, Bill Perkins and his partner, Selwyn Skeels as Skeels and Perkins. They were based in Argyle Street, next to Minty's, a sheet metal workshop that is still in operation today. Skeels and Perkins manufactured some of John's first casting patterns and castings for winches and anchors.

The global Muir legend was born. It would be a decision to visit an international boat show to show the world what he could make that would change the business and the life of John Muir and his family forever.

THE START
of
SOMETHING NEW

It was in the very early 1970s when John Muir discussed with two of his long-time friends and engineers, Bob Harper and Chris Michael, the idea of developing and making a Muir range of manual and hydraulic commercial and pleasure boat anchor winches and line haulers. At the time the trio agreed that the existing range of winching equipment available within Australia and overseas had some serious shortfalls.

The discussion followed a couple of years spent repairing other manufacturers' equipment. Armed with this background knowledge and his own skills and expertise, John Muir knew they could build a more reliable and more versatile range of winches.

Many of the work boats and fishing vessels that used this type of equipment were plying and working the unreliable and rough waters around Tasmania and Bass Strait. Tasmania lies in the belt of the Roaring Forties, a zone in the Southern Hemisphere that is home to strong, many times gale force westerly winds. The gales can strike suddenly with wind speeds from 80 kilometres per hour (km/h) to 150km/h, sometimes higher. This is the zone the Tea and Wool Clippers and Windjammers plied during the mid-to-late 19th century. It is still regarded as part of the fastest sailing route around the world.

In 1885, for example, the *Cutty Sark*, one of the fastest sailing ships of her time, took just 67 days to sail from Sydney to the English Channel, driven by strong westerly winds. The region is not without its dangers; many ships and sailors have been lost in the wild storms that come and go without warning.

"Because Tasmania dangles down from Australia, it's more exposed to the westerlies. All of southern Australia experiences these winds, but more often than not Tasmania is within the scope of those westerlies," says Ian Barnes-Keoghan from the Bureau of Meteorology's (BOM) Tasmania and Antarctica Regional Office.*

* Source: ABC Science Documentary 2011

Fellow BOM weather gurus Kenn Batt and Bruce Buckley, in an unpublished draft article on the weather sailors could have to cope with in a typical Sydney to Hobart yacht race, suggest:

"Sailors need to be prepared for Southerly Busters, they can be very nasty. Be aware of the possibility of cyclogenesis, the fast and sometimes explosive generation of an East Coast low. Thunderstorms are one of nature's terrors, with savage squalls, waterspouts, winds from every direction, hail and heavy rain. Beware the weather when crossing Bass Strait, one of the most changeable stretches of water in the world, even though its nickname is 'The Paddock.' Be very aware that when a big swell hits a strong cross current and is opposed by a large wind wave train, you can see very dangerous wave conditions, as we did in the 1998 race."

This draft was submitted as part of the evidence into the coronial inquest into the 1998 disastrous Sydney to Hobart Yacht Race.

Using data derived from Antarctic ice cores and other sources, Australian researchers at the Australian National University published a study in 2014 that found Southern Ocean winds are now stronger than at any time in the past 1,000 years.

"Greenhouse gases are what are causing the winds to intensify," said Nerilie Abram of the Australian National University's Research School of Earth Sciences and lead author of the research, published in Nature Climate Change.

The research suggests that the wild weather of the Roaring Forties may be shifting southward into the 'Furious Fifties.'

Cray fishing boats from Tasmania, abalone boats and deep sea fishing trawlers need reliable winch and anchor equipment to withstand the most horrendous storms, as on both the east and west coasts of Tasmania there aren't many anchorages where boats can shelter safely during a storm.

West Coast fishing legend and Tasmanian sea dog, Max Hardy: "When you are laying there at sea, west of Tasmania with the waves breaking over the bow and you can't see out of the wheelhouse windows, it's time you weren't there. It's not about being brave, it's more about being bloody silly!"

Survival is all about how well built and strong the vessel is and how rugged its anchor gear and associated winches are.

Ocean going sailing yachts are no different, as was the case with the three masted schooner, superyacht *Adix*, helmed by Tasmanian-born Paul Goss. In December 1996 *Adix* was caught in an Antarctic gale while anchored in a lonely, mountainous area at the southern end of Chile. If the heavy duty vertical Muir anchor winch and chain stopper securing the 26mm stud link anchor chain had failed, Paul, along with his crew and passengers on the 65m super-yacht, could have perished.

Rugged and reliable anchoring equipment can mean the difference between life and death. John Muir knew this from his own and his family's experiences at sea.

On one occasion his father Jock was delivering a re-furbished fishing boat to the mainland and was anchored offshore from a beach near Cape Barren Island, part of the Furneaux Group that lies to the north-east of Tasmania. They were sheltering as best they could from a nor-westerly gale with wind gusts up to 60kt (nearly 130km/h).

The boat was yawing from side to side with a single anchor chain out. Suddenly, the anchor chain jumped clear of the chain roller as the boat swung beam onto the wind. The anchor chain stretched tight and with a big shudder, the uncontrolled chain sawed the bulwarks off from the stem back to the mast. (Bulwarks are extended topsides and ribs, solid and sturdy, designed to keep water off the deck, the crew safe and to secure the likes of fishing gear. Rails and lines are used on sailing yachts and are of much lighter construction, not solid timber as was the boat in question.) Fortunately it was dusk and Jock fired up the engine, turned the vessel's head to wind and as he did the crew hand hauled the slackened chain back onto the roller and lashed it securely in place.

John Muir: "Dad told me about this incident when we were building a new chain roller anchoring system for another more modern fishing boat. He insisted we make the roller side plates higher, to stop the chain from jumping off."

John was smart enough to know when to listen to advice from his Dad and not to ignore him. A new design was drafted, incorporating a U-shaped loop that totally retained the chain within the roller area.

WILD SOUTHERN WATERS

*John and crew on deck on **Shonandra** as part of a round Tasmania cruise in 1991. The weather was so rough that most of the yachts took respite in Port Davey.*

*Greg Muir recounts: "John Sutcliffe and I joined **Shonandra** at Melaleuca Inlet, Port Davey, after an early morning flight from Hobart. After a day collecting several crayfish from craypots set outside the harbour at Breaksea Island, an enjoyable dinner and a few wines was had by the crew. Forecast was for strong winds next day so we headed off at 5 am in a 35 knot NW breeze and large westerly swells. The wind increased to 40 to 45 knots as we headed down the west coast and moved to a westerly direction. After some debate we decided to gybe over to port tack off South West Cape, hearts in mouths. The winds and swell continued to increase to 60 knots and as we headed outside of Maatsuyker Island, it became more difficult to steer. With John and I both on the wheel, we broached on several occasions. At one point, **Shonandra** was laid flat on a wave face and we heard a loud whimper from below as 20 stone Tim Watts was thrown from the port bunk, over the table and into the starboard side bunk, where he stayed for the rest of the trip! John Sutcliffe, feeling sick, stayed below for the rest of the day, but revived as we approached Partridge Island. He hooked onto a few couta, which livened everyone up, and we ended up enjoying it for dinner. It was a great day of 11 hours' sailing. With only one gybe for the day it was a most memorable trip."*

" *Sailors need to be prepared for Southerly Busters, they can be very nasty. Be aware of the possibility of cyclogenesis, the fast and sometimes explosive generation of an East Coast low… Beware the weather when crossing Bass Strait, one of the most changeable stretches of water in the world, even though its nickname is 'The Paddock.' Be very aware that when a big swell hits a strong cross current and is opposed by a large wind wave train, you can see very dangerous wave conditions, as we did in the 1998 race.* "

SAFETY FEATURE

Westward II's H2500 installation has a hinged anchor roller with retaining loop, to prevent chain jumping off. Muir equipment is offered standard on Buizen yachts.

Listening to the tales of sea dogs like his father and others with international sailing experience is critical if you are to design equipment that is sturdy enough to withstand the demands of whatever mother-nature throws at you when at sea. To this day John Muir is highly regarded within Australia and around the world as a manufacturer who 'knows his stuff,' who is hands on, always willing to listen, to design suggestions and on occasions incorporate something that could improve new designs.

David McQueen, internationally renowned megayacht builder and the Managing Director of Oceanfast in Western Australia, is just one of many 'Muir winch true believers.' He says it's the constant high standards of the product, its strength, reliability, quality and performance that does it for him every time.

"Until I retire I'll still be unofficially selling Muir winches because it's the best product in the world. I recommend it because it's my reputation riding on everything in a build. You have to be able to put your hand on your heart – based on reputation, trust, loyalty, communication and history – when you recommend a product. I have history with Muir now, I don't check any of their specs or equipment, or their quotes and I just trust them 100%. I know the gear will turn up and is going to work and if there is ever a problem – which I've never experienced – there'll be no trouble fixing it. Even when someone doesn't want to specify Muir winches to begin with, they always come on board once they do their research and ask around. It's the number one marine product in Australia and one of the best in the world."

Business references don't come much better than that.

However in these early days it wasn't an international reputation that John was chasing. It was continuity of work, his passion for engineering and work for the growing number of employees at his Battery Point workshop, albeit finding the cash needed to finance expansion and the latest machine tools to increase throughput and efficiency was a necessity too.

Another long-time family friend and workmate, Rodney Jackman, with his wife Angie purchased the Retlas Bronze foundry property in 1996 and remained one of Muir Engineering's preferred casting suppliers for many years. Rodney Jackman started working for John's father, Jock, when he was just 15. He was taken on as a shipwright's apprentice, a trade that is steeped in history.

There is, to this day, a Worshipful Company of Shipwrights, based in London, where early records suggest that there have been apprentice shipwrights going back to 1199 and maybe even earlier.

"London being an ancient port on a formidable river, it was entirely natural that shipwrights should have been one of the oldest trades there – so old in fact that there are no records of the origins of the Worshipful Company of Shipwrights, which was officially recognised five hundred years ago as being 'prescriptive' (that is, before things were written down) generally recognised as before 1199."*

* Source: The Worshipful Company of Shipwrights website: http://www. shipwrights.co.uk/company/history/shipwrights-history

> 66 *Until I retire I'll still be unofficially selling Muir winches because it's the best product in the world. I recommend it because it's my reputation riding on everything in a build. You have to be able to put your hand on your heart...when you recommend a product. I have history with Muir now, I don't check any of their specs or equipment, or their quotes and I just trust them 100%.* 99

– DAVID MCQUEEN, MOTOR YACHT BUILD

TOP: LAUNCHING MY *ILONA*, 2004
David McQueen, right, of Motor Yacht Build, with Rob Luijendijk, Amels Managing Director. Photo: Amels Holland.

ABOVE AND LEFT: AUSTAL ORDER
Patrick Roberts and Nick Dale (above) loading a massive SD450 drum winch for Austal in the late 1990s at the Muir Kingston factory.

MY *HEY JUDE*

44m, launched in 2014. One of the many Motor Yacht Build vessels fitted with Muir equipment. Muir supplied two VRC8000 anchor winches and combination chain stopper, roller and devil claw assemblies, and VC8000 mooring capstans aft.
Photos: Motor Yacht Build

OPPOSITE PAGE: WARREN 120

Built by Warren Yachts. Muir supplied two VRC6000 anchor winches and anchoring systems, forward, and two VC4000 tall drum mooring capstans, aft.
Photos: Motor Yacht Build

> ## John manufactured the stainless steel for all the boats Jock built. These fittings were highly polished and precision built. John's pursuit of perfection was clearly evident to me even in these early days. "
>
> – RODNEY JACKMAN

Rodney Jackman: "I started work for John's father, Jock, at age 15 as a shipwright in 1968. At this time John was working out of a steel shed the size of a double garage. This shed was/is situated north of Jock's main slipway. Soon after starting work for Jock I got to know John, in fact I was warmly welcomed by John's entire family – Ernie, Mollie, Max, Wally, Don, Ross, Greg, and of course Jock.

"I recall John manufactured the stainless steel for all the boats Jock built. These fittings were highly polished and precision built. John's pursuit of perfection was clearly evident to me even in these early days. The three yachts that I worked on and that were built in the yard were the *Lady Nelson* for a New York-born owner launched in 1969, *Trevassa* for a Sydney owner, Russell Duffield launched in 1971, and *Astrolabe* for Bob Gear, launched in 1973."

Within the extremities of John's new 12m x 6m smallish workshop, beginning in 1968, he installed several lathes, a universal milling machine with many attachments for multi-purpose machining and boring operations, grinders, pedestal and bench drills and several welding machines. The driving force behind this investment in capital equipment was the increasing demand for winching and hauling equipment on older fishing vessels. It was a new opportunity so the business began to design their own anchor and fishing winches, gear that was to prove better than most of the equipment that was available 'off the shelf.'

Even at this early stage, John's business was working polished stainless steel, manufacturing balustrades, spiral staircases and other contracting work. It's a far cry from the eventual production of stainless steel anchor windlass components and castings. At the time there were only a handful of stainless steel fabricators in Hobart and demand far exceeded supply. It was a lucrative time for Muir Engineering. Most of that work took place in nearby rented premises. John's business was growing and by the mid 1970's had more than 20 employees. The 48ft *Trevassa* was the last large sailing yacht built at Jock Muir's boatyard (launched in early 1971) and the 31ft *Astrolabe*, launched in 1973, was the last yacht built there. It was to mark the end of an era for John's father, Jock.

Trevassa was one of the finest yachts of her type built in Australia. Though construction began on spec, the buyer, Russell Duffield of FR Duffield Manufacturing in Sydney, had owned *Patsy* of Island Bay which Jock built in 1950. Russell Duffield went on to own *Trevassa* for 41 years. When the time came to sell her, he contacted John and said he wanted the boat to go back to Hobart and to the family that had built her. The boat is now owned jointly by the Muir family and is moored at the Royal Yacht Club of Tasmania's marina in Sandy Bay.

THIS PAGE: STILL SHINING

Trevassa competing in racing on the D'Entrecasteaux Channel during the Barnes Bay Regatta, Tasmania, 2014. Trevassa won the first race of the event, from Castray Esplanade to Bruny Island.

OPPOSITE PAGE: CELEBRATING 40 YEARS OF BUSINESS

Rodney Jackman, left, presents John in 2016 with a Retlas Bronze cast plaque, marking 40 years of the Muir Winches business, from 1968 to 2008.

When *Trevassa* was being built, John's business carried out all of the engineering work, including provision and installation of the main engine and propeller drives, all the stainless steel fittings, water and fuel tanks. They fabricated all the above deck polished safety rails, rigging, external and internal fittings.

It was another of those 'breaks' John talks about. The break of setting up next to his dad's business and being able to feed from it and in turn provide support to it. The break of having a father, brothers, uncles and extended family who were all 'hands on' strong individuals, who encouraged risk taking, setting up on your own and who were only too happy to provide support when needed.

The *Trevassa* project was critical to the future direction of John's business.

John Muir: "Following a discussion with Jock we decided to design and build a 12 volt electric (VRC2500) vertical anchor windlass for *Trevassa*.

"Back then we made the tooling for the bronze castings, then the machining and cleaning up for

nickel and chrome plating was done by well-known Hobart Plating Co. in Elizabeth Street, in the city. This new design with an inline planetary drive and 1500 watt motor became the forerunner of the ever popular 'Easyweigh' range.

"We also commenced manufacturing hand hydraulic and power assisted steering systems for a variety of boats, branded Hydnautic. We manufactured a range of long line and drop line winches for the new trevalla deep water fishery, followed by a range of drum winches for the Tasmanian and Victorian scallop industries.

"By now we had in production a range of pleasure and workboat ('manual') anchor winches, first a single speed model Samson, then Bob Harper came up with a first class design by making a simple and no fuss new chain drive assembly that was branded as Neptune. A larger size lever action two speed Hercules was underway, then an enquiry came along for a larger two speed anchor winch that led to the aptly named Triton, and it wasn't long after that a good lot of these were installed on the Sydney Harbour Ferries.

"The first of our horizontal DC electric winches followed in 1975, the 1000 watt Cougar, and then came 1200 watt Cheetah and Jaguar. And lastly 2500 and 3000 watt Thor.

"Things were going very well locally, and Jock and I had a talk about selling our winches interstate."

Jock said he knew someone (of course he did!) and mentioned a business by the name of Inglis Smith, who at the time were one of Australia's oldest marine businesses, beginning in 1858. They had a solid reputation in the Australian marine market.

"At the time they were representing a Scottish based company called Simpson Lawrence. They had a good share of both the Australian and international marine winch markets. Jock suggested we might be able to break into the mainland market with anchor winches.

"Dad knew the Melbourne based manager at Inglis Smith, and suggested I go and meet him. Having introduced myself, I mentioned that I had some of our equipment in the boot of the hire car. (Remember this story; it too will be repeated over and over again.) While we were walking down through his store, he asked me if I was Jock Muir's son, to which I replied, 'Yes' and he said, 'If your equipment is anything like your dad's boats, they should sell well.'

"I opened the boot and showed him the anchor winches, then we carted them into his warehouse to take a closer look. We discussed pricing and availability, and he mentioned he was importing anchor winches and they were doing well, but they had back orders they couldn't fill. As it turned out, I didn't need to go and see anyone else – he purchased all the winches and gave me an order for another six."

Suddenly the world changed for John Muir. Not only did he realise that he had a market in Tasmania with his gear, but there were a myriad of boat builders over the ditch (Bass Strait) who were now, suddenly, potential customers. His eyes must have lit up, his heart rate must have risen as he travelled home, complete with orders in his pocket. His future customer base had risen by a factor of anything from 50 to 100. Australia was his oyster and he was to grab that oyster and devour it soon after.

One of John's earliest and newest interstate based winch customers was a family owned Sydney based business Stebercraft, run by its founder Bruce Steber. The business began in 1946, building timber clinker hull boats. In 1959 it changed course and began using the new product, fibreglass. Steber is one of the pioneers in the construction of fibreglass vessels in Australia. It has remained at the forefront of the industry and is now regarded as the premium manufacturer of commercial fibreglass vessels and composite components. These days they produce pleasure and commercial vessels from 6m up to 15.8m.

EARLY WINCH PRODUCTS
Top: John with a VR1000 vertical anchor winch with an in-line drive.
Above: Muir HR1200 (Cougar) horizontal anchor winch.

Bruce's son, Alan, runs the family business today. Some years ago Steber relocated production and sales operations to Taree on the north coast of New South Wales.

Alan Steber: "John Muir and I go back many, many years – to the 1970s. We built our first large cruiser back in 1975-76, and we were dealing with Muir Winches back in those early days. We bought not only anchor winches, but we purchased hydraulic trap winches and hydraulic steering systems."

Bruce Steber was one of the very first fibreglass powerboat manufacturers in the Australian marine industry. He is one of the country's best known boat builders and a pioneer in his field. The company manufactures a range of commercial and pleasure boats and exports throughout Australasia. Steber's well-known range of commercial boats are in use far and wide, and fish the continental shelf, in some cases up to 30km off shore.

John Muir: "Stebercraft vessels are built to rigid design and exacting marine survey engineering standards. The Australian Government operates Steber vessels for Water Police, fisheries and research. In the early days of building up Muir Winches, I would twice annually drive north through Sydney on to Taree and further to northern Queensland, always calling in on Bruce or Alan, just to see how things were going and to let them know if we had any new equipment they might be interested in."

**ALAN STEBER,
STEBER INTERNATIONAL**

Alan's father, Bruce Steber, founded Stebercraft, one of John's earliest customers. Steber International continue to supply Muir equipment on their commercial vessels shown below.

> **66** *Stebercraft vessels are built to rigid design and exacting marine survey engineering standards… we will still be supporting Muir Winches 'til the cows come home.* **99**
>
> – ALAN STEBER, STEBER INTERNATIONAL

The Steber family and their business command John's highest respect. They are after all, one of his company's oldest and most loyal customers.

Alan Steber: "John Muir is a personal friend of my father, Bruce. I'm the boss here at Steber Group now as Bruce is 86. He's still hands-on in the factory every day tinkering, talking to staff, walking through, but not physically doing anything. He's still part of the business and it's part of his life. By the way, you might want to know that we will still be supporting Muir Winches 'til the cows come home."

Stebercraft were one of the first small powerboat builders in Australia. The Steber name was synonymous with good design and quality craftsmanship. They have a large following in the boating industry and amongst amateur fishermen.

> **66** *Make sure the winch you design and build is stronger than the deck it's bolted down to.* **99**

To this day, Jock's words of wisdom remain in the back of John's mind when designing winches and anchor equipment. Words that had a defining effect on the future reputation of his then fledgling international business.

"Make sure the winch you design and build is stronger than the deck it's bolted down to. Make sure that if anything fails it's the deck or the anchor chain and not the winch!"

There was another astute insight to come.

"If you are unsure about the diameter of a shaft or a fastening, make sure you go up to a larger size!"

Those few words might seem like simple common sense, but as we all know from experience, there is an uncommon lack of common sense in this world.

Jock's advice (that John religiously followed for years) emanated from experience, when life-threatening moments happened at sea.

John's many trips selling winches and anchor gear up the east coast of Australia included another renowned boat builder at Ballina on the northern New South Wales coast. Well north of the Steber operation.

John Muir: "When we commenced manufacturing fishing winches in the early 1970s, initially for local fishermen, it gave us a leg up into the winching business. I particularly recall Bob McLaren, a lovely bloke and boat builder based in Ballina, NSW, who was producing a large number of timber boats up to 60ft. At the time there were a couple of other equipment manufacturers along the coast who produced bespoke winches, but I wanted the business. Bob liked a beer, so on one occasion, I approached him about having a bite and a beer at the local pub, and used the opportunity to discuss Muir supplying all his winch and steering equipment.

EARLY MUIR PRODUCTS

This page, clockwise from top left: SGC2 and SGC1 commercial anchor and warping capstans;
Waubs Bay*'s tubular galvanised hydraulic line hauler fitted with two different size hauling heads, late
1980s; Shona with a VR800 Easy Weigh low profile manual windlass for rope and chain, mid 1990s;
Early VRC5000s, late 1980s; M2 hydraulic anchor winch and hydraulic pedestal line hauler,
mid 1980s; SGC2 400V twin-gypsy anchor windlass, still manufactured by Muir today.*

*Opposite page: 1970s and 1980s Muir brochure with the majority of their product range,
and the first professional brochure the company produced.*

"Over the ensuing years I was able to secure all of the McLaren business, and retained it until the yard ceased manufacturing almost a decade later. In McLaren's heyday, they were one of the largest boat builders on the east coast of Australia."

This is a classic insight into the tenacity of the Battery Point Blue Heeler in action. It would become a scenario that would be endlessly repeated over the years. Not just jaunts up the Australian coastline, but sales trips, breaking new ground and knocking on stranger's doors throughout Europe, Scandinavia, Canada and the USA. Once he was on the road, there was no stopping John Muir, well, not till he'd completed what he had set out to do, or secured a sale and that could take weeks, in one case, ten years till hitting pay dirt.

Through the 1970s and 1980s Muir Engineering workshops at the Battery Point slipway and boatyard made, supplied and installed a range of equipment in commercial and fishing vessels.

There is another story that reveals that tenacity in action and it is centered on Jock Muir's attention to detail and his habit of keeping accurate records.

Through the 1970s and 1980s Muir Engineering workshops at the Battery Point slipway and boatyard made, supplied and installed a range of equipment in commercial and fishing vessels.

The project in question involved the installation of custom designed and manufactured scalloping gear including a drum winch, hydraulics, tray, tipper and scallop dredge, for a 50ft fishing boat. It was an unusual project for another reason, there was no upfront payment made at all.

TOP LEFT: DRUM WINCH TEST BENCH

Drum winch production in the 1980s started to pick up so much it took over the rigging shop. Boat slipping plans, drawn on plywood, are hanging in the background. The boatyard had around 500 of these plans.

TOP RIGHT: *GAYE GLENN* 1990

*Later renamed **Stormboy**, owner Sam Gregg – one of Tasmania's top fishermen throughout the 1980, 1990s and 2000s.*

ABOVE: MUIR'S BOATYARD 2002

*Brett Evans's 18m work barge on the slip and **Shonandra** further up.*

PROGRESSING IN THE 1980S

A photo taken in the 1980s of Muir's Boatyard from the water shows the mooring punt.

The owner was keen to get the job done as quickly as possible because the scallop season was about to open. There was a tight build schedule made even tighter when the owner purchased more new equipment Muir had to install.

John Muir: "In good time we were ready for commissioning and had the vessel alongside the wharf for testing the following morning. However when we arrived to begin work the next day, the boat was no-where to be seen. Unbeknown to us the owner had left and gone fishing using untested gear. He decided, without telling us anything, to test the gear himself.

"We weren't angry with the owner, but did attempt to find the boat to check in and see if the equipment was working OK. We contacted the vessel via radio and arranged to meet up while it was in port re-fuelling up the east coast. Fortunately all the gear was performing properly, and after making some minor adjustments the crew was able to continue scalloping.

Months later the owner had still not settled the bill, hadn't even made a part payment. A discussion with solicitors followed, as John was concerned that he was never going to see the money that was owing. Legal action began but after several years had passed it became too complicated to sort out, so the solicitors advised John to abandon the legal action and cut his losses.

John Muir: "Nine years later a new solicitor joined the company and had a look at the abandoned case, suggesting we had a good chance to win this but we would need to employ a QC. Eventually we had our day in the Supreme Court when the owner, under oath, claimed that the equipment had broken down shortly after the first scalloping season, requiring his vessel to be moored for a period of time while repairs were carried out and preventing him from fishing. Because he claimed he had been paying for repairs to the vessel, he felt he should not have to pay the outstanding balance."

After a week in court with the QC arguing the Muir side of the case, the Judge advised they would have 24 hours to prove that the vessel had not been tied up in the Hobart docks at the time the owner claimed, otherwise Muir would lose the case. John said everyone was wracking their brains trying to figure out what proof they could find to counter the owners claims.

The owner had given a definitive week when he said the scallop boat was tied up. Jock was semi-retired, and his home overlooked the River Derwent where he could readily see movements of boats up and down the river. He used to sit and watch the boats for hours and make notes in his day book of what vessel was going which way and what time it was.

John Muir: "To our jubilation and our surprise we came across an entry in one of Jock's day books where he had noted the vessel's name and observed it steaming down the river heading to work on the very date the owner said it had been in dock and unable to work.

"The next morning the day book was presented to our QC and then to the court. A QC cost a thousand bucks a day back in those days, not cheap by any means. The Judge asked the owner to come forward to look at the note book, and to confirm whether or not he knew Jock Muir. The owner confirmed he did in fact know Jock very well. He was then asked to read what Jock had entered in his day book on that date, and to tell the court what was written there. The owner conceded that if Jock Muir had written that his vessel had been heading down the river on this day, then it must have been true."

The Judge ruled that the owner was liable for the outstanding payment; all monies owed plus interest, as well as all Muir's legal costs. The amount was substantial. John said those were some of the sweetest words he could ever want to hear, especially after so many years.

John's time at Battery Point boatyard was coming to an end, car parking and access for big trucks was being restricted from next door on the right of way.

Throughout the time Jock was building boats, his business employed an average of 12 permanent employees, with a back-up of sub-contractors for electrical, machining, refrigeration and other outsourced skills. On bigger yachts built by Jock, such as *Balandra*, *Waltzing Matilda*, *Van Diemen* and *Trevassa*, there would have been another half a dozen full time contractors working on the build.

John Muir: "I realised soon after my business started to grow that the boatyard operation meant Jock was restricted to building one or two reasonable sized boats per year. It meant he had most of his eggs in one or two baskets and relied on the payments from those one or two owners.

"In Muir Engineering we were building a solid and broad customer base and I came to realise that the more customers we had, the better. Simple business economics at work. Create our own range of products with a fixed material, overhead and labour cost that we could then add a margin to and hey presto, when a customer wants a winch, we can tell them the price upfront, and make some money."

To John Muir money is important, but in his early days it rated second to his desire to 'make something.' To put his head and hands to work, to design and build 'things,' in this case winches, capstans and related boating gear. Not just to make it, but make sure it is world class, the best money can buy. The sort of gear that yachties and fishermen can rely on when the going gets tough.

John Muir: "Starting your own business is about a number of things, independence, making your own decisions and running your own race, the opportunity to prove your worth and the value of what you make. However, as time progresses there comes a need to make good money in return for all that hard work and effort. You need to start with a goal in sight. That goal could be retirement to do other things or selling your business."

John and Wendy still own the boatyard at Battery Point and the original Muir Engineering buildings. The boatyard is presently undergoing an upgrade, with Doyle Sails and their new ship chandlery in place. It's also a new location for another business, Boat Sales Tasmania.

John Muir: "You have to find the best customers and then you have to work hard to keep them as a bird in the hand is worth two in the bush."

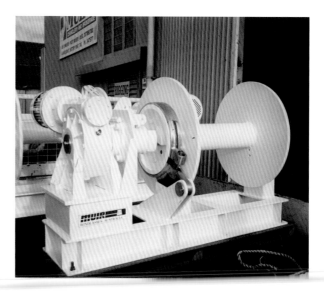

TWIN SD50 DRUM ANCHOR WINCHES
Outside the Battery Point boatyard engineering shop, ready for shipping to Singapore, late 1980s.

BOAT SHOWS
and the
MOVE TO KINGSTON

Boat shows, both national and international, were to play a pivotal role in the expansion of the Muir business. Boat shows are unlike any other trade shows. They are an important social and commercial event in the yachting and boating world's calendar, particularly the international shows. To compare something like the Singapore Boat Show with another car or caravan trade event is like comparing cheese and chalk.

International boat shows are where the beautiful people are seen, where you can rub shoulders with the rich and famous, where the parties are legendary. A place where mega-luxury yachts, superyachts and pleasure cruisers of all shapes and sizes are on display and in many cases, for sale. Where agents hope that prospective buyers with buckets of money come to see what bargains can be had. Where the atmosphere is fuelled by glitz and glamour.

Yet beneath that glamorous surface is where the real action lies. It's where the prospective clients, naval architects and shipyard representatives meet and mix with the representatives of marine equipment manufacturers and suppliers of various other marine products. The myriad of amazing commercial booths selling their wares include engines and propulsion equipment, winches and anchor systems; those that fabricate stunning boat interiors; electronic marine and safety equipment, deck machinery and stabilisers, hi-tech sonar and radar; marine cranes and boarding ladders, all manner of industry providers from across the globe.

John Muir had a gentle introduction to the size and scope of boat shows when in 1972 he was an exhibitor at the Melbourne Boat Show. That was another turning point, because suddenly he saw the size of his potential market expanding exponentially. Prior to Melbourne, John was supplying his locally made winches and commercial fishing winches throughout Tasmania. Now mainland Australia beckoned and the possibilities seemed endless.

Just prior to going to Melbourne, John began producing his own line of marine winches. This followed several years spent making repairs to other makes of equipment that had either broken down or weren't capable of doing the job at hand. John's winches were one-off units, not a specific range of purpose designed equipment. They were manufactured on demand on a vessel by vessel basis.

One of the more critical turning points in the development and growth of the Muir Engineering business was a conversation John had in July 1971 with a mentor and family friend, Russell Duffield. (Russell passed away in 2014 and is sadly missed by many, particularly the Muir family.)

John and Russell used to talk to one another when the need arose and on this particular day, following the delivery of Russell's boat *Trevassa* to Sydney, he said to John, "Why don't you specialise in the production of a range of marine products like steering gear and the anchor winch you made for *Trevassa*?"

It took John less than ten seconds to think about that idea before he made a decision to design and build anchor winch equipment. Remember yachties make split second decisions all the time, so even in business John Muir does just that. If you make a wrong decision, you can just as quickly change it again. He sat down with two close work mates, engineers, Bob Harper and Chris Michael, all agreed it was a great idea and the work was set in motion.

Within a few months new designs, casting patterns and prototypes were developed and modified and final parameters settled. Prototype production began in 1972. There was close collaboration with the local Hobart foundry Skeels and Perkins.

Andrew Perkins: "Back then we were Skeels and Perkins Pty Ltd, and our primary business was manufacturing brass plumbing fittings from our premises in Argyle Street in Hobart. I remember John approaching us and reckoned if we could cast the plumbing fittings in brass we should be able to cast his winch parts in bronze and aluminium. We gave it a go and began casting some smaller parts which went well. I remember it because they required small batches of a wide range of different types of castings; it was more interesting than making thousands of the same boring plumbing fittings but we had to battle with existing tooling that wasn't always perfectly suited to the job."

In those early days in the 1970s and into the 1980s there were three local foundries to choose from: Retlas, Skeels and Perkins and the Derwent Foundry. Now there is only one, Apco, which was formerly Skeels and Perkins.

Andrew Perkins: "Apco are the only company casting stainless steel in Tasmania and about ten years ago began producing large superyacht winch castings. The requirement of Muir for a very high quality casting was extremely demanding, due to being machined and polished to a mirror finish without any blemishes, which is very difficult with a casting as large as 400kg.

"John could be a hard man to work with in some ways, yet totally soft in other ways. I always used my experiences with John as a learning tool. If I was faced with a problem, I'd ask myself, 'How would John deal with that?'"

Reeling in big 'uns

TEN-TONNE pull winches designed and built in Hobart will soon be reeling in fish around the coasts of Australia.

Muir Engineering won the order for two winches from Victorian deep-sea fishing company Lakes Entrance Pty Ltd. The winches will be fitted to two of the company's 27-metre ocean-going trawlers.

The managing director of Muirs, Mr John Muir, said

yesterday the winches, each weighing about two tonnes, would be driven by 120hp hydraulic motors made by Robbins Pty Ltd of Hobart.

The winches alone were worth $33,000 for the pair, he said. They were the biggest his company 'had supplied.

Muirs in 10 years has emerged as one of Australia's major makers of high-class industrial and marine winches and windlasses.

● Fitter and turner Mr Bob Harper puts the finishing touches to a new 10-tonne winch at Muir's Kingston factory.

Its annual production in this field is worth $750,000. About 80 per cent of the products are exported to markets in New Guinea, Fiji, Hong Kong, Singapore, Manila, Tonga and New Caledonia.

ABOVE: THE INIMITABLE BOB HARPER

Bob Harper, shown here in a local newspaper article, was one of Muir's best ever engineers. Described by most who knew him as a 'very clever bloke,' he was well regarded by Muir Engineering and in the saw milling and marine industries. Prior to working for Muir, he had run his own mill. Both Bob and Alan Perkins are described by John as 'a rare breed and god's gentlemen'. Bob's skills included product design, engineering and product development, fabrication and machining. Steam power was his passion and when he retired from Muir's he built his own steam engine and train in his backyard workshop.

OPPOSITE PAGE: SECOND AND THIRD GENERATION FOUNDRY WORKERS

Apco Engineering's Alan Perkins, brother Andrew Perkins, and Andrew's son Oliver Perkins, 2016.

> **❝** *I always used my experiences with John as a learning tool. If I was faced with a problem, I'd ask myself, 'How would John deal with that?'* **❞**

ANDREW PERKINS, APCO ENGINEERING

Decades on, Apco and the Perkins family remain actively involved in a multitude of pattern development and the supply of ferrous and non-ferrous castings. The volume of business over the years from Muir Engineering would run into the millions of dollars.

Back to the early 1970s, John travelled to Melbourne for his inaugural boat show on his own and set up his first trade show pavilion. It was a mere 3m by 3m space, with a couple of spotlights. Those who know John and know how he operates at these sorts of events will tell you that he doesn't just sit at his stand waiting for the world to come to him. He manoeuvres around the other marine display stands ferreting for any new products or ideas. He picks up or swaps brochures, he asks questions, he takes photos and carefully looks over competitors gear. The down time before opening and after closing a show is the perfect opportunity to peruse what's on offer. His competition have also been caught out doing the same thing many times over.

Alan Steber, son of Bruce Steber, founder of the well known boat building company Stebercraft, first met John at the Melbourne Boat Show in 1972. The business association that was formed then is still strong, 44 years later.

Alan Steber: "John is a lovely likable man. At every boat show that we've been to, John is always a thorough gentleman, always knowledgeable and always supportive. I know from personal experience that he would wander around the boat show with a large quantity of little metal plates – I think they might have been blue – with 'Muir Winches,' or 'Anchor Winch Supplied By Muir Winches' on them, and a bundle of cable ties.

> **❝** *As he wandered around the show, looking at all the boats on display, if they had a Muir winch, he'd ask permission to put the little cable tie and the note on the rail so that, let's say, 50-60% of the boat show would have had little Muir notices on them.* **❞**

– ALAN STEBER

"As he wandered around the show, looking at all the boats on display, if they had a Muir winch, he'd ask permission to put the little cable tie and the note on the rail so that, let's say, 50-60% of the boat show would have had little Muir notices on them. It's like Dick Smith, you've got to promote your own product. I'd have to put him in the category of Dick Smith, where he's out there promoting, promoting, promoting – Australian made, and promoting Muir Winches.

"How or when he found the energy, I don't know, because he's still there packing up after a boat show finishes, and he's there assembling the boat show before the show starts. So he's a hands-on boss and he's not scared of hard work. He operates much the way we do at Stebers, because we're exactly the same. We don't get crew to go and deliver the boats, we do that ourselves, and we set things up ourselves, and we do the brochures ourselves and we get everything all set up ready the way that we're comfortable with. It saves paying others, covers costs.

"We've never had any major warranty issues with Muir Winches. If there were issues, they've always been dealt with. I've visited their factory on several occasions – always well organised, and I think John's always had that respect. I remember sitting in his office one time and he's pulling his hair out. Some things weren't going quite right at the time, obviously, but the phones were ringing and he was jumping to attention dealing with all the matters."

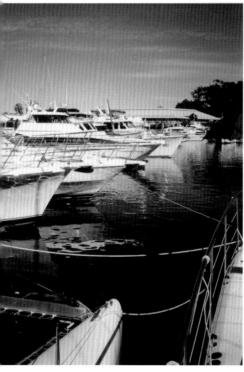

This was Muir Winches' first Sydney Boat Show, and a young Richard Fader went along to help. On the right is Craig McNaughton, on the left is the ABDEC representative.

The Muir display at one of the earlier Sydney Boat Shows. ABDEC were Muir's first Sydney agent in the early 1980s.

TOP: PERTH BOAT SHOW, C. 1988

Michael (left) and Malcolm Flintoff, sons of Rob Flintoff of AMI Sales, a long time distributor (40 years) of Muir winches in Western Australia.

BOTTOM: CHICAGO BOAT SHOW, 1986

Powerwinch were the first US distributors of Muir products.

If you have ever seen a Blue Heeler at the start of the working day, they are a mirror image of John. They bark furiously, get excited about the prospect of working their guts out all day, they spin in circles, hoping they will be out the gate and off to the distant paddocks to chase cattle or sheep, they can't wait to get stuck in. They will work flat out all day, chasing stock, looking for a pat and a drink of water and nothing else. They don't stop 'til the job is done. Sometimes when John was away on sales trips or at an international boat show, he would work the stand all day, work the dinners at night and then, back in those days, prepare faxes longer than some of the boats on show, to send back to the office.

The first Melbourne Boat Show that John attended was held from the 7-15 July 1972 at the Exhibition Building. The very first Melbourne Boat Show had been held in the early 1960s. Despite bad weather, the 1972 show was attended by over 60,000 people and catered mostly for fibreglass pleasure boats rigged for recreational fishing. There were also several boat builders present selling their smaller commercial fishing and work boats. Sizes varied from 4m to 8m.

The sign of a successful business is getting sales, generating cash flow to more than cover the costs of employees, manufacturing, rent and the myriad of other business expenses payable every week or month. Cash is king!

John Muir: "When you start making something you need to sell it. Back then just about all the boats on show were mono hulls, some with small internal prop shafts and Stuart Turner and Blaxland water cooled single and two cylinder petrol engines.

"Most of the anchor winches on show were from the Scottish manufacturer Simpson Lawrence. They had a worldwide reputation for good gear. From New Zealand there was also a Kiwi anchor winch and capstan exporter, Lucas, along with me and my new Muir range.

"I shipped a range of gear we were making at the time to Melbourne for the show: Samson, manual, single speed anchor winch, Hercules, two speed manual anchor winch, hydraulic steering, our own brand 'Hydnautic,' a line hauling winch with components, steering wheels and electric capstans."

At this show John met boat owners, boat builders, component part suppliers and, as chance would have it, a few boat builders from southeast Asia. He managed

to sell the winches and gear he shipped to Melbourne and made many important contacts, some of whom were to become lifelong friends and colleagues.

One of those long friendships survives to this day, Alistair Murray, Chief Executive Officer (CEO) of Ronstan Marine, Melbourne.

Alistair Murray: "I've known John Muir for a bloody long time... close to 40 years. We're more peers than competitors. I don't buy or sell any Muir products, and he doesn't buy or sell any Ronstan products; we're just two leaders in the industry, in the export side of things particularly.

"I've been seeing John for many years at international boat shows all around the world. Back in the mid 1980s I even entertained the idea of working for John. John and I discussed me being his freelance export manager and a representative in the southern states of Australia. My business had been through a bit of a difficult period, but was coming good, so I decided to stay where I was. So he's been the CEO of Muir and I've been the CEO of Ronstan and we've been seeing each other all round the world and we've become good friends."

When he saw the opportunity to have someone like Alistair onto his team, John was keen as mustard.

John Muir: "I approached Alistair about coming to work for Muir because I knew he was not satisfied in his current job. It would have made him happy if he could of bought into Ronstan but that wasn't a possibility at the time. I wanted him at Muir in a management capacity, looking after sales and marketing, as we had our sights set on expansion into the USA and Canadian markets where Alistair was well established. Although Alistair eventually made the decision to stay on with and buy into Ronstan, he ultimately helped me a lot with North American contacts in the market place."

The friendship remains as strong today as it ever was.

Alistair Murray: "When I went to Tasmania to talk to him about working for him, I stayed at his house with his wife Wendy and daughters Alex and Shona. Years later I ended up serving on the board of AIMEX [The Australian International Marine Export Group] with Alex. She subsequently married Matthew Johnston, who was the CEO of Muir for many years. John was one of the founding members of AIMEX with me, so I started with him, moved through with Alex and now with Matthew. I've worked with the whole family on that board.

"I've been to Kingston a few times and visited the factory and followed John's progress very closely over the years, and admired what he's done and what he's achieved. Probably the most amusing aspect of my relationship with John is that between Ronstan and Muir, we've won virtually all of the Marine Industry Export Awards on offer. I'm getting sick of going to export award nights and hoping to win a category and hearing the words read out, 'The winner of Exporter of the Year is...' and I'm waiting for 'Ronstan' but it's 'Muir Winches' again. I reckon he's pipped me in a lot of awards!

"He and I are both Austrade Export Heroes which is quite an honour. I think there are only four people in the marine industry in Australia that have been conferred with that honour. I was actually the one that nominated John. I'm not sure if he nominated me!

"That's a program run by Austrade which acknowledges and honours Australia's export leaders or pioneers. There are some pretty famous names on that list.

ABOVE: RONSTAN EARLY DAYS
Alistair Murray at Miami Boat Show in 1993.

BELOW: EXPORT HEROES
Alistair and John are both Austrade Export Heroes, an Australian government commendation for export leadership.

> 66 *I've known John Muir for a bloody long time... close to 40 years. We're more peers than competitors. I don't buy or sell any Muir products, and he doesn't buy or sell any Ronstan products; we're just two leaders in the industry, in the export side of things particularly.* 99

– ALISTAIR MURRAY

"But as you can see our relationship runs pretty deep, through running parallel to each other over many, many years."

The Muir product is different to Ronstan's. John's business makes windlasses for anchors and Ronstan's make sheet winches for controlling sails and halyards. That gear is more sailing oriented and John's is more power and work boat, fishing boat, fast ferry and superyacht oriented. Both men see one another frequently as they travel the world.

Alistair Murray: "When I go to Tasmania, in particular for the Wooden Boat Festival, I always catch up with John. It's always a chance to relax and go out on his sailing boat, and eat the finest seafood that Tasmania has to offer, with John, and more lately with Alex and Matthew. It's been a great association.

"I've also been with John in some pretty funny social situations. One that comes to mind is a little bar in Amsterdam where we were relaxing after METS [Marine Equipment Trade Show], which is the biggest trade show in the world. John and I have been seen late at night singing songs together, and I think there were a few

times we may have even been dancing on the bar together. He's been known to let his hair down a bit, as have I, but we always find time during any show to sit down and have a serious chat about how life's going, and how our businesses are doing, and what the latest developments are, and we always try to help each other. Everything we've done together has always been in the spirit of cooperation and friendship; he's one of my closest friends in the industry, and I am his. It's been a relationship I've really enjoyed."

Ronstan and Muir are unquestionably the two leading Australian manufacturers of marine equipment and both export throughout the world. Ronstan would be about twice the size of Muir in terms of employees. It was started in 1953, by two blokes called Ron and Stan, that's where the name comes from. (It's the sort of name association that could easily become the makings of a good Australian comedy, the Ron and Stan show.) They were both sailors and started building fittings for the boats they were sailing. Even though the Muirs were also sailors with an international reputation, the business John set up moved into winches, windlasses and anchor equipment, while Ronstan concentrated on sailing boat hardware. Both businesses grew together as successful Australian exporters.

Alistair Murray: "Ronstan manufactures a full line of a couple of thousand items of deck hardware and rigging for sailing boats, from 3m to 50m in length. We produce blocks, cleats, shackles, turnbuckles and travellers, and we sell sailing clothing and rope and wire, but nothing that competes with Muir at any time.

"I like going to Hamilton Island Race Week because the Muir boys are almost always there. These days they sail a boat together, that's Ross, Greg and John. They always charter a boat and have a huge Muir logo on their spinnaker, so they're the most blatantly commercial of all of the sailors there, and when you see them in action, they tend to be the ones who are partying the hardest at the end of it and having a good time, as three brothers should. I've always enjoyed seeing the Muir team and the Muir boat – and that big spinnaker – in action at Hamilton Island Race Week, and I think it's great that they get away and do that each year.

John Muir is a legend of the Australian marine industry... and a good mate!"

In good old Australian slang terms that comment would be put this way: 'He's a legend in his own lunchtime, mate! That's our John!'

John Muir: "Alistair often visited Tasmania and we met on occasions at the Muir boatyard and chandlery. My brother Ross and I would always try to catch up with Alistair for a beer, a bite and a gossip about the marine business in general.

"The first boat show I did with Alistair was the Tokyo Boat Show in the mid 1980s. At this time we were ably assisted by Austrade and the local Trade Commissioner. We both did well and Muir was fortunate enough to set up with the well-known Okazaki family who were manufacturing on an island two hours offshore from Osaka. They

FORGING INTERNATIONAL PARTNERSHIPS

Above: John with Mr Okazaki of Anchorage Marine in Osaka, 1996.

Opposite page, left: John with Yoshitaka Sugimoto of Anchorage Marine, Osaka 1993.

Opposite page, right: Yoshitaka Sugimoto at Miami Boat Show, 1998.

BELOW: WINCHES SOLD TO OKAZAKI MARINE IN JAPAN

For pleasure and commercial vessels. Okazaki is one of the biggest buyers in the world of Muir's freefall winches. The original freefall patent was developed by John Muir and Bob Harper in the late 1990s.

Below, VFF1000 Vertical Automatic Freefall anchor winch, de-clutched by reversing the motor and engages to freefall pawl anchor and chain.

Bottom, Freefall drum winch, operation as above for the VFF1000.

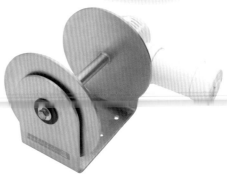

operated under the company name of Anchorage. The Okazaki family were building a range of sailing yachts up to 14m and gave us orders for the anchor winches for these vessels. We are still associated with the Okazaki family and they have purchased more freefall anchor winches than any other customer,and have also helped us develop line and spooling techniques.

"Alistair and I have both successfully skippered sailing yachts in the Hamilton Island Race Week series, sometimes in the same class. He is one of Australia's more experienced yachtsmen, having been sailing from a young age and is as tenacious today a he was when I first met him."

Another one of John's mates who also lent a helping hand around the boatyard and with the business when he could was a bloke called Paul Hurd. He has had a close association with the entire Muir family, in the early days helping build and crew the racing lightweight sharpies.

John Muir: "Paul Hurd was a good friend, and still is. We co-built a 12ft Rainbow, I think in early 1960 named *Goldilocks*, with a hard chine flat bottom and a big spinnaker. I was the gun forward hand and Paul was the sea anchor. With the assistance of some good mates in the mid-1960s I also built two lightweight sharpies in John Griggs's backyard in Quayle Street, Sandy Bay.

"Paul was always around my engineering business at Battery Point and the nearby boatyard. He was hands on, an innovative artist with no end of marketing ideas. He designed the first and subsequent advertising brochures I needed, including some for my father, Jock, to use with his boatyard. For the 1972 Melbourne Boat Show and later for the Singapore Boat Show he designed a compact modular display pack.

"The display featured the 1972 Bicheno storm photos that had fishing boats in varying states of distress, some rolled over, others with bent spars and some with seaweed and kelp hanging from the top of the masts. The main components of the display unit were anchor winches, fishing winches, line haulers and the new 'Hydnautic' brand steering gear.

"As times were tough and money short, we made the display stands in house and Paul utilised his facilities at the College in Hobart. We purchased a 50 m roll of large photographic paper and processed the large photos in our bath at home. We squeegeed them (dried them) and mounted them with the help of Mum's hair dryer and Wendy's feet. We never really knew if it was going to work but the display exceeded ours and others' expectations."

You can see the attitude of 'Yeah, we can do that mate,' coming out in spades. It's why John Muir and his employees have managed to do what they have from where they are, at the bottom of the world, thousands of kilometres from their main markets. Nothing is too hard, anything can be done, even if it isn't in existence already, they will make it happen and in most cases they did. Much of who is the real John Muir comes from that rough and tumble background growing up in Battery Point, learning to be tough and look after himself, or else suffer the nasty consequences.

Paul Hurd: "From my earliest recollections of John or Nhoj (remember his secret sailing name was pronounced Nodge) was his desire to master the ancient art of Queensberry Rules above schoolwork and chores. He could ably defend himself in a fight being the first kid on the block, and to this day, he has had more wins than losses.

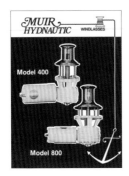

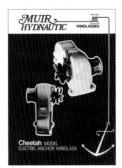
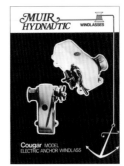

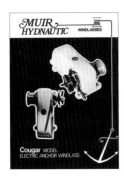

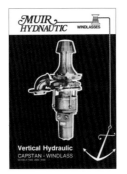

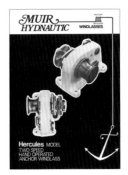

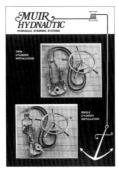

MUIR HYDNAUTIC HYDRAULIC STEERING SYSTEMS

Brochures from the late 1970s and 1980s show the range of Muir Hydnautic products. The hydraulic steering systems were available in four sizes: 38mm, 50mm, 65mm and 75mm, all in bronze. Available as hand- or power-assisted for vessels from 10 to 28m. The pumps on both model types models used a Charlynn hydraulic motor, which was mounted in a cast aluminium reservoir on the manual steering models.

The majority of hydraulic winch drives in the Muir range at this time were Charlynn. The Muir philosophy was to base manufacturing around the supplier's gear, which meant choosing suppliers that had the best worldwide range, availability and servicing support.

"This single-mindedness stood him in good stead when it was first applied to business some 48 years ago. It's quite evident his father's and mother's work ethic and commitment had a strong influence on John and his brothers as all three have excelled on the water as well as in business. An understanding mother and wives may also have had something to do with it."

Paul is right on the mark on with that acute observation. John had Wendy supporting him all the way. She was the one who brought up the two girls, who always had John's bag ready when he needed to travel at short notice. She was the one who sorted out his medication packs when he was travelling after his bout with life threatening acute pancreatitis.

John, in his inimitable style made many contacts and successful sales to mainland and southeast Asian boat builders from his visits to both the Melbourne and subsequently Sydney boat shows. His world was growing fast. One of those new customers was Craig Whitworth, AM. (Member of the Order of Australia.)

Craig Whitworth: "Whitworths commenced dealings with Muir Winches in the 1970s, and have continued the association through to the present day. In that time we have sold thousands of Muir winches to satisfied customers, including my own personal boat requirements.

"John can be rightly proud of the esteemed position the company now enjoys in the international marine market. I know first-hand that this success was hard earned by John's continuous diligence.

"Over the years I have attended many overseas boat shows, some major, many others quite remote. I was always amazed that I would turn into an aisle and there would be John on his Muir Winches stand, testing the market."

Never give up, never show weakness, never say die, never say no until you know absolutely that the deal is not worth it. In other words 'say no more than yes!'

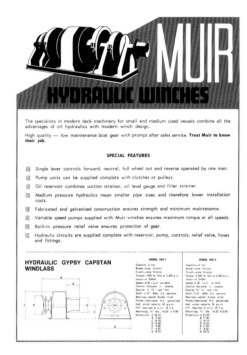

MUIR HYDRAULIC WINCHES

A Muir brochure from the 1970s and 1980s.
Designed around a Robbins hydraulic motor, ideal for Muir's commercial winches as the motor had a hollow bore to pass a main drive winch shaft through. Robbins, a US company founded by Dick Robbins, were renowned for their hydraulic tunnel boring machines which were well ahead of their time. A huge bonus was that their Tasmanian factory, part of their global manufacturing operations, was 200m down the road from Muir in Kingston.
Ross Scrim was one of John's good friends and worked at the Robbins manufacturing plant, and he brought to the fore a renowned hydraulic engineer by the name of Tony Peach. Tony went on to establish Terratec, manufacturers of tunnel boring equipment.

> ❝ *From my earliest recollections of John or Nhoj (remember his secret sailing name was pronounced Nodge) was his desire to master the ancient art of Queensberry Rules above schoolwork and chores.* ❞

– PAUL HURD

John Muir: "I've been known to postpone my trip home by a week or two to get an order because life is all about perseverance. Sometimes you're knocked back, sometimes you're knocked over, sometimes you've got to get up and you've got to get going again, but take a different way.

"Another saying you probably haven't heard, but one of my sayings is when you're looking for new business you go in the front door. If you can't get in, you go to the side door. If you can't get in there, you go to the window. If you still can't get in there, go down the chimney. Sometimes there might be a way into the attic so you can get in that way. There's no end of ways of getting your toe in the door that allows you to keep on going.

"We've had obstacles to overcome all our life, like being told we shouldn't do something. Some people know me pretty well at work and know that if they tell me there's something that can't be done and I'm bloody sure it can, we will get it done.

"There's times when you are behind the eight ball on a job and you're going to get into strife. Well you've certainly got to do something about it, but don't take no for an answer. A good way to be."

At every boat show people would come up to John, or one of his sales people wanting to buy gear or represent the Muir business. Names like Peter Hickey, who represented Muirs until a couple of years ago, Barry Spooner of Caribbean Cruisers, and Stebercraft, who Muir have been supplying for almost four decades.

John Muir: "Usually the Melbourne boat shows went for at least a week and following the event, when I had cleaned up and dismantled whatever gear I had left over, I would take it with me and spend a few days driving and visiting the timber boat builders from Williamstown in Melbourne to Mordialloc and across to Lakes Entrance in eastern Victoria, calling on the boat builders and retail shops along the way.

"A year or two later when the Adelaide boat show kicked in straight after Melbourne I would spend over a week there with our gear on a stand before heading home. In my first or second year at the Adelaide boat show, in the mid 1970s I met with Mr Milde of EJ Milde and Co. who represented Muir for many years."

CRAIG WHITWORTH

Rigging up his yacht, 1968. Undoubtedly one of Australia's best yachtsmen and sailmakers, John describes Craig as an extremely dedicated man and he still has controlling share of his company, Whitworths, the largest marine retail chain in Australia.

66 *Over the years I have attended many overseas boat shows, some major, many others quite remote. I was always amazed that I would turn into an aisle and there would be John on his Muir Winches stand, testing the market.* **99**

– CRAIG WHITWORTH

EJ Milde and Co. were an Adelaide based importer/wholesaler of marine products mainly supplying the South Australian marine industry, specifically the recreational power and ski boat market and the commercial fishing and yachting industries. EJ Milde did well and expanded the Muir business throughout South Australia.

Adding up these new connections, boat builders and agents, there is, without exception, a single thread that connects them all. They have had or still have a strong and lengthy connection to the Muir family and business. Muir Engineering is known across the world as a manufacturer of the highest quality equipment that can be relied upon when the going gets tough. Ask *Adix* skipper Paul Goss.

There is one employee who John managed to get on board at a Sydney boat show who rates more than a passing mention. He's an inspiring Welshman who was approaching 60 years old when John first met him. He has written his own biography that is worth a read in itself. He has spent his very colourful life sailing the globe, racing single handed across the Atlantic in yachts he and his son built. His book details some of the more lurid of those adventures, that are, at times, wickedly funny. He is Valentine (Val) Howells.

John Muir: "Val Howells, a Welshman and entrepreneur, is now 89 years old. I first met him at the Sydney Boat Show in August 1986. He was on the stand next door selling Hempel Paints. Val was intrigued by our product and spent more time on the Muir stand than he did on his own. Being a seafarer he was more interested in the nuts and bolts of the winches than paint.

"Following the end of the boat show, Val arranged with his boss for us to rent some floor space in the Hempel showroom which was located on the main road at Spit Bridge, on Sydney's North Shore.

"I couldn't believe we could be so lucky as to have a Muir Winches sign on the window in such a prestige location as Spit Bridge. Over the next week I looked around for somewhere to rent with the intention of setting up a showroom. Luckily, I found a small warehouse we could justify in Manly Vale. Val provided a trailer and a vehicle and helped me relocate all the Muir gear.

"When Val returned to the Hempel office his boss made a lighthearted observation about how much time he'd spent on the Muir stand while at the Sydney Boat Show, and asked if he'd maybe prefer to work for Muir. Val called me and mentioned in passing this conversation with his boss. I'd been thinking Val was the perfect bloke for a sales job, as he had the gift of the gab, and Welsh charm in spades, so I told him he could start anytime!

"I must say, from the first time I met Val I was taken by his vitality, attention to detail, and his charming manner. He was nearly 60 years young at the time, and when I was a young bloke 60 seemed old, but nothing about Val was old. Most importantly, he had a lifetime of extraordinary yachting experiences, which I'd gleaned throughout our conversations at the boat show.

"To my elation, Val gladly accepted my offer and he started the following week. Back in those days Val's wife Eira and their children were living in the northern suburbs of Sydney, having recently emigrated from Wales. On Saturdays Val would drive all over Sydney and walk all the slipways north and south, visiting chandleries to have a chat to prospective customers and boat owners.

SETTING THE BENCHMARK HIGH
The inimitable Val Howells, pictured above with John in 2001, and below John with Val's beloved wife Eira.

SYDNEY BOAT SHOW, 1985

In the days before the Sanctuary Cove Boat Show.

"The Sydney Boat Show we'd just attended had been our first and ran for 10 days over two weeks and we set up and manned our own stands. We were already supplying various marine retailers and boat builders in Sydney and along the east coast. Meeting Val had been serendipity and him working for us, with all his experience, was a real coup.

"Val had not long been in the country, having arrived here on his 26ft Scandinavian Folkboat which he sailed single handed from Wales, without an engine and only a hurricane lamp for navigation. To my knowledge Hempel was Val's first job in Australia.

"Val really got our business on a roll, within a few days new orders were coming in to Hobart. Back in those days our main competition was Nilsson from Auckland, New Zealand, and Simpson Lawrence from Glasgow, Scotland. Nilsson commenced their business around 1968, the same time as Muir, and over time had several owners, eventually being bought out by Maxwell Cundy who renamed it Maxwell. For some time the new business sold Cundy sheet winches, but the growing anchor winch business was an obvious adjunct."

When Muir started building pleasure anchor winches, Simpson Lawrence had the biggest market share around the globe. John could now see remarkable market opportunities for his business globally. The Blue Heeler from Battery Point was sniffing about, checking out the scene, sensing opportunities where others may not be as quick and sizing up the situation to work out his best means of attack.

In the 1990s Simpson Lawrence wanted to buy the Muir business and approached John to see if he was interested. However, he didn't want to sell as he had ongoing plans for new and larger winching products and even though the price offered was very good, John knocked it back.

John Muir: "They told me that if I didn't want to sell and they couldn't buy Muir they would buy Lewmar Marine, a large UK based manufacturer, which they did."

Simpson Lawrence of Glasgow was another family owned company, involved in the manufacture and distribution of yacht equipment and chandlery since the early 1900s. In 1980 it was acquired by Clyde

Marine; the equivalent of David buying Goliath! By 2000 Clyde Marine also owned Whitlock Steering and Lewmar Winches. Operations were moved from Glasgow down to Havant, Hampshire, in the UK, and it wasn't long before Simpson Lawrence was divested and became Lewmar Scotland (Anchoring & Windlass Division).

John Muir: "I was Val's main contact at the Kingston facility, but it wasn't long before Val set up a great and close working relationship with our sales management and factory production manager, Don Di Martino, who worked with us for 28 years.

"A big plus for Muir was that Val had constructed his own sailing yachts, and had extensive racing, sailing and cruising experience across the Atlantic. The first yacht he built was a 26ft Folkboat, launched as *Eira* (Val's wife's name), which he raced in the first Single-Handed Trans-Atlantic Race in 1960. The race left from Plymouth, England, and ended in Newport, Rhode Island, USA. Val completed the race in 62 days, 5 hours and 50 minutes.

"The second Trans-Atlantic Race, held in 1964, saw Val sailing in *Akka*, a 35ft timber cutter that he also built. He came in third behind Eric Tabarly and Sir Francis Chichester, and his position would have been improved if his boat hadn't been rammed by a harbour cruiser near the start of the race, which caused serious damage.

"Another sea-faring experience of Val's was skippering a large staysail schooner in the Caribbean with up to 70 passengers, mostly American tourists looking for adventure. Following, he decided to leave his maritime life behind, changed tack and returned to Wales to become a freelance journalist for the BBC and some of the national papers, while helping Eira run a riding stable.

"Val and Eira also owned a succession of restaurants, and along with other pursuits, led a far from boring life. Val participated in the 1976 Single-Handed Trans-Atlantic Race that involved the building of two identical vessels – *Unibrass Brython* and *Fromstock Filius* – with the intention of he and his son enjoying the honour of being the first family to have built and raced their own boats in the event.

"Val and his son both competed in the event, but after a near-fatal accident, retired early. Val was extremely disappointed by the failure and subsequently suffered bouts of depression that were only cured by more sailing. His ensuing adventures spawned the book 'Up That Particular Creek,' a fascinating tale of solo yachting and high sea adventures on his Folkboat.

"Solo, without an engine or a battery for lights, Val told me on several occasions he was almost run over by a steam ship that obviously couldn't see his lonely navigation light, being just a single hard to see hurricane lamp.

"Val's the author of a number of yachting books and has featured in several films presented by the BBC in the UK.

"Craig McNaughton joined Val in Sydney in 1989, just prior to 'the recession we had to have.' Val remains one of my closest friends, and was a valuable mentor to me during his early days at Muir."

Muir's first overseas boat show was also Singapore's first international boat show, held at the national stadium from 17-22 June 1977. The event uniquely brought together exhibitors from the USA, England, France, Japan, Taiwan, Hong Kong and Australia. It was also one of the first times that buyers from both eastern and western countries were present at a single venue. On display were commercial and fishing boats and gear, as well as work and pleasure craft and equipment.

> 66 *A big plus for Muir was that Val had constructed his own sailing yachts, and had extensive racing, sailing and cruising experience across the Atlantic. The first yacht he built was a 26ft Folkboat, launched as **Eira** (Val's wife's name), which he raced in the first Single-Handed Trans-Atlantic Race in 1960.* 99

> **❝** *I will never forget what I saw as we flew in, there must have been a hundred ships at anchor, many were huge. I had never seen anything like it. Many fishing boats of various sizes, however not many yachts and pleasure cruisers.* **❞**

Coinciding with an increased global demand for pleasure boats and advances in manufacturing technologies and processes, particularly fibreglass craft, the event precipitated further interest in the marine companies that exhibited, many noting marked increases in sales and brand momentum.

The Muir display included a range of two types of manual anchor winches, mechanical and hydraulic pot and line haulers, hydraulic steering systems, stainless steering wheels and rope capstans.

According to John, Muir Engineering was there at the right time with equipment to suit the various marine markets. Most of everything they shipped to Singapore sold at the inaugural show or within a matter of weeks via the Singapore family agent, whom John met and came to an agreement with, an agreement that lasted almost two decades.

As Singapore has expanded and become a significant player in the international business community over the decades, so too has the Singapore boat show, superseded by the Singapore Yacht Show several years ago.

Today the event is one of the flagships of the international boat show arena, bringing together the world's finest superyacht and international yacht brands in one location, the well-appointed Sentosa Cove.

This was John's first overseas trip. Up until then he had travelled to Melbourne and Sydney and like many Australians, had never ventured beyond its shores, unless he was delivering boats to the mainland with his dad, or sailing in one of his 16 Sydney to Hobart yacht races. Can you imagine what that first overseas plane trip must have been like for a young businessman, busting his butt to do well and expand his operations, coming as he did, from a small island state where the tallest building was about seven stories high?

Landing at the international airport in Singapore is an experience in itself and John still has vivid memories of it.

"I will never forget what I saw as we flew in, there must have been a hundred ships at anchor, many were huge. I had never seen anything like it. Many fishing boats of various sizes, however not many yachts and pleasure cruisers."

ABOVE: FIRST COMMERCIAL WINCHES
Nick Fleming with a Muir M2 hydraulic anchor winch and a hydraulic reservoir to suit, at Battery Point in 1993.

OPPOSITE: MUIR'S FIRST VRC10000 HYDRAULIC ANCHOR WINCH
Getting ready to be shipped off to the Nice Boat Show, 1994. Muir Battery Point employees, left to right: Glenn Gleeson, Stuart Woolley, Bob Harper, Lindsay Groat. This same winch is presently on display with PSI Feenstra in the north of Holland.

John was not on his own for this trip, travelling with him was Bob Harper, also on his first overseas trip. John describes Bob as 'One of God's gentlemen and one of Muir's best ever all rounders and engineers.'

Bob had served his apprenticeship as a fitter and turner at the IXL jam factory, located in Hunter Street near Victoria Dock in Hobart. (It is now the site of the University of Tasmania's Centre for the Arts, as well as home to several art galleries, up-market restaurants and a boutique art hotel.) In those early days, it was Bob Harper and Chris Michael who undertook the majority of the in-house component design work, machining patterns and following through with the castings.

John Muir: "Bob worked with Muir Engineering for over 30 years, mainly at Battery Point and sometimes at Kingston. Chris Michael also worked at Muir Engineering in the early days, at Battery Point and then transferred into engineering and design at Kingston. Chris had his own engineering business for a few years, then came back to Muir in Kingston. He travelled extensively throughout Australia and New Zealand and throughout most of northern Europe and was also with us for almost 30 years. Chris was one of our most widely travelled and best sales warriors.

"Bob and I put together a really good display in Singapore to show off our products, particularly our pleasure and fishing boat winches and steering gear.

"We received a lot of interest from boat builders and set up several new Asian distributors in Taiwan, Singapore and Hong Kong. After the show I visited these new prospective agent/distributors to look over their operations.

"We were there at the right time with equipment to suit the various marine markets. It was a resounding success and led to substantial growth in our business."

Business growth, however, comes at a cost. It's not cheap to travel across Australia, attend expensive boat shows, and then travel round the country seeing how many more customers you can drum up. It's even more expensive to do that internationally. Sales expenses were rising. Still, John and Wendy had managed to put away $20,000 from the business to re-invest and used it to purchase industrially zoned land in Kingston, 15 minutes drive south of Hobart, to build a purpose-built factory with room for expansion. As John says, "Nothing ventured, nothing gained." Expansion costs money and is part of the growing pains of any new business.

John Muir: "The business at Battery Point was at a stage where we needed to expand, but we were lacking the capital to finance everything, land, buildings and equipment from our own funds. I would regularly speak to Russell Duffield for advice. Prior to building the Muir workshop at Kingston I asked his advice, as I intended to build this new workshop twice as big as what we needed at the time.

"We mortgaged the land we'd bought outright in Browns Road, Kingston, to allow us to purchase an existing structure from a defunct juice factory in Hampden Road, Battery Point. We dismantled the steel structure with the assistance of Elliot Brothers, and transported it to the Kingston block. Later, we undertook modifications to increase the height and laid it all out for blasting and painting. Within a short while, we had well known identity Don Hazell, of Hazell Bros. come and help with his big D8 caterpillar dozer and over a few days

John Muir: "When I spoke with Russell Duffield about our plans, and my concerns over committing to a much larger workshop than we currently needed, all he said was, 'If you're sure you'll fill it up within five years, don't worry and just get on with it'

"While another friend, mentor and contractor, Don Hazell was working on site, I asked his opinion on our expansion. He was a fellow business owner and had grown a large business with his brother Rowley through civil road and construction work and property development, as well as farming, so his opinion was valuable to me.

"He raised his three middle fingers and told me if I owned this much, then I should only borrow one (he folded two fingers down). Only borrow one third as much of what you already own. Another important thing he said was that it was unwise to have all your money tied up in one asset because if you get tight

> 66 *When I spoke with Russell Duffield about our plans, and my concerns over committing to a much larger workshop than we currently needed, all he said was, 'If you're sure you'll fill it up within five years, don't worry and just get on with it'.* 99

he levelled off the block and then set about digging foundations with his backhoe. Then over a couple of weeks the contractors poured the slab and footings, and followed with the erection of the steelwork.

"The new building ended up 20m wide and 80m long. We maintained the existing roof truss width at 18m but spaced the trusses out so the building was quite a bit longer. We also increased the height of the shed by another 2.5m. All the steel work was carried out on site by Muir Engineering employees."

This sort of DIY (do it yourself) behavior is not surprising. It embodies the work ethic John had been brought up on. Why go out and buy a new shed at what could have been a huge cost, compared with buying a solid second hand one that you can re-design to suit your own needs at a quarter or less of the cost of something now? It is all about 'Do it yourself' because you can. Because you like doing that sort of thing, building stuff from scratch.

for cash you're better off having several smaller assets you can sell to free some cash up."

It turned out to be sage advice. Even though the Muir business would have to weather economic storms, particularly 'The Recession We Had to Have' in the late 1990s and the 'Global Financial Crisis' (GFC) of 2007, John's business was resilient. Muir Engineering survived and grew.

John Muir: "We split the cladding work between ourselves and another contractor and did the same with the roofing, again to save precious capital.

"By the time we had completed the building with two mid-height mezzanine floors on the north side, it had cost us around $300,000, which we had progressively mortgaged as various construction stages of the bare building were completed.

"At the time Wendy was very nervous about the financial commitment it took to build this premises, and I remember we sat up in bed one night talking about it."

ROOM TO GROW, 1976

The new Muir workshop at Kingston provided room for growth into mega winch development. Photos are taken from the opposite side of the newly constructed Southern Outlet, a major highway project built to connect Hobart's emerging southern suburbs to the city more efficiently than the previous coastal route through Sandy Bay and Taroona.

This workshop was 80m x 20m, with two raised floors running its full length on the northern side. In 2002, a second workshop was added for fabrication, big winch testing, polishing and assembly of the fabricated winch components.

The authors of a book called 'The Millionaire Next Door,' Tom Stanley and William Danko revealed that, as most of us know, starting and running your own business can be very liberating, and an excellent way to secure your financial future. It can also be very stressful.

According to the Australian Bureau of Statistics, more than 60% of small businesses cease operating within the first three years of starting. It's an incredibly daunting figure and it's something that's thrown at many an enthusiastic business person who announces to the world that he/she is about to start a new venture. It might just help to keep those enthusiastic feet more firmly planted on the ground of reality. Likewise it can happen the other way.

Starting a new small business is a risky venture, because obviously it can and does lead to disaster. With a failure rate of over 60%, it's a wonder anyone does it at all. That's probably because many new small business owners don't do their homework, don't test the market first and don't start small the way John Muir did. He and Wendy already had a strong and successful business, with a reliable cash flow, a growing number of customers and an expanding market share. Any bank worth its salt would want to lend to them and John and Wendy's bank did.

After attending the Melbourne, Sydney and Singapore boat shows in the early 1970s, the business was on a roll. New customers were constantly coming on board, production was flat out at Battery Point and pushing the limits of what could be produced within the confines of available space. The push was on to get the Kingston facility up and running and equipped with newer machinery as quickly as possible.

Even though the Muir business would have to weather economic storms… John's business was resilient. Muir Engineering survived and grew.

During this period of transition, starting to sell nationally and internationally, attending boat shows and building the business, John met another businessman, Malcolm Lewis. It was another commercial marriage made in heaven.

Malcolm was the CEO in Australia for the huge Italian industrial engineering business, Bonfiglioli.

Malcolm Lewis: "We are accustomed to dealing with world-class clients with specialised needs – including some of the world's biggest mining and energy companies – so we know what tough and reliable performance means and we expect that from the people who supply us with products."

Ms Sonia Bonfiglioli is the current Chairman, second generation and CEO of this vast family owned business, designing, manufacturing and distributing gear motors, drive systems and planetary gearboxes for industrial processes, automation, mobile and renewable energy applications. It began back in the 1950s building gearboxes for agricultural equipment and motorcycles.

"SOME OF THE BEST"

Above: Joe Didocha, left, and Lyndon Potter in the workshop, 1998. John describes them both as 'two of the best all rounders'.

Opposite page, top left: Hans Iseli, whom John describes as "One of the best all-rounders – machinist, tool maker, fabricator, designer and perfectionist.

Opposite page, middle: Lyndon Potter, left, and Dave Webb, working in the Mega section of the workshop, 1990s.

Opposite page, top right: Dave Webb and Lyndon Potter with another employee, 1990s.

Opposite page, bottom left and right: David Oates (in safety glasses) packaging up another large winch shipment for the USA.

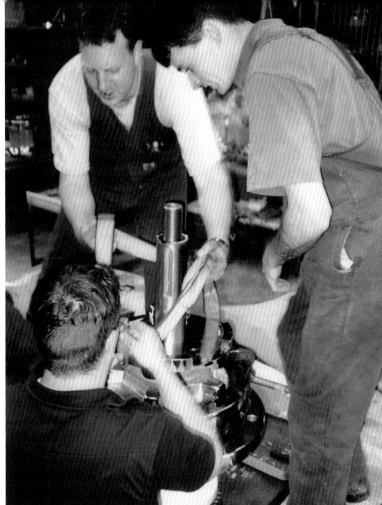

Malcolm Lewis: "The marine environment for which John Muir engineers his windlasses and anchoring systems are every bit as demanding as the environments for which we engineer wind turbines and port technologies, for example, so we are an excellent fit.

"What makes it a truly special relationship is the focus we share on quality, performance and innovation – John is always innovating and always inviting us into the process where we can add value from a local and global base of knowledge."

The relationship between the two businesses is one of Bonfiglioli's longest 'Down Under.' Muir was the first direct customer for Bonfiglioli in Australia and the association continues to this day. Muir Engineering is still one of their most important and consistent customers.

Malcolm Lewis: "John is a great believer in established quality, but also a champion of innovation.

"Over this time Muir has gained and expanded a strong market share with their global customers, despite all the low-cost alternatives finding their way into the marketplace. They have led their market with quality, performance and reliability, factors which are prized in maritime applications.

FIRST INTERNATIONAL BOAT SHOW
This page and opposite: Muir's stand at their first overseas boat show – Singapore Boat Show in 1977. Bob Harper, pictured right in glasses, was John's right-hand man and attended the show with him.

> ❝ *There is no doubt that the driving force and continued growth of Muir Engineering's business over the years can be attributed to the tenacity and business skills of John Muir.* ❞

–MALCOLM LEWIS

"There is no doubt that the driving force and continued growth of Muir Engineering's business over the years can be attributed to the tenacity and business skills of John Muir, who is one of those unique entrepreneurs who has achieved continued success through hard work and belief in his product.

"We have always shared his scrupulous attention to enduring performance. When we started, we looked very closely at the torque and load capacities of our gearboxes, to match the various models within the vast Muir range of marine winches, windlasses and capstans, all of which need strong and reliable gearboxes. These selections were checked and double checked with our engineers to ensure that they were capable of handling the duty cycles and arduous marine conditions, which can change dramatically depending on the tides, sea conditions and operators of the equipment.

"Muir products are shipped around the world and on occasions where something needs to be checked or inspected overseas, we have usually been able to assist John Muir by calling on our vast network of branches and distributors worldwide."

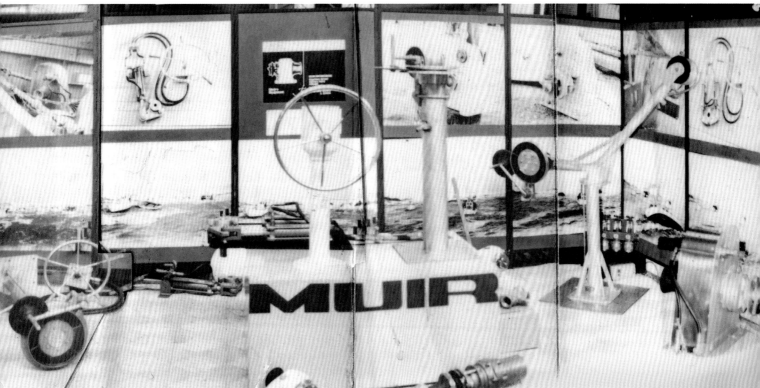

Malcolm Lewis started work with Bonfiglioli as a young engineer, involved in engineering sales and service and, according to John, worked extremely hard with his team to grow the Bonfiglioli business throughout Australia and New Zealand. John is also glowing in his support for the company and the standard of the products they supply to him.

These years of boat shows and building the Kingston operation from scratch were filled with new people, new commercial contacts, people to meet, people to assess and decide whether or not to do business with, or put them on the payroll.

John Muir: "40 years ago, back in June 1977, I met Alan Brooker and Rob Flintoff at the very first Singapore Boat Show. This was also the first overseas boat show I attended. We had been preparing for the show for 18 months, and by this stage we had developed a range of hydraulic steering gear, hydraulic line haulers, small to medium size pleasure anchor winches and a range of heavy duty commercial anchor winches.

"Myself and Bob Harper were setting up our comprehensive display when we were approached by Alan and Rob from Plymar Sales out of Perth. At that time they were representing Maxwell Winches from New Zealand, who were our major competitor in the small to medium winch business. Alan and Rob were impressed by the range of equipment we had on show and visited us several times. On their last visit they asked me if I would fly home via Perth to visit them and discuss the possibility of their business representing Muir products in Western Australia."

Instantly John changes his flight arrangements and travels home via Perth in Western Australia. This would become a pattern of behavior that his wife Wendy would soon get used to, gone one minute, then his stay extended without warning.

"I visited Plymar on my way home and we agreed on the new representation arrangement and I went home with a substantial order for anchor winches, as well as line haulers and capstans. As of 2016 AMI Sales, as Plymar are now known, are still representing Muir products."

There are some very interesting times to reflect on with the booming Western Australian boat scene; pleasure boats, patrol boats, small and large commercial and fishing vessels, and the likes of Austal ships with their large ferries, all in full swing.

Austal were building motor yachts and established a company called Oceanfast, managed by a young naval architect from the UK, David McQueen. Oceanfast built some of the world's best motor yachts over the next 20 years including internationally famous golfer Greg Norman's yacht and several vessels launched under the name *Mercedes*, all fitted with Muir winches."

The 1980s and 1990s were boom times for Western Australian boat builders and subsequently Muir. In those days there was as much boat building going on in this state alone as there was in whole countries overseas. John's reputation as a hard-working, driven man was spreading as was the reputation of his gear.

Rob Flintoff: "It has been an incredible journey over many years. John used to visit Western Australia on many occasions to assist with sales and boat shows, and he had an incredible appetite for work which resulted in long hours, often finishing with a good meal and a cold beer. My association with John started 40 years ago when I was with a former company Plymar Sales, then a leading distributor of marine equipment

PERTH CONNECTIONS

Left: Chris Michael (left), Sales and Technical Manager for Muir, with Phil Cass of Alec's Marine, sometime in the late 1990s at the Perth Boat Show. Handing over a bonus for best retail sales in the area.

Above: Alec's Marine stand, Perth Boat Show, mid 1980s.

Below: John in 1995 presenting Alan Brooker (right) with a painting of the Hobart docks he had commissioned to celebrate AMI and Muir partnership spanning 20 years (since 1976), accompanied by Margaret Terry and Rob Flintoff, centre.

Opposite: Rob Flintoff, 1995. Plymar, later known as AMI Sales, have had a long and successful relationship with Muir.

> **AMI, which has now been in the industry 30 years, will always be a loyal supporter of the Muir brand, as it is part of AMI's foundation as a company and one of its original start up agencies.**

– ROB FLINTOFF

in the Australian Industry. This association continued when I later started a new company AMI Sales in December of 1986. John tells me that this is the longest distribution arrangement that Muir has had – 40 years."

Rob says there was one particular Italian restaurant called Roma at the bottom of High Street in Fremantle where they would often go after a long day. These meals often became entertaining sales sessions, pleasure hand in hand with work.

Rob Flintoff: "I recall on one particular occasion we entertained Phillip and Darryl Cass from one of John's biggest Western Australian clients, Alec's Marine. It wasn't our usual haunt, this time the restaurant was called the Conti on Collins in West Perth. That night a deal for 22 winches was negotiated.

"AMI now has international branches in Singapore and Vietnam, and has been successful in assisting Muir with its marketing and sales of winches and anchoring systems for workboats and defence vessels built in the local yards of these regions.

"AMI, which has now been around 30 years, will always be a loyal supporter of the Muir brand, as it is part of AMI's foundation as a company and one of its original start up agencies.

"John Muir and his team can be extremely proud of their achievements in an extremely competitive environment against other major corporate brands. From a remote place called Hobart, he had the tireless courage to take on the challenge and did it very well."

ROB AND MALCOLM FLINTOFF
Left, with the Muir display at the AMI Sales Perth head office. Right, outside AMI Sales' O'Connor WA office, 2015.

THE WORLD
is our OYSTER *in the*
EIGHTIES

It is the early 1980s and it's well after midnight in Hobart, Australia. Andrew Perkins, one of the joint CEOs of Skeels and Perkins, a casting and foundry business that supplies Muir Engineering with bronze and stainless steel components, is sound asleep. His phone suddenly rings, with the persistent, jarring trill that only a call in the middle of the night can bring.

Startled, Andrew scrambles for the phone, fearing the worst. Calls at this time of night usually come with bad news attached, a member of the family injured or worse. Not this call. Not this time. This one was from 12,000km away.

"Andrew is that you?"

"Yes."

"It's John Muir here, mate, I need a price on castings for a winch deal for a bigger yacht than we have ever supplied before."

There is a brief moment of relief for Andrew before John's conversation ramps into top gear and he reels off the list of what he wants. How much bigger the castings will be, what the price limits are. He's in a boardroom somewhere in Europe, furiously negotiating a deal to supply winch gear and he needs an answer now. He hasn't got time for Andrew to do his sums, or check the profitability of the job. Are you in or are you out?

"John, do you realise what time it is here?"

"Yeah mate, I know, I'm sorry, but I need this price and I need it now so I can seal this deal. So what do you reckon, do you reckon you can do it for…"

This is John in full swing, having got his foot in the door of some prominent European shipyard, he now has to put his money where his mouth is and put together some meaningful numbers. European shipyards shop hard for the very

LEFT: STOCKTAKE 2002

Chain gypsies by the score! The majority of these were supplied by Apco Engineering.

OPPOSITE: ADOPTING NEW TECHNOLOGY TO COMPETE

Fitting & Machining apprentices Lyndon Potter, left, and Paul Rodgers, right, around 1990 operating the new Colchester lathe.

best prices and expect the very best quality. John has six weeks delivery time to factor into his calculations, unlike European winch makers that don't have a shipping time or freight costs to contend with. The figures have to be right; even though John's winches and equipment have a great reputation now, it is still early days. Right now, having been given an opportunity to supply a larger model anchor winch system, John needs this deal more than he ever needed one before.

This prospective order means new winch designs developed from scratch. John has already looked into the sizes required, knows what the customer wants and has sketched it up. (Hand drawn sketches.) He knows that there would be new casting patterns to be made by either Muir or Skeels and Perkins. The next hurdle, once things are under way back home, is to meet the customer's shipyard arrival deadline.

There was no time to stop and ponder the possibilities. It had to happen, do or die.

Andrew Perkins: "There were quite a few late night/ early morning calls from John on the other side of the world, frantically doing a deal with a buyer. John talking to the customer in the background, trying to seal the deal, to discover if we were in and could agree to the terms offered."

John knew how to play one business off against another to get the best price and quality he could. Nothing wrong with those business practices. On his own turf he could buy from three local foundries: Retlas, Skeels and Perkins and the Derwent Foundry.

Andrew Perkins: "Working for Muir has improved our quality, as John has very exacting standards. Muir is always after ever-better quality. Some of the other foundries just thought, 'Nah, stuff it,' but we've worked hard to improve our quality to meet Muir's demand. They helped drag us kicking and screaming out of the 'She'll be right' mindset."

Meanwhile engineering operations at the new Kingston site were in full swing. The building had proven to be far bigger than required, so John successfully rented out the rear third, with the rent paying off most of the building's mortgage interest.

The biggest centre lathe at the factory was an Australian made Macson, which was moved from Battery Point to Kingston to machine bronze, stainless steel and cast iron. Various other equipment was purchased, as and when needed, some paid for by cash reserves, others financed. Muir bought several new Colchester lathes and various other milling

machines. It was the early 1980s and the computer age was not yet with us, even though it was getting closer, so all working drawings and winch patterns were all hand drawn.

Back then, Colchester lathes were among the best in the world. Made in the UK, they had a great reputation for being able to withstand heavy use and for giving years of trouble free service. When (like Muir) you are manufacturing from a base that is thousands of kilometres from your markets, you have to adopt new technology early to give you an edge over your competitors.

In the period leading up to 1983, Australia was again in the throes of political change. The Prime Minister was conservative Malcolm Fraser, who had led the country from 1975 following that defining moment in Australia's political history when the Governor-General, the Queen's representative, had sacked Labor Prime Minister, Gough Whitlam. However things were not going well for Malcolm and the elections of 1983 were looming. The Labor party, led by a bloke whose nickname was 'the Silver Bodgie,' Bob Hawke, won a landslide victory and the party held power until 1996. During that time, while Paul Keating was the treasurer, Australia went through an exciting period of economic

stability and growth. Union wage claims were contained by an agreement brokered by Bob Hawke. Paul Keating oversaw the floating and the free falling of the Australian dollar and extensive financial de-regulation.

An editorial in one of the nation's biggest daily newspapers, The Sydney Morning Herald, in December 2013 described the floating of the dollar thirty years before as:

"One of the most dramatic changes in our economy's history. Global financial markets, rather than government officials, set the value of the Australian dollar from December 12, 1983. Since its float, the dollar has been on a wild ride, from levels of US55c in the eighties up to the record highs of US110.8¢ in 2011. When the exchange rate was fixed, the Reserve Bank could not effectively control the amount of cash in the money markets, which hampered its ability to set interest rates.

In being freed of its obligation to set the exchange rate, the Reserve Bank was able to focus on keeping inflation in check. This, in turn, has underpinned the past two decades of economic stability and lower borrowing costs."

In those early days at Kingston, before the international winch business took off, two of John's respected employees, Joe Didocha and Don Di Martino, were interested in finding something else Muir's could make and sell. At this time making winches was a seasonal operation and to fill a production gap in winter it was decided that wood heaters were a smart product to manufacture, particularly in a cold place like Tasmania.

Joe Didocha: "I started working at Muir in 1979 and have been with them 29 years. I had a lot to do with the initial design of the Steelfire wood heaters. We started making the wood heaters, because winches slowed in the winter and we needed to maintain a steady workforce of around 35 people, plus a further 10 engineering people at Battery Point. Another employee, Don Di Martino and I had built our own wood heaters and John agreed we could make them in the factory as long as we told him what materials we used. Mind you, he never charged us for anything that we built for ourselves!

"We discussed the idea with John and he agreed. Everyone wanted heating, especially in Tasmania,

where firewood was abundant, so we agreed to make wood heaters of really good quality that home owners would like to buy. We had five different designs by the finish. The business was so successful that in the first year we sold almost 500 heaters and over a period of almost 20 years we manufactured thousands and thousands."

Joe was a leading hand and Don was the production/factory manager. At that stage wood heaters were fast growing in popularity.

Joe Didocha: "I'm a fitter and turner by trade. I did my four year apprenticeship with Purdon Engineering in Sunderland Street, Moonah. I continued working at Purdon for a further six years. I was interested in diversifying. I called in at the Kingston workshop one day and I started working for Muir."

John Muir: "Joe's first job at Muir's Kingston was machining a big batch of anchor winch main drive shafts. He had one of the brand new Colchester lathes going 'hell for leather' and in full swing. Joe could machine a batch of these winch shafts twice as fast as anybody else!"

The new Kingston factory had plenty of space available, even though the back section was rented. At first several wood heaters were manufactured and used in the factory. Then, as local demand kept rising, Joe, Don and John agreed to expand production to include their own range of wood heaters. The brand 'Steelfire' was born.

Joe Didocha: "Don made the first prototype wood heater, and then I made one and I still use it in my home today. We made models for factories sold as 'Factory Fire'. Another model contained a two-speed fan while another allowed for air-ducting. They were particularly useful for double-storey homes.

"We were struggling to keep up with orders and business was booming, and as John was always looking ahead we constructed a large purpose-built fabrication workshop at the rear of the property purely for heater and metal fabrication. John around this time had his sights on carrying out more stainless steel work for the marine industry."

A production line was set up – three long welding benches, one long assembly bench and close by, a parts bench. On a new raised mezzanine floor in the main workshop a storage area for heaters was made. The new second workshop had a good sized paint spray booth and a modern metal polishing shop.

GROWING RAPIDLY

Photos from the Kingston workshop in the late 1970s show the scale of the operation. Pleasure winches are assembled on a long bench (above) and modern time-saving equipment is adopted early.

Up until 1985, Muir's big winch gear was being manufactured at the Battery Point workshops. After this, production gradually migrated to Kingston.

John Muir: "The Steelfire wood heater business expanded and overgrew the space intended. We seriously went into production mode, making up to 40 mobile assemblies to move the heaters around between different processes as they were being constructed and assembled. Finally, heaters were sprayed, assembled and relocated to the stores area on the top floor."

At the same time as wood heater production was ramping up, John and Chris Michael started developing another larger range of purpose built, fabricated drum anchor winches for Austal Ships in Perth and Incat in Hobart.

John Muir: "By now we were really into the pleasure boat windlass business. There were two manual models to begin with, the Samson (a one speed winch) and the Hercules (a two speed winch) and a range of vertical and horizontal anchor windlasses with a capacity of up to 1700kg lift.

"Within a year Bob Harper developed and patented a figure eight chain drive (the first in the world) which allowed a manual lever to rotate 180 degrees, preventing any excessive handle load breaking the Samson manual drive. I knew this was a great idea and arranged to pay Bob a royalty on the patent, even though the winch was developed in Muir time. Over the same period, larger vertical winch models were still evolving from Muir Engineering at Battery Point, including the VR7000 and VR10000. The last big

ROARING SUCCESS
Above: Mark I and Mark II Steelfire wood heaters complete and stored on the newly built mezzanine level of the Kingston workshop.
Below: An image of a Steelfire Mark I slow-combustion heater alight used in marketing material in the 1980s.

OPPOSITE: FOLD-AWAY GANGWAY, 1995
Designed and fabricated by Muir from aluminium, at Battery Point, at a time when the rigging shop was converted into a winch testing and fabrication workshop because of a lack of space and a rapidly growing work load. The engineering team at Battery Point were highly skilled and so able to tackle a wide range of design and engineering projects.
Left, Matthew Williams in the foreground. Right, class rules testing at Macquarie Wharf.

model vertical anchor winches to be developed and manufactured at Battery Point were VRC13000-15000 in polished aluminium bronze. They really looked a treat. These were installed on the three masted schooner *Adix*. (The yacht mentioned in the Introduction to this book.)"

Other winches that were developed at Battery Point before the move to Kingston were the Panther, Cougar, Cheetah, Jaguar, Thor and Goliath range.

For a decade Muir developed and manufactured a range of hand and power assisted hydraulic steering equipment, the brand was 'Hydnautic.' They were sold within Australia, New Zealand and throughout Asia.

Meanwhile, John Muir had realised the peak of the wood fire market might be getting closer, as there was growing environmental concern about air pollution from wood heater emissions. Environmental standards were being tightened and wood heaters were being increasingly scrutinized. Sales of wood heaters were also seasonal. Additionally, the sales team were asking John "What business are we in, wood heaters or boat winches?"

John Muir: "It wasn't long before I talked to Don and Joe and informed them we were going to wrap up wood heater production at the end of autumn. Neither could understand my decision to move away from wood heaters, as they'd been so successful and had created full-time employment for up to ten people. They were also rightly worried about whether this meant terminations. I was confident we could engage these employees in the stainless fabrication

area that I knew was about to expand into the large megayacht winches and anchoring systems market."

For over 20 years, Muir had sold a lot of wood heaters, amazingly many are still in service to this day. The Kingston factory still uses one of the earlier Steelfire Mark II wood heaters in the middle of the machine shop and on cold winter days this provides a cosy hub for the employees to enjoy their cuppa.

John Muir: "I could see quite a bit of work on the horizon if we tooled up to go down the route of stainless steel fabrication, but this would mean we'd have to cease production on the wood heaters that year. I made the decision to cease production on the wood heaters and focus more of our efforts on expanding the megayacht and commercial drum winch business."

When wood heater production stopped, the Northern Hemisphere was coming into spring and the windlass manufacturing operation was going to be flat out all year round. Sales doubled over the next three years.

John was often away, with more to do now looking for new business and customers to offset the 1990s recession. Travelling on his own or working and travelling with locally based agents interstate initially, and as the recession took more hold, John spent a lot of time in the USA and Canada seeking new winching business. Some of those trips became legendary, as did John's reputation for his late night demands on hotel staff and their fax machines. They were also the topic of much conversation, as were the length of those faxes when they arrived at the factory in Kingston.

OPPOSITE PAGE: THE LAST BIG JOB AT BATTERY POINT

*The last big model vertical anchor winches to be developed and manufactured at Battery Point were VRC13000-15000 in polished aluminium bronze for the sailing yacht **Adix**. Second from right in the main photo is the inimitable Bob Harper, who was a long time employee and staple of Muir's innovation in the early years of large winch development.*

*Centre photo: **Adix** team, left to right: Left to right: Bill Baun, Mick Temple, Nigel Bruce, Brett Ross, Unknown, Nick Fleming, Bob Harper, Glenn Gleeson.*

THIS PAGE: STEELFIRE WOODHEATERS

A brand of wood heater developed at the new Kingston workshop, Steelfire was intended to fill a production gap in the winters. Displayed in 1993 at the Derwent Entertainment Centre (above) by Glenn Gleeson, and David Wright, the brand was a roaring success. About this time, however, an opportunity to expand into the lucrative megayacht market had John asking, "What business are we in?"

On the right, top to bottom: the Muir Gas Marine Fire; Steelfire Mark II wood heater; Steelfire Factory Fire, which proved very popular in Tasmania.

Trips were either new business, sales or visits to international boat shows, such as Miami and Fort Lauderdale in Florida, USA, METS in Amsterdam or Nice in France, which later became the Monaco Boat Show. More often than not John was carting with him, as excess luggage, brand new winching products, mostly new pleasure anchor winches to countries as diverse as Holland, Germany, the UK, the USA, Canada, Japan, Singapore, South Korea and even just across the ditch to New Zealand.

Closer to home, just as things were starting to improve, John and Bob Harper had to sort out a serious problem. The factory had received a big order from Melbourne for six sets of scallop boat winches, power steering equipment and anchor winches. The order was valued at around $65,000 per ship set with commissioning. It was a big order and very important to Muir's financial situation.

> **66** *I could see quite a bit of work on the horizon if we tooled up to go down the route of stainless steel fabrication, but this would mean we'd have to cease production on the wood heaters that year.* **99**

– JOHN MUIR

John Muir: "It was a substantial order, but the customer also wanted our help to fit and commission the gear. That was a mistake we made, it became a nightmare due to the vessels being built in Melbourne.

"At the time, there were probably half a dozen boat builders in Melbourne involved on this project doing different work. Some were steel fabricators, others were contractors. Then we found out that it was one of those end of financial year, whatever you call them, tax things.

"There wasn't just one boatyard, there were five different engineering firms involved and to make matters worse a few were not professional boat builders. We started to build the six ship sets and when progress payments were received, we shipped them over to Victoria. Some of the businesses, we found out too late, definitely shouldn't have been building or fitting up hydraulic equipment on boats.

"We learnt our lesson after that experience. Never install anything unless it was on our terms. At the same time, in early June, we had our family's 48ft sailing yacht *Shonandra* under construction. She was just a hull, deck and basic bulkheads and was sitting at the rear of the Kingston factory. The plan was to get her finished and head away as a family on Boxing Day, the day after Christmas Day.

ABOVE: WORKING AROUND THE CLOCK
John in his hotel writing extensive notes to fax back to headquarters. The faxes tended to be very long and required a fair bit of deciphering.

TOP: WENDY'S PARENTS
Cliff and Betty Harwood both served in the UK RAF in the Second World War. Cliff was an aeronautical engineer and was involved in maintaining the UK warplanes. Prior to his retiring from Forestry Tasmania, Cliff worked for approximately 20 years as a plant superintendent.

It left us just six and a half months to fit her out, install an 80hp Ford diesel engine, fit all the stern gear and propeller and attend to the rigging and new sails. They were being made in the sail loft at the Muir boatyard. We had on hand a mast and boom section that came with the boat.

"I arranged with Bob Harper to go to Melbourne to manage the scallop boat project. He should have gone with at least one other person, but he said, 'I'll be right for a while.' So Bob was hands on, supervising the installation of all the gear, and once it was all installed we had to commission it. As time got closer to June, the builders were getting testy about getting their boats in the water. I got several calls from Bob getting anxious.

"To keep a very long story short, the so-called fabricators turned engineers told Bob the hydraulic reservoirs of three engines had been flushed prior to starting. Unfortunately he took their word for it. He washed the other three systems himself. It was a disaster, because the three systems that Bob didn't do himself ended up with sand all through them. When they were started, the motors seized."

Back in those days it cost around $4,000 to replace each motor, plus time spent on the job. The three redundant motors were scrapped and replaced at Muir's expense! Following, John decided to seek reimbursement from the boat builders.

John Muir: "'Crikey', I said, when Bob called and told me what had happened. 'We'll get some more motors from Malcolm Moore's Melbourne branch and put it in the boats'. At the same ruddy time, we had *Shonandra* being fitted out and we were flat out in the factory. One night when I was home, I received a call from the project manager for the overall company handling this really tight operation. They had six different boat builders on the go, desperately trying to get these boats finished by June 30.

"He said, 'One of the boats your bloke's working on caught on fire. You'd better get your backside into gear and get over here by the morning'. That's the way he was talking. He was a bloody arrogant foreign bloke, so I get on the plane the next morning, taking with me my overalls and some gear.

"When I arrived I found the newly completed wheelhouse had burnt out. Fortunately, we didn't make the hydraulic hose that caused the problem. I ended up talking to our Hobart solicitors and they talked to another solicitor over in Melbourne. I wasn't sure whether I should fix the gear up or just turn my back on it. Reputation is on the line in a situation like this. I decided we couldn't afford to turn our backs on the project. Bad news travels fast on the fishing industry wireless."

The stress of the project was really hard on Bob Harper, in two months his hair went from brown to white and John was feeling it too. It was a scary situation for both of them.

With John's attention fully on the Melbourne project, he talked to his wife Wendy and Don Brown, one of Muir's best shipwrights about what to do with the *Shonandra* boat building project.

They both agreed they would continue on with the fit out and John arranged for several extra tradesmen to assist, as the yacht was still at Kingston.

John Muir: "Don and another of the shipwrights pushed ahead with the fit out of *Shonandra*, while Wendy continued sanding and varnishing the fore and aft bulkheads, along with preparing and varnishing the mid ships saloon, galley and aft single and double bunks. We were fortunate to have Wendy's parents, Cliff and Betty Harwood pick up our daughters, Shona and Alex, from school and look after them.

I was very fortunate to have Wendy on side with the work on the new boat, as she proved on many occasions since then that when given a job that had to be done she would get on and do it.

"I said to Bob after a week in Melbourne, 'I need to go home.' It was the time when these Melbourne blokes were commissioning another boat. They blew that big hydraulic motor up too! We ended up replacing four of these motors. We paid for them. Some valves and fittings had grit blasting sand all through them. After a couple of days I went back to Melbourne and worked with Bob until we finished the commissioning of the scallop boats and luckily picked up some payments. All six vessels were launched and commissioned by the end of June.

"I came back and talked to my solicitors. We took legal action and sued several of the boat builders and eventually we were paid. Four ended up paying us in full, another one paid us for the original equipment balance but went bust before we got to sue for the damage to the hydraulics. The sixth one went bust and we didn't recover anything to speak of. That deal cost us a lot in lost time and components. From then on we only installed our equipment when the job was in Hobart."

SHONANDRA, ALEXANDERS BAY 1995

Getting her finished was a challenge, but the Muir family enjoyed many sailing trips away with friends and extended family on **Shonandra***.*

Thankfully very few of Muir's business deals went the way of the scallop boats.

Another of the many long term business relationships John cultivated in the 1980s was with the Spooner family and in particular Barry Spooner. Barry's father, Arch, had purchased a large tract of swampland near the Dandenong Ranges, southeast of the city of Melbourne. On a visit to the UK in 1958, he saw the possibilities of a new product called fibreglass. Realising its potential in the boat building industry Arch established the Caribbean Boat Factory soon after returning home. The boats that were built needed to be tested, so what better use for swampland than to create a man-made lake. In the early 1960s Lake Caribbean was created. It's now known as Caribbean Gardens.

The factory Arch Spooner (known as the father of Australian boating) built and then used to pioneer Australia's fibreglass marine technology is still in existence. Today the factory is more than ten times the size of the original building and has churned out over 50,000 boats from 3m to 15m since it began operations.

> **❝** *I was very fortunate to have Wendy on side with the work on the new boat, as she proved on many occasions since then that when given a job that had to be done she would get on and do it.* **❞**

ANOTHER BOATING DYNASTY

Barry and Richard Spooner at the Caribbean factory in Scoresby, Victoria, 2016.

Barry Spooner: "John and I have had a very long association [since 1983]. It's been very harmonious, he's always tried to do his very best in every respect with his business. We've never had an argument about anything. I remember that in the early 1980s we worked together to pioneer the design of some of his winches. John was always receptive to new ideas.

"He's done extremely well as an Australian manufacturer, to go out internationally and sell his winches in various parts of the world. He's put a great effort into it and I respect him for it."

There is a defining moment in this business relationship when in the mid-1980s Barry asked John to come to Melbourne as soon as he could as he had something he wanted to talk to John about. Without knowing what was in store, John jumped on the next plane to Melbourne and drove to the Caribbean factory at Scoresby.

John Muir: "I discovered that Barry proposed to carry out pull tests on a Muir horizontal winch and one of our competitor's horizontals. They were trying hard to get

the Caribbean/Bertram anchor winch business, having recently delivered a 1,000 watt horizontal anchor winch for appraisal.

"When I got there we went straight to the factory where Barry had the competitor's anchor winch set up on the test bench. He told me that he was going to carry out identical pull tests on both winches to see if one was better than the other. I was glad I was there to oversee what subsequently happened.

"The test would compare pull loads, clutch cones and sizing and anchor chain matching. I would be able to keep an eagle eye on my competitor's winch and also see how mine performed. We would both be looking for any distortion of the winch components, particularly when the winch was close to stalling. Maker supplied circuit breakers were fitted for protection of the 1,000 watt 12v DC winch motors, to stop them from burning out.

"The dual drive clutch cones driving the chain gypsy were slowly tightened to increase the pull load."

This is the ultimate test for a winch to see if it will do what the makers claim it can. This is the 'do or die' moment to see if and when a winch will fail. If it does fail when it's been fitted to a boat and that boat is caught in a storm, then the subsequent events could be disastrous.

John Muir: "As the pull load on the competitors winch was increased it was obvious it was struggling to pull to expectations. The problem that showed up was mainly due to slippage of the smaller sized clutch and drive cones. The test continued and as we exerted more pressure on the drive the winch pulled again and to everyone's dismay the main drive shaft bent!

"When we tried to disengage the clutch, the two part clutch nut assembly split open and the flat bar lever handle fell out. I must admit I was now wondering how our winch would handle the test.

Barry said, 'Pull it off the bench and put yours on John.' Before we put it back in the box, we had to measure the shaft diameter. Ours had a larger diameter shaft and our clutch cone drives were also larger.

"We ran the Muir winch through its paces, checked the speeds, pulls, drive cones and main shaft. The Muir winch came up to Barry's expectations, having reached the stall load without any component failing, nor was there any noticeable shaft deflection.

"Barry smiled and said, 'You retain our business John.'

"There was never a sweeter moment than that. I packed up, we had a cuppa and I headed back to the airport. I reckon you would have had trouble wiping the smile of relief off my face. I'm sure that positive test result didn't do our business reputation any harm at all."

ABOVE: INDUSTRY STAYERS

International Marine's stand in the 1972 Melbourne Boat Show held at the Melbourne Exhibition Building, displaying Bertram pleasure boats.

OPPOSITE: LONG ASSOCIATION

Muir has been supplying winches to International Marine since 1983. Left, a 'Storm' VRC1200 polished stainless steel anchor winch fitted on a Caribbean cruiser. Right, a custom clutch handle atop a VRC1200 vertical anchor winch, preferred by Barry Spooner because there is no loose handle to go over the side. Note the snubbing line and chain hook for securing the anchor on the chain roller.

> 66 *John and I have had a very long association. It's been very harmonious, he's always tried to do his very best in every respect with his business. We've never had an argument about anything. I remember that in the early 1980s we worked together to pioneer the design of some of his winches. John was always receptive to new ideas.* 99

– BARRY SPOONER, INTERNATIONAL MARINE

John Muir: "I found working with Barry very interesting; he was personally involved in installation and testing of all new products. He was always forthcoming with new ideas, and on occasions suggesting changes to something at the design level if he thought there was a better solution.

"Barry was very safety-conscious. He preferred a slower speed anchor winch, as he'd once had a customer lose the end of his finger in the chain of a winch. It was Barry's idea to make an integral handle on the top of the windlass vertical capstan, thus saving the inconvenience of a loose or overboard handle.

"Barry's son Richard, like his dad, is carefully spoken, technically minded and has maintained his father's thoroughness and eye for detail."

The Bertram/Caribbean boats have a long-standing reputation for being excellent sea boats. International Marine, along with Steber, Maritimo and Mariner (then Riviera) are a handful of Australian power boat builders that have operated continuously since they started. These longstanding boat builders have been fitting up Muir winches from the outset. Over the years John has maintained a close personal relationship with the founders and directors of all of these companies.

A brief perusal of John Muir's diaries, such as they are, from the late 1970s to early 1980s shows a man who has a lot of responsibility and more than his share of stress! John kept a good tab on his finances with Wendy and his bookkeeper.

There are myriad fascinating quotes to choose from:

> *"Flat out, money is tight, overdraft in place, hard to keep up with demand."*
>
> *"It's not easy to keep on top but if I don't give up we will."*

What John is referring to is the constant need for the global sales team to get new business and meet or exceed projected budgets. Then you have to balance those sales against the costs of doing business from isolated Tasmania. Combine that with a currency that has yet to be deregulated and the competition from New Zealand that always seem to have a cheaper production base than Australia and you can see why at times John was getting frustrated.

However as the months passed, his comments grew more positive:

> *"Very busy November."*
>
> *"Stock and debtors have never been higher, if we can get them both down we will be looking good."*
>
> *"Coming up I have two weeks in the USA, they are coming out of recession, and the market there is good."*

Many of the quotes are in affirmation form, as if John is telling himself to believe that everything is possible, that the conversations he has in his head are as important, or more important, than the ones he has with clients, friends or employees.

Author of the book, 'Mind Power,' John Keogh, tells us that affirmations are critical to ensure success, in whatever you do.

"Affirmations are statements that you say either out loud or quietly to yourself. You affirm to yourself whatever it is you want to happen. For example, if you have an important interview coming up, you could affirm to yourself, 'A great interview,' and you would repeat this statement over and over again for several minutes. Or, let's say you're recovering from a leg injury, you could repeatedly say to yourself, 'I have strong and healthy legs.'

"Why do affirmations work? Keogh says they work because whatever you verbally repeat to yourself will influence your thoughts. Say to yourself, 'A great interview,' and you will automatically begin thinking about your upcoming interview as 'A great interview.' Repeat to yourself, 'I have strong and healthy legs,' and your mind will begin imagining strong and healthy legs. What you focus your mind on, you attract, so begin focusing on whatever it is you want."

in the yachting world as the impossible. After the win, the cup was shipped to the Royal Perth Yacht Club in Western Australia, but first it had to be unscrewed from its pedestal at the New York Yacht Club where it had sat for the past 132 years.

Australia was on an economic high and John Muir was getting on with his growing winch business. He talked to his friend and mentor Russell Duffield from time to time. In his diary notes of one such chat, Russell warned him against thinking that tariffs in Australia, protecting businesses from cheaper imported products, would ensure John's business survival. "You have to be internationally competitive to survive," he said. It was sage advice that John took seriously. He realised that to be competitive within Australia and overseas you had to constantly stay ahead of the design, research and development game, produce winches that would build your reputation and contain costs at home.

Boat shows were now an integral part of John's travelling and sales calendar. It was on one of these trips in 1983 that he met another marine distributor who was to prove a real asset and friend for John and the Muir business. He is Jeroen Jeltes from a business called Belship, based in Holland.

Jeroen Jeltes: "I met John on a European tour a long time ago in the early 1980s. I was in distribution and

Knock on the door, if that doesn't work, climb in the window. If that fails, go round the back and if it all fails, climb down the chimney.

Back in Tasmania the green movement was born in 1978. It remained small until 1983 when there was a huge groundswell of support for an anti-dam campaign. A Liberal conservative government, led by Robin Gray, wanted to dam the Gordon and Franklin rivers on the west coast and build another hydro-electric power scheme. The campaign gathered force and it won the support of the new Hawke Labor federal government. The culmination of community opposition and federal government intervention in the High Court stopped the dam in its tracks.

In 1983, an Australian high roller called Alan Bond, made headlines around the world. We had done the impossible; we had beaten the Americans and won the America's Cup. No-one had ever managed to achieve what was regarded by almost everyone

selling other winches made in Scotland. When Simpson Lawrence (later Lewmar) merged, I lost distribution rights, so I was looking for a replacement supplier. I knew about Muir winches so I contacted John to see what was possible.

"There were other companies who'd been selling Muir winches, but I knew he wasn't satisfied with their representation in Holland. Being a sailor, I knew I could do a good job for him.

"Economically, there was a lot of competition, especially in the smaller winches, mainly from Italy and Scotland, so it was difficult to compete. To make matters worse, freight costs made it even more difficult for John's products to be competitive. They were being shipped from Australia as opposed to their competitors that came mainly from the UK and Europe.

"Oceanco's Technical Director, Gary Bradshaw, an ex-Australian living in Holland, gave us a chance, but he said 'If you screw this up, we both get fired.'

"Muir pleasure winches were not competitive in Italy at the time, because of the lower costs of European manufacturing. Anyway, I picked up John at Schipol Airport in Amsterdam. We would knock on every door and every shipyard in Holland, and also visit many naval architects."

Knock on the door, if that doesn't work, climb in the window. If that fails, go round the back and if it all fails, climb down the chimney. That's a John Muir motto and that's what he and Jeroen did, not just in Holland and Germany but also in Italy.

John Muir's winches may not have been cheaper, but they were higher quality. According to Jeroen that made it more difficult but not impossible to drum up business.

John Muir: "There were fewer competitors in the mega winch business in Europe, the design and quality of Muir products was superior, it was all above deck highly polished equipment. Some of our competitors were still using galvanized, painted steel components on above deck equipment. As we progressed with sales in Scandinavia, Holland, the UK and Germany, I was asked several times by Dutch and German yards why they should buy winch gear made in Australia.

EUROPEAN CONNECTIONS

*Above: John in his element onboard **Sycara V** at Monaco Boat Show in 2013.*

Below: Jeroen Jeltes visits the Muir Kingston factory in 2015, and posing with an SD3 drum winch.

"I replied, 'In Australia we buy German and Dutch vehicles, like Mercedes, BMW, and DAF trucks, which are well represented, supported and serviced by the importer and their sales service agents. Until you purchase an Australian made Muir winch, you won't know how good it is.'

"In the early 1980s we had Cramm in the north of Holland looking after Muir sales and service, providing after-sales service, which we've always had available throughout Europe."

Cramm first began supplying another Dutch motor yacht builder, Moonen Shipyards with Muir anchor and mooring winches in the early 1980s. It is a business relationship that remains to this day. Of the 70 motor yachts launched from 1983 up to 2009 the majority of the Moonen motor yachts were fitted with Muir anchor and mooring winches.

Moonen Shipyards is regarded as one of the world's best builders of small to medium motor yachts. The business is situated in the picturesque medieval Dutch town of Den Bosch, and began operations back in 1963.

Between 2009 and 2016 Muir supplied anchor and winch equipment to many Moonen constructed vessels.

John Muir: "Construction of a new 36m motor yacht got underway at Moonen in 2016. FEEBE marine equipment will be supplying and installing two Muir vertical hydraulic VRC8000 anchor winches and two VC4000 hydraulic mooring capstans."

The majority of Moonen motor yachts were designed by renowned Dutch naval architects like Willem Stolk, René van der Velden and Emile Bilterijst.

"In breaking new ground, there has always been a customer or a shipyard willing to opt for the Muir product. In particular, several well-known European boat builders gave us the opportunity to initially supply Muir winches to suit larger motor and sail yachts of around 60m. As the vessel length increased towards 100m we had support and service firmly in place. That gave the shipyard the option of choosing Muir over and above other well-known northern European winch makers."

Jeroen Jeltes: "We spent five days in shipyards in Holland, then three days in northern Germany and made a few sales. I dropped John off at Bremen Airport on the Friday, and he headed off to Italy to visit Bonfiglioli in Milan. I would go home over the weekend then fly to Florence on the Monday to meet John. We then picked up where we had left off."

This is a journey that Jeroen will almost certainly never forget. John was doing what he does best, meeting people, talking about his winches and being a thorough gentleman. They travelled to Viareggio, the main city of the northern Tuscan Riviera area of Versilia, then onto other boat builders and component manufacturers including Bonfiglioli.

ABOVE: LONG TIME EUROPEAN DISTRIBUTOR

Jeroen Jeltes of Belship outside the Muir Kingston factory with John during a 2015 visit to Hobart.

OPPOSITE: FOOT IN THE DOOR IN EUROPE

Top: Benetti 45m motor yacht, coming back from sea trials off Viareggio, southern Italy, 2001. This yacht had fitted two VRC11000 anchor winches and two VC8000 mooring capstans. This was the first time John had been on the Mediterranean on a yacht, and it was one of many orders resulting from John and Jeroen's visits to Benetti in the early 1990s.

Middle and bottom: When Cramm Hydraulics decided to take on selling Muir pleasure winches in the 1980s, it provided a real foot in the door of the European luxury yacht market. Photos: Cramm Yachting Systems.

Jeroen Jeltes: "We rented a little car and visited maybe 30 shipyards in Italy. I had been selling deck cranes to the local shipyards so I knew the area. Once we were on the road, we didn't stop for lunch, unless we could get a quick meal at a service station.

"You have to be a terrier. Don't give up at the first door that gets slammed in your face. I remember, at one shipyard, John was asked when his flight home was. His response was, 'Not before I get your order.'

"On another trip like this one, we managed to get into Benetti Shipyards.

"John's energy is quite remarkable and I think he is half gentleman and half streetfighter because he never gives up.

" *John is half gentleman, half street fighter.* "

– JEROEN JELTES, BELSHIP

"You have to work hard to keep these customers. You can'tjust assume because you got one order that you'll be the first choice next time. There might be a different purchasing or project manager next time. Relationships are very important. People move about in this industry, they leave shipyards and go elsewhere, or they retire, and then it's somebody else who likes to be respected as well. If you're lucky the old contact shows up at a different shipyard, so you manage to get a foot in the door there."

In the 1980s, Europe managed to create over 6 million new jobs, in the USA it was more like 10 million. 1983 was a year when the world economy was recovering from the global oil shock of 1979-80. It was good news for the hard working John Muir, as world trade began to recover after two years of stagnation. The boat building industry is very susceptible to changes in economic conditions, as much of its demand is driven when the world is having 'good times.' When people have plenty of money and confidence is high, they spend.

Jeroen described John Muir as "half gentleman, half street fighter." According to John that description of half gentleman and half street fighter may be right.

"Jeroen certainly has seen me in some pretty tight conditions, he's never seen me in a fight. But he knows if I make my mind up I'm pretty determined.

"I think what he's getting at is a bit like sticking with it. Sticking with it until the end, until you get the business, until you get it done. I know if you want a better deal and your margin of profit, you've got to negotiate it and that's the same with selling and sales and you just have to work harder, don't you?"

Two of the many people John met early in northern Europe and subsequently did business with were Mr Reinhardt Heimstra and Hessel Rienks, two of the directors of a very successful and growing

ABOVE: MY *ISSUE*

27m, launched in 2001. Muir VRC8000 hydraulic anchor winches and VC6000 mooring capstans. Photo: Moonen Shipyard.

LEFT: MY *DARSEA*

Moonen 97. Muir VRC11000 hydraulic anchor winches and VC8000 mooring capstans. Photo: Moonen Shipyard.

BELOW: MY *BIJOUX*

At Monaco Boat Show in 2016, Moonen's latest motor yacht **Bijoux** *displayed a set of polished stainless steel VRC4000, vertical hydraulic anchor winches, and VC4000 mooring capstans. Photo: Moonen Shipyard.*

OPPOSITE: GENOA BOAT SHOW

Luigi Pomati, left, with John and Rob Flintoff from AMI sales at Genoa Boat Show in 2002.

Dutch business, Cramm Hydraulics. The business trades now as Cramm Yachting Systems and is a trusted supplier to the megayacht industry worldwide. Over time, as John was starting to set up a network of contacts from 'The Big End of Town,' they would prove to be invaluable in the years ahead.

When John was introduced to Cramm, he managed to convince them to take on selling Muir winches into the European yachting and boat building market. Cramm supplied, installed and serviced a complete range of hydraulic equipment from bow and stern thrusters, boarding steps and ladders, deck cranes, as well as Muir hydraulic anchor and mooring winches and steering systems. In 1982 Cramm took on selling the Muir pleasure winch range.

Another in the long list of Dutch work boat, motor and sailing yacht builders John successfully gathered into his client fold in the early eighties was the Damen Group. These days Damen is an international shipyard group but, like John, it had humble beginnings. Established by two brothers back in 1927, today it boasts over 9,000 employees, operates in over 32 countries and is highly regarded in the international shipbuilding world. It is still run by Damen family members.

John Muir: "The Damen family business offers its customers a wide variety of tugs, work boats, patrol vessels, high speed craft, cargo vessels, dredgers and offshore support vessels.

"Muir have been supplying Damen with anchor and recovering winches since the early 1980s. It was another Dutch operator, Belship, who first introduced

me to Damen with the supply of a range of horizontal DC anchor winches for their production work boats. Over the years Muir have supplied many polished stainless steel anchor and mooring winches to this company."

Under the Damen ship building umbrella is the world renowned mega motor yacht builder Amels, based in Vlissingen in the south west of Holland.

John Muir: "When Mr Damen senior, the founder of Damen, built his own sailing yacht for extended world cruising he chose to purchase a Muir VR4500 anchor windlass.

"He also purchased another Muir 4500 as a spare! Not that he envisaged having trouble with the windlass. That said the yacht travels to many remote places and Mr Damen has on standby a container with that spare anchor windlass located strategically close to where he is cruising at any given time."

The list of people John met on his endless travels is long and varied. Take Luigi Pomati, who met John at the Genoa Boat Show in 1985. John was wandering around, doing what he did best, checking out other competitors stands, making sure he wasn't in for any nasty surprises from new entrants into the business and just 'pressing the flesh.' This boat show was then the largest in the world, so you can imagine its size and scope and the hundreds of thousands of people who would visit.

Luigi Pomati: "John was perusing the many small to medium size power boats, sailing yachts and several of the competitors winch gear. The Genoa Boat Show was the largest of its type in the world with over 400,000 visitors.

Hydraulic SD450 drum anchor winch installed on an 80m Austal fast ferry.

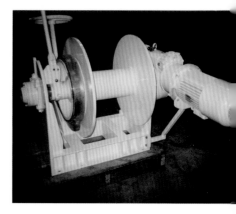

SD250 drum anchor winches were supplied to Austal Ships in large quantities throughout the 1990s and 2000s for their 42m fast ferries.

Super Sea Cat *with SD5 drum anchor winch and 4 tonne mooring capstans.*

Austal Ships built Customs patrol vessel fitted with Muir VRC11000 vertical bronze anchor winches with electric 400V drives.

SGC2 twin gypsy, twin capstan electric anchor winch with manual drum brakes.

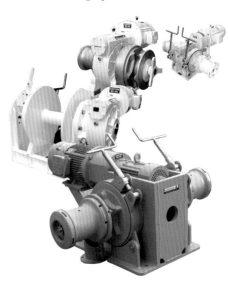

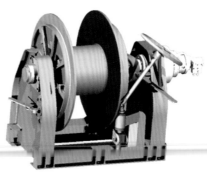

*Austal Ships **Delphin**, an Auto Express 82m high speed vehicle-passenger catamaran ferry fitted with SD450 drum anchor winch.*

Muir SD450

The types of products supplied to Austal, front to back: VCC750 6 tonn gypsy capstan electric anchor winch; SD250 drum anchor winch; SGC250 electric anchor winch; SGC2 twin gypsy, twin capstan electric anchor winch with manual drum brakes.

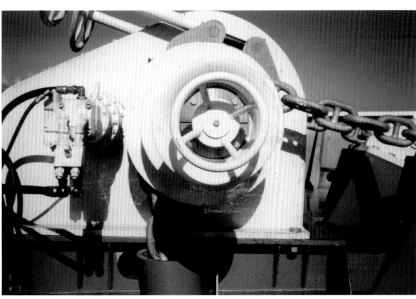

NQEA HYDROGRAPHIC SHIPS, LATE 1990s

Muir designed and manufactured two sets of custom 10,000kg horizontal anchor winches for two 80m hydrographic ships being built by North Queensland Engineering Associates (NQEA) in Cairns, Queensland.

Above: Positioned aft of the H22000 winch are two vertical turning rollers to redirect the mooring lines from the anchor windlass to the mooring scuppers.

Forward, H22000 10,000kg horizontal hydraulic anchor winches to suit 38mm stud link cable. On the outside of the chain gypsies, large rope-warping capstans for forward mooring purposes. Aft deck, two 4 tonne vertical mooring capstans with hydraulic drive.

The internal bulgear and pinion were machined in-house at Muir's workshop Kingston, although the gear cutting on the bulgear was done interstate.

Right: Talented engineer and fabricator Patrick Roberts supervised the manufacturing with the assistance of Chris Michael, Sales and Technical Engineer. He poses here with the winches during Lloyds class testing.

DAMEN SHIPS

Belship got Muir in the door at Damen Shipyard in the early 1980s, and they now supply Damen with a range of winch gear for their work boats and fast ferries. The above equipment is for Damen Singapore. Top: Damen high speed support vessel **MarineCo Shamal**.

POLICE AND PATROL BOATS

Top and middle: Turkish Coast Guard patrol vessel; Qatar Emiri Naval Forces patrol vessel. Vessels built by Yonca-Onuk Shipyard, Turkey. Photos: Yonca-Onuk JV
Bottom: Left, rescue patrol boat with a Muir VRC600 anchor winch, New Zealand 1990s; right, Chinese patrol boat with a Muir VRC6000 anchor winch, 1990s.

PV *VAN DIEMEN*, TASMANIA POLICE

23.5m police patrol vessel built by Geraldton Boat Builders, Western Australia, in 1995. All Muir hydraulic drive equipment. Aft capstan: VC1600; Anchor winch: HR4000; Pot hauler: 18"/450mm diameter aluminium with stainless steel pedestal.

ABOVE, LEFT AND RIGHT: ITALIAN CONNECTIONS

Luigi Pomati, of CIMA. Left, outside hotel in Milan 2000, ready for a sales tour with John; Right, in Genoa for the Genoa Boat Show, 2002.

OPPOSITE: CHICAGO BOAT SHOW, 1980s

The Muir display on the Powerwinch stand, featuring images of a teenage Alex Muir onboard **Shonandra***.*

"Towards the end of the boat show it became obvious to me, after talking to John, that he was intending to go after marine business in Italy. I mentioned to John that Lofrans windlasses, at that time were right up there on the numbers and likely the biggest globally in volume, with a spread of anchor and mooring winching products selling world-wide. Later on I introduced John to the Lofrans family and on several occasions he visited their works. They have remained good friends ever since."

In those early days John travelled alone, to destinations all over the globe, attending boat shows, setting up displays, visiting boatyards and customers, and seeking out new distributors. Muir had already set up distributors in North America, Canada and Scandinavia.

That same year John decided to travel to the USA to attend the Long Beach Boat Show in southern California. The Muir sales booth was part of the Australian Trade Commission display. Just before he left, John travelled to Sydney and visited the Newport marina of Fleming Marine. Another long term friendship began, this time with one of the owners, Kevin Fleming.

Kevin Fleming: "I first met John in 1984 when he came by my Newport marina north of Sydney. He was going to the USA, to a boat show sponsored by the Australian Government for Aussie businesses. I tagged along with my new stainless steel Fleming self-steering gear.

"The booth setup was a large area with about 20 other booths, internal space incorporating a lounge/bar setup with lots and lots of Aussie beer and wines. It was certainly appreciated by all. They did it well."

Australian born Kevin Fleming spent his childhood in the small South Australian fishing town of Port Lincoln, learning to sail and, like the Muir family, developing a deep respect for the sea. It was during the early 1960s when the cruising bug saw him sail his 32ft yacht to the Great Barrier Reef and back to Sydney. The voyage was a test run for his first self-steering wind vane system. The Fleming Marine business is still going strong today. Kevin and John often find themselves competing for national export awards.

Kevin Fleming: "I still smile recalling some of those experiences. We met many USA agents and clients, it would have been in the hundreds! Long Beach at that time was the biggest indoor sail boat show in the USA.

We went with a guy from Seattle. Peter Rachtman was just starting out as an agent for John and was located in Seattle."

From this boat show, John's USA business volume began to grow and over many years became substantial. That growth was mostly a result of Peter's hard work, ably assisted and financed by John.

During the show, John sold the same winches that were on display at Long Beach over and over again. When the show ended and clients (who had been promised those winches) turned up to collect them there was some angst over this unfortunate screw up. (John had sold many more winches than he had available.) Kevin Fleming took over the negotiations and in the end, he says, there wasn't a problem. New winches would be flown direct to the clients who missed out and all were happy. According to Kevin they seemed to love dealing with Australians.

> **66** *I still smile recalling some of those experiences. We met many USA agents and clients, it would have been in the hundreds! Long Beach at that time was the biggest indoor sail boat show in the USA.* **99**
>
> – KEVIN FLEMING

Kevin Fleming: "I also remember an invite for breakfast with a Muir client. He picked us up in his Roller [Rolls Royce] and then showed us two 54ft yachts he had just imported. They needed winches of course and John had sold them to him. He was a big land developer and on the way back to the boat show we were shown his latest project. It was a whole block of old church buildings sitting on waterfront land. Years later, a multi-story complex sat there.

"I sold more wind vanes in 11 days at that show than I had in the previous 12 months. After coming to my wits I realised I was holding deposits for more units promised to buyers than my factory could possibly build. John and Muir Engineering took over the build of the initial design and construction, and dug me out of a giant hole, and a lifetime friendship has ensued."

According to John, his mate Kevin Fleming was a hell of a salesman. He sold the Fleming Wind Vane business four times, because every one of the new owners couldn't get it right, so he bought it back again. It was always a deal that saw Kevin buy it back for less than he had been paid for it.

John Muir: "Kevin and I were at the Chicago Boat Show in September 1983 with Peter's who was looking after the distribution and sales of Muir Winches. At this time, *Australia II* (owned by Alan Bond, and skippered by John Bertrand) was sailing in the America's Cup in Newport, Rhode Island. The event coverage in Chicago wasn't so good and after two days we were both becoming frustrated that we weren't in Newport. Kevin and I decided, unbeknownst to Peter, to take a plane to Newport to see what we could of the race. We left him on his own with the stand.

ABOVE: FISHING TRIP
2001 fishing trip with the Imtra guys in the D'Entrecasteaux Channel, Tasmania. Left to right: John, Chip Farnham, Muir staff Ian Stocks, Chris Collings and Chris Michael.

BELOW: EUROPE
Muir windlasses on display at METS in the 1990s.

BOTTOM: POWERWINCH STAND
Muir gear on display at Miami Boat Show, mid 1980s.

"When we arrived in Newport, it was down to the last race that day, and when *Australia II* won the Cup, it was something we'd never experienced before. One hell of a celebration ensued. In the pub we were approached by a writer from The Australian newspaper, and being Australians, he asked us what we thought of the win. By this time we were in full celebration and the Budweiser was flowing We were in The Australian newspaper back home the next day showing our exuberance."

At the Long Beach Boat Show John also met and started another long business association with Jerry Truax from a business called Tatoosh Marine based in Seattle.

The Tatoosh website describes Muir winch gear as: "A range of anchoring and mooring systems that is globally renowned as today's leader in anchoring systems for a large variety and size of luxury motor and sailing yachts. A Muir anchoring and docking system provides long term reliability, durability and dependability.

"Muir equipment is manufactured in Hobart, Australia and globally distributed and serviced in over 60 countries. Their dedication to support provides the confidence demanded by cruising and charter operators the world over.

"Muir's success in designing and building anchoring and docking systems for the luxury yacht market has come from a longstanding commitment to work closely with naval architects, designers, builders, captains, engineers and owners in the pursuit of excellence."

Jerry Truax: "I first met John at the Long Beach Sailboat Show in 1982. I was production manager at Tatoosh Marine and we were displaying one of our 40s built by Ta Shing in Taiwan. As I recall, the Australian Trade Commission had a group display and Muir Windlasses had a booth. One of my responsibilities was to manage the commissioning and outfitting of our new boats, and as a result, I purchased a lot of anchoring equipment. I had never seen the Muir windlasses before and I was impressed with the quality and appearance. At that time, the majority of our sailboat customers preferred manual windlasses, and we purchased mostly the SL555 2-speed."

The SL555 is a Simpson Lawrence product, made in Scotland. Simpson Lawrence were at that time a world renowned anchor windlass and marine equipment manufacturer and one of John's biggest competitors, although there was literally half a world between Scotland and Tasmania.

Jerry Truax: "At some point in early to mid-1983, I received a call at Tatoosh from Peter Rachtman the owner of So-Pac. He talked about Muir Windlasses and wanted to come over and talk about the products. He came by and left a Muir Hercules 2-speed manual windlass next to my desk in the hopes that I could find an interested customer. Business was pretty tough at that point with very high interest rates and our boat sales had slowed down. I don't remember having an opportunity to try and sell the Hercules before he came back and picked it up.

"Moving to the autumn of 1984, I had left Tatoosh and was looking for a new opportunity. One of my old college buddies was working at a local marine distributor (Kolstrands) and apparently mentioned to Peter Rachtman that I was looking. He called and asked if I would like to come by and have a talk with him about joining So-Pac. We came to an agreement in mid-October, with a starting date of 1st November. My first day duties were to fly to Long Beach, California, and work the So-Pac booth for the final weekend of the 1984 Long Beach Sailboat Show. No better way to find out what you don't know about the products.... It was all 'on the job' training that weekend.

"That was when I started to get to know John Muir. We were displaying a good range of the Muir windlasses along with other products, and John was around the So-Pac booth quite a bit and also spending time with Kevin Fleming, who was displaying his Fleming wind vane steering units. I don't remember many details from that first weekend as I was getting a crash course, but I do recall that John and Kevin were working pretty hard."

Even though both John Muir and Kevin Fleming fell out with Peter, John says "He was a hell of a salesman, you might even describe him as a swashbuckler." It's the latter description that might come from Kevin Fleming.

It transpired that Peter was living up to his reputation and description. He spoke to John after the boat show and said "If you can make me those horizontal 1000 watt DC Cougar windlasses for US $500 I will sell 600 every year!!" John made the winches and Peter sold them. In order to be able to meet that price line, John had the winches cast, machined and powder coated in New Zealand. It was cheaper than getting the job done in Tasmania because the New Zealand currency was 30% lower than its Australian equivalent. The gear was tested, passed and shipped to Bayliner, a boat building operation in the Pacific Northwest of the USA, on the border of Canada. Within three years John managed to reduce his cost of production and sold another few hundred a year elsewhere. He was also able to increase the selling price to US $600 each. That was a good price back then, especially when the US dollar remained high and the Australian dollar was weaker.

At one of the METS boat shows in Holland where Muirs had a stand, John caught another European winch manufacturer taking photos of his gear, having pulled a winch top works down without his permission. Before the bloke could react, John surprised him, grabbed the camera from him and told him to, "Bugger off. You can come back and get your camera when you are going to apologise to me. By the way there won't be any film in this camera when you do come back!"

Following the Long Beach Boat Show, Peter suggested the trio should visit some ship chandlers and importers of winch gear in Los Angeles and in wider California. They set off in search of new customers.

John Muir: "Kevin came along with us. It was usual in those days to pre-arrange a meeting, however on most occasions this didn't eventuate, so we cold called with a carton of beer on Peter's shoulder, and a winch under each one of our arms. He would knock on the door, put his right foot forward, then his head and shoulders in the door, and to be honest we only got refused once.

"This became the way we proceeded to set up around the west coast of the USA. Peter, being single-minded, up against Kevin, caused a furore on several occasions. I recall Kevin saying to him, 'You're only a friggin' rock star.' By the way, prior to being in the marine business, Peter managed some of the best known rock bands in the United States!

At one of the METS boat shows in Holland where Muirs had a stand, John caught another European winch manufacturer taking photos of his gear, having pulled a winch top works down without his permission. Before the bloke could react, John surprised him, grabbed the camera from him and told him to, "Bugger off. You can come back and get your camera when you are going to apologise to me. By the way there won't be any film in this camera when you do come back!"

ABOVE: SALES DINNER
John with Peter Rachtman, centre, and Murray Morten in the mid 1990s.

BELOW: AUCKLAND BOAT SHOW 1998
Muir horizontal anchor winch range.

"Travelling with these two blokes was highly stressful. We went to Seattle, where Peter lived, and worked around the marine markets, setting up with the well-known Seattle retailers. Kevin was readying to get back to Australia. We were both weary from being away for almost five weeks. On the last day, Peter was to settle with me a substantial amount, however, it wasn't to be. Only a small part of this amount got paid up front, the balance came later."

Later that afternoon John Muir wasn't feeling well and he decided to book a flight home as soon as possible. John was not at all well, he had thrown up in the basin of his hotel room and saw blood, lots of it. He thought, "I better get home." He was really wound up trying to cope with the arguments and tensions between Kevin and Peter. He didn't go to the doctor or a hospital. Instead he caught a taxi to Seattle airport and took the next available flight to Hobart, via Los Angeles and Melbourne.

After a two hour wait in the airline lounge in Los Angeles, he was fortunate enough to be upgraded to a business class seat for the flight to Melbourne. He remembers having dinner and sleeping for most of the duration of the 14 hour flight. In Melbourne there was another two hour wait for his flight to Hobart.

What John did not realise was that he was suffering from a bout of acute pancreatitis, a life threatening illness. At one point in his life, John had planned to build the business to the stage where he could stand back more and not be so heavily involved.

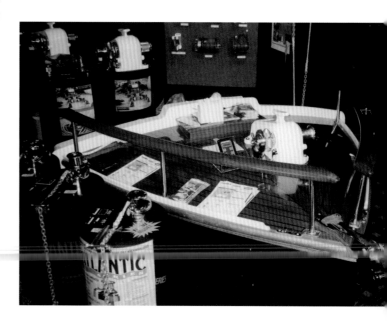

He arrived home and thought he would just have a rest for a couple of days and then get back to work. It was not to be.

A STORM GATHERS
AND BREAKS

We left John Muir at the end of the last chapter, deciding to fly home to Hobart from Seattle, via Los Angeles and Melbourne, even though he had been vomiting up blood and wasn't feeling at all well. No visit to a doctor, no visit to a hospital emergency facility.

John Muir: "Looking back now I should have gone straight to hospital when I was in Seattle. I was angry and upset because Peter owed me money and had told me he couldn't pay me the full amount straight away, as was promised. I decided to get on the next plane and come home. I know now that I was really lucky to survive."

When John finally got home he went to bed. He didn't tell Wendy about the blood he had coughed up, behaving just like many men of his age and background. Don't whinge or complain, get to bed, get some rest and it will all be OK in the morning! Next day Wendy was up early, got the girls ready for school and went to see Skeels and Perkins in the city, leaving John asleep in bed.

An exhausted John had slept well, but was still not right. It was more than just being tired from travelling and selling for five weeks, much more. By mid-morning he was restless and decided to get up.

John Muir: "I took several steps down the hall and experienced one hell of a shock. My stomach blew-up. It happened so fast, it bloated about a hand span outward. I thought I was having a heart attack. I called our doctor and said he needed to come and see me quickly, and I left a message at Skeels and Perkins for Wendy to please come home ASAP.

"Wendy arrived just before the doctor, they bundled me into the car and took me straight to St John's Hospital emergency department. I ended up in intensive care, and promptly passed out. I was there for an hour or so, before I woke up. I had tubes hanging out of me everywhere. When I came to I heard the doctor ask Wendy, 'Where has your husband been?' She told him I'd been in the US for five weeks on business and had only arrived home the previous evening.

"I heard him say, 'He's lucky to be alive. He's had an attack of acute pancreatitis and if he wasn't in intensive care within another 20 minutes he would have died.'"

After two days John was whipped into surgery and had his gall bladder and two opaque gallstones removed. One of the gallstones was blocking the duct between the gall bladder and the pancreas. It was this blockage that caused the swift swelling of his stomach. He was sent home to recover and prepare for another more serious operation. After several weeks it was back to hospital to remove a large cyst that had grown over part of the pancreas that secretes insulin.

John Muir: "What I didn't realise was that the part of my pancreas they removed was the part that is responsible for producing insulin, so I was on the way to becoming a full blown type I diabetic."

The UK based website, 'Drinkaware.co.uk' sounds a grim warning: "If you're diagnosed with chronic pancreatitis, the most important thing you can do is to stop drinking alcohol. This should help with the pain and stop your pancreas being damaged even more. If you carry on drinking, you're likely to experience huge amounts of pain. Worse still, you're three times more likely to die from complications of the condition."

Never a heavy drinker to begin with, after the operation John was instructed not to drink any alcohol, an instruction that he has religiously followed. If he had continued to drink, even in small quantities it could have killed him, as alcohol can poison the pancreas. It was the gallstones that caused John's pancreatitis, not alcohol.

> 66 *'I heard him say, He's had an attack of acute pancreatitis and if he wasn't in intensive care within another 20 minutes he would have died.'* 99

With acute pancreatitis, even if its not been caused by alcohol, you should avoid drinking completely for at least six months. You need to give your pancreas time to recover.

John Muir: "Prior to leaving the hospital, my surgeons, Dr Terry Horne and his assisting doctor, Dr Michael Wertheimer, advised Wendy not to mother me but to leave me alone. I needed to learn to look after myself again. I was as weak as a kitten.

"I was anaemic, I'd lost a lot of weight. I'd gone down from about 83kg to 60kg, and I had to learn to get up and walk and do things for myself. At this stage I could only really crawl, and it took some weeks to gather the energy to attempt walking upright. Over this time my prime focus was my health and recovery."

ABOVE: GETTING UP AGAIN
Following a bout of acute pancreatitis, getting back on the water helped the healing. John had lost a lot of weight, as is obvious in this photo from a trip on the water not long afterwards, with good friend Bob Cowle.

BELOW: FISHING WITH FRIENDS
John's friend Winston Bevis holds a freshly caught Tasmanian crayfish near Wineglass Bay on Tasmania's east coast. Winston and John Griggs enjoy a freshly caught and cooked meal onboard **Westward II.**

> **"** *He said, 'John forget what I just told you, from here on, if you look after your health better than your mates, you will most likely out live them!' That was the best advice I had ever received about my health and I took in on board 100%.* **"**

Can you begin to imagine how frustrating that must have been to the Blue Heeler of Battery Point? All he could manage was to lie there, try to crawl to the toilet, wag his tail, smile and try to keep a positive outlook. Blue Heelers never complain about their lot in life, they just get on with it. So did John.

Several weeks after John was discharged from hospital, he was up and about again. John, Bruce Darcey and three friends departed the Royal Yacht Club of Tasmania to sea trial a brand new 12.5m motor sailer, on a 145km run, circumnavigating Bruny Island.

It was a boat designed, built and fitted out by the talented Tasmanian shipwright and multi-skilled tradesmen, Bruce Darcey, for Frank Collins of Collins Marine in Sydney. Bruce had worked with Jock and Max Muir at the Muir boatyard and fished for abalone commercially with Jock on the *Mara Jane* and the *Strathleen*.

John Muir: "Being a responsible bloke, I took along a carton of non alcoholic apple cider and mineral water, that was the extent of my refreshment for the trip. When we got back to the Royal Yacht Club, we were scrubbing down the decks and a chap on the fuel wharf, whom I'd not seen for several years, noticed me and asked why I had lost so much weight. I think he was a nurse, but I can't remember his name. I told him about my operations and he, quick as a flash said, 'Hop up to the chemist and buy some urine test strips. You need to check if you have diabetes mate.'

"I slipped up to the nearby chemist and when I came back he was still on the dock and told me to pee on the strip and see what happened to it. He said to me, 'If it goes black there's a good chance you have diabetes.' It did and when I consulted my Doctor soon after, it was confirmed. I was now a full blown type 1

diabetic. That was a hell of a kick in the guts I can tell you. I didn't realise the high sugar content in apple juice, so that didn't do me any good at all."

"A month later I went to see Dr Tom Kirkland, a well-known and experienced Hobart based physician.

"I asked Tom to give me a good examination as I wanted to know one way or the other, how many years I may have lost off my life, and after many questions about the health history of my parents and grandparents, brothers and sister he told me, 'It could be five years John.'

"Well that was bad news, frightened the blazes out of me, anyway Tom went out for a few minutes to let me ponder things. When he came back I was standing up getting ready to leave and he suggested I sit down. I thought, 'Cripes, what's he going to tell me now?'

"He said, 'John forget what I just told you, from here on, if you look after your health better than your mates, you will most likely out live them!' That was the best advice I had ever received about my health and I took in on board 100%."

John's second time in hospital was meant be about treatment and recovery, but it was not all plain sailing. While he was lying in his hospital bed, not long after the operation, he received an unexpected phone call.

"It was from Peter Rachtman. Obviously word had spread that I was in a bad way. He was ringing from Seattle. First of all he said he'd heard I wasn't at all well, and was taking on selling Lofran's Italian made winches as well as Muir's, no doubt thinking I wasn't going to be around much longer. Words cannot describe what I told him on the phone. He still owed me money."

"He said he'd arranged to send me the money he owed me and asked me whether I would continue to supply him with products. I told him when I received his money that I would get back to him. I was slowly feeling better, and in terms of what was good business for Muir meant I should keep him on selling our gear. I later agreed to continue the supply on the proviso he paid me within 14 days of shipping, which he did until a couple of years later when he sold the business to Imtra. Imtra had both Muir and Lofrans winches that they continue to sell to this day."

John's life threatening illness is a timely reminder that business related stress can take a heavy toll on anyone. It knows no boundaries and can strike when least expected. John's great plans for backing off at 40 were in tatters. In fact, had it not been for the efforts of his staff at Muir Engineering and the hard work of his wife Wendy, the business might have struggled while John was seriously ill and laid up.

Shona Prior (née Muir): "Dad could have died if mum hadn't supported him when he was sick. Mum helped with the business while he was out of action for at least six months. I was eight years old when it happened and I thought my Dad was going to die.

"I can remember him just lying flat in the bed, he couldn't get up or do much. Mum told me that Dad was saying 'If I do get better, we may sell the business, life's too short for me to be in this state.' So Mum helped Dad get better but I don't think she wanted to keep the business at that time."

AMERICAN CONNECTIONS
Muir products have long been sold by US agents Imtra.

ABOVE: MIAMI BOAT SHOW 2000
Jerry Truax, left, and Paul Elskin.

BELOW: FORT LAUDERDALE BOAT SHOW 1993
Bill Farnham, father of Ted and Chip Farnham. Bill was the second generation of Farnhams in Imtra.

> ❝ *Mum helped with the business while he was out of action for at least six months. I was eight years old when it happened and I thought my Dad was going to die.* ❞
>
> – SHONA PRIOR (NÉE MUIR)

To give some perspective as to why John Muir suffered the attack of acute pancreatitis, a glimpse of his travel schedule from Hobart, during the early 1980s, across the world to boat shows, visiting prospective and existing clients, reveals a punishing schedule that would have taken a toll on any individual, let alone a driven man like John Muir.

John had full product displays and his own sales booth at numerous Australian and international boat shows. They proved to be a critical part of existing and future client education and outreach, as they all slowly began to realise how reliable and well-built Muir windlasses were.

ABOVE: IMTRA GROUP

Left: Chip Farnham displaying their Muir inventory at New Bedford, Massachusetts in the 1990s.
Centre: Jim Studley and wife Corkie, Fort Lauderdale Boat Show, 1998.
Right: The Imtra crew at Fort Lauderdale Boat Show in 1998, left to right: Ted Farnham, Jerry Truax, Chip Farnham, Jim Studley, Paul Elskin.

John's early 1980s travel schedule included Singapore in 1981/82, Chicago in 1982/83, New Zealand in 1985, Seattle in 1986, Europe, Scandinavia and Taiwan also in 1986 and visits to Melbourne, Sydney, Brisbane and Perth many times every year.

For John, it wasn't a case of why he went travelling the way he did, but simply because that's what he had to do to make Muir the international success he wanted and that it became.

John Muir: "As the days and weeks went by I was gathering more strength and agility. After contemplating the future, I decided to move the business in a different direction. I was unable to travel alone, as it was dangerous considering the surgery and punishment my body had taken in the previous year. I was advised to take Wendy with me to Europe, as we intended to set up distributors there."

Wendy Muir: "John was so sick and it took him several months to get back on track. When he was back into the business, of course it ended up bigger and better than it was before. When John started travelling again, I didn't travel with him apart from a long trip in 1986 to Europe and a couple of interstate trips. At that time he needed someone to look after him when he was away."

While John and Wendy were away in Europe, their two daughters, Alex and Shona stayed with their grandparents, Wendy's mother and father, Betty and Cliff Harwood.

Wendy Muir: "I didn't get totally involved in the business simply because, I guess, like a lot of women, a lot of families in our age group, I kept the home fires burning and looked after the kids. I did work in the business at Battery Point for almost ten years and from then on I helped out when John was away, but mostly I worked from home."

A year after John's frantic dash to hospital, he was on the road to recovery and there wasn't any talk of slowing down, only of expansion and more travel. The problem was that John had been warned by his doctors that he was not – *not* – to travel on his own, so Wendy agreed to go with him to Europe.

John Muir: "We were away four weeks in northern Europe. We appointed new agents in Spain, France, the UK, Holland. [It was Cramm, a hydraulic sales and service operation.] We had six winches with us that we had air freighted on our flights to our destinations. We visited a large French yacht builder, Beneteau, and discussed the possibility of supplying anchor winches. We came away with an order for ten units.

"Without doubt the best two nights we had away was when we stayed in an old waterfront castle come hotel in France at La Rochelle. It was located within a large marina complex, we had never stayed anywhere as nice as that. It was absolute waterfrontage, with the marina full of sailing yachts up to 20m in length. In the morning I asked why were there so many yachts there and I was told that France has more sailing yachts per capita than anywhere else in the world."

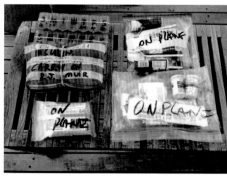

TRAVELLING AS A DIABETIC

The amount of travel John was doing when he was diagnosed with Type I Diabetes was potentially problematic. His wife Wendy has been packing for him and thoroughly organising his travel needs ever since. Everything is triple-checked, and back-ups or vital medicines are always packed in hand luggage in case the suitcases get lost.

On the way home John and Wendy stopped at Hong Kong for two 'rest days.' A rest day to John Muir is an opportunity to wander around the local docks and boatyards to see what was going on. He scoured marine retail outlets, fishing and boat yards. He noticed there weren't many anchor winches around, but a competitor's product, Simpson Lawrence, was most noticeable. Wendy flew home and John went to Taiwan on a sales trip and appointed his first local agent, who was an emerging marine distributor. They settled on the sale of a stock order there and then. Another success.

While John and Wendy were away, selling and attending boat shows, John left the management of the Muir operation in the capable hands of senior management like Don Di Martino and John Sattler.

The 1980s had also been a decade when Muir Engineering was being increasingly recognised for its achievements. That recognition began in 1980 when they won the award for 'Tasmanian Small Business of the Year' from the Advance Australia Foundation. Five years later, just as John was in recovery mode from his illness, the business was highly commended for achievements in domestic and export marketing by the Australian Marketing Institute.

Now that John was recovered and feeling stronger physically, his next step was to go to Western Australia and install a Goliath horizontal anchor winch on the old America's Cup boat *Cambria*, spend seven to ten days on the water, then it would be off to the Tokyo Boat Show to seek a new distributor.

The decision to travel to Tokyo followed a period of evaluation. John had decided to go to Japan to set up a Muir display with a group of other emerging Australian marine businesses under the banner of the Australian Trade Commission. John and the other seven exhibitors, including long-time friend Alistair Murray from Ronstan, were out to find a Japanese marine distributor. John also wanted to purchase a computer controlled multi-tool lathe and another computer

SMALL BUSINESS AWARDS, 1982

John Muir accepts the State Finalist award from Michael Hodgman.

CAPABLE HANDS

John trusted the operation of the Muir business to his highly capable team at Kingston, including Sales and Marketing Manager Chris Mackel (left) and Workshop Manager Don Di Martino (centre), above, with new Easy Weigh vertical anchor windlass, model 2000, in the late 1980s. Photo: The Mercury

controlled machining centre. He had his sights on Hitachi Seiki, one of the best computerised machine tool manufacturers in the world. The two machines would do the work of ten people

John Muir: "We needed to speed up our production and throughput. Following the boat show in Tokyo and a visit to our new agent in Osaka, I went to the Hitachi Seiki factory and observed their machine tools manufacturing the computerised equipment I was intending to buy. I purchased our first computer-operated centre lathe and milling machine. I spent about a quarter of a million dollars on those two machines, with tooling and freight.

"When the machines arrived at our Kingston factory, Don Di Martino commented, 'What the hell are you

gonna do with these things?!' My response was, 'Do the work of ten present operators, and we won't be laying anybody off.' He asked, 'How come?' and I answered, 'We will increase our production and productivity so much we'll have work for those eight people.'"

John's travel schedule in the early 1980s, that had been punishing enough before his illness, was ramped up as he began to realise the potential markets for mega-winch gear. It included Europe and Scandinavia in 1986. Then Tokyo, Chicago, London, Paris, Hamburg, Seattle and Miami in 1987. Chicago, Paris, Hamburg, Genoa, Seattle, Miami and Annapolis (near Washington, D.C.) in 1988. Then another burst in 1989 to Chicago, London, Dusseldorf, Tokyo and Miami. Not to mention the myriad of regular trips to and fro across Australia.

Winched to success

● John Muir, managing director of Muir Engineering Pty Ltd, of Kingston . . . 'a company famous for its winches.

QUALITY-BASED Tasmanian manufacturer, Muir Engineering Pty Ltd, is Australia's Small Business of the Year.

The Hobart company makes high-performance winches which are in international demand from shipping companies and serious yachtsmen.

It gained automatic entry into the national awards last year following its victory in the Tasmanian section of the Small Business of the Year Award.

The awards — the only national small business awards — are designed to recognise the outstanding achievements of Australia's small Businesses.

They are presented in three categories: manufacturing, non-manufacturing, and smaller business. The Australian Small Business of the Year, is selected from one of those categories.

Muir Engineering won the overall award for the 1989 Small Business of the Year, as well as the award for manufacturing.

The Tasmanian company started off as a partnership in 1968 specialising in a range of diesel services.

Today, 21 years later, the company has become a major exporter, with markets in the United Kingdom, Sweden, Norway, France, Austria, Germany and New Zealand.

Muir Engineering has diversified and now designs, manufactures and markets marine winches and windlasses for commercial and pleasure craft.

Muir's success is based on the quality of the products, as well as quality organisation that enables the winches to be cost competitive on world markets.

The managing director, Mr John Muir, attributes a lot of his success to "blood sweat and tears", as well as a policy of listening to clients in order to work out their requirements.

Muir Engineering receives ongoing support from the Tasmanian Development Authority and the Tasmanian Productivity Council — in production methods, plant and equipment layout, staff training and financial planning.

Mr Muir sees a bright future for his company. "There is increased interest in pleasure craft here and overseas," he said.

"I am confident my company can match any competitor anywhere in the world," he said.

THE MERCURY Friday, December 15, 1989 — 5

Business winner exposes our dire Strait

The managing director of the award-winning Muir Engineering, Mr John Muir, with the Australian Small Business of the year trophy presented by the Treasurer, Mr Paul Keating.

TASMANIAN businessmen who wanted to succeed still had to overcome the hurdle imposed by Bass Strait, award winning businessman Mr John Muir said yesterday.

Hobart-based Muir Engineering was named the Australian Small Business of the Year yesterday at a ceremony in Sydney.

Managing director Mr Muir, 45, said the company started 21 years ago as a "one-man show" but had grown to employ 50 people.

He said the barrier imposed by Bass Strait was a definite disadvantage but he had no plans to leave Tasmania.

Instead, Mr Muir said the business had set up offices in Sydney and Brisbane and planned to open an office in the US next year.

Muir Engineering makes and exports marine equipment for pleasure craft including winches and windlasses.

The world's third largest exporter of marine equipment, Muir Engineering exports to Britain, Sweden, Norway, France, Austria, Germany and New Zealand.

"In Tasmania you have a stable labour force which can not easily move all over the place," Mr Muir said.

"Tasmania also has a lower rate of pay to the mainland but the market is not as competitive as it is on the mainland in some areas of manufacture."

Mr Muir said Tasmania did not lack the expertise but there was little competition for business.

As an example, he said there was only one chrome-plater in Hobart compared with 16 in Auckland — which is the major competitor for marine equipment.

"Luckily, we have been able to work with that chrome-plater but if not then we probably would have been forced to open up our own plant," Mr Muir said.

He said there needed to be more incentive for small business to export its products and pointed to the Export Development Initiative grants as a positive step.

But, Mr Muir said the high interest rates were having a bad effect on small business.

He also criticised payroll taxes and penalty rates as disincentives to small business.

"Payroll tax is a disincentive to employing more staff, while penalty rates are a disincentive to working longer hours," Mr Muir said.

Other award winners were ABW Tools of Salisbury, Queensland, which won the non-manufacturing category and WA-based survey equipment supplier, Haefeli-Lysnar Survey Equipment which won the smaller business category.

SUCCESS AFTER SO MANY YEARS' HARD WORK

Muir Engineering won 1989 Australian and Tasmanian Small Business of the Year. John was presented the national award by then-Treasurer Paul Keating.

Top: Left to right, John Muir, Muir Engineering; Paul Keating; Mark Wilson, ABW Tools; Richard Lysnar, Haefeli-Lysnar Survey Equipment.

Articles: The Mercury

OPPOSITE: TASMANIAN WINNER

Top: John proudly collecting the Tasmanian division win for the Australian Small Business Awards, 1989.

Bottom: John being presented with the Tasmanian award by then state Premier Michael Field.

During the period 1987 to 1989 when John was fully recovered and firing on all cylinders, sales and output of the business almost doubled.

In 1989, another award from the Australian Marketing Institute was received, Muir Engineering earning a silver award for achievements in domestic and export marketing. Later that same year, came the biggest award of them all, first recognition as Tasmanian Small Business Manufacturer of the Year. Then at the national awards, held in Sydney in December, Muir won both the Manufacturers' National Award and Australia's most outstanding Small Business of the Year.

In an article written at the time of the award for the Telecom Yellow Pages/Advance Australia Foundation, John was extensively quoted as saying: "There really is no substitute for hard work. The business has grown from modest beginnings since the first employees, to a staff of 50 people. We attribute much of our success to a long-standing commitment to product research, development and innovative design. Significant improvements in alloy-casting technology and electronic Master Controls have been incorporated in all popular models."

> 66 *There really is no substitute for hard work. The business has grown from modest beginnings since the first employees, to a staff of 50 people. We attribute much of our success to a long-standing commitment to product research, development and innovative design. Significant improvements in alloy-casting technology and electronic Master Controls have been incorporated in all popular models.* 99

– JOHN MUIR, 1989

The way John did business when he was on a sales trip had obviously rubbed off on some of his sales staff and sales representatives.

Murray Morten has never forgotten his first association with the name Muir and the winches they produced. The occasion was another boat show near Sailor's Corner, which was the major marine chandlery in Auckland's Westhaven. It was 1985.

Murray Morten: "Sailor's Corner had been selling New Zealand made Maxwell Winches with considerable success for a number of years, however the relationship was becoming strained. This was a worry, as winches were a very important and strategic product line for any chandlery worth its salt. A winch sale was usually accompanied with chain, anchor and, if the salesperson was any good, quite a number of other products at the same time.

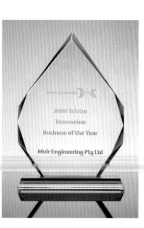

AWARDS AND HONOURS

Muir has earned a massive range of awards and honour spanning four decades under John's ownership and direction.

Some of John's best memories are of winning the Australian Small Business Awards in 1989, the Australian Export Heroes award in 2011, and the Australian Marine Export Hall of Fame award in 2013.

"In early August of 1985, a marine trade show [IMTEC] was staged in downtown Auckland. Sailor's Corner was among the exhibitors and had a couple of Maxwell winches on display. John Muir had despatched his International Sales Manager – a big fella by the name of Richard Box, whose main goal was to find a New Zealand distributor for Muir Winches.

"As it transpired, the timing couldn't have been better. Richard stationed himself on the Maxwell stand in order to glean for himself a bit of a New Zealand customer profile and came away knowing that on the whole, most Kiwis had a pretty good idea of what to expect from a winch. In fact Richard carved his name into immortality by selling one of the bigger Muir winches to a fellow called Brian Bambury, when he was hanging around the Maxwell stand.

"Brian promptly walked down to the Sailor's Corner's stand to announce his purchase. Shortly after, Richard Box introduced himself to Rex and Evan Innes-Jones [Sailor's Corner owners]. I was also there at the time and we proceeded to evaluate the truckload of models Richard had brought across the Tasman and which, he assured us, he had no intention of taking back. We agreed on pricing and Richard was able to return empty handed as planned.

"Some months later across the Tasman for a visit [for another boat show] and after a number of big lunches followed by even bigger dinners, a long and fruitful relationship began between myself, John Muir, Sailor's Corner and later, Lusty & Blundell, a relationship that is still going strong today."

A keen observer of human nature, particularly when selling winches and attending boat shows, John had noticed that the ladies who sailed in many cases knew as much about yachts as their male counterparts.

John Muir: "Ladies would often walk up and forthrightly ask questions about anchors and chain, weights and sizes, and or course anchor winches. In some cases, this would become a sale for me, as I spent time explaining the advantage of having an anchor winch up forward.

"I would ask a lady who steered their boat and who looked after the anchor, what did they do in situations where there is no anchor winch? They'd say they struggled like hell to pull the anchor and chain up, while the other party (husband or partner) would be yelling and screaming at them to get it up quickly. It can be and almost always is a highly stressful job in rough or windy conditions.

"My suggestion to these ladies, who obviously did not like being yelled at, was to, 'Tell the other party you're not going to pull the anchor and chain anymore, you're going to steer.' Do this several times, and you'll very likely have agreement on getting an anchor winch installed. If you do, ensure it's a Muir."

ABOVE AND CENTRE: MURRAY MORTEN

Muir's long time New Zealand ally, Lighthouse Marine. Top: At Sydney Boat Show 2005 with Duncan Norton. Above: Working hard onboard a 60ft America's Cup motor cruiser in 2002.

BELOW: NORTHPORT TUG BOATS

On the slip in New Zealand, late 1990s. Muir supplied three ship sets of SGC twin gypsy anchor winches.

Muir's New Zealand distributors – Lusty & Blundell, Sailor's Corner and Lighthouse Marine – worked tirelessly to gain and maintain new business. They went out of their way to beat our competitors on their home ground.

John Muir: "Murray was an experienced and knowledgeable design engineer, and certainly had his mind around the anchor winch and marine business. Without doubt, he was one of the very best people I've ever worked with in regard to selling and persisting to win business. I also consider him a very good long-time friend."

Murray Morten also had direct input into the design and operation of Muir winches. The waters around New Zealand are deep, the seas are rough and it's often very windy. Murray generally recommended a winch with additional capacity, or a larger size winch, motor and anchor rode to prospective customers. (The anchor rode is the chain or cable that connects the anchor to the boat.) Murray Morten is also known for his wicked sense of humour.

"Anyone familiar with offshore sailing would also be familiar with an essential piece of kit called a 'grab-bag' – when everything turns to custard and you are stepping up from the sinking yacht into the raft, you have managed to snatch the 'grab-bag' on the way which contains everything you need for your short term survival.

"I've always believed John's wife Wendy had one of these ready for John's business trips because part of the reason he has been so successful is his readiness to jump onto an aircraft at the drop of a hat should there ever be any risk of losing a sale. In one period of the early 2000s, out of six superyacht yards in New Zealand, Muir Winches were spec'd on five of them and John was present at the signing of every one of the orders."

Over the next few years, Muir Winches were supplied to the bulk of the New Zealand custom boat builders and many of the smaller trailer boat production builders. There was [and still is] a winch model to suit any boat between 10m and 140m. On top of that, Muir has an extensive range of commercial winches for tugs, trawlers, defence vessels and ferries. One of the many different commercial sales was a set of big SGC commercial winches for four tugs being built in New Zealand in 1999; this was a coup at the time as most of the commercial yards preferred to build their own winches.

John Muir, once again quoted in the Telstra business award article: "Rigorous testing programs occur for new winch models that incorporate design changes and for the many custom winches where clients require extra features whilst fully complying with international standards. Standards such as those set up by Lloyds (UK), Det Norske Veritas (Norway) and the American Bureau of Shipping. Muir's quality assurance system was put in place in 1985."

> 66 *Anyone familiar with offshore sailing would also be familiar with an essential piece of kit called a 'grab-bag'…I've always believed John's wife Wendy had one of these ready for John's business trips because part of the reason he has been so successful is his readiness to jump onto an aircraft at the drop of a hat should there ever be any risk of losing a sale. In one period of the early 2000s, out of six Superyacht yards in New Zealand, Muir Winches were spec'd on five of them and John was present at the signing of every one of the orders.* 99

– MURRAY MORTEN, LIGHTHOUSE MARINE

One time when John was in Norway, he was talking to the Norwegian Managing Director of Det Norske Veritas. He gave John some valued advice on the cost of quality control and how to keep it as low as possible without affecting the quality of production:

"John, if you and your quality officer run a tight ship and keep track of everything that costs Muir and your customers $100 or more an incident, you will be staggered at how much this will add up to."

John Muir: "At that time, before we set up our quality control process, I used to identify everything that was a quality cost in my note book. When I added it up it was substantial and a bit scary. Within a year we had reduced our quality control cost by almost half. Quality control systems don't work well if they are managed or interfered with by production people. And the quality control person needs to report directly to the Managing Director.

Whilst in Europe in 1986 John and Wendy returned to Milan to visit CIMA, at the invitation of Luigi Pomati.

Founded in 1915 by Giovanni Pomati, CIMA built ignition magnets for truck starter motors. In the 1930s they opened a factory in Via Fabio Filzi producing injection pumps for diesel engines. With the outbreak of the Second World War and the beginning of allied air strikes on Milan, both plants were bombed and burnt to the ground.

Despite many tough times and dark years after the end of World War II, the company was resurrected and began producing electric DC motors. In 1985 Luigi Pomati joined the company and introduced new technology and production lines.

Crisis struck again in recent years when the Italian economy was in meltdown and pushed the Pomati family to renew efforts to save the company. CIMA now designs, manufactures, tests and exports a wide range of high quality motors for industrial and marine clients.

> 66 *At that time, before we set up our quality control process, I used to identify everything that was a quality cost in my note book. When I added it up it was substantial and a bit scary. Within a year we had reduced our quality control cost by almost half.* 99

"International and domestic sales and marketing has always been very important at Muir. We have maintained a policy of working with clients worldwide to precisely identify their winch and windlass requirements, many of whom found from their own experience that there really is no substitute for a quality product that is built to fully comply with acceptable performance standards. There is a definite pre-sales and post-sales policy in place that our regular clients appreciate."

John had already met Luigi Pomati, one of the owners of Compagnia Italiana Magneti Accessori (CIMA), early in 1985 and was to see him again when travelling through Europe, on the first international sales and boat show trip since he was ill. It was Wendy who did all the travel arrangements, packed clothes and medical supplies, for John who was now a full blown diabetic and needed insulin shots twice a day.

The company and the Pomati family are obviously long term survivors who don't give up easily. Sound familiar?

Luigi Pomati: "I had only recently received my driver's license. It was 1985 and I was driving a small Panda motor car, really designed for two people, we had three squeezed in. I remember we had some time to spare that day so we decided to drive to Portofino in Liguria."

Liguria is widely known as the Italian Riviera. It is a crescent-shaped region in northwest Italy. It includes five famous fishing villages, set beside the sparkling blue green waters of the Mediterranean and backed by dramatic cliffs. It is without doubt one of the most beautiful coastlines in Italy.

Luigi Pomati: "It was raining heavily, plus strong winds made it difficult to drive. I was driving fast and John insisted I slow down as he and Wendy were hanging on to the back of the front seats. John was calling me Fangio!"

Wendy Muir has a somewhat different memory of the trip: "When Luigi collected us, he restarted the tiny car, took off his hat and his seat belt and *vroom!*, off we went at an alarming speed. Luigi didn't seem at all fazed by the driving conditions, even though we found out later he had only just managed to get his driving licence." The car in question was a Fiat Panda. In Australia they were sold as Fiat Niki, a tiny, two door, 600cc motor vehicle, cute as a button and barely big enough for two small Italian people.

Luigi Pomati: "The rough journey ended with a beautiful dinner of pasta and pesto in a restaurant by the sea. The weather had much improved on the way back and we made it safely back to their Milan hotel.

"I have a dear friend in John. I have labelled him as, 'The man who always writes his notes in a pocket book, and crosses the tasks off as they are attended to.' I like this in a man like John. As I drive the car John continues to work on various projects in his notebook, on his phone or email!"

Luigi recalls that trips and meetings with John were always interesting. It didn't matter if they were travelling to Milan, Monaco, Genoa, Amsterdam, London, Sydney or even when Luigi flew to Hobart to visit the Muir Factory.

"The first time I visited the Muir works I observed how well laid out and clean it was. John said, 'Luigi, there is no reason why an engineering works like this one should be any different to a hospital!'"

Visiting the factory is also about seeing how CIMA motors are fitted to Muir winches, to look at the overall operation and check on technology adoption. Everywhere Luigi looked he saw things that pleased him. The latest computerised lathes, testing equipment, polished stainless steel and bronze finishing machines.

"In particular I wanted to see the way our motors were coupled to the winch drives, and on occasions it allowed me chat to production and assembly staff and give suggestions about improvements, how to reduce assembly costs when fitting our motors.

"I like that Muir always has new products under development, with their engineering and design people. John has said to me on occasions, 'There are four things to remember about any business for retaining the valued customer, and not necessarily in this sequence: Price, Quality, Service, Relationships.'"

John Muir: "Over many years we have become really good friends with Luigi and his family. Luigi is always really accommodating and he is a great communicator and keeps in touch with key personnel at Muir. On occasions we get a surprise package with some of our CIMA shipments that arrive in Hobart. He carefully packs in with the motors a couple of magnum bottles of the very best of Italian Camargi from Agricola Fabbriche Palma from Lucignsno – Toscana.

"CIMA and Muir have a lot in common, like our own product sales and respective and extensive knowledge of all our own products.

ABOVE: LUIGI POMATI, CIMA ITALY

A long-time friend and business associate of John's, Luigi has visited Hobart and spent time on the water with John (here in 2006).

BELOW: STELIOS SAKIOTIS, SAKIOTIS GROUP GREECE

John and Stelios aboard Stelios's 28m motor cruiser, in 2015. Sakiotis Marine was one of the largest Greek marine distributors and retailers, and John met Stelios at one of the European Boat Shows in the late 1980s. Muir supplied an initial large order of winches to Sakiotis Marine and they maintained a working relationship after that. Stelios liked to let his hair down and along with being a successful businessman was also a member of a Greek rock band along with famous Greek performer Demis Roussos.

"Luigi can always be contacted when we need him and in the past we have always looked forward to meeting up for a chat, somewhere in Europe or when he comes to Tasmania on his way to or from Auckland. We always used to enjoy having something nice to eat along with a cold beer and a red wine. These days, I have to be careful with what I eat and drink, but my health has improved so much that I can manage a low-carb beer or a glass of Chardonnay."

Luigi Pomati: "John has been all over Europe and Scandinavia on many occasions, spanning 35 years. He has traversed the entire Italian coastline, where a variety of different motor and sailing yachts of all shapes and sizes are built, serviced or berthed. I like that he remains 'hands on', always willing to lend a hand to a customer or someone in trouble.

"Just recently we both visited Bonfiglioli in Bologna for a tour of their very interesting gear box operations. I was pleased to hear Muir has been using Bonfiglioli products non-stop for 47 years!"

John Muir's relationship with Bonfiglioli, and the company's Australian boss Malcolm Lewis, also goes back a long way. Each holds the other in high regard. John says: "I have known Malcolm for a long time, and he drives a well-oiled machine in Bonfiglioli."

Malcolm says: "John is a great believer in established quality, and a champion of innovation."

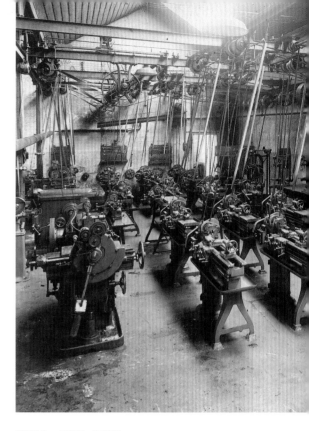

CIMA, EST. 1915

A 1930 photo (left) and a current photo of the CIMA workshop show the remarkable changes in technology during the company's 101 year history.

> ❝ *The first time I visited the Muir works I observed how well laid out and clean it was. John said, 'Luigi, there is no reason why an engineering works like this one should be any different to a hospital!'* ❞

– LUIGI POMATI

Malcolm Lewis points to a number of occasions when John has incorporated design changes suggested by engineers from Bonfiglioli. Malcolm says durability of Muir technology has been given a further lift by the introduction of Planetary Trasmital drives as suggested by Bonfiglioli.

"Particularly in the larger drives, the advantage of planetary over worm drives can include much better efficiency (especially for the higher ratios used by Muir, as worm efficiency worsens the higher the ratio) and, of course, greater torque density than large worm gearboxes in these applications.

"An example is where we suggested some years ago the use of Trasmital planetaries engineered to John's specific requirements. They deliver outstanding torque densities and reliability, all within

MUIR HORIZONTAL CHEETAH

Powered by a CIMA 1200 watt DC motor. CIMA motors are proven to be the best in the world, according to John Muir.

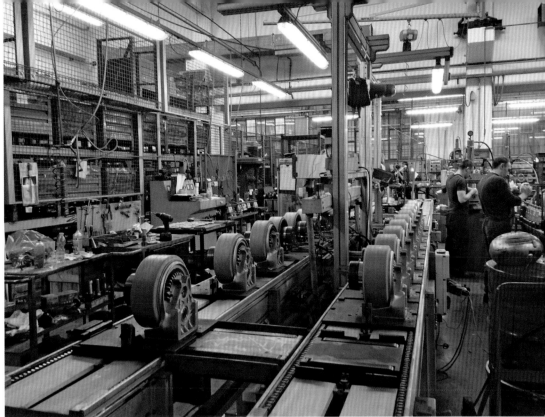

the compact spaces so precious in marine environments. We have also used energy-efficient variable frequency drives where these provide a performance edge and additional features.

"Such engineering and correct application of the product has worked to ensure optimum reliability and performance of the Bonfiglioli ranges used by Muir which have served them well across a diverse range of gearboxes.

"In order to support Muir with a swift service, we keep large quantities of stock locally in our Melbourne branch to ensure that Muir are able to supply their winches on time. The larger planetary gearboxes are also built to order in our Melbourne branch. All this is backed up by the extensive inventory held in our head office following investment of more than $A20 million in stock and facilities."

In case you are left wondering just what Malcolm is talking about, let me clear up any confusion amongst those of you who don't have a degree in marine engineering, as I don't.

The boat building and yachting world is large. It is a truly global industry and yet there seems to be this close knit, quite small community of people, like John Muir, who all seem to know one another. If they don't specifically know everyone, they have certainly either met them or heard of them and know how to get in touch when required. It is an amazing network of key people. John Muir is a critical part of that complex web, because of who he is and what he has designed, built and sold.

Yacht owners and skippers all attest to the quality of the Muir product, because John had the foresight to take advice from his father.

> *"Make sure when you build a winch that the winch never fails, that when it gets really rugged, it's best that something else fails, not the winch."*

It was in his early years in his business when Jock gave him that advice and John took those words of wisdom and experience on board and followed them to the letter.

David McQueen is a classic example, another member of the complex marine industry contact web.

David McQueen: "I met John 27 years ago. We got on extremely well and I realised that his product, which was already on Oceanfast boats, was the best that I'd ever seen. I have to say that to this day, I've never built a boat without Muir winches on it. John has always said I'm the most prolific and effective unofficial salesman of Muir winches that he has in the world."

David McQueen has been in the superyacht industry since he was 18. He's now in his mid-50s. David spent the first eight years of his career working for a famous wooden boat building company on the Isle of Wight in England, called W.A. Souter and Sons. He finished his

apprenticeship and soon moved into management, because as he said, "I was better at telling people what to do than doing it myself."

David then travelled through India and Asia to arrive in Perth, Western Australia in 1986, just in time for the defence of the America's Cup. There was a boat building company in Perth called Austal Ships who he'd never heard of because there weren't many luxury boat builders around the world at that time building superyachts. A big superyacht in those days was around 50m, possibly a 60m motor yacht.

David McQueen: "I decided to stay in Perth, and I saw one of the Oceanfast boats called *Part VI*, which John had supplied winch equipment for. This boat had been chartered by someone to watch the America's Cup. I decided to stay a bit longer in Australia, but I only had a 12 month Visa. I contacted Oceanfast to see if I could get some temporary work, because obviously you run out of money all the time when you are living as a backpacker. Within a couple of weeks of talking to them, they offered me a job as an estimator as they didn't have one at the time.

"I'd been involved in some big boat builds – previously in England the biggest build I'd been involved in was 32m. Oceanfast had never heard of anyone who was involved in the superyacht industry, with Perth being the most isolated city in the world (maybe Hobart people would dispute that), but what they were doing as a company was world record breaking. They were using designs from Jon Bannenberg, who unfortunately had died a few years before. Jon Bannenberg was an Australian who lived in London most of his life, he was a prolific boat designer, and he was 20 years ahead of anyone else. He designed a gas fire (he won a design award for that), he was a pianist, and he designed beautiful boats which were way ahead of their time. He designed a famous boat for Donald Trump."

The website 'Yacht Forums' traced the boat's history: "It was known as Trump's floating home, the *Trump Princess*. Built in 1980 by Benetti Shipyards in Viareggio, Italy, at a cost of $100 million (equivalent to over $250 million in today's dollars), this 85m superyacht was originally built for Saudi billionaire Adnan Khashoggi and named *Nabila*, after his daughter. Designed by the legendary Jon Bannenberg, *Nabila* was featured in the James Bond movie 'Never Say Never Again.'"

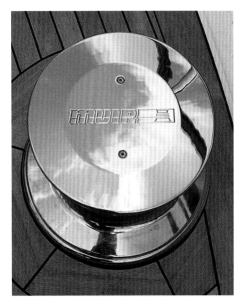

Engineer anchors an elite market

WORLD BEATER: Managing director John Muir with some of Muir Engineering stainless steel windlass devices yesterday. Picture: EDDIE SAFARIK

By JOHN BRIGGS

HOW many Tasmanians know Greg Norman's wildly expensive yacht Aussie Rules contains parts made at Muir Engineering in Kingston?

The golfing multi-millionaire is but one happy customer of the company that is fast becoming a world leader in manufacturing anchoring systems for export markets.

Executive managing director John Muir proudly displayed the latest products bound for the US as part of a million-dollar package.

The order left yesterday for Seattle-based Delta Marine, which is building the largest

HAPPY CUSTOMER: Greg Norman's luxury yacht Aussie Rules is fitted with Tasmanian-made parts.

private yacht in the US for more than 70 years.

"The 73 metres luxury ves-sel will be fitted with our complete stainless steel an-choring system, comprising windlasses and docking cap-stans, electrical controls, sys-tem accessories and other parts," Mr Muir said.

"We also have nearly ready for despatch a similar system for a 72-metre super yacht under construction in France, also in completely polished stainless steel."

Mr Muir said success had not come easily and most of the clients for these big pro-jects were based in the north-ern hemisphere.

"We're in a highly competi-tive market and have people on the ground in England and Belgium to market our prod-ucts," he said.

Muir Engineering was in competition with a large Dutch firm to win the US contract.

Mr Muir paid tribute to his large workforce of 63 people at Kingston, along with local and interstate suppliers.

Muir's anchoring winches and systems will be on dis-play later this month at the prestigious Monaco Super Yacht Show and Internation-al Fort Lauderdale Show.

The size of the 30-year-old company has doubled in the past five years and exports have risen 30 per cent in the past year.

There is to be further ex-pansion, including factory ex-tensions at Kingston.

MY *AUSSIE RULES*

69m vessel built by Oceanfast (in David McQueen's time). Fitted were Muir's first VRC18000 anchor winch and mooring capstans, all in polished stainless steel.
Article: The Mercury

David McQueen: "I stayed at Oceanfast, and after three months decided I really liked Perth, and they didn't want me to leave. My Visa only allowed me to work for six of the 12 months, and only a maximum of three months with any particular company. They'd had a great summer, so they sponsored me to get residency, and eventually I got my citizenship years later. I stayed at Oceanfast for 15 years and became the Managing Director running the place with a staff of 350.

"We built about 20 big boats over those 15 years. Eventually I met John Muir through his sales pitches and visits to the yard. Since then I've run other companies in Australia, and I'm consulting to major clients from Australia and around the world. I'm building boats all around the world because unfortunately the industry in Australia, aside from parts, is not cost effective because we haven't got cheap labour.

"Annual worldwide production of these vessels has tripled over the past decade and competition for facilities to accommodate them has intensified, resulting in opportunities for new cruising destinations. The State Government recently called for expressions of interest to establish a super-yacht service and repair facility at the Australian Marine Complex (AMC). The aim is to provide the super-yacht industry and commercial shipbuilders with a common use area to facilitate maintenance and repair, refits, launch and retrieval and sea trials.

"WA is fast becoming a popular destination for visiting super-yachts and the AMC is perfectly placed to incorporate a super-yacht cluster to refit and maintain these exclusive vessels. The strength of the burgeoning super-yacht industry in Australia can be seen with the establishment of Super Yacht Base Australia (SYBA) in 1999."

> **❝ I'm always looking around at boat builders with clients of mine, and I tell them there are a few simple things to judge a boat builder by, and that's quality of plumbing and piping, ventilation and wiring, and one major thing – if they don't have Muir winches on the bow of the boat, then it's not a proper boat. ❞**

DAVID MCQUEEN, MOTOR YACHT BUILD

"We didn't have a foothold in the industry, and we didn't have a foothold in the market – the market being America and Europe – so unless you were very cheap, clients wouldn't look to Australia, and we just can't be that cheap. To make matters worse the global recession in the early 1990s killed our industry. There are a couple of boat builders left and they're doing ok, but they're owned by overseas people."

Edition 4 of the Australian Superyacht News (published in 2007) championed the burgeoning boat building business in Western Australia like this:

"The superyacht sector is one of the fastest growing in the marine industry and Western Australia is leading the way with an internationally recognised industry and a proposed new super-yacht cluster.

WA is home to one of the most innovative and experienced superyacht manufacturing industries in the southern hemisphere, boasting several internationally acclaimed builders who are constructing quality vessels for rich and famous clients all over the world.

Obviously marine industry exuberance was alive and well in 2007. These days boat building in Western Australia has shrunk from the glory days when there was much talk and enthusiasm over superyachts and superyacht clusters, to the reality of fibreglass and aluminium runabouts.

David McQueen: "I'm always looking around at boat builders with clients of mine, and I tell them there are a few simple things to judge a boat builder by, and that's quality of plumbing and piping, ventilation and wiring, and one major thing – if they don't have Muir winches on the bow of the boat, then it's not a proper boat. So this boat I'm overseeing the build of right now [in Turkey in 2015] we've written the specification for, there's Muir winches on it, anchoring system, and there's Muir docking winches on it, and I wouldn't have anything else. I know without even considering it, that it's going to work every single time, forever.

"Six weeks ago I signed up to build another 38m sports fisher in Auckland, and in the negotiations for that we've got a New Zealand yard building it, for a New Zealand client, using a New Zealand designer. I got recommended as an Australian – or some people still call me a Pom – but one of the major debating points of finalising the contract and specifications was that I said I wouldn't build the boat unless we had Muir anchor winches and docking winches on it. They wanted to put a competitor's products on the boat, because you can see their factory from the boatyard, their argument being that it was so close by.

"I said I don't care if the winches come from the across the world or the next door office, we're not having anything but Muir. The client was apprehensive, but they did a bit of research and made some phone calls and agreed the consensus was Muir is the best. So now it's written into the specification."

MY *RUYA*

41m luxury yacht fitted with two VRC8000s and two chain stopper-roller anchoring systems, forward, and two VC8000 mooring capstans., aft. Photos: Gökhan Çelik, Alia Yachts

> **66** *I said I don't care if the winches come from the across the world or the next door office, we're not having anything but Muir. The client was apprehensive, but they did a bit of research and made some phone calls and agreed the consensus was Muir is the best. So now it's written into the specification.* **99**

– DAVID MCQUEEN, MOTOR YACHT BUILD

This final quote from David McQueen is worth repeating, particularly at this stage of the Muir story.

"We continue on wanting to use the right product, because we know even though it's not the cheapest, it's cost effective anyway. It's come out of this little place called Tasmania, which half the world don't even know exists, out of a place called Kingston which people definitely don't know of, and it's sold by these funny Tasmanians who are dogmatic, passionate and brilliant at what they do. They're the ultimate product."

So you can imagine now why when David rings John in late 2004 and says: "I've got a problem and I need you to help fix it, can you fly to Sydney and meet me there?" John says: "Yes mate, I'll be there tomorrow."

A very well-known Australian had commissioned the construction of a superyacht *Ilona* from a well known Dutch shipyard, *Ilona* was launched in early 2004. David's company had completed a major refit on the boat some years later. About 12 years ago David got a call from the owner who asked if his company could do some work on it while the boat was in Sydney. He asked if David could come down to Garden Island to take a look at a problem they were experiencing with the anchor windlasses and mooring capstans.

David McQueen: "I think this was mid-December, and he wanted to use the boat on Good Friday, the following Easter. There was a problem with the anchoring equipment and it needed to be changed. I drove down from where I was on the central coast of NSW to speak with the captain. He said they'd been having problems with the German made anchoring system. Twice they had to drop a chain because they couldn't get the anchor up. (That means losing the entire chain and anchor each time.)

"I wasn't really sure until that point how they wanted to resolve the problem, but the captain said what they really wanted, and he knew it was going to be basically impossible with timing, was to swap out the gear for some new systems. They knew I had a great relationship with John Muir and asked if I could call John to come up and have a look because they specifically wanted Muir equipment."

It is now late December and the owner wanted the job completed before Easter. These are very big winches, not something Muir have just sitting on a shelf waiting for someone to say 'I'll buy that one please.'

John's response was "I'll meet you at the boat tomorrow, I will be with Alex. We will be coming down from the Gold Coast as we are about to go to the Export Awards dinner tonight."

David McQueen: "So John and Alex came down to Sydney and I met them at the boat with the captain. John looked at the gear and he looked under the deck and he looked at this and that, the whole thing, and said, 'Give me a couple of days.'

"He and Paul Hollingsworth had the quote to replace the gear to us within a couple of days. I had a team of guys who could bolt it on, we set the date when it would be bolted on, we set a date when Lloyds classification society would test the equipment in John's workshop in Tasmania, and then re-test it when it was bolted on the boat.

"The Muir team worked through Christmas and New Year that year, to make the equipment to the kind of world class standard that they normally do, and delivered it to Sydney. My team of guys were there, and they were very good as well, they'd unbolted and removed the other gear ready for the Muir stuff to arrive."

MY ILONA

The stunning 74m superyacht, built by Dutch shipyard Amels, was launched in 2004.
Photos: Amels Holland

This is the stuff of legend, when superyacht owners and boat skippers meet their mates and contacts, their complex web of people and the Muir name is passed into folklore. Not only did the gear arrive on time, it fitted exactly in place and then came the big moment. It had to be tested by Lloyds. John and his team had worked like navvies, manufacturing the special designed anchor winches and capstans that would align with the existing holes in the deck that had been drilled for the old winches. The faulty gear was packed into Muir boxes and shipped back to the manufacturer. One wonders what the conversations were like back there when the boxes were opened and the story told.

David McQueen: "The new winches were bolted on successfully. Deadlines were tight. A few days later [two days prior to Good Friday] we headed out to sea, out through the heads at Sydney, we were 30km offshore ready for a sea trial.

"We were all on the bridge of the boat, and the guys from Lloyds gave us directions to go out to the shelf, to deep water. So we powered straight out and stopped in water too deep for the anchor to hit the sea bottom.

"Ilona had 1000ft of anchor chain on each windlass. The instructions from Lloyds were to drop one anchor and chain, so it's just dead weight. The whole weight

of the chain and anchor is just hanging in 400-500m of water. It's the hardest possible test for this gear, and as they were letting the chain out I turned to John and asked, 'Is this going to work?'

"I was feeling very anxious, I'd seen this test done other times, but this was big gear. He replied with absolute confidence, 'It'll be fine David.' And that was that.

"The chain was right out and the skipper hit the button for slow anchor recovery speed, and up she comes, 9m per minute. Passed the first test. The surveyor said, 'It's ok.'

"John was a bit impatient to try the second one so we pressed the button for the second gear, and the chain was coming up at 18m per minute as though it was just nothing. It was absolutely perfect.

"So that was all good, signed off, I went to tell the owner we'd changed it all over successfully in 12 weeks. That's the best story, but the stories are still going on forever and ever, and until I retire I'll still be unofficially selling Muir winches because it's the best product in the world. I recommend it because it's my reputation riding on everything in a build.

"You have to be able to put your hand on your heart – based on reputation, trust, loyalty, communication, history – when you recommend a product. I have

MY ILONA

*Left: John onboard **Ilona** in Sydney after the new Muir VRC22000 equipment was fitted. Middle: Photo courtesy of Amels Holland. Right: Craig McNaughton onboard Ilona during commissioning of the new Muir gear.*

history with Muir now, I don't check any of their specs or equipment, or their quotes, I just trust them 100%. I know the gear will turn up and is going to work, and if there is ever a problem with it – which I've never experienced – there'll be no trouble fixing it. Even when someone doesn't want to specify Muir winches to begin with, they always come onboard once they do their research and ask around. It's the number one marine product in Australia, and one of the best in the world."

John Muir: "It's only natural to feel apprehensive when testing winching products, especially in deep water. With the anchor on 1000ft of 30mm of stud link chain hanging vertically in the water you have to be able to raise it. It is normal practice for Muir to design a winch drive capable of lifting the anchor and all the chain, 50% at low speed and 50% at high speed. This is the ultimate test for serious motor yachts or commercial vessels.

"In earlier discussions with David and the owner, the owner insisted on us overbuilding the gears and the AC electric motor in order to guarantee there would not be any failure of the drive gear assembly, as was the case with the competitor's original equipment. Rather than have an 11kW motor, we fitted a 15kW motor, and a two-size-up extra heavy duty planetary drive.

"For those with an interest in engineering specifics, the equipment supplied included two VRC22000 vertical anchor windlasses for 30mm U3 stud cable, three VC20000 vertical mooring capstans, and a VRC20000 combination above deck capstan with a below deck dog clutch drive stern anchor windlass. All had variable speed 'soft drives.' Speeds vary between zero to full speed at the touch of a hand-held control. These soft frequency drives are similar to those used in an elevator. There is no jerk whatsoever when engaging the soft variable speed drive, unlike single and two speed 'direct drives' that start with a jerk.

"In the case of *Ilona*, all original drives were removed, control cabinets were removed, and new all new control cabinets were installed and commissioned.

"This was a really big project to be completed and commissioned in what would normally require twice as much time. We were already under the pump, crews working six days a week, when this order came through. The Muir design office staff, machine and fabricators crews upped the effort and the majority of our people worked around the clock through Christmas and New Year until the large order was shipped out."

> *It's only natural to feel apprehensive when testing winching products, especially in deep water. With the anchor on 1000ft of 30mm of stud link chain hanging vertically in the water you have to be able to raise it. It is normal practice for Muir to design a winch drive capable of lifting the anchor and all the chain, 50% at low speed and 50% at high speed. This is the ultimate test for serious motor yachts or commercial vessels.*

- JOHN MUIR

When the consignment left it was 10m³ in size. It was road freighted to Devonport on Tasmania's north coast, shipped across Bass Strait then road freighted to Sydney. All that in 36 hours to meet the crucial Good Friday deadline.

One of John's Sydney based employees, Craig McNaughton, who had started work as an over qualified junior in 1989, working with Val Howells, remembers this event well.

Craig McNaughton: "One of the things that always stayed in my mind was back in late 2004, the Sydney owner had a megayacht being built in Holland, a big 74m motor yacht called *Ilona*, and we quoted to replace the anchor windlasses and mooring capstans. John had been to Holland and met with the management of the shipyard."

John was in Sydney and tracked down the captain's name and arranged to meet him in Hobart to discuss the quote.

John Muir: "When I spoke to the Captain he indicated he'd be in Tasmania in a few days time. We met on a Sunday and showed him some large anchoring and mooring equipment recently completed for Greg Norman's 69m motor yacht *Aussie Rules*, built by Oceanfast."

Craig McNaughton: "The captain was shown around the works and the yacht club, then when he was leaving he said he would be ordering Muir equipment.

"We quoted a competitive price and short delivery, but somehow we didn't get the job. Within three months after the boat was launched, it was back in Sydney with an issue with the windlass drive shafts that they had to remove. At that stage fellow Australian, Dave McQueen, was doing some consulting for the bigger superyacht people, and they'd had issues with the anchor winches failing, so Dave told them to contact Muir Winches. He said they were made in Australia, and the owners response was, 'Well why didn't I have these on my boat to start with?'

SEA TRIALS ON *ILONA*

*Below: Craig McNaughton with the **Ilona** crew, heading out for deeper water to test the new Muir VRC22000 anchor winches.*

*Opposite: **Ilona** crew in Sydney Harbour, preparing to take the yacht out for its Lloyds classification sea trial of the new winches at a depth of 400m off the coast of Sydney.*

"I remember John got on board the huge boat and started crawling all over it. He measured up the winches that were fitted on the boat. They were held down with 32mm stainless steel bolts, and there were probably twenty around the base of these winches. John got in underneath them, and he measured them up and new winches were built to fit into those existing holes.

"Once the replacement gear arrived they removed the old winches, and we had these new winches – and they're huge, they're big 22000 winches which are monstrous big things as tall as a man. We're lowering them in with a crane, and I'm looking at the twenty studs on the bottom of these winches thinking, 'There are twenty holes, it's gotta fit, there's going to be an issue here.' We dropped the first one into place, and one of the holes was out maybe 5mm.

"We opened up that hole, lowered the winch down and bolted it up. Lowered the next one in, it went straight in, didn't even have to modify it. I was just scratching my head, how accurate! Crawling in, measuring things up with a tape measure then building a winch to fit in the exact same holes. There was a new skipper involved by this time, I'm not sure what happened to the one we spoke to originally.

"That was something that always stuck in my mind – John would build these things that were completed in a timeframe that was considered impossible in the Muir works, and Muir built them so they fitted into the same holes of the opposition's winch that had come out, he just measured everything up himself. That's the sort of guy he is, he doesn't take no for an answer."

That's the essence of the Muir business philosophy on show. Do it now, do it well, do it again and again.

I L O N A

12 June 2005

<u>To Whom It May Concern:</u>

I am the Captain of the motor yacht 'Ilona', 74m & 1836grt. 'Ilona' was built in Holland and fitted with anchoring and mooring equipment made in Holland. The windlass main drive shaft failed on several occasions, resulting in Ilona requiring replacements either from Muir Australia or Steen in Germany.

In December 2004 Muir Engineering based in Hobart, Australia were commissioned to build two VRC22000 anchor windlasses, one VC20000 capstan and one VRC20000 stern windlass/capstan along with 3 variable speed control cabinets or 'soft' controls.

To my knowledge Muir Australia and Steen in Germany are the only two winch makers capable of manufacturing large and reliable equipment for yachts of this size and larger. We decided to go with Muir because of their reputation for the highest quality and user friendly operation. I understand that Muir windlasses are now being fitted to yachts under construction at Lurssen, Feadship, Delta, Alstom, HDW, Oceanco, Pendennis and other well known yards in Europe and the USA.

Muir was able to design and build the equipment for retrofit within a 3 ½ month period from order to sea trials. Muir is able to supervise installation of all deck equipment including the electric VSD drives. The windlass installation was speedily achieved due to Muir's eye for detail and planning ensuring the original and new windlasses would interchange seamlessly.

The original AC DOL controls were replaced with the much softer VSD controls. The advantage of VSD controls is their infinite, slow, medium or fast speed from a hand held 24V pendant. VSDs are ideal for easing the anchor home into the pocket, lining up the chain compressor, capstan to chain gypsy to drive gear. Whereas the DOL stepped drives are hard, overrun and can do damage to the equipment.

Muir windlass design incorporates a torque limiter/clutch between the AC motor and the heavy duty planetary drive gear which protects the motor from excessive overload in case of stalling of the anchor windlasses.

'Ilona' departed Sydney, Australia in April 2005. Anchoring has since been confidently accomplished, I can highly recommend Muir as a company who build superior equipment and who stand by their product anywhere in the world.

Please feel free to contact me for any further information

Yours sincerely,

Captain Peter Oddie
Motor Yacht 'Ilona'

HIGH PRAISE

*Captain of **Ilona**, Peter Oddie, sent a letter in 2005 to John Muir praising the anchoring and mooring equipment installed on **Ilona**, and wrote that he considered Muir products to be 'superior'.*

SURFING
into the
NINETIES

The late 1980s and early 1990s were good to John Muir. Not because he was lucky or fortunate, or because the winds of economic trade blew favourably, but because in his usual inimitable style, John had been doing the hard yards to ensure his business was growing.

The growth was not just in the standard anchor and fishing winch gear he sold to small and medium boat builders, but also in his capacity to design a range of drum anchor winches for the booming fast ferry market. Added to that was the growing demand by the rich and famous for 'megayachts'. Huge, beautifully crafted and expensive sail and motor yachts.

In 1989 a brief glimpse of one of John Muir's many diaries reveals another unbelievably punishing schedule of sales calls and boat shows lasting 24 days. Not one day during this trip was designated for 'time off,' for sightseeing and relaxing, that wasn't in John's makeup.

The trip began with a flight to Melbourne, where John realised, because of industrial action, his flight to the USA was delayed. Undeterred, he had time to whip down and visit International Marine. It's always about making hay while the sun shines. Then it was back to the airport, off to Los Angeles and on to Chicago for the boat show. Here he met Brian Brain, the Manager of Plastimo USA. (By sheer coincidence his wife's name is Mary Muir.) Next on John's itinerary were Baltimore and Atlanta on the east coast, Seattle on the west coast, Tampa on the east coast, Houston and Albuquerque in the southwest and then back to California. Next he flew to Seattle to meet with representatives from Retfort Marine, South Pacific Associates (So-Pac) and Bayliner. At Port Townsend, on the Olympic Peninsula that lies north of Seattle and south of Vancouver, he visited businesses like Wellcraft, Endeavour Yachts and Catalina Yachts, to mention just a few.

Prior to the existence of the Monaco Boat Show in the late 1980s John travelled alone. On several occasions he criss-crossed the globe, attending boat shows in Nice (later to become Monaco), Fort Lauderdale, USA, then to the METS in Amsterdam. Each year Muir Engineering would have several new models, be they pleasure or

US REPRESENTATION

So-Pac (later purchased by Imtra) was an early US representative for Muir equipment. Above, Jerry Truax at a USA Boat Show. in 1995.

megayacht windlasses to put on display. The models due for display would be air-freighted, to save up to six weeks shipping time between each destination. One trip that comes to mind was in the late 1980s when John took a brand new VRC18000 windlass (weighing over half a tonne) as a full working model first to Nice, then air-freighted to two more shows, one in the USA, and the other in Europe. John would follow them around, unpack them, put them on display, pack them up at the end of each show and ship them onto the next one. They often came with two or three crates of other new equipment, brochures and promotional material.

It's that determination of John Muir's, to do what you have to do, to focus totally on the task at hand, to keep going when many others would fall by the wayside or even worse, just give up because it is all 'too hard,' that sets him apart from mere mortals.

Alistair Mant, when penning the unauthorised biography of Robert Clifford, 'The Bastard's a Genius' said:

"There is no doubt Robert Clifford (read John Muir) is a 'character.' Anybody born with such single-minded determination and extraordinary talents will make some kind of mark on the world. As Robert McKee notes in his screen writers bible: 'True character is revealed in the choices a human being makes under pressure – the greater the pressure, the deeper the revelation, the truer the choice to the character's essential nature."

David Ryder-Turner, an employee of John's father Jock Muir, a British based yacht designer, who also once worked as a woodwork teacher at Hutchins School for Boys in Hobart, met John at a boat show in the UK in December 1999. In the letter he subsequently wrote to John, just a few days after seeing him at the show, he tells of Jock Muir's extraordinary generosity, keeping him on when times were tough and imparting his extensive knowledge of yacht design. He also tells of his time teaching at Hutchins: "When I came to Tasmania for the first time in the early 1950s, I stayed at the Shipwrights Arms Hotel, near Jock's Battery Point boatyard. They were just about to finish building a boat called *Fantasy*. She was launched on 12 December 1953. It was a 33ft UK-designed racing sloop built to the order of Dudley Burridge and Stan Brown, both of the Huon.

Not only was Jock exceptionally kind to me in giving me employment in the yard — and the teaching of how to use tools properly, and yacht building in general — but he went further than that. There was a time — in the middle of the year as I remember, when there was not much work on, and Jock had to lay off one or two of the staff. But, he kept me on, doing odd jobs and cleaning up the place etc. It was extraordinarily generous of him.

LETTER TO JOHN

In a 1999 letter to John, David Ryder-Turner, once an employee of Jock's, wrote about his apprenticeship under Jock and later a trade teacher at Hutchins Boys School where he taught woodwork to David Jones, Alan Perkins, Jock Campbell, Trevor Sharman and Robert Clifford, among others. He said, "All they wanted to do was build boats and go sailing."

It's that determination of John Muir's, to do what you have to do, to focus totally on the task at hand, to keep going when many others would fall by the wayside or even worse, just give up because it is all 'too hard,' that sets him apart from mere mortals.

"When I first arrived I taught at Hutchins, class 3C, a collection of apparently 'useless' clods who could not be taught anything. Twelve of these kids lived for boats, so we all got on very well. I taught them maths, English and social studies and everything was based on boats and the water. They were a great crew, one was Robert Clifford... I loved those boys and teaching them was an adventure. I think I was just one lesson ahead of them every week."

David Ryder-Turner is obviously not the teacher at Hutchins who classed Robert Clifford as a 'dunce' and unlikely to amount to anything.

Many of the people John counts as friends – boat builders, designers, owners of large marine businesses – are of the same ilk. What they see in John is a mirror reflection of who they are, why they have succeeded when many have failed. Risk takers all. They are men and women of the sea, where you will almost certainly, one day, confront your fears. Where you will, like John and like his brothers, his sister, his father, his grandfather, his great grandfather, even his great-great grandfather, be confronted by life and death moments, when you realise what it is to be human and what it means to survive.

John Muir could have taken the easy way out. He could have sold his business, taken the money and retired to a life of some luxury. No. Not an option, especially when in a rare moment of reflection he admits that, "I love the chase, I love the adrenalin rush of success, of reaching and exceeding targets, of seeing the gear we have made on the decks of some of the biggest and most advanced yachts and cruisers in the world."

In the last chapter we detailed the story of how the team at Muir Engineering was successful in re-equipping a 74m yacht, the *Ilona*, with new and very large winches, windlasses and capstans at very short notice. The production crew in Kingston worked like navvies over the Christmas and New Year break to build the gear then ship it to Sydney, to have it installed and tested before Good Friday, so the owner could take his yacht out for a family break over Easter.

This timeline would never be repeated, it was extraordinary. A similar project would normally take six months to complete.

A few months after installation and successful testing John Muir and his team received this letter from John Venter, the Chief Engineer of the *Ilona*.

> From: Engineers Ilona M.Y Ltd
> Sent: Thursday, 30 June 2005 4:10 PM
> To: John Muir; Paul Hollingsworth
> Subject: M/Y ILONA Anchor Capstans
>
> Dear John, Paul and everyone else @ MUIR
>
> I would like to take a moment to give you some feedback now that your Anchor Capstans have been in service here on ILONA for a couple of months. We arrived back in the Mediterranean nearly a month ago and we have pretty much spent all of it around Southern Greece.
>
> Most of the islands have pretty deep anchorages for a vessel this size and to top it all off, it has been extremely windy this summer. It then comes as no surprise that we have had to anchor in deeper water than we'd like, with winds of 50 knots battering us. The winds have been so strong that we've been dragging anchor even with 5 to 7 shackles (130m to 200m of anchor chain) out on both sides and often having to move as a result of this.
>
> In all of this your winches have been working faultlessly and so far, as you can imagine I have kept a keen eye on them, making sure the initial setup worked as you intended it. Your winches haul anchor under the most extreme conditions without so much of a squeak from any of the MUIR equipment. We are truly happy for the huge improvement it has brought to us on board. The winches most definitely passed their deep water hauling test (60+ metres), which was one of the issues I know Paul wanted some feedback on.
>
> Once again thank you very much for the effort from everyone involved with the project here from our side and ultimately providing us with "Peace of Mind".
>
> All our very best regards
> John Venter, Chief Engineer M/Y Ilona

HIGH PRAISE
*Johan Venter, Chief Engineer of MY **Ilona**, in 2005 during commissioning and testing of the Muir anchor capstans.*

That testimonial is worth gold to any business that seeks to produce the highest quality product. It came as a wonderful surprise to John and others when this letter arrived, unexpected and uninvited. Johan Venter, his skipper and the boat owner are obviously all 'happy chappies.'

For John Muir, the wise council he received from his father, Jock, bears repetition, "Make sure when you build a winch that the winch never fails, that when it gets really rugged, it's best that something else fails, not the winch."

> **66** *Even the very first Muir winches were better designed and built than our competitors. Over the years we have been able to continually produce better and better anchoring systems. I know there is no better built or finished product on the market and that makes me proud.* **99**

– DON DI MARTINO

Don Di Martino started with Muir in 1978 and within the year he took over management of all the company's manufacturing operations and service. Don was one of the key personnel at Muir who John relied on to keep the factory floor operating flat out, particularly when John was away interstate or overseas. That letter made everyone's day, because for all the production crew who had worked long hours over the Christmas break and into January to produce the large winches and gear, in record time, it made the hard work worthwhile. It reinforced their belief that the anchor winches, capstans and other winch gear they churn out under the Muir brand are 'the Best in the World.'

Don Di Martino: "Even the very first Muir winches were better designed and built than our competitors. Over the years we have been able to continually produce better and better anchoring systems. I know there is no better built or finished product on the market and that makes me proud.

"This small company in Tasmania has been able to grow and grow and be a world power in marine anchoring systems. Growth based on hard work, good ethics and real team spirit. This is a company that is prepared to take a chance on new designs if they are based on proven research and development. We are always aware of the trust placed in us and our anchoring systems by boat owners and skippers, that's something we take very seriously indeed.

"The amount of change I have seen here is incredible, but one of the strengths of this company is its ability to embrace technology, and quickly adapt to make better products for our customers. We are driven by innovation, but having said that we are quick to discard any development that does not have a

genuine purpose. For us to adopt it, it must increase reliability, safety, performance or good looks!"

Take the brand new technology of mobile phones and faxes. When they were first introduced into Tasmania, some years later than the big cities of Sydney and Melbourne, John was hot to trot.

To aid with communication and make him instantly accessible, John purchased the first of the Telstra "brick size" mobile phones and coincidentally was second behind Robert Clifford when he purchased his first fax machine.

At that time Muir Engineering were supplying Incat (the burgeoning International Catamarans) with all their winch gear and machining, including propeller shafts and couplings. John was always interested in new technology and was constantly looking at ways to speed up production. He and his team were innovators. He developed an enviable reputation for his constant search for new ideas and processes. It was hard enough competing against the best in the world, but when you are producing and selling from a base half way round the world from your markets in Europe and North America, the adoption of new technology is critical and is the first stage of keeping abreast if not in front of your competitors.

A former Australian dairy farmer turned boat builder, Wes Moxey, understands better than most the importance of 'getting it right and doing it well.' At a young age he left the family's dairy farm near Newcastle in New South Wales and scored a boat building apprenticeship. He worked for Bill Barry-Cotter and went onto senior management positions at Riviera and Belize.

Wes Moxey: "Being from a dairy farm, I'd seen the hard work involved in making a living from the land. My father said to me, 'There's no future here son, go and get an apprenticeship.' So I did; in 1976, I started as an apprentice Shipwright at Carrington Slipways, Newcastle. After doing my trade it was not really exciting to return to milking cows for a living. However I still have a strong connection to my roots and have today a small family farm in northern NSW."

There is a wonderful Australian saying that says, 'You can take the boy or girl out of the bush but you can't take the bush out of either of them.' One of the most critical lessons anyone will learn when owning and running a dairy farm is that time and cows wait for no man. The cows know when it's milking time, they have full udders and they need to be milked at roughly the same time every day, twice a day. They have to be fed while being milked. There are strict washing and hygiene protocols when dealing with milking equipment and the storage of bulk milk. Do it wrong and you lose thousands of dollars. You have no alternative but to get stuck in and do it on time and do it right, every day of every week of every season.

Wes Moxey: "In 1981 I moved to Queensland having completed my trade and looking for new challenges in life. The first year was hard but in 1982 I began working for myself, sub-contracting to Riviera. By 1987 I was appointed Production Manager, right after the stock market crash. Some years later I progressed to General Manager and then CEO in 2002 when I led a private equity backed management buyout of Riviera.

ABOVE

Wes Moxey, CEO Riviera. Riviera have been dealing exclusively with Muir since the early 1990s.

OPPOSITE

Rodney Longhurst and Wes Moxey celebrate the world premiere of the stylish Riveiera 4800 Sport Yacht at Sydney International Boat Show, 2016.

BELOW: APPRENTICE AWARD

Wes presents a Riviera apprentice the Muir award for apprentice of the year in 2001.

> 66 *Once Riviera started exporting in the late 1980s, lifting our quality standards and needing larger products, we started dealing with Muir. We've kept the relationship going ever since.* 99

– WES MOXEY, CEO, RIVIERA

"Riviera saw some boom times in the early 2000s up to 2006/7, however I could see a slowdown coming prior to the GFC [global financial crisis] in 2008. There were some signs preceding this in the marine industry, forward orders slowing and deposits not coming through. Our private equity owners did not want to hear of this so I left Riviera in August 2008. (I had no real idea but my departure was about six weeks before the collapse of Lehman Bros.) In May 2009 the company was placed in receivership by the banks.

"Once Riviera started exporting in the late 1980s, lifting our quality standards and needing larger products, we started dealing with Muir. We've kept the relationship going ever since. I've been dealing exclusively with Muir since the early 1990s, and one thing I'll say about

John is he always kept to the highest moral ground. I've had numerous other companies approach me to stock and use their winches but I don't ever shop on price. We have a strong relationship with John Muir and the whole Muir organisation. Even the new blood in the organisation upholds John's honesty and trust in how they do business.

"What they've done is incredible, really. They've built a global brand from a little place like Tasmania, and it comes down to John's willingness to jump on a plane and travel wherever he needed to go – he was at every trade show, every boat show, and he always made a point of coming to see his customers on their stands to say hello and ask 'is there anything you need.'

"The Muir business' success is a direct result of the endless air travel and hard yards John has done attending boat shows and visiting customers. It's hard work in the marine export business; at times with the high Aussie dollar it's been a real struggle to compete, the cost of doing business from Australia is high. Australia really can't afford to see the dollar much above US$0.75 because exporters find it hard to compete, particularly against cheaper Asian manufacturers. So it's hats off to John and the whole Muir organisation for what they've accomplished."

Wes Moxey: "I often rate John Muir as the hardest working man in the marine industry. Wherever I am in the world, there's John at trade or boat shows peddling the Muir brand with passion and commitment. I have the utmost respect for him.

"Despite all this travel and tiring foot work, I've never heard John whinge or complain about anything. He always has a positive thing to say about any negative. The Muir brand has a stellar reputation globally and I cannot remember the last time we had a warranty issue."

John Muir: "I've known Wes since the early days of Riviera's move to the Gold Coast and I don't think he has ever lost his innate sense of urgency, to get things done, to meet deadlines and targets. The same production quality and service ethos was apparent at Riviera, making sure boats were delivered on time.

"Wes is very much a hands on bloke, he must have learnt that from his days on the farm, where you learn to become a jack of all trades, because you have to. He, like me, spent a lot of time at boat shows across Australia and around the world as their business grew."

Riviera remains one of Muir's best customers globally, in the boom times they were producing up to 400 boats per year.

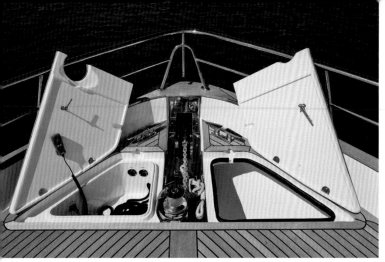

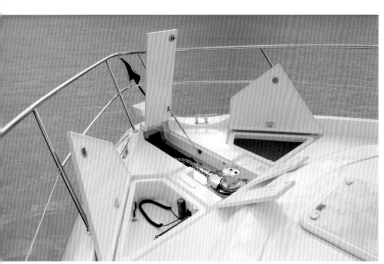

RIVIERA SUPPLY MUIR GEAR ON THEIR YACHTS

Top left and top right: Belize B54 Sedan anchor well showing Muir VRC3500 anchor winch; Bottom left: Riviera 6000SY Sport Yacht anchor well with Muir VR1000 winch; Bottom right: Riviera 3600 Sport Yacht model.

John Muir: "This was another reason why we established our facility in Coomera, at the top end of the Gold Coast, almost opposite the Riviera complex, as there was so much activity with winches, capstans, anchors, chain, servicing and call-outs. This required at least one full-time employee who would be on stand-by. We stocked two months' supply of equipment for Riviera, and on occasions this facilitated sales to other boat builders in the area. The largest motor yacht at present is 21m and has installed VRC4500 vertical anchor winch, the small end of our mega-yacht range."

Riveria's new chairman and owner, Rodney Longhurst, purchased the business in March 2012 after it had been placed in receivership. He invited Wes Moxey to return to the business as CEO. As a result, the Belize marque (a brand of luxury cruising motor launch) was brought under the company's banner. Subsequently, the Longhurst family purchased the world-class Riviera site in May the following year (2013), securing the company's future in Australia.

Represented by a growing dealer network spanning the globe, Australia's largest and most-awarded builder of luxury motor yachts has an unparalleled commitment to customer care, which includes exclusive invitations to regular Experience trips – cruising in company with fellow members of the global family of Riviera and Belize owners – and also hosts regular educational and social events.

Each May, the Riviera Festival of Boating is held at the home of Riviera, the 14 hectare world-class facility, on Australia's Gold Coast.

In November 2012, the 5,000th Riveria was launched. CEO, Wes Moxey, said it was a very memorable and momentous occasion. "It was very moving to see the first Riviera model and the 5,000th Riviera side by side, and to share this moment with more than so many Riviera owners was one of the most rewarding experiences in my entire career."

When flying on one of his many overseas trips, this time from Houston to Albuquerque on a USA sales trip in 1989, John got chatting to an American stockbroker who told him, "The US and Australian economies are both strong and the stock markets are as well. We should do well this year and next."

In his diary John writes himself a reminder: "Let's not count on a weak AU$, let's push on with sales to the US and Europe." Adding "I need a new distributor for the Chicago area, shouldn't have much trouble finding one."

His new best friend and stockbroker mate was spot on with his observations about the US economy, that's according to two members of the US-based Federal Reserve Bank of Kansas City.

"After completing its sixth year of uninterrupted expansion, the US economy enters 1989 and beyond in remarkably good condition. The nation's output of goods and services is expanding at a moderate pace, employment is showing strong growth, unemployment is steady and inflation seems to have stabilised."*

Meanwhile in Europe the formation of the European Union was forging ahead. Well, maybe 'forging' isn't the most appropriate adjective to use, 'steadily moving ahead' might be more accurate, even if still an exaggeration.

"At its meeting... in 1988, the European Council confirmed the objective of economic and monetary union. The council will meet in June 1989 to examine the means of achieving this union."

RODNEY LONGHURST
Chairman and Owner of Riviera

indeed turned out to be a great leader. He has sensed the pace of history and helped history to find a natural channel."

Earlier the same morning, Marc Kusnetz, from the US-based news organisation, NBC, reporting from Berlin, goes back to his hotel to freshen up. As he bends over the bathroom sink and splashes cold water on his face, he notices a thick grey powder washing off him. Then, of course, it hits him: he is watching the Berlin Wall go down the drain.

The article went on to say: "The Iron Curtain was being swept aside. Europe would never be the same again. What many maybe did not know was that as the dust

Two years after the fall of the Wall the entire Soviet Union as we knew it was dissolved... Europe was filled with enthusiasm for life and liberty and the possibilities of the future.

One of the biggest changes to affect the entire European community and the nations that made up the USSR was brewing. The Cold War was coming to an end and so was its biggest symbol, the Berlin Wall.

The British tabloid, the Daily Telegraph on 10 November 1989, quoted from the diary of Anatoly Chernyaev, an advisor to USSR President Gorbachev: "The Berlin Wall has collapsed. This entire era in the history of the socialist system is over. The PUWP [Polish Communist party] and the HSWP [Hungarian Communist party] are both gone. That is what Gorbachev has done, he has

from the collapsing wall was settling, somewhere in the chaos a young woman, Angela Merkel, made it through from the East to the West via the Bornholmer crossing. From the west side of the Wall, she phones her aunt in Hamburg – and then, presumably, joins the celebrations. This is the night that sets Merkel on her path to be chancellor of Germany. She will later join the new East German party, Democratic Awakening, and begin her political career."

* J.A. Casy and Richard Roberts, Federal Reserve Bank of Kansas City. December 1988.

After 10 years hard work Muir winches are known worldwide

His winches pulled off a marine engineering win

THE HARD YARDS ARE FINALLY START PAYING OFF

Local newspaper articles from 1989 and 1990 celebrate Muir's Small Business Awards success. Articles: The Mercury.

While the Christmas decorations were going up and Australia was on the cusp of summer, Keating had to tell us that bad times were here and that a necessary economic adjustment had to be endured. It was to be some adjustment but it changed the nature of the Australian economy.

Two years after the fall of the Wall the entire Soviet Union as we knew it was dissolved. The major concern of the then Prime Minister of Great Britain, Margaret Thatcher, was the re-unification of the two Germanys, she saw it as a threat to peace. That threat did not eventuate and her concerns have evaporated.

Europe was filled with enthusiasm for life and liberty and the possibilities of the future now that countries like East Germany, Poland, Czechoslovakia and many others were no longer under the yoke of communism and the control of Russia. More than 20 countries emerged from the dust of the fallen wall of control.

Despite these events, not much changed in Australia. Even when the Chinese Communist government brought the tanks into Tiananmen Square in 1989 and brutally crushed a student uprising, our trade volume with them didn't change one iota. Of course we were happy that so many people in Europe were tasting freedom, but we also saw increased trade opportunities coming. Yet, an ill wind was beginning to blow.

John's new friend, the US stockbroker that he'd met on that flight from Houston to Albuquerque 18 months earlier, who had predicted things would be rosy for two years, didn't see the changes that were coming internationally and had no idea what Australia's Treasurer was up to.

In late 1990 and for the next few years, the Australian economy and to a lesser extent, Asia and the USA, were buffeted by recession. In our case it was brought on by Treasurer Paul Keating who later coined it as 'the recession we had to have.' Good of him wasn't it?

John Muir: "Out of the blue in November 1990 came the storm clouds of recession that we were told we had to have. It wasn't only boatyards and marine businesses throughout Australia and New Zealand that felt the winds of change and tough conditions, but because most boat purchases are regarded as 'luxury' items they were among the hardest hit. Boat builders in the USA and Canada slowed, as they also did in Australia."

John's wife Wendy later remarked that throughout the early 1990s John was away for months on end, travelling, selling, reinforcing contacts and supporting clients. It was a tough time for all concerned.

It was certainly a time to keep in close contact with the key people he had working for him across the globe, selling Muir winches and continuing to attend boat and yacht shows around the world.

In a review of the life and times of Paul Keating the Sydney Morning Herald newspaper, in December 2015 put it this way: "It will be on his epitaph. It's already the stuff of fridge magnets, postcards and tea towels. And, to paraphrase him, walk into any saloon bar and every punter will quote that line whenever his name is mentioned." The line? "This is the recession we had to have." Paul Keating immortalised it 25 years ago, on 29 November 1990. Of course that quote from the then Labor Treasurer is in stark contrast to the one attributed to his mate and former Prime Minister Bob Hawke, when Australia won the America's Cup in 1983: "Any boss who sacks a worker for not turning up today is a bum."

While the Christmas decorations were going up and Australia was on the cusp of summer, Keating had to tell us that bad times were here and that a necessary economic adjustment had to be endured. It was to be some adjustment but it changed the nature of the Australian economy.

It was Keating's response to the release of the national accounts which showed that for the September quarter of 1990 there had been a 1.8% fall in gross domestic product (GDP). Keating canvassed the line about the 'recession we had to have' with Bob Hawke before going public. It was memorable but way over the top. Every figure on the economic scorecard showed the Australian economy was in deep trouble.

There were business failures, bankruptcies, negative equity, falling investment and mounting unemployment. All the debt-financed business carpetbaggers like Russell Goward, Christopher Skase, Abe Goldberg and Alan Bond were put out of commission. Australia was, as Keating put it, "de-spivved." Inflation was exorcised from the Australian economy. It was a policy-induced recession though it was not meant to be; the econocrats were aiming for a soft landing but it all went terribly wrong.

The double-digit interest rates that were intended to give us that transition went awry, with the economy sent crashing. Keating wanted interest rates brought down far quicker, but the Reserve Bank was too cautious. Even now Keating believes he had a greater instinct of where the economy was heading than the people who were advising him.

When asked about it recently by ABC TV's Kerry O'Brien, whether Keating had any remorse about landing the economy into recession, he responded that, "I will take the blame for it so long as I also get the credit for the subsequent flowering of the Australian economy where real incomes for middle Australia have grown more than for those in most of our trading partners."

In the USA, through the constant travelling of John and his sales representatives, Muir Engineering was building its client base. Jerry Truax from Imtra, a big player and marine industry systems supplier, servicing the entire North American continent, had just begun selling Muir 'Cougar' winches and windlasses to a client company, Bayliner. It was to become standard equipment on their 38 and 45ft motor yachts. Muir were selling 600 windlasses a year to Bayliner alone.

Jerry Truax: "This was volume business and we were trying to ramp up to stay ahead of Bayliner's usage. There were many times when the Bayliner driver would show up to pick up their order just an hour or so after we had received the shipment all the way from Tasmania. I didn't like the stress because it's a long way from Tasmania to Seattle and the Bayliner business was growing rapidly. We were also working with Doc Freeman's and fisheries in the Northwest, and having some success in California.

"I remember that initially John had a couple of other distributors. I think they included The Moorings in Texas and a small operation run by a couple of brothers in the South San Francisco Bay area. Kevin Fleming was also involved for a short period of time, but So-Pac (I worked for Peter Rachtman in the So-Pac business before joining Imtra) soon had the distribution sewn up for western USA.

"I had the good fortune to be able to visit Muir Engineering in May of 1987. I had been in New Zealand on business prior to that and flew from there to Hobart via Sydney. John and Wendy were very gracious and put me up at their home. I had a very interesting couple of days at the factory learning about their production and meeting everyone. They had the chandlery on the waterfront, then in addition to the factory, had recently started building some large yacht windlasses in the 7,000lb to 10,000lb range. It was a while after that when I made my first sales call to Christensen Shipyards with a vertical 7,000lb windlass sample in the back of the So-Pac van. I can tell you it sure made an impression.

"Travelling with John was always interesting. He never travelled light. He always had a full complement of printed literature, suits and ties and frequently a number of very heavy windlass parts. He was never without plenty of pocket size note pads that he would fill with notes during our meetings. These notes got translated into numerous hand-written faxes that he would send from my office or from his hotel room at night. This led to a very well done caricature of John… 'Fax Man… Faxing the world from down under.'

"Looking back, I have spent many hours with John over the years stretching from 1984 into the mid-2000s. Lots of customer visits, particularly in the Northwest of the US, but also in Wisconsin, Florida and California. Not to mention the boat shows from IMTEC in Chicago to Miami and Fort Lauderdale, as well as the Long Beach shows, and meetings in New Zealand on a couple of occasions."

John Muir: "There was one particular incident that comes to mind in my early days when travelling with Jerry Truax around Seattle and the Northwest. I was staying in a motel in Seattle and I can tell you it was nothing flash, very basic.

"I went out for an early morning stroll before breakfast and being a diabetic type I always take along my grab bag of medicines and particularly my glucose in case I need a boost when my blood sugar levels are low.

"I arrived back at the motel after a stroll to realise I had left my keys and my diabetic gear in my room. I looked around for the owner but he was no-where to be found. I found his business card and called him from reception and he said he was on his way back. He didn't arrive and so I called him again but he didn't answer.

"By now I could feel my blood sugar level was dropping and that can very quickly make me go weak in the knees and legs. I was getting desperate and realised I needed my diabetic kit and an insulin injection within a few minutes or I could quickly collapse and drop into a diabetic coma.

THE ADVENTURES OF FAX MAN

Muir employee Steve Arnold (above right), talented with tools and the pen, created these hilarious cartoons in the early 1980s reflecting John's ambitious faxing and one particular diabetic incident in Seattle (the title of which is a parody of the 1993 movie 'Sleepless in Seattle'). "Nuclear Nick" refers to Muir employee Nick Dale (pictured above), who worked in purchasing at the time.

"There was no one around, so I charged headlong into my hotel door and knocked it clean off the hinges and unfortunately did a bit more damage than just that. I grabbed a hand full of glucose and ate a banana and had to sit down before I flaked out. When I came to the owner was in my room yelling at me and then he called the police.

"Two police officers arrived, I humbly apologised, explained what had happened and said in my defence that I really had no option but to do what I did. Otherwise they may have found me dead outside the hotel room door.

"In the end I paid for one night's accommodation which was about $40 US and another $200 US to replace the door. If I recall right Jerry Truax came to pick me up. Back in those days we had no email or text, however news still travelled fast and it wasn't long before the factory and Wendy knew I was lucky not to be locked up in gaol.

"This story went round like wildfire, the next day I arrived at Jerry's Seattle office and on the fax was a very descriptive sketch faxed from Steve in the factory back home."

Living with diabetes is not easy, but it's made a whole lot harder when you combine the lifestyle of John Muir with the disease. John has been a type 1 diabetic for 33 years, however he wasn't diagnosed formally until the mid-1980s when he suffered an attack of acute pancreatitis. In simple terms having diabetes means the body has too much glucose in the blood.

"Glucose is your body's main source of energy. It comes from the carbohydrate food and drink you consume. You need a steady supply of glucose each day to fuel your body. Insulin, a hormone made by your pancreas, assists the glucose to move from the bloodstream into the cells of your body to be used for energy.

In diabetes, the pancreas cannot make enough insulin or the insulin it does make does not work properly. As glucose needs insulin to move easily into the cells, the lack of insulin results in a build-up of glucose in the blood stream."*

Diabetes is made worse by stress, by travelling between time zones, working constantly to tight deadlines and by lack of exercise. Since his diagnosis John has had to constantly check his sugar levels and inject with insulin as and when needed. If his insulin levels go seriously astray, things can go badly wrong, as they almost did on a flight to Singapore once. John fainted while waiting to go to the toilet, the crew applied oxygen, he was hospitalised at the airport in Singapore, stabilised then allowed to catch his next flight to Nice. There is no stopping John Muir when he is on a mission.

* Source: Diabetes Queensland: (http://www.diabetesqld.org.au/about-diabetes/what-is-diabetes.aspx)

TRAVEL TAKING ITS TOLL
John says of this photo taken at his 50th birthday party in 1994, "Already starting to show signs of the toll travel and Type I diabetes was taking.."

QUANTUM HYDRAULICS

Left: John Allen and Pete Florence at METS 2002. Right: The Quantum team with John at Monaco Boat Show, 2013. From left: Sharon Allen, Peter Florence, Robyn Florence, John Muir and John Allen.
Opposite page, bottom: John and Matthew Johnston enjoying a meal with the Quantum team during Monaco Boat Show 2009.

John vividly remembers another funny, but not life threatening, incident when Jerry Truax was in Tasmania on a visit and was in John's office. John had left him to attend to a problem elsewhere and when he arrived back in the office, there was Jerry taking photos of the filing cabinet!

John Muir: "He had his camera out and he was photographing the filing cabinet. I asked what on earth he was doing. He said, 'I want to show the boys that you do actually have a filing system.' In the early days of expansion, there likely were some shortfalls in our administrative systems. Faxes used to be on rolls of paper at that time, and I used to fax a lot of designs, notes and order information."

The Muir business was now selling more winches than ever before, the cash flow was good, enabling them to pay the costs of developing bigger and better winch equipment and importing marine accessories like anchors, anchor chains and more. For Muir Engineering the late 1980s was a time of rapid growth. The sales from December 1986 to December 1989 increased at 30% each year and turnover doubled in just three years. The 1990s looked just as promising, that was until the recession hit.

Somehow, as he criss-crossed the globe, John managed to find remarkable individuals, with a wide range of marine industry contacts, who become Muir representatives or Muir ambassadors. One such individual is an American, Pete Florence, a director and the CEO of Quantum Hydraulics based at Fort Lauderdale, Florida.

Pete Florence: "Many years ago I drew the short straw and had to pick John up at the Miami Boat Show and transport him to his hotel on Miami Beach. I had just brought a brand new Land Rover Discovery and when I picked up Johnnie he was so excited to be in my new car. He kept touching the leather, checking out the radio and just admiring everything. I was so pumped that I was transporting the famous John Muir in my new Land Rover, so I thought I might go a bit further by asking John what he drove back in Australia to which he replied 'A Range Rover' and totally destroyed my ten minutes of fame. John, mate, you are the best!"

Quantum today is a global success story – they are the leading marine stabiliser (anti-roll) manufacturer in the world, with headquarters in Fort Lauderdale and manufacturing and servicing operations throughout northern Europe.

MIKE PERKINS, QUANTUM HYDRAULICS USA

Above, Mike hand-lining flathead on a fishing trip in Hobart with John and Greg Muir in the 1990s.
Below, at METS 2002 doing what he's best at – sales and service.

John Muir: "Over the years, I've participated in boat shows all over the world and at almost every one there has been a Quantum booth. The Quantum guys are unpaid Muir salesmen and a wonderful strategic alliance. We have worked together closely on many projects where Quantum hydraulic stabilisers and Muir hydraulic winches have been plumbed and commissioned by Quantum.

"Pete Florence is a charismatic guy and very knowledgeable on mechanical and hydraulic systems, having spent his early days in the British Navy. He's also a specialist on stabiliser systems.

"There are two other friends at Quantum I've had a lot to do with – the founder and entrepreneur John Allen and sales maestro Michael Perkins. Sadly in October 2015 Michael passed away at his home in Fort Lauderdale."

John Muir discusses one of his early meetings with John Allen in the early 1990s: "I was travelling the mid-east coast of the USA, following up winch gear leads. John Allen had a hydraulic workshop set up in one of the larger shipyards. We really hit it off from day one and John told me where the best opportunities were for new business and what new megayacht and larger vessels were going to be built that could be possible clients for Muir.

"We have remained good friends ever since. From those very early days, Quantum have spread across the globe. Quantum have their head office in Fort Lauderdale, and strategic servicing locations around the world. Their large stabiliser components manufacturing sites are strategically located in several places in northern Europe as well as the USA."

"Michael Perkins was affable and well-liked by all the marine industry. I met Michael and John Allen at one of the early Fort Lauderdale boat shows, in the late 1990s. They were supplying and installing stabiliser equipment to Austal Ships in Western Australia, including for Greg Norman's 69m *Aussie Rules*. We had the winch contract for that motor yacht. I arranged for Michael and John to visit us in Tasmania and have a look over the Muir operations in Kingston. They had been doing a lot of travelling and decided to take a well-earned week's break in Hobart."

"We decided to go fishing with my younger brother Greg on his 34ft Mariner powerboat. Michael and John tried their hand-lining skills, resulting in a good feed of flathead. We set two mesh nets and landed a 1.3m hammerhead shark that was tangled in the net and took a lot of time to release. It caused a bit of excitement.

"The following year I met up with Michael and we travelled to Germany to visit several yards. This was my first visit to the larger German yards, which were primarily building large motor yachts. At one yard in particular I was with Michael while he was discussing supply of Quantum stabilisers for a new yacht. Unfortunately, I was a few weeks late, as the supply of deck machinery was already under negotiation and close to being awarded to a local winch maker. However, I decided overnight to quote and provide several specific drawings.

"When our meeting finished I was invited along for dinner. All up, there were about ten of us – the captain, engineer, shipyard directors, and interior decorators. The conversation became very casual very quickly. However, I learned this was a great way to unwind any tension that had developed during the project negotiations, and it became easier to discuss details of the project as the night progressed.

"The next morning Michael and I were back in the shipyard and I was introduced to the Chief Naval Architect of the project. We discussed putting in the Muir offer, which I put together overnight. However he said

yachtswoman and crewed with Michael for several years early in her career. "

The Australian economy had been and was going through tough times, as were numerous others of our international trading partners. Ian Macfarlane was the governor of the Australian Reserve Bank from 1996 until his retirement in September 2006. In an edited transcript of his first ABC Boyer lecture, run in The Age newspaper he said: "In the early 1990s, Australia went into a recession. I believe that the financial excesses of the 1980s reached such a scale that the 1990 recession was inevitable. At the end of the 1980s expansion, the Australian economy was overstretched in a number of ways and the country was extremely vulnerable to any contractionary shock to the economy itself or to confidence. The shock duly came in the form of the international recession of the early 1990s."

It remains a controversial subject, and one where political feelings still run high. In large part this is because so many people associate it with the catchphrase of the then Treasurer Paul Keating, that "this was the recession we had to have". In his 1992 assessment, journalist Paul Kelly said of the Keating phrase: "It was perhaps the most stupid remark of his career and it

Despite the state of the Australian economy, by the early 1990s, the global megayacht business was back on its feet and expanding.

he had gone too far to make changes, and the owner and captain were settled on the equipment. He did assure me we would have an opportunity on the next vessel and he would be in touch in a few weeks time.

"During this meeting, Michael got frustrated, pulled me aside and told me to back off as this was his meeting not mine. Which was right, because he felt I was taking over. I learnt a hell of a lot being with Michael and observing the way he did business. Over the next week he introduced me at other shipyards in Germany and Holland, where we were able to meet the right people and get a foot in the door.

"I had the utmost respect for Michael Perkins. He was a tenacious go-getter, extremely well versed in all facets of sail and motor yachts, and didn't take no for an answer. Michael captained and skippered several large sailing yachts, having crossed the Atlantic on multiple occasions. Kim Mayer was also a seasoned

nearly cost him the prime ministership. However — it is largely true — the boom begat the recession."

We take up the story with one of Australia's most respected newspapers, The Age, in December of 2006.

"Of the 18 Organisation for Economic Co-operation and Development (OECD) countries of reasonable size and development, 17 experienced a recession in the early 1990s — a similar situation to the mid-1970s and early 1980s global recessions. Why? First, any boom built on rising asset prices financed by increased borrowing has to end. Second, the relentless pressure of high interest rates on businesses, which in many cases were borrowed up to the hilt.

"In the event, the cash rate reached 18% in the second half of 1989, the mortgage rate 17%, and many loans to businesses well in excess of 20%. But rates as high as this, or nearly as high, had little effect in stopping the rapid growth of credit earlier in the 1980s.

"There had been falls in inflation after the 1970s and 1980s recessions, but the falls were not large enough to leave us with an ongoing low rate of inflation. This time, inflation fell to around 2%, which meant that for the first time in 20 years, Australia had an inflation rate in line with world best practice. We had returned to being a low-inflation country.

"The events in Australia were mirrored elsewhere."*

Despite the state of the Australian economy, by the early 1990s, the global megayacht business was back on its feet and expanding. It was getting to the point where Muir Engineering had too much work in fabrication. At the same time they had some serious international enquiries about components in fabricated and polished stainless steel, in preference to the traditional sandcasting method. In discussion with several large megayacht builders in Europe, it was suggested Muir could do well if they got into the market early.

That suited John Muir, so he talked to his crew back home about what it would take to move into stainless steel and mega winches.

John had a versatile workshop crew, but he would also need interstate based Muir sales staff. Thankfully, he had the expertise at hand. Several years prior, in 1988, John was sailing *Shonandra* in the first Pipe Opener Cruise for the Royal Yacht Club of Tasmania's season. They berthed at Geeveston for the overnight stay and a dinner come party at the nearby Geeveston Hotel (owned by Mike Wilson, who would become Ross Muir's brother-in-law). A fellow called Ken Padgett and a couple of others came on board for the leg back to Hobart.

By January 1990, several customers were in financial strife and by early February some of them had closed their doors and left Muir with considerable unpaid invoices.

John Muir: "We had a cabin full of people and I heard Ken Padgett talking to a friend, David Turner, and to be honest it was very hard to get a word in. At the time, I was impressed with their ongoing discussions, and I thought to myself, 'This bloke could sell ice to Eskimos.' Ken mentioned he was relocating to Queensland as we were discussing our Queensland business, and we agreed to stay in touch."

The following year (midway through 1989) John was visiting his Queensland distributor in Brisbane, looking over the inventory that was on consignment and came across several customised anchor winches they had shipped north, a special order for a Gold Coast boat builder. John discovered the gear had been sitting on the shelves for almost a year and had never been delivered to the client. He was not a happy man.

When John asked "Why haven't these been delivered?" he was told "We overlooked them, sorry."

* Source: The Age Newspaper, 2 December, 2006.

EXPANDING INTO QUEENSLAND
Ken Padgett became a valuable Muir resource as the business expanded into the Queensland market.
Top: Ken showing customers around at Sanctuary Cove Boat Show, 1999.
Above: Ken briefing Matthew Johnston, left, and Don Hoban (Muir Canada representative), at Sanctuary Cove Boat Show, 2005.
Opposite Page: Ken (centre in white shirt and shorts) on the Muir stand at an earlier Sanctuary Cove Boat Show.

"The stock was shipped to another location. I went home and the next day, out of the blue, came a call from Ken Padgett, saying he was interested in representing Muir equipment in Queensland. It was unbelievable, but that's how it happened.

"My response was, 'Yes, you can start tomorrow, and we'll need some storage.' Ken replied, 'I have a double garage at home, we'll use that to kick off.' The rest is history."

Ken immediately set about finding more customers. With some excellent sales over the ensuing months, business was going up and up. The operation closed over Christmas and the New Year. However the tremors of the imminent recession were about to take effect.

By January 1990, several customers were in financial strife and by early February some of them had closed their doors and left Muir with considerable unpaid invoices. Times were tough for the next couple of years, but as the economy improved, business picked up again and Muir were on another roll.

Ken Padgett had worked for the Boral Group for 20 years across Tasmania, Victoria and Queensland. He was in Hobart in January 1975 when the Tasman Bridge collapsed after being hit by the bulk ore carrier, *Lake Illawarra*. That split the city into east and west and launched the ferry operation that precipitated the huge boat building career of Robert Clifford and his business, International Catamarans (Incat).

When Ken took on the Muir distributorship in Queensland, Val Howells came up from Sydney for a couple of days to do the rounds and show him the ropes.

Ken Padgett: "Val was a real rum'un, a one off. I can remember it was June 1989 when I started as the Muir Winches salesman."

(I hear many readers asking, 'What on earth is a rum'un? My research suggests it is a saying that originated in the Yorkshire/Lancashire regions of the UK and was transported, particularly to Tasmania, by convicts. The expression was often used fondly to describe the person as being a 'bit of a character.'

Children were often referred to as being a bit of a 'rum'un' when they had done something quaint. It has nothing to do with that beautiful fluid in those bottles of Bundaberg Rum.)

Muir Engineering's advertising in magazines was extensive and Muir enjoyed a reputation for quality and reliability. That reputation, coupled with the fact that it went hand in glove with respected boat manufacturers, helped enormously.

Ken Padgett: "I was asked by one fellow once why he should use a Muir winch, and I said well Bertram use them, Riviera use them, I went through the whole list, and he thought that was a pretty good recommendation."

But it wasn't all plain sailing. In those early days Ken noticed they were experiencing problems with some of the winch motors. Muir was using an Australian manufacturer and by comparison, the motors Muir were importing from CIMA in Italy were streets ahead.

Ken Padgett: "The situation for us was saved by two things, one was that I was Johnny-on-the-spot up here, and the second was the production bloke they had down there in Tassie, an engineer by the name of Don Di Martino. Don was not only brilliant from a production and mechanical point of view, but he had really good people skills and was excellent in dealing with problems. Don was very much a part of Muir.

"John used to spend an awful lot of his time overseas, promoting his winches. Don looked after the factory and he was well thought of and well respected within the industry. So he was a lot of help. For me it's always a case of 'selling service.' That's what it's all about."

John Muir is fulsome in his praise for Ken Padgett, both the man and the Muir company representative.

"Ken was well-versed in financial matters, and was great with numbers. A big plus was his technical aptitude with mechanical items. He was shrewd and quick on his feet. He was a real people person and introduced me to everyone he knew in the boat building yards. He made it his business to know everybody in the boatyards, from the cleaner, to the sweeper, the receptionist, the accounts payable people, production manager, R&D, sales people, management, directors, right through to the big boss."

In the early 1990s, a lot of boat and yacht manufacturers had moved to Queensland because it was the place to be, particularly on the Gold Coast. Bill Barry-Cotter

moved Mariner (later to become Riviera) up from New South Wales. It was a big operation and soon got even bigger. They went from doing a couple of boats a month, to 30 or 40 a month. Muir was their preferred supplier. It became a great business referral, 'if Mariner was using Muir winches, others should be too.' Mariner and later Riviera were large operators and held in high esteem within the industry.

Ken Padgett: "Within four to five years we'd outgrown our original dual warehouse facility, so Muir purchased a new and larger dual warehouse in Coomera, one of fifty built by Bill Barry-Cotter of Marina and Riviera fame."

The new Muir premises were located across the road from the big, bustling Coomera marina and boat builders on Waterways Drive. The boat show at Sanctuary Cove went from a village affair to a very big and impressive show. It now attracts over 40,000 visitors annually and has over 300 exhibitors with hundreds of boats of all shapes and sizes on show. It has hard stands and floating marinas and is held in May each year when the weather in invariably warm, but not hot. It is so successful that it rivals the Sydney Boat Show.

Ken Padgett: "I personally, along with my wife Leonie, built up strong and lasting relationships with people in the boat building business right through Queensland. As in any business, it's relationships that make the difference.

"I hardly ever saw John, but one day when he was up here I took him to Runaway Bay to meet a guy from Hervey Bay, Danny Drager, who did boat maintenance. I introduced John as John Muir, and Danny's response was, 'Muir?! You mean there is a real Muir? I thought that was just a name you'd thought up for your winches.' The funniest part about that was after seeing Danny we went down to see Bill Barry-Cotter's business, Riviera. It was massive, and there's John introducing himself around and handing out business cards left right and centre, it was a bloody scream.

EARLY ADVERTISING

The 'Porsche' ad is a company classic and John still talks about this now.

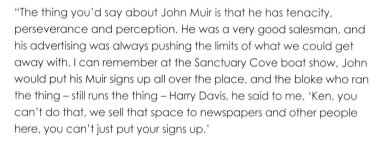

"The thing you'd say about John Muir is that he has tenacity, perseverance and perception. He was a very good salesman, and his advertising was always pushing the limits of what we could get away with. I can remember at the Sanctuary Cove boat show, John would put his Muir signs up all over the place, and the bloke who ran the thing – still runs the thing – Harry Davis, he said to me, 'Ken, you can't do that, we sell that space to newspapers and other people here, you can't just put your signs up.'

"There were times when the signage got ripped down. When John wasn't going to be there, he'd want us to put the signage up and send him a photo to prove we'd put it up. So the group of us would put the sign up, all stand in front of it and take a photo, send it to John, then take the signage back down. You know, I had to live there, you just couldn't do what John wanted.

"But the absolute dogged determination of the man is amazing, he was like a terrier – he got something in his teeth and he just wouldn't let go."

Ken was seeing John in action, working the job the only way he knows how, flat out from dawn to dark, only stopping when the work is done.

"He'd never say die. I can remember we had to go and look at a boat here at Sanctuary Cove. John was up here because the owner wanted him to have a look at something he was having a problem with. So we got there and it's all locked and no one could get in. I said, 'Oh it's locked and he's not on his boat, I'll just go and get security.' As I'm walking away I turn around and there's John scaling the fence, barbed wire at the top, and I said, 'John you can't do that! You'll get arrested.' He didn't care, climbed the fence, went round the other side, opened the gate and told me to come in! Just do it."

Remember this quote from a previous chapter? It reveals the real John Muir at work.

TOP LEFT
Kevin Fleming assisting with sales of the Fleming self-steering products, Sydney Boat Show 1998.

TOP RIGHT
The Muir team at the 1998 Sanctuary Cove Boat Show, from left: Duncan Norton, Hobart; Craig McNaughton, Sydney; John Muir.

MIDDLE
The Muir display with a variety of winches at the 1998 show.

BOTTOM
A Muir Winches sign proudly displayed on the marina.

"When you're looking for new business you usually go in the front door. If you can't get in, you try the side door. If you can't get in there, you go to the window. If you still can't get in there, try the back door. There's no end of ways of getting your toe in the door and keeping on going."

According to Ken Padgett the Muir name became synonymous with quality and reliability. That's one of the reasons the business was successful. Over the years there were some rocky patches, but the Muir name, the quality of the gear and the reports of how well it stood the test when it mattered, built the company brand name.

Ken Padgett: "I can remember talking to a bloke from Simpson Lawrence, the Scottish based winch makers, one of John's biggest competitors, it was back in the early nineties at the Sanctuary Cove Boat Show. He told me how embarrassed he'd been to have a bloke from the company out from England to look around, and, wanting to have a look at one of their winches on a boat. He hadn't been able to find one example – they were all Muir winches! Which was true in those early days, we were just Johnny-on-the-spot, we happened to be here."

The anecdotes are almost endless, but there is one more that is worth the telling. It's an example of how businesses live or die, based solely on reputation and word of mouth.

Ken Padgett: "I didn't ever have a Muir company car, John would pay me my expenses, so I'd just drive my car but it had no signwriting. Muir's advertising was always very good, and they used to have these big blue Muir signs they'd stick on windows in shops. I went and got a bit of that magnetic sign material and stuck it on the car and stuck the Muir sign on.

"John always encouraged me to take my wife Leonie on selling trips. We were in Mackay, on the north coast of Queensland and we were driving down to the marina along the pier past all the boats, to see someone I'd arranged to see who was waiting at the end of the pier. On the way back up the pier, all these fellas had popped up out of their boats to see 'The Muir Man' because they'd seen the sign on the car.

"Then when we'd stopped for a coffee, we came back to the car, and there was a guy leaning on it. He said, 'I've been waiting to see you, you're the Muir Man!'

"John used to stay with us when he'd come up for a visit. We had a little two-story townhouse and he stayed upstairs, we had our bedroom at the bottom of the stairs. In his pockets, John used to have all these air tickets to all manner of destinations because he could never make up his mind where he'd be going next – New Zealand, overseas or home. This trip he had an early morning flight to catch. He always had big bags full of all sorts of anchor winch gear with him. It was the middle of the night and I was woken up to banging and crashing on the stairs. It's John coming down the stairs with all his luggage. I asked, 'What are you doing?!' and he replied, 'Come on I've got a plane to get at half past seven.' And I said, 'John, it's only –' and I looked at the clock and it was 1:30 or something, 'the middle of the bloody night!' 'Bugger me!' he says, 'I've got my watch on upside down!' So we went back to bed.

"But a really good bloke, and was well thought of even by people he'd had a falling out with, and there were falling outs, because of John's sheer doggedness."

> 66 *I can remember talking to a bloke from Simpson Lawrence, the Scottish based winch makers, one of John's biggest competitors, it was back in the early nineties at the Sanctuary Cove Boat Show. He told me how embarrassed he'd been to have a bloke from the company out from England to look around, and, wanting to have a look at one of their winches on a boat. He hadn't been able to find one example – they were all Muir winches!* 99

– KEN PADGETT, MUIR QLD

Sydney based Craig McNaughton, who has been working for John Muir for almost 30 years, agrees with those sentiments.

"He's just so tenacious, but he can be difficult. I said to John many years ago, 'John you're a lovely man, and I love to work with you but I couldn't work in the same place as you, I'd have to be arm's length away.' He just expected things to be done immediately. He'd want things done a certain way because that was his way, and you'd have to try and divert his focus so you could get it done the right way. I didn't mind doing that, because I could see where he wanted to go, but he just wanted to be there immediately. His intentions came from a good place.

"John would come up and he and I would do boat shows. I remember at the Sydney boat show one year, it ran over two weekends so it was ten days straight, nine o'clock in the morning until ten o'clock at night every day. It was John and me on the stand, and you know he's not a young man now, but he wasn't much younger back then. He just had that ability to get it done. He's a very interesting man, because it rubs off on you. It doesn't rub off on some people, but I don't think they're the type of people much would rub off on.

"I've worked for the company for a long time, and if people ask me about the product I tell them I wouldn't sell it if I didn't have faith in it. It's easier for me to be honest about a product than to try and tell stories about it. I have no issues selling our product because it's always been a quality product, and that's due to John. He tended to over engineer things, but I say to people, 'It's designed in Tasmania, they make things heavy-duty down there. It's not going to break.'"

Meanwhile, in the late 1980s back in Europe things were looking good for Muir. John and his sales engineer, Chris Michael, had begun designing and manufacturing much larger anchor and mooring winches and a range of chain compressors. Domestically, they had already supplied and fitted some of this gear to big yachts and cruisers, particularly for Oceanfast in Perth and most of the megayacht builders in New Zealand.

Also at this time came several ground breaking sales for commercial vessels, in particular two 80m hydrographic vessels being built by NQEA in Cairns, Queensland. Following several visits to Cairns by Chris Michael, Muir was awarded the contract to supply the two vessels. The team at Muir Engineering set about designing and manufacturing the internal bull gear and pinion drives along with every other component and the large anchor winch outer housing to fit the vessels. These winch and anchor sets became the first in the horizontal H22000 series with chain gypsies to suit 38mm stud link anchor chain.

In 1990, quotes were called by the UK based Pendennis Shipyard for the complete refit of one of the world's biggest superyachts, *Adix*, a 56.1m three masted schooner. Its overall length with the bowsprit is 64.8m.

GOOD PEOPLE MAKE THE COMPANY

Top: Chris Michael with Paul Rienks from Cramm Hydraulics at the Fort Lauderdale Boat Show, mid-2000s. Chris was a long-time employee of Muir and one of John's right-hand men.
Bottom: Craig McNaughton, during preparations for **Show Me** (**Westward II**'s *original name when purchased) to be sailed back to Hobart in 2002.*

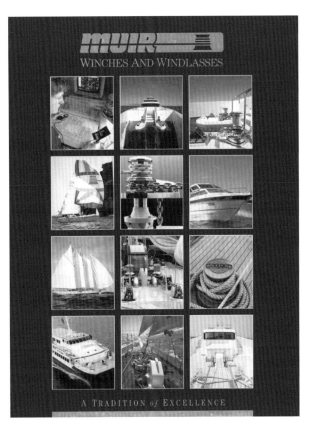

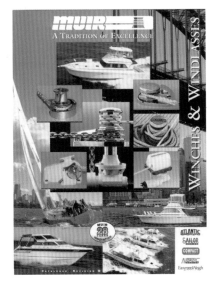

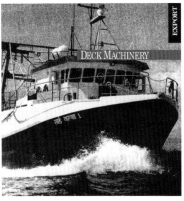

ABOVE: MOVING INTO THE BIG GAME

Various Muir 1980s and 1990s advertisements and brochures.

Fortunately for John he was in Amsterdam at the time, exhibiting at the 1990 METS, the world's largest marine equipment trade show. Visitors were just starting to come by and one of them looked up at the display and noticed the Muir name and asked John if this Muir came from Tasmania. It was Paul Goss, the Project Manager for the *Adix* rebuild and the man who was to become the vessel's skipper. It was a case of, 'Gooday John, Hello Paul, long time no see mate.'

John Muir and Paul Goss not only knew each other, they were both born in Tasmania. They would spend time remembering happy days sailing dinghies at the Sandy Bay Sailing Club when they were in their early teens. A classic case of a single degree of separation. Paul was another of many Tasmanians, who as a young man, had left home to seek adventure and made a career sailing the world. He was living in Europe and managing the huge re-fit of *Adix*.

Adix was originally built in Spain and launched as *Jessica*. Australian businessman Alan Bond bought *Jessica* in the mid-late 1980s and renamed her *XXXX* in promotion for his brewery. ('*XXXX*' stands for Four X, a popular brand of Australian beer, particularly in Queensland.) Pendennis Shipyard undertook a complete refit of *Adix* in 1991.

John Muir: "It was really great to meet up with Paul Goss again at the METS boat show. I hadn't seen him since he left Hobart as a young lad to crew on European motor and sail yachts. After METS was over and our gear packed up, I went down to Cornwall to see the boat and chat to Paul. He told me our competition were aggressively chasing the *Adix* order.

"Before seeing the yacht and when working up our quote, I had priced up smaller anchor winches, VRC10000 and VC10000 mooring capstans, suitable for anchor chain up to 22mm. This was based on what Paul said Maxwell was quoting. The quote was around $80,000. However, when I flew to the UK after METS and visited the Pendennis Shipyard to check the scope and size of the boat, I am so glad I made the visit because it turned out to be critical in the end. I was checking whether or not the gear I had included in the quote was the right gear for a vessel of this size.

"When I climbed up on the stern of Adix and looked along the deck to the bow I saw she was a monster of a sailing yacht, and to be honest I felt quite sick and could not get up the courage to tell Paul I had priced up winches that would be too small. However, they were a similar size to the models he proposed to buy from our competitor."

METS BOAT SHOWS
Some typical Muir displays from the early 1990s at the METS (Marine Equipment Trade Show) held annually in Amsterdam.

John and Paul bid farewell, John held his tongue and flew home. When he arrived back in Hobart he went straight to the waterfront engineering workshop adjacent to Muir Boatyard at Battery Point to meet Bob Harper. John had with him several sketches of the *Adix* foredeck and some larger sizing ideas drawn over a copy of the original VRC10000 plans. Bob Harper was a long time employee, a knowledgeable and very capable all-rounder who could turn his hand

GROUNDBREAKING

The 26mm chain stopper for **Adix** *was a new design pioneered by Bob Harper and developed at Battery Point.*

❝ To boot, we now had two new models in one: VRC13000 with a 14 inch brake and a VRC15000 with an 18 inch brake. ❞

to virtually anything. He had served his apprenticeship as a fitter and turner at the well-known jam maker, Henry Jones IXL, located on the Hobart docks. Bob had also owned and operated his own business in the timber sawmill industry prior to joining Muir.

John Muir: "We looked over the sketches and after some head scratching Bob looked up at me and said, 'John why don't you leave this all with me. You go home, rest up for a few days, and when you come back I will have looked into the Lloyds rules for the size of the anchor chain because as you know that determines the chain gypsy sizing. Then I'll lay everything out on an 8 x 4 sheet of plywood and we can look over it.

"Back in those days we didn't have CAD software at Battery Point although we had just started using it at Kingston. At this time, all winch design and development was done at Battery Point. CAD was still very new, and computers were not as ubiquitous as they are in our business now.

"On the morning of my third day home I went to see Bob and revisit the project. To my delight he had drawn up full size plans by hand – every component for the aft mooring capstan and the anchor windlass. On the other side of the plywood – was a design for a 26mm chain stopper complete with locking pawl and curved chain pipe. There were even two different brake bands for stud link chain in 22mm and 26mm

sizes. To boot, we now had two new models in one: VRC13000 with a 14 inch brake and a VRC15000 with an 18 inch brake."

"You might find it hard to believe but we didn't have a 26mm chain sample, Bob actually cut to size, using scissors, the 26mm standard and joiner links out of thin cardboard, eight links in total. He used them as the anchor chain for the chain gypsy pattern. We still use this same 26mm pattern for other projects without any changes since that time. Further proof of Bob's ingenuity."

After agreeing on a couple of minor changes, Bob got underway building all the patterns in wood. Everything was completed and ready to cast within two weeks. Muir grabbed the opportunity, built the patterns and tooling for a new, larger range of winches, VRC13000/15000 and VC13000/15000, all hydraulic drives with other accessories such as chain stoppers and chain pipes. All the patterns were made at the workshop in Battery Point, with the assistance of one of the boatyard shipwrights. It was quite a challenge because *Adix* was a very large three-masted schooner. All the winch gear was cast locally at Retlas Bronze in Hobart, then machined and polished in the Battery Point workshop.

Polished aluminium-bronze maintains a gold-like appearance. The *Adix* logo, which was designed by Paul Goss who had previously worked as a graphic designer, was cast in the same material and affixed to the drum tops of the windlasses and capstans.

Big order for a queen of the seas

A CHANCE meeting at the Metz marine exhibition trade show in Holland at the end of last year has resulted in an order for Tasmanian-made winches for one of the largest and most lavishly appointed yachts in the world.

It is the Spanish-built, steel-hulled Adix, built as Jessica and once used by Alan Bond, a 61.8-metre, three-masted topsail schooner with upper and lower square topsails and gaff-rigged on all three masts.

Adix has a beam of 8.6 metres, teak decks and teak-clad deckhouses with aluminium masts, topmasts and yards and sitka spruce booms and gaffs.

The superb yacht also has a working sail area of 1391 square metres and such extras as air-conditioning, double cabins with separate showers and a crew of 19.

Now, as part of a refit, Adix is to have two 10,000 vertical hydraulic winches and two 5000 hydraulic aft capstan winches custom-made in aluminium bronze by Muir Engineering Pty Ltd at Kingston.

Managing director of the company, Mr John Muir, said the winches were the largest ever made by his company.

The order came after a former Tasmanian, Paul Goss, who left his home State 20 years ago and has since been master on many large yachts, saw John Muir at the Metz marine show and told him about the refit of the giant Adix.

Mr Muir said landing the contract was part of Muir's major export business which has helped offset the slump in the Australian pleasure boat industry.

● The Adix under full sail. This 61.8-metre, three-masted topsail schooner is beautifully fitted out.

John Muir: "After just 14 weeks it was time for workshop testing of the equipment by the local Lloyds surveyor Chris Wells. It passed, then followed final buffing and polishing, we packed everything really well and shipped out these magnificent polished aluminium-bronze winches bound for Pendennis Shipyard in Cornwall.

"Following shipment, I called Paul Goss and told him we *had* to make the winches 40% larger, in both size and capacity, due to the larger 26mm stud link anchor chain required and according to Lloyd's class rules."

John had not contacted Paul Goss at all during this time. He, Bob and the crew had simply charged on regardless, building winch gear that they knew a yacht of this size would need. It was only when the order was shipped out of Hobart John rang Paul to let him know what had transpired and why.

John Muir: "Paul's reply was, 'Ok John, when the gear arrives I will show The Boss.' Paul called me eight weeks later when the gear arrived by sea at the Pendennis Shipyard in Cornwall. The owner was with Paul when he called me, and he was ecstatic, as was Paul, and couldn't believe his eyes. He asked me to let him know what the extra cost was and I later told him if he could just cover the cost of time, tooling and larger castings that would do us. This was an additional cost of around

66 *The owner was with Paul when he called me, and he was ecstatic, as was Paul, and couldn't believe his eyes.* 99

ABOVE: MAKING NEWS
The Adix refit and subsequent Muir winches order was a big deal. Article: The Mercury

OPPOSITE: UNDER FULL SAIL
Adix during the 2014 Pendennis Cup. Photo © Nick Bailey courtesy of Pendennis Shipyard.

40 percent, but the owner paid up willingly. This project opened the door for more and larger vertical windlass sales going forward."

John Muir is obviously not your average businessman. He could have jacked up the price of that new and larger gear, to ensure a hefty profit. No. That's not the way he does business and his clients would all soon know that. It would help any client to relax when dealing with Muir Engineering, to know that they are not racketeers, driven by corporate greed, but true craftsmen intent on supplying the best possible product to the highest possible standard.

On her way back from a voyage to the Antarctic Peninsula in 1995, the beautiful lady *Adix*, with skipper Paul and crew, arrived in Hobart on the morning of the Sandy Bay Regatta. She was an amazing sight to see, full sails set as she came up the River Derwent towards the Hobart Docks.

12 months later, as we read in the Introduction to this book, the Muir anchor systems would be tested to the limits when *Adix* was anchored in the Chilean Archipelago and a katabatic storm hit.

Paul Goss again: "Although we heard all the stories about the weather, it is hard to be prepared for the ferocity of it until you are actually there. What is a still, attractive bay on arrival, can very quickly transform into a spume blown cauldron. The anchorage we chose was virtually land-locked with a narrow entrance, outside of which was a tight and complicated waterway where every stony wall has the potential to be a lee shore. This particular night we decided to swing to the anchor as the weather looked settled and quiet. However, by nightfall, the wind banged in quickly, and by midnight it came out of the darkness with great force. It is always a katabatic wind with no settled direction due to the rocky, mountainous terrain, and although we anchored with a lot of scope, we were now at its mercy with no room to escape.

"We will never know if the anchor was in sand or not, but it was a very rocky bottom, and it was probably a combination of this and the right ground tackle that kept us secure that wild night. With no constant wind strength and direction, the heavy moisture-laden gusts were coming from different quarters, and the boat would accelerate away until the chain took up and arrested her motion. We stood watch all night of course, but there was really nothing we could do except hang on and bear it. When the chain came up hard, it would pull you off your feet if you weren't prepared for the sudden snatch of the cable. All night she yawed, juddered and snatched at her anchor, while the noise of the chain over the rocks meant no rest for the off-watch.

"By 0830 hours the next morning there was not a breath of wind in the cove. We set about hauling the chain, and miraculously, it came aboard in one piece and undamaged. We marveled at the bright spots of raw metal covering the chain where it had been scoured by the rocks, stark evidence of the torture the cable endured all night long.

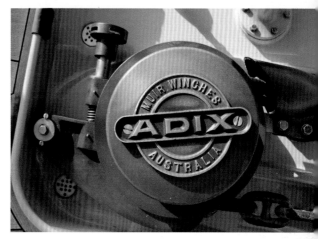

ABOVE: NEW DESIGNS

*Cast in aluminium bronze, the mooring and winch gear for **Adix** was designed to develop a patina over time, appropriate to the style of the yacht.*

OPPOSITE, TOP: MAGNIFICENT

***Adix** during the 2014 Pendennis Cup.*
Photos: © Andrew Wright, courtesy Pendennis Shipyard.

"In thirty five years at sea as a professional, the experience of that night remains as the greatest endorsement of good gear. Our Muir capstans and windlasses have served us well over the years, and will continue to do so for a long time to come. Give me plenty of good chain and the right gear to handle it, every time."

It is the combination of John Muir, his workshop team and support staff who have built the business' enviable winch and anchor gear's global reputation as one of, if not the, best in the industry. Not only did they storm into the mega winch market with installations on boats like Adix, but they also built a really solid reputation as Australia's best winch maker. It's one of the reasons why, in Australia, nationally acclaimed boat builders like Bill Barry-Cotter and many others ended up as solid Muir customers.

A brief potted history of Bill Barry-Cotter, an extraordinary man, and his businesses, is warranted. In 1960 a young Bill started work as an apprentice boat builder with Neville Steber, brother of Stebercraft's Bruce Steber. Neville ran a Sydney based company called Clinker Craft.

So began a remarkable and life long association with the global marine industry, culminating in Bill Barry-Cotter becoming one of the world's most respected and internationally renowned boat builders.

A few years after Bill had finished his apprenticeship, he moved from Clinker Craft to work with another Australian marine industry stalwart, Cedric Williams. Bill's story is all about seeing opportunities

ABOVE: BOATBUILDING AND PROPERTY LEGEND

Bill Barry-Cotter and John have had a long business relationship.
Photo: Mike Batterham / Newspix

BELOW: VRC4500

The most popular type of winch model designed for motor cruisers up to 20m.

OPPOSITE: MUIR QLD

Muir's Coomera warehouse and distribution headquarters. The drums are full of anchor chain of various sizes.

and taking them. 'Carpe Diem' or Seize the Day could easily be Bill's motto. When Cedric Williams decided to stop boat building and retire, the young entrepreneur got his first real break.

"Cedric did me a real favour because when he stopped boat building, he gave me a lot of workshop machinery and it was from this point that Mariner Cruisers was born in 1966."

Bill was 22 years old. He started building boats the traditional way, in timber, the way he had been taught as an apprentice. Timber boats soon gave way to the new technology of fibreglass, Mariner Cruisers built its last timber boat — a 40 footer in 1968. With the arrival of the new fibreglass age, the company forged ahead, taking on the Sydney based competition that included old stagers such as Halvorsen, Griffin, Quilkey, Bracken and Swanson.

In 1968, when he first set up Mariner, Bill moved the operation to Darley Street, Mona Vale (in New South Wales), and just a few kilometres from the original facility. Two men who are still on the staff of Riviera Marine today joined the company — Bob Haygarth and Peter Brown. (Several other employees from the early days are still involved more than 33 years on.) Now that alone tells you something about the man in charge, low staff turnover usually comes with intense job satisfaction. In 1975 Bill purchased the original Garden Street premises and built his first boat manufacturing facility to his own design, eventually employing a staff of 60. The first 'glass boat

MARITIMO MODELS

Maritimo have been using Muir equipment on their yachts since the company was founded.

was really 'half and half', a 25 footer with a fibreglass hull and timber cabin. The first all-fibreglass boat, the 30ft Mariner, was followed by a range that really set Mariner Cruiser soaring. More than 400 Mariner Pacers up to 26.5ft were sold. Two fly bridge cruisers were then introduced and became synonymous with the Mariner name — the 31 and 34. The company also delivered more than 100 Mariner 43s — the dreamboat of game fishermen of the day.

The business was up and running and the marine world was at Bill's fingertips.

John Muir first met Bill Barry-Cotter in the early 1970s when he visited Mariner Cruisers large fibreglass production complex in Mona Vale, on the northern beaches of Sydney. He hadn't seen a pleasure boat production facility of its size and layout in any of his travels throughout Australia. The two began what is still to this day, an enduring business relationship and friendship.

John Muir: "My father Jock Muir was well known in Sydney boat building and sailing circles and had met Bill in Hobart after a Sydney to Hobart race.

"At the time there were quite a few other boat builders in Sydney that I was starting to do business with, so when I found out how big Mariner was getting, I decided to pay them a visit.

"By the time I re-visited the facility, Bill had sold the business. Mariner's Production Manager was a Tasmanian who

John knew from his sailing days, Nick Wells. Nick had spent a decade or more crewing on the big sail boat racing circuit in North America. I think Nick and another Hobart sailor, Andrew Crisp both crewed for Jim Kilroy, owner of the big American racing yacht, *Kialoa III*."

Tasmanian dinghy sailors enjoyed a good reputation for offshore racing and were much sought after and also well rewarded in US dollars. Andrew Crisp and two other Tasmanian sailors, including Robert Vaughan, who is mentioned in an upcoming chapter, were on board *Kialoa III* on 29 December 1975 when she took line honours in the Sydney to Hobart race. Andrew Crisp returned to Hobart in the early 1990s and took up a sales management position with Muir Engineering in Kingston. Nick kept working at Mariner.

"US maxi ketch *Kialoa III* set a benchmark elapsed time record for the 628 nautical mile race, a record that was to stand unchallenged for a remarkable 21 years. *Kialoa III*, a Sparkman & Stephens design owned by Californian yachtsman and Silicon Valley corporate executive Jim Kilroy, was already a world champion maxi yacht when she came to Australia in December 1975."*

John Muir: "I was fortunate to meet up with Nick again at Mariner Cruisers, now under new ownership and he showed me around the factory. Bill had sold Mariner in 1970, having established the business in 1966. Bill later bought the business back in 1988 for a song."

* Source: http://www.rolexsydneyhobart.com/news/2005/pre-race/kialoa%E2%80%99s-race-record-remembered-30-years-later/

John had with him a car boot full of winches, as he was keen to get Mariner's business. At that time he remembers they were fitting Vetus anchor winches, made in Holland. He sent a detailed written offer to Mariner and Nick - and was successful, even though he had to reduce his price by 15% to counter the competition.

John Muir: "In a short time we received a good stock order from Mariner. After Bill had sold the company, I made a follow-up call to Mariner. It all progressed from there and within six months we were fortunate to have all the Mariner winch business."

In 1980, Bill Barry-Cotter returned to the marine industry business with a vengeance, establishing Riviera, with a large manufacturing plant on the northern end of Queensland's Gold Coast at Coomera. Ironically 10 years after selling Mariner for several million dollars he purchased it back from the liquidators, and moved the entire operation and its equipment to Queensland to form part of the Riviera stable.

All of Bill Barry-Cotter's boats manufactured at the Riviera plant were fitted with Muir winches and gear. There were a handful of exceptions, one in particular was when the Queensland agent for a European company sold Riviera an anchor winch for Bill's own motor cruiser. Ken Padgett got a call from Riviera following tests undertaken by Bill Barry-Cotter who evidentially said it wouldn't pull your hat off! Should've been a Muir!

John Muir: "Business was going well for Muir and in discussion with our Queensland Manager, Ken Padgett and his offsider (and future son-in-law) Michael Trickey, we agreed Coomera was to be our next move! By this time Michael Trickey had taken over the management of the Queensland operation from Ken Padgett, who retired after more than two decades with Muir.

> 66 *After Bill had sold the company, I made a follow-up call to Mariner. It all progressed from there and within six months we were fortunate to have all the Mariner winch business.* 99

– JOHN MUIR

"We eventually purchased one of Bill's larger dual warehouses. It was right across the road from the Gold Coast City Marina and we moved in several weeks later. It was fantastic to have a new and much larger facility and our customers driving in and out of the marina couldn't help but to notice where we were! We had a second smaller warehouse at the rear which we rented out to a marine fit out business and they have been there ever since."

After a brief and well-earned break Bill Barry-Cotter launched into the next stage of his boat-building career starting Maritimo in 2002. It was established in a state-of-the-art manufacturing centre virtually across the road from Riviera in the Gold Coast Marine Precinct of Coomera.

ABOVE: CHEETAH, JAGUAR, THOR
The H2500 'Cheetah', H3500 'Jaguar' and H4000 'Thor' – three of the Muir horizontal anchor winch models used on Maritimo motor yachts.

Bill Barry-Cotter: "They were the heady pre-GFC (Global Financial Crisis) days and at the Sanctuary Cove International Boat Show in 2007 we released a new model, the Maritimo 52 sky lounge, we sold 15 at the show. But it kept getting better because in the weeks after the show our orders doubled to a total of 30. Things were really firing."

The GFC's impact on the boat manufacturing industry worldwide is well documented and in the years after the financial meltdown Bill Barry-Cotter downsized his operation and stuck rigidly to his core strengths of producing high quality, high performance vessels that were perfectly suited to the tough Australian boating conditions.

In the years since the GFC, Maritimo has grown, improved and been at the forefront of international boat building delivering a range of new models with unsurpassed levels of luxury, fit-out, design and performance. In the past few years Maritimo's international dealer network and sales have increased significantly.

John Muir: "When we discussed which anchor winches we could supply to Maritimo, Bill's preference back then (and remains the same today) is for horizontal anchor winches. Bill maintains horizontal winches are better for his boats because the winch housing is all above deck, and encloses the gearbox and motor assembly. Everything is above deck, and clear from the chains vertical fall to the chain locker below deck. He also wants detachable emergency manual override handles that can be used standing up or bending over if required, with a 'back and forward' lever operation. Finally a horizontal capstan on the port side of the winch gives the user the ability to stand up and 'tail the line off' while using the capstan.

"I have had a continuous and congenial association spanning almost 40 years with Bill Barry-Cotter from the early days of Mariner, Riviera then Maritimo and beyond. The same goes for other major Australian boat builders like the Spooner family and Caribbean and the Steber family and Stebercraft."

John's former manager for his Queensland operation, Ken Padgett, sums those times up beautifully.

Ken Padgett: "They were the halcyon days of boating in Queensland. I remember boating was very big; Riviera used to tell me they'd get the real estate salesmen in there and they wouldn't ask how much a boat was, they'd just say they want to buy it and ask how much a month was it going to cost them. They were living off real estate inflation, the Gold Coast and southeast Queensland were booming."

MARITIMO AND MUIR
A Maritimo 60 fitted with a Muir H4000 in 2004.

"Wendy Muir stayed with us sometimes while John was here, he'd pop in from overseas somewhere, and then he was going off somewhere and he couldn't make his mind up whether he was going to New Zealand, or overseas or somewhere else, or back home to Tassie.

"He confessed to me that he was never more relaxed or happy than when he was getting on an aeroplane to head overseas. I think he liked to get away, and in those days of course he had Don Di Martino down south to rely on, the factory was happening alright, and he'd go away pushing his mega winches."

THE NINETIES ROLL ON

Before we sail on through the 1990s and reveal more of the trials, tribulations and successes of John Muir and his business, Muir Engineering, it strikes me that it is a timely moment to reflect on who this John Muir fellow really is.

He has been variously described as dogmatic, passionate, brilliant, focussed, relentless and driven by a bloody minded determination, obstinate, half street fighter, half gentleman and extremely passionate.

John admits he can be hard and fierce, but also says he has a soft and gentle side. However, throughout the anecdotes and recollections of the many people from all over the world who have met and either worked for or been a client of John Muir, there is an underlying level of respect and admiration.

"John Muir is a legend of the Australian marine industry… and a good mate!"

"John is a great believer in established quality, but also a champion of innovation."

"I have never heard John whinge or complain."

"The Muir brand has a stellar reputation globally and I cannot remember the last time we had a warranty issue."

"John is a lovely likable man. At every boat show that we've been to, John is always a thorough gentleman, always knowledgeable and always supportive."

"He's just so tenacious, but he can be difficult."

One wonders if these are the characteristics you need in order to build a successful global business? Especially when your business is based in Tasmania, thousands of kilometres from the largest markets and up against other globally successful winch manufacturers, located virtually next door to the boat builders John wants as clients.

In an article written by Steven Benna, for the magazine Business Insider Australia in August 2015, Steven quotes Ray Carvey, Executive Vice President of Corporate Learning at Harvard Business Publishing, a subsidiary of the

Harvard Business School at Harvard University near Boston, USA, listing eight critical leadership traits that are essential for global business success.

1. Effective leaders manage complexity. Leaders who know how to manage complexity are skilled at solving problems and making decisions under fast-changing systems.

2. Effective leaders manage global businesses. This includes assessing what's happening with consumers, competitors, the economy and the politics of the markets in which their businesses operate.

3. Effective leaders act strategically. Leaders must always be prepared to adjust their strategies to capture emerging opportunities or tackle unexpected challenges.

4. Effective leaders foster innovation. Regardless of how successful something may be, there can always be an emphasis on innovation. Effective leaders understand this and are focussed on taking a business to the next level.

5. Effective leaders leverage networks. Successful leaders take networking as a way to benefit the organisation and create relationships with customers, suppliers, strategic partners and even competitors.

6. Effective leaders inspire engagement. It's absolutely crucial to keep employees at all levels of an organisation interested and engaged in the work being done.

7. Effective leaders develop personal adaptability. Adaptable leaders steer clear of a 'that's how we've always done it' mentality.

8. Effective leaders cultivate learning agility. Effective leaders take the initiative in finding opportunities to learn. They take time to reflect on their experiences so they can learn from successes and failures.

Of course no one business leader is perfect and would be able to tick every one of those eight boxes, but as you read, mark, learn and inwardly digest the stories, anecdotes and experiences of John Muir, you can see that many of these qualities are embedded in his business operating DNA. In particular his capacity to establish networks, foster innovation and spread his Muir passion.

Ray Carvey describes today's business world as "volatile, uncertain, complex and ambiguous," and says it's crucial to stay productive through this time of change. John Muir and most of his senior people would certainly attest to that. Muir Engineering has successfully negotiated its way through a 'Recession We had to Have', the GFC and a very volatile Australian dollar.

A classic example of many of these leadership skills at work is evident in the next narrative centered on another international and very important Muir customer, mega ship builder Oceanco and the suggestion that Muir get into stainless steel fabrication early.

… You can see that many of these qualities are embedded in his business operating DNA. In particular his capacity to establish networks, foster innovation and spread his Muir passion.

ABOVE AND OPPOSITE
Oceanco's shipyard in Alblasserdam, Netherlands, 2013.

Oceanco is a privately owned custom motor yacht builder. The company boasts that it does not focus on quantity of builds, but rather the world's best quality. Since its inception in 1987, the Dutch firm has built around 26 full displacement hull megayachts, ranging from 50m to over 110m in length.

Without doubt these are stunning motor yachts. Beautifully engineered and fitted out to perfection. Muir gear fits that description as well.

Oceanco operates from a large shipyard in Alblasserdam, near Rotterdam, in a newly completed facility (2013) and is regarded as 'state of the art,' equipped with a private harbour and a climate-controlled building for new construction and refitting of superyachts, and very large motor and sailing yachts, up to 130m. In January 2016 Oceanco launched an 85m dyna rig ketch, then more recently a 106m three-mast sailing yacht. Like the best of Dutch shipyards it thrives on innovation and the pursuit of excellence. One quick glance at the images of the yachts already launched bears strong testament to that business ethos.

The company lends its name to some of the yachting world's most recognisable vessels including *Indian Empress* and *Anastasia*. Remarkably, both vessels are fitted with Muir anchor and mooring winches.

John Muir: "Around 1998 I received a phone call from Gary Bradshaw, the Technical Director for Oceanco, later to become Oceanco's Managing Director. Gary mentioned he was in Australia managing the construction of two steel luxury motor yachts, a 52m and 55m and was interested to buy Australian made Muir anchor and mooring winches. He specified he wanted them made in 316 polished stainless steel and not chrome on bronze. That meant a significant change of direction for us and our stainless steel supplier, Skeels and Perkins. It wasn't just innovation, new tooling was also required.

"Skeels and Perkins (now Apco Engineering) had never worked stainless steel before, so we were all on a steep learning curve.

"This marked the point where Alan and Andrew Perkins decided to move Skeels and Perkins into stainless steel components and we shook hands on the understanding that this would be a long term business arrangement with Muir Engineering."

'We shook hands.' Note that. No contracts, no lawyers, no weeks of delay while contracts are drawn up, it was a case of 'let's get on and do it!' They did.

Surveying those leadership skills above, reveals this is a chance for John Muir to use four at once. Building the global business, acting strategically, fostering innovation and expanding and leveraging his networks. Of course this text book description of what would have been going on in John's head bears no resemblance to the reality of his brain and thought processes at the time. Quickly surveying the new opportunity, John realised it was another chance to expand his capacity, work a bit harder and longer and get excited in the process. John loves building things!

This is not the moment to pause, reflect on questions such as, "Am I following my leadership plans and format?" No it is a time for quick reflection, decisions and action. Just what any old sea dog worth his salt has learnt to do.

John Muir: "Gary was looking to purchase two ship sets of polished 316 stainless steel VRC15000 vertical hydraulic anchor winches, VC13000 mooring capstans, anchoring systems (chain stoppers) and chain pipes. Anchor chain size was to be 20mm for stud cable. All this was for the construction of the 52m and 55m steel motor yachts.

"At the time we were manufacturing several sets of vertical VRC15000, hard wearing, aluminium-bronze anchor winches and mooring capstans."

Quickly surveying the new opportunity, John realised it was another chance to expand his capacity, work a bit harder and longer and get excited in the process. John loves building things!

Gary Bradshaw: "I had a number of discussions with John Muir in 1998, regarding the development of a range of non-cast 316 stainless steel anchor and mooring systems for large luxury yachts. My experience, over 20 years of building and engineering of luxury yachts, is that 316 castings can bleed on anchoring systems. The corrosion appears from areas where it's not possible to machine away the surface.

"I remember I advised Muir Engineering that, should they pursue manufacturing a range of stainless steel anchoring and mooring systems, it would greatly enhance their business worldwide. The owners of these large luxury vessels do not like to see any contamination of the expensive stainless steel equipment on their yachts.

"I also told John that if Muir do proceed and develop this new range of windlasses for luxury yachts manufactured from bar and flat stock, machined and welded, they will have eliminated the possibility of bleeding which will be a big boost to their megayacht business and the windlass industry as a whole."

John Muir: "These were to be our first medium size mega winches in polished stainless steel. We spoke to our long-time local supplier, Skeels and Perkins (now Apco Engineering), managed by brothers Alan and Andrew Perkins, as they would need to re-tool in order to meet our needs for the stainless steel components. This marked the point where Skeels and Perkins extended their capabilities to supply stainless steel, on the understanding that there would be long term business from Muir Engineering.

"We agreed to modifications to some of our existing patterns and made several new tooling patterns due to the different shrinkage and tolerances of cast stainless steel. In a matter of a few weeks we received the valued order for two ship sets from the shipyard, for the 52m motor yacht *Sunrise* and the 55m motor yacht *Lady Christine*. Within three months of receiving the order all the equipment was machined, tested and approved by the local Lloyds surveyor.

"Following the test approvals we commenced polishing in-house and sub-contracting out some to our local polisher, Hobart Plating Company, with whom we'd worked continuously for more than 40 years under three owners/operators. All external surfaces on all above deck components were polished to the highest quality mirror finish."

Muir received another order from Gary Bradshaw for two ship sets of much larger anchor and mooring equipment, for two large 80m motor yachts being constructed under Gary's supervision in South Africa. These yachts were later launched as *Stargate I* (now named *Constellation*), 1999, and *Stargate II*, 2001. At that time the VRC22000 anchor windlasses and capstans were the largest vertical units Muir had manufactured and supplied at the time. Just as the orders from Oceanco were ramping up, another unexpected bonus and substantial new customer was just around the corner.

John Muir: "I was with Duncan Norton, Muir Sales at the METS boat show in the late 1990s, the largest marine equipment trade show in the world. We had one of our very large, highly polished stainless steel VRC22000 electric anchor winches on display. It was just there for the boat show and would then be shipped to Oceanco for the new build *Stargate* motor yachts.

"Around the corner came a familiar face, it was Mr Tom de Vries whom I had got to know very well from my ongoing visits to the Feadship shipyards. When Tom sighted the big gleaming vertical anchor winch, he said to me, 'Well Mr Muir, it looks like you have finally arrived. We want to talk to you about an order.' "

There was never a sweeter moment for John Muir's professional career. He had arrived. He now had a chance to become a supplier to one of the world's most respected megayacht builders. This is the moment when John realised what all his hard fought efforts over the preceding years were all about and for John Muir it doesn't get any better than that.

John Muir: "It was mentioned to me that I would need to liaise with the owner's representative, an American, AJ Anderson, who I was informed would ultimately make the decision about what equipment would be installed on his owner's motor yacht.

"AJ Anderson was the most discerning owner's representative I had ever worked with. After some protracted negotiations he agreed to order Muir products for the boat in question, MY *Rasselas*. This was to be a new chapter for Muir winches and for me. It still remains as one of my proudest moments when the order finally came through, complete with the title, de Vries purchasing office!

"There is another side to AJ Anderson, he was fair and reasonable if there was a problem, but it needed to be rectified quickly."

It had taken John Muir almost ten years of hard slog and ongoing visits to Europe and the Netherlands, meeting with engineering and purchasing and members of the de Vries family.

That's what you call persistence!

TOP LEFT
METS 2001, left to right: Simon Pettitt, John Muir and Chris Michael.

ABOVE AND OPPOSITE
*Motor yacht **Rasselas**, the first winch order from Feadship, which had taken nearly ten years to secure. Opposite photo: Feadship.*

Getting a break with new business — for any manufacturer — entails some risk for the manufacturer as well as the customer. For Muir Engineering, having customers like Oceanco and Feadship was a big leap into polished stainless steel megayacht anchoring systems. Customers like Gary Bradshaw of Oceanco gave Muir the opportunity to enter the big boat market by having faith in Muir Engineering's quality. Delivery and local service was arranged well ahead of time with Cramm Engineering in the North of Holland.

John Muir: "There have been instances where our level of service and commitment to a customer have been stretched to the limit. We have always managed to deliver. Take this example. When Oceanco were taking delivery of the *Stargate* ship sets, each weighing over a tonne, one of the big vertical windlasses fell off the delivery truck, damaging the gear drive. As soon as I received a call alerting me to the accident, I rang Reinhardt Heemstra, one of the directors from Cramm, told him what had happened. Next morning the Cramm service truck was at the shipyard repairing the damage. That's the level of service customers expect us to deliver."

Fortunately Oceanco were to become long term customers and using another of those leadership principles, 'leverage,' John was in a position to say to other megayacht builders, no matter where they were located, hand on heart, "Muir supply complete anchor and mooring systems for large sail and motor yachts in highly polished 316 grade stainless steel," and John could look them straight in the eye when he did. Having a satisfied customer almost always leads onto new business. Keep in mind that Europe was the home of some of the best and long established anchor and mooring winch makers in the world, so reputation and customer satisfaction were key factors in Muir's sales success.

Gary Bradshaw: "As an Australian I was interested in the possibility of John's company being able to build anchor winches and capstans of a high quality to suit our luxury motor yachts. At the time we were using winches from Steen, a European Company.

"I was convinced that John's company would deliver the quality I expected, and when the first winches and capstans arrived in our shipyard in Alblasserdam, Holland, all personnel were totally amazed at the quality of the equipment from Down Under.

"It was evident to our Purchasing Department, and it was my conviction that Muir would become our primary anchor handling and capstan supplier."

The first orders to Muir Engineering from Oceanco had been for what are now regarded as small motor yachts, 52m and 55m. The following year Gary contacted Muir again about supplying anchor and mooring winch gear for a considerably larger 96m motor yacht. He wanted a complete ship set of dual installation VRC22000 two speed vertical anchor winches, VC22000 mooring capstans two speed AC electric, chain compressors to suit 34mm grade 3 chain and mooring capstans for a motor yacht launched as *Al Mirqab*.

At the same time as the orders for megayachts were arriving, Muir was also producing hundreds of sets of small to medium size winches for pleasure and work boat builders within Australia and overseas. It was a time of frenetic activity at the Muir works in Kingston.

John Muir: "Fortunately we had all the tooling and patterns to hand, and the main technical difference was the requirement to fit up larger capacity gear drives, larger electric motors and controls. Now, with these larger windlasses and capstans, we were on the cusp of the 100m plus megayacht market.

"In 2009 came an enquiry and subsequent order for the 85m *Anastasia*, another ship set of 400 volt three phase electric drive anchor and mooring winches, and anchoring systems (chain compressors and turning rollers). Chris Michael and I worked through these interesting times of design, development and testing of the larger units. Chris was actively involved in commissioning Muir equipment, including the larger units manufactured for Oceanco. He was a lateral thinker and unafraid to try new ways of doing things."

The rest for Oceanco, as they say, is history. Muir Engineering went on to supply equipment for a number of luxury megayachts built by Oceanco including:

- 80m *Stargate I*, now named *Constellation*, (launched 1999) – one ship set: two VRC22000 anchor winches, two VC20000 mooring winches and two anchoring systems, electrical control cabinets and switch gear.

- 95m *Al Mirqab*, now named *Indian Empress*, (launched 2000) – one ship set: two VRC22000 anchor winches, two VC20000 mooring winches and two anchoring systems, electrical control cabinets and switch gear.

- 52m *Sunrise* (launched 2000) – two VRC13000, two VC13000, two anchoring systems, electrical control cabinets and switch gear.

- 56m *Lady Christine*, now named *Queen Mavia*, (launched 2001) – two VRC13000, two VC13000, two anchoring systems, electrical control cabinets and switch gear.

- 59m *Pegasus*, now named *Helios*, (launched 2001) – two VRC13000, two VC13000, two anchoring systems, electrical control cabinets and switch gear.

- 80m *Stargate II* (launched 2001) – one ship set: two VRC22000 anchor winches, two VC20000 mooring winches and two anchoring systems, electrical control cabinets and switch gear.

- 56m *Ambrosia* (launched 2006) – two VRC13000, two VC13000, two anchoring systems, electrical control cabinets and switch gear. Construction of this yacht was begun at Oceanco, but when the shipyard was sold the vessel was finished by the new owners, at Benetti's shipyard in Italy.

- 85m *Anastasia 3* (launched 2012) – one ship set: two VRC22000 anchor winches, two VC20000 mooring winches and two anchoring systems, electrical control cabinets and switch gear.

Around the world, including the Americas there are other well-known large yacht builders who had taken a liking to Muir anchor and mooring equipment.

As Henk Wiekens (the current Joint Managing Director) from the large Falmouth based British superyacht builders, Pendennis, can attest.

"Pendennis Shipyard in Falmouth has enjoyed a 26 year-long relationship with Muir Engineering in Tasmania. Unbelievably we started our relationship in the faxing era despite the fact you couldn't create a farther distance between two companies.

"There is one thing both Pendennis and Muir Engineering have always had in common, it's the ability to create products that can't be bought off-the-shelf. Over the years it's been a pleasure to have John and his team at Muir working with us, to tailor-make supplies for our yachts, even when the request was often not only outside-the-box but a couple of boxes away!

"Thanks for all your help John."

John knew very well his business was only as good as the Muir team back home and is quick to praise his team who 'worked their hearts out' to finish orders on time.

Bob Harper, Don Di Martino, Chris Michael, Joe Didocha, Patrick Roberts, Lyndon Potter, Brett Ross, Rodger Dixon, Lyn and Wayne Carter, John Sattler to name but a few, were all part of the team John relied on so much, particularly as he was away travelling for many months of every year.

John Muir: "Take Lyndon Potter, he's a hands on supervisor. Lyndon has been with Muir for over 25 years, he supervises the rear workshop where the fabrication, painting and polishing sections are.

He doesn't believe in sitting in the office like some people do. He never stops and he's a highly productive guy and without doubt he's one of the best chaps I've ever worked with. Lyndon prefers to be on the shop floor, and he's always out there when the

ABOVE
52m **Sunrise**

OPPOSITE, TOP TO BOTTOM
85m **Anastasia**
95m **Al Mirqab** (now named **Indian Empress**)
56m **Lady Christine**
59m **Pegasus** (now named **Helios**)
80m **Amevi**

pressure is on, be it testing winch gear with the marine surveyor, assembling, machining or pushing things along in the polishing shop, and anywhere when there is a bottleneck.

"Lyndon is on the same competency level as Brett Ross. Brett started with us as a fitter-machinist at the main works at Kingston when he was 15, after four years when he'd finished his apprenticeship, he relocated to Battery Point. 12 months later he took over running the engineering workshop from Bob Harper. Like Bob, Brett could do anything. It's great when people run things like it was their own business. Weld, machine, diesel work, make patterns, haul boats up on the slips, put on his dust coat to paint or sand a completed winch and keep his eye on the weather and the boats on moorings. He never complained, was always in early. Hard to find and that's the sort of commitment and dedication that made Muir Engineering thrive and prosper."

ABOVE: "ONE OF THE BEST"

Long-time employees like Rodger Dixon are, in John's opinion, what's made the company what it is today.

BELOW: LEARNING FROM THE BEST

Brett Ross, former Engineering Manager at Battery Point, has gone on to own his own successful businesses since leaving Muir.

There are many others who have worked the hard yards for Muir Engineering who would attract this sort of accolade from the Boss. One is Rodger Dixon, whose working life with Muir's began in the early 1980s.

Rodger Dixon: "I came down from Queensland with my parents in 1982, and we moved to Howden. I worked in the Cripps apple orchard. I used to drive tractors around and prune the trees. It was a good job, I enjoyed being outside. When I first started at Muir's I worked in the castings area and eventually I was put in charge. Then I moved from castings to the pleasure winches section."

John Muir: "Back in those days there were four key people assembling the range of pleasure winches. Rodger re-arranged the assembly process and re-organised the components storage area. The pleasure winch section was expanding, but Rodger's aim was to streamline the assembly process and reduce the manpower needed down to two, including himself. The result was much higher productivity with significant cost savings."

Rodger Dixon. "I left Muir for a couple of years because my Mum bought a take away in Kingston. This was just after my father had been killed in a tragic car accident."

John Muir: "Rodger has always had a sense of urgency in everything he does, he sets high standards and is one of the businesses most respected employees, always ready to lend a hand to anyone who needs it, particularly with new and younger staff, including budding design personnel like Jeff Taylor. Rodger is one of a handful of employees who have been with Muir for over 30 years."

Throughout the 1980s and early 1990s John and his crew raced on the family yacht *Shonandra*, in three Sydney to Southport races. (Southport is at the southern end of the Queensland coast.) There were great benefits for the business from the Muir Windlasses sponsorship images on the hull and the spinnaker. On one of the races, both Alex and Jock were part of the crew.

With dedicated and focussed sales, marketing, production, design and accounting personnel hard at work in both locations, John and others were out and about and travelling all over, drumming up new orders. With the Muir reputation growing it's no wonder John or one of the sales team couldn't resist sneaking across the Tasman Sea to successfully take on Maxwell Winches on their home turf.

In the mid 1980s Murray Morten was John's unofficial sales representative through his role as General Manager of Sailor's Corner (in Auckland) and later Sales Manager of Lusty & Blundell and then Lighthouse Marine. Murray, together with Richard Box, another Muir salesman from Sydney worked together and took Maxwell winches on. John followed up with a visit to a New Zealand boat show and the relationship with Murray was cemented over a few long lunches and on occasions even longer dinners.

Murray Morten: "Over the next few years, Muir Winches were supplied to the bulk of the New Zealand custom boat builders and many of the smaller trailer boat production builders as well. There was [and still is] a winch model to suit any boat between 5m and 150m+. On top of that, Muir has an extensive range of commercial winches for tugs, trawlers, military vessels and ferries. One of the many different commercial sales we pulled off was a set of big SGC Commercial Winches for four tugs being built in New Zealand. This was somewhat of a coup for Muir, as most of the commercial yards preferred to build their own winches."

Even when it was time for hard work, focus and making sure that orders were filled and delivered on time, occasionally there was time for 'play.' Well, just a little and in almost every case 'play' involved something to do with yachts and racing.

In 1999 Auckland and Team NZ staged New Zealand's first defence of the America's Cup, which was a huge event for Auckland, New Zealand and world yachting in general. It was to be a showcase for international yachting and the publicity surrounding the event was inevitably accompanied by huge advertising and sponsorship opportunities.

This unique sales and advertising opportunity was not lost on John Muir, who had somehow smuggled a massive Muir Winches banner into his luggage and trotted across the ditch (the Tasman Sea) with future son-in-law Matthew Johnston, to watch the racing. His initial plan was to find a suitable vessel on which he could to display the huge banner. John saw an old NZ boating magazine lying around, that he immediately leapt on and leafed through, finding an ad for his vessel of choice in the 'For Charter' section at the back.

Murray Morten: "'How much do think it will cost you mate?' I asked. 'Aww, should get away with a couple of slabs of Steinlager – maybe a bottle of rum,' said John."

No-one was sure how he would get on. John rang the owner of the boat who turned out to be quite accommodating, but the cost was a tad more than a couple of slabs of Steinlager and a bottle of rum. It turned out the owner needed a new winch and he knew the name John Muir. What would any enterprising boat owner do when provided with an opportunity like this? Ask for a new winch as rent for the boat of course.

TOP: LIGHTHOUSE MARINE
Murray Morten with John in Auckland for the America's Cup, 2002.

ABOVE: IN WITH A WINNER
Muir couldn't lose, with Sailor's Corner in Auckland Harbour taking on Muir Equipment.

A BARTER AGREEMENT

John underestimated his side of the barter offer for hiring this charter to advertise during the America's Cup television coverage from New Zealand. But it turned out to be worth it in the end!

Murray Morten: "As I remember the conversation went something like this:

'What size winch mate?' asked John? We were all listening to this phone conversation.

'I dunno, what do you reckon? You're the expert.'

'Aww, from the picture of the boat looks about 40ft, 12 tonnes — reckon a Cheetah will do it,' said John.

"Next day an ashen-faced John Muir rocked up to my work.

'What's the matter mate?' I asked. 'That flaming charter boat,' he says. 'Its closer to 60ft and 40 tonnes — looks like a Thor.'

"First time I've seen a grown man cry — Matthew and I were howling with laughter.'"

One assumes from this conversation and John's anguished response, that there is a significant difference in cost between a Cheetah winch and the next stage up, the Thor. That assumption is correct. The cost is double and John had to wear it.

However, in the end the laugh was on everyone else, as John scored a significant advertising coup. The promotion turned to gold when, at the end of the regatta with a triumphant Team NZ returning to base escorted by a massive flotilla of all sizes and types of craft, there was on old charter boat with a huge 'MUIR WINCHES' banner displayed along its starboard side about as close as you could get to the winning yacht, without touching. The images went out internationally and therefore for John Muir everything was alright with his world after all.

Murray Morten: "There was a lot of fun during this period and John and Muir Winches have always been one of the best and most loyal of suppliers in an industry renowned for constant change and innovation. Muir has always been at the forefront of innovation and continual product development and this, coupled with John's and later Matthew's ability to build relationships, is why Muir Winches will always be a major player in the international marine winch market.

"If there is anyone who reads this book who has never been to Hobart, get yourself down there. It's a great city, full of tradition, history and wonderful characters and you never know… John Muir might even buy you a beer!!"

Spoken like the true Muir Man he is. Of course, John also has a reputation for taking on what others might regard as 'mission impossible.' He liked to remind everyone that when all five production sections and the design team were feeling the heat and under the pump, John came out with one of his well-known sayings!

John Muir: "Guys, as I've said before, we (Muir Engineering) are just two engine rooms in a big Incat ferry.

"At times Incat have multiple ferry orders on the go. They are pretty well always delivered on time.

"We are no different. When there's a big new order on the books, it's all systems go, with a commitment from us all, we can and will get the work done."

But John didn't leave it at that, he was always walking the shop floor, checking on the progress of large and small orders, that's how he and his supervisors got things done. The last thing he usually expected was a phone call from one of his customers complaining about a late delivery. It did happen, once.

met the project manager and amicably talked about all the angst involved.

In some situations, when the work overload was bordering on the ridiculous, Muir would outsource work to local machine shops, like Apco Engineering, Saunders and Ward, Emu Bay railway workshops, Fogarty and former employee and friend Dave Webb, who operates his own engineering works in Hobart.

Incat (International Catamarans), the extremely successful Hobart based ship builder founded by Robert Clifford, was first established close to Victoria Dock in Evans Street. At this early stage Muir Engineering were supplying Incat with all of their anchor and mooring winches along with machining and small component fabrication, machining propeller shafts, couplings and various other marine components.

John Muir: "There was a hell of a lot going on at Incat in those early days, the size of the ferries was expanding exponentially and orders were starting

> **"** *When there's a big new order on the books, it's all systems go, with a commitment from us all, we can and will get the work done.* **"**

On a large and unidentified project, John got a call from a new project manager telling him that he expected the order for the equipment for his vessel to be delivered in Amsterdam by the time the shipyard crew were back from holidays.

John Muir: "This came as a helluva shock because we understood sea-freight delivery would have met the originally agreed deadlines. However the only way the equipment could be delivered earlier was to use air-freight and that was six times the sea shipping cost.

"We contacted several air-freight companies, including China Airlines who turned out to the cheapest and could meet the deadline. The gear was sent, via Singapore and arrived on the due date. The bridge deck was due for installation on the same day and the anchor winches had to be installed first, hence the hurry.

"A week later the shipyard agreed to pay part of the air-freight cost."

For Muir Engineering, this was another example of the customer comes first. The last thing they could afford was to compromise a good customer. John eventually

to come in thick and fast. Sometimes Robert Clifford would arrive at the Kingston factory and look over whatever project the Muir machinists were working on. He had an enviable reputation as a fisherman, ferry operator and now fast ferry builder and innovator.

"Robert Clifford could be very demanding, certainly was the sort of customer who knew exactly what he wanted and got straight to the point when he needed to. When International Catamarans first moved to their new home in Prince of Wales Bay, Bob asked me on two occasions to build a fabrication workshop out there. He even offered me a block of land to set up. However we had a lot of anchor and mooring winch work from Austal Ships in Perth plus much more, almost more than we could handle, so I declined his offer."

John also knew that Apco, formerly Skeels and Perkins, had plans to set up near Incat and were about to move. John was concerned some of the work he would be asked to do would be in direct competition with Apco and thought there might be a conflict of interest detrimental to one or both businesses.

TOP LEFT: *SPIRIT OF VICTORIA* (HULL 016)

*The 28m long, experimental **Spirit of Victoria** was launched on June 15 1985, designed primarily to test the Wave Piercing Catamaran concept. Photo: Incat*

LEFT: *TASSIE DEVIL 2001* (017)

December 20 1986 was the vessel launch date, with fitting out progressing with urgency so the craft could journey to Fremantle, Western Australia for the finals of the 1987 America's Cup. Photo: Incat

ABOVE: SGC150

Single gypsy, single capstan AC electric anchor winch, as fitted to Spirit of Victoria and Tassie Devil 2001.

BOTTOM: *KEPPEL CAT 1* (011) *AND KEPPEL CAT 2* (010)

*Catamarans were proving their worth servicing the islands of North Queensland and **Keppel Cat 1** was launched in September 1984 to service Keppel Island from Yeppoon harbour and she was later joined by **Keppel Cat 2**. Fitted with Muir H4000 horizontal DC anchor winches. Photo: Incat*

BELOW: SD100

3-phase electric drum winch.

TOP: *GALAXY CLIPPER* **(075) &** *NEPTUNE CLIPPER* **(076)**

Delivered in 2015, the 150 passenger, 35m long ultra-high specification twin catamarans are owned and operated by MBNA Thames Clipper for service on the Thames River, UK. Muir SD100 drum anchor winch fitted. Photo: Thames Clippers

ABOVE LEFT: *OCEAN TRACKER* **(078) &** *OCEAN WAVE* **(079)**

Built for Manly Fast Ferry, the vessels operate a frequent daily service on Sydney Harbour, NSW. The 24m ferries have the capacity for 260 passengers plus crew, with indoor and outdoor seating on both the main passenger deck and upper deck where the bridge is located. Muir SD100 drum anchor winch fitted. Photo: Manly Ferries

ABOVE RIGHT: *2000* **(019)**

With a hull length of 31m, and the ability to carry 390 passengers and crew, the vessel was launched in 22 February 1988, for service in Hamilton Island, Whitsundays Queensland. Photo: Incat

RIGHT: *FRANCISCO* **(069)**

*At 99m in length, **Francisco** was launched on 17 November, 2012. The vessel is the world's first high speed passenger Ro-Ro ship powered by LNG (liquified Natural Gas) and operates between Buenos Aires, Argentina to Montevideo in Uruguay. Photo: Robert Heazlewood*

ABOVE: FROM SMALL BEGINNINGS

Toby Richardson, left, and Ron Devine, owners of Richardson Devine Marine, at their shipyard in Prince of Wales Bay, Tasmania.

OPPOSITE PAGE: VESSELS

*Clockwise from top: The launch of **Kilimanjaro VI** in 2016; **Eagle**, a 35m catamaran ferry operating in the Tasmanian Wilderness Region and built to strict environmental requirements for wash and vessel emissions. Photo courtesy of RDM; **Annabelle Rankin**, third new generation Sydney Harbour Ferry and part of the Captain Cook Cruises Fleet. Photo courtesy of Captain Cook cruises.*

John Muir: "I had been approached by a senior staff member of the Tasmanian Development Authority (TDA), and asked if I could assure the TDA (in writing) that Muir Engineering would continue to purchase castings from Apco for a minimum of three years. I agreed. That decision helped the government decide to go ahead with an expansion loan to Alan and Andrew to offset the relocation expenses of the business. Within a couple of years Apco had set up a new foundry and machine shop and were up and running."

The Muir business with Apco was significant.

Closer to home, not far from Robert Clifford's vast operational centre, there is another, smaller but no less successful Tasmanian success story, boat builder, Richardson Devine Marine (RDM). This business was established in 1989, the same year that Incat moved to its new production hub in Prince of Wales Bay. Its two directors, Toby Richardson and Ron Devine, have extensive experience in aluminium fabrication and have a "hands-on" approach to closely monitor the construction of every vessel they build. Like John Muir they deliver high quality catamaran ferries with the help of a very talented workforce.

Toby Richardson: "I started this company with a guy called Ron Devine, when I got a job to build a sailing catamaran in 1989. It turns out there wasn't anywhere to build the boat in Sydney, where I lived, but I knew we could build it down in Tasmania.

"I came down and I never ended up going home. I've always liked it here. People use their boats here. I love the lifestyle but I hate the cold. That first sailing catamaran we built is now plying the Gordon River on Tasmania's west coast as a powerboat.

"We started the company at the end of that boat build, and we struggled for a long time, with bits of work here and there. Then in 1994 we got a job to build a charter fishing boat for a customer in Sydney, called the *Alley Cat*. The year after that we started building boats for the Grinings family, who operate tour boats on the Gordon River. So far we've built seven boats for them.

"After we built a handful of boats for clients within Australia, we started branching out overseas. We've built ferry and tour boats for New Zealand, Japan, Tanzania, and countries around the world. We also build offshore services boats for the oil and gas industry (including three for Offshore Unlimited), and they all have Muir winches on them."

When your production facility is a mere 20 or so kilometres from one of the best winch makers in the world, why would you go anywhere else?

John Muir: "I came across Toby Richardson and Ron Devine when they were working for Parry Boat Builders in Perth, Western Australia. Parry were building the America's Cup boat *Kookaburra* 3 for Alan Bond in Perth in 1986. Now they run a very successful boat building operation in Hobart.

"Toby and Ron have developed a wonderful long time relationship with a Tanzanian customer. The last was the 39m *Kilimanjaro VI*, launched in 2015.

"From small beginnings in Hobart, they soon outgrew the facility on the Hobart wharves (Macquarie Wharf), and relocated to a larger purpose-built premises at Prince of Wales Bay, capable of building much larger boats and two at a time."

Toby Richardson: "We've built quite a few boats with John's winches. When you're building a boat it's very important that you can trust the equipment. It's your reputation. John's stuff is incredibly good quality, and clever. I'd heard of the Muir family (before knowing John and using Muir equipment) through sailing and boating, but it wasn't until 1989 when we built our first catamaran in Hobart that I really met John properly, when we put one of his winches on that boat."

Apart from the commitment to quality and craftsmanship at RDM, another reason they have been so successful is their close link to Naval Architect Phillip Hercus, from Incat Crowther. There is no current connection between Incat Crowther and Robert Clifford's Business, Incat or International Catamarans. Not now, but there was once.

Both Incat and Incat Crowther can trace their lineage back to the original Clifford business in the 1970s. Back then International Catamarans was a joint design venture between Robert Clifford the ship builder and Phillip Hercus, the naval architect. The partnership was dissolved in 1988 and a new company was started by each partner: Incat, in Hobart, by Robert Clifford and Incat Designs, in Sydney, by Phillip Hercus. Incat Designs then merged with Crowther Design to form Incat Crowther.

Since then RDM has continued to expand and do well in this highly competitive international market.

Unfortunately, another boat building venture, North West Bay Ships, building small (23m) to medium (61m) sized boats located south of Hobart, closed its doors in 2010. The shipyard was later sold to a well-known steel worker from Launceston

Boat building success is big news in Tasmania. It has been since the early days of European settlement. The industry got formally underway in the 1830s and in

1847 attracted nationwide attention when the 562t full-rigged ship *Tasman* was launched from Battery Point, she was at that time the largest ship ever built in Australia and compared favourably with other large sailing vessels built overseas.*

In May of 2013 the Tasmanian state government website, Brand Tasmania, was trumpeting good news to all:

EXPORT SHIPS OFF TO THREE CONTINENTS

"Three gleaming new aluminum ships were tested on the Derwent Estuary in April as Richardson Devine Marine (RDM) and Incat Tasmania put the finishing touches on big-ticket exports bound for three different continents.

"RDM's 45 metre **Kilimanjaro IV** *passed with flying colours and will soon be loaded on to a heavy-lift ship for transport to Zanzibar, off Africa's east coast. She will be the fourth – and biggest – RDM passenger ship to be bought by Tanzanian business Azam Marine for its busy shuttle service between Dar es Salaam and Zanzibar.*

"RDM Sales Manager, Roger Janes, told The Mercury 'Shipbuilding is always about the next contract, but through what has been a quiet time for a lot of boat builders, we've managed to get that next contract.'

"The next contract was exactly what Incat's Chairman Robert Clifford had in mind when he left for Asia, after two successful sea trials for vessels bound for Argentina and Denmark. An Argentine crew was in port to test the world's first high-speed passenger Ro-Ro ship powered by LNG (Liquified Natural Gas). The 99m gas-propelled catamaran, **Lopez Mena**, *was commissioned by South American company Buquebus, in November 2010, for operation on their River Plate service between Buenos Aires, Argentina and Montevideo, Uruguay.*

"The eighth ship built by Incat for the Buquebus group is the largest catamaran the South Americans have operated and is considered the fastest, environmentally cleanest, most efficient, high speed ferry in the world."

That really is something to crow about. (If something's 'to crow about,' it's particularly good and special and well worth boasting about.)

Think about it for a moment, from this tiny, isolated island, Tasmania, lying in the belt of the Roaring Forties, sitting under mainland Australia, thousands of kilometres from most other countries, are being produced the fastest, most environmentally clean, most efficient, high speed ferries in the world, many with deck machinery from Muir.

These remarkable vessels and winch gear come from three separate businesses, whose founders grew up in the same city, who also grew up sailing and racing little boats on the Derwent and who do not have between them a university degree. It really is a remarkable story.

* Source: 'Spirited, Skilled and Determined, the Boat and Ship Builders of Battery Point.' Nicole Mays 2014.

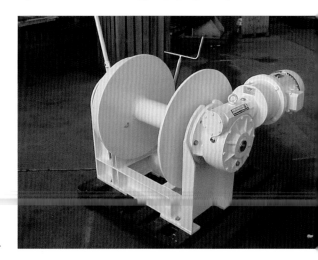

ABOVE: LONG AND SUCCESSFUL PARTNERSHIP

Ron Devine and Toby Richardson onboard their new launch, **Kilimanjaro VI**, *during sea trials in 2016. The vessel is the sixth ferry build for the same Tanzanian ferry operator.*

BELOW: SD100 400V

Popular drum anchor winch supplied for fast ferries up to 30m.

Toby Richardson: "We've always had a good working relationship with Muir. Never a problem, and never any reason for there to be one, because their product is very good. John's always run an amazingly tight ship, and the three brothers are all the same. Probably Jock (their father) was the same too, he did very well to survive those hard times. You had to have that toughness because when you've done it tough you know everything counts."

Australia's economy is one of the top 20 in the world. We are also among the world's biggest exporters and importers. It is not regarded as unusual for small businesses, like Muir, RDM or others to expand their operations across Australia, from a base in Tasmania and expand further to take on the rest of the world.

> ❝ *We've always had a good working relationship with Muir. Never a problem, and never any reason for there to be one, because their product is very good.* ❞
>
> – TOBY RICHARDSON

We are a very successful trading nation, pushing far above our weight. Tasmania is also the nation's smallest state and the only one isolated by water from the rest.

It might seem amazing to some who know a different John Muir than the one Toby Richardson and others of his ilk talk about. But the more we explore the businesses and people John has dealt with over the decades, the more you realise that he does have a way with people, he does have a capacity to empathise with a client's needs, to understand in some depth, what size and type of gear will work well for each particular vessel. He has been known to crawl round under decks, in cramped spaces, with a tape measure and a notebook in hand, scribbling measurements down that later on prove to be accurate to less than a few millimetres.

Fred Mayer (Muir USA): "Johnny was hands on all the way, from the engineering and design, to production to the installation and sea trials. This was no more apparent than it was for the installation of VRC20000 windlasses and anchoring systems on the MY *Laurel*. During dockside commissioning Johnny could be found adjusting the brake band supports, running back and forth from the boat to Delta's machine shop where their machinist allowed him to work. That is the kind of respect he received from yard personnel.

"John takes pride in engineering, designing and building his windlass systems to last. The motor yacht *Sea Falcon* was one of the first US yachts that put on a Muir windlass system back in 1979. Years later the Captain on *Sea Falcon* wanted to replace the existing VRC7000

MUIR VRC4000 ANCHOR WINCH WITH CAPSTAN

Toby Richardson recently fitted a DC electric version of this winch to his Riviera cruiser.

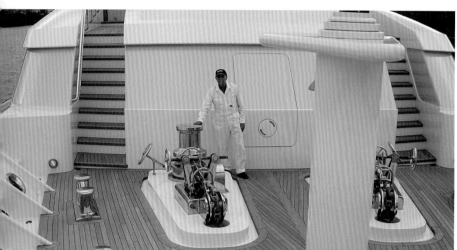

windlasses with new VRC8000 windlasses as they were about 30 years old. When I spoke with John about quoting the new windlass set, Johnny says to me, 'Freddie boy, Muir builds their equipment Caterpillar strong, we will refurbish these windlasses'. And so we did and I lost out on a large windlass sale!"

I hope you are not surprised by that event, because you should not be. That is so typical of John Muir. 'Waste not, want not.' You would almost think he was a product of The Depression years. No, but he did belong to a family that for the most part, lived frugally. There was never an excess of cash around in the Muir home and that's why John, his brothers and sister are all innovative and made good with what they had.

Fred Mayer and his wife Kim represented Muir Engineering in the USA and were successful in selling Muir winches onto the large motor yachts being built at shipbuilders like Trinity Yachts in New Orleans, Louisiana, (located along the southeast coast) and Christensen near Seattle on the west coast and more.

Muir has supplied many ship sets to Delta shipyards via Imtra in Seattle. The Delta built yachts equipped with Muir anchor and mooring winches include the motor yachts, *Affinity*, *Jamie*, *Princess Gloria*, *Triton* and the 74m *Laurel*.

Further east in the Wisconsin the well-known shipyards, Palmer Johnson and Burger Boat Coy. The two shipyards were busy building motor yachts throughout the 1990s and early 2000s. Palmer Johnson built some prominent sailing yachts over the years including the 61m *La Baronessa* and *Anson Bell*, all equipped with Muir anchor and mooring gear.

Over the same time period Muir supplied Burger with a variety of ship sets of anchor and mooring equipment, including mooring winches for *Sycara IV*, a beautiful classic new build of a 1930s style motor yacht.

Delta Marine are still going strong and build very large custom made motor yachts. Trinity Yachts was one of the world's largest builders of superyachts (up to 74m) and in-house designed motor yachts.

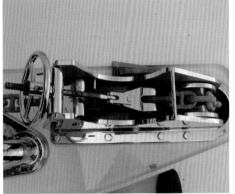

THIS PAGE: MY *ZOOM ZOOM ZOOM*
Trinity Yachts' shipyard in Gulfport, Mississippi.

OPPOSITE: MY *LAUREL*
Fred Mayer during commissioning of newly fitted Muir VRC20000 windlasses and anchoring systems, 2007.

66 *Johnny had actually dropped down into the engine room to tinker with the Volvo diesel. This was his form of relaxing...* 99

– FRED MAYER, MUIR USA

Fred Mayer: "When I had my first meeting with John [in the late 1990s] I had to pick him up at the Residence Inn on 17th Street in Fort Lauderdale, Florida. After our good morning hellos and how are you and nice to meet you, we got in my car to get some breakfast and talk about selling winches. First thing John says in the car is, 'I need to get some health into me.' He proceeds to pull out his insulin kit and gives himself an injection in the thigh right there in the car right next to me. I had only met this fellow a few minutes before and here he was wielding syringes near me!"

John was diagnosed as a type 1 diabetic in 1984. He was fortunate to visit the Miami Diabetes Institute in 1985 where he learnt first hand about the realities of diabetes and how insulin works in the body. After his illness, John's body had lost the capacity to produce insulin.

Fred Mayer: "It was right then that I realised he was comfortable around me and vice versa.

"During my first visit to the Muir factory in Tasmania John planned a weekend boat trip on his sailboat

with a couple of his mates from when he grew up. We didn't depart from the dock till 11:30 pm and sailed out into a pitch black night in fairly calm water. As soon as we pulled away and cleared the yacht club John asked me to take the wheel and he went below. I thought he was going down to do what he had to do for his diabetes.

"Johnny had actually dropped down into the engine room to tinker with the Volvo diesel. This was his form of relaxing, being the engineer he is. Well an hour or so later he resurfaces back up to where I was at the helm.

"Meanwhile I had been sailing around in a place I had never been before, didn't know what was up front or nearby that might lead to disaster, in pitch black conditions and just a few miles from the open southern ocean. I was a little wound up but John seemed totally unfussed."

John Muir: "Although I was down below for a while, I gave Fred some stars to follow – the Southern Cross – and I didn't hear anything from him. There were another

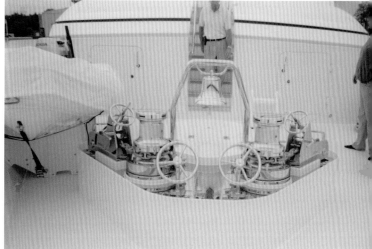

BURGER BOAT COMPANY, 2006
*45.5m Burger motor yacht fitted with Muir VRC11000
anchor winches and VC4000 tall drum mooring capstans.*

two mates on deck who knew the river well. He'd spent a good amount of time boating in various places so I wasn't worried about his ability to navigate in the dark."

Fred Mayer: "I will never forget, John was always speeding. He got 'flashed' as they say in Tasmania. One morning John and I were on our way to the factory and John was on the speaker phone when, as we came off the highway, Johnny drove straight through a stop sign. Coming the other way was a cement truck traveling at about 70km/h. Johnny didn't hesitate, floored his Range Rover, the turbo diesel kicked in. Between the cement truck horn, my 'Watch out' scream and Johnny yelling 'Oh…', Muir's production manager Ian Stocks caught all this on the phone and thought we had been run over.

"When we arrived at the factory a few minutes later Ian met us in the parking lot laughing his ass off saying to me this was my orientation to Johnny's driving habits."

When Fred started selling Muir winches, he said John was all about faxing. "It was not unusual during road trips where Johnny would be communicating back and forth with the factory in Tasmania during the wee hours of the morning, driving hotel staff mad and sending hotel faxes that were sometimes very long.

"The fax charges cost more than the room charge. Then John got his first Blackberry mobile phone. Oh boy, he would take his glasses off and hold that phone about 6 inches from his face as he used one finger to type copious amounts of emails.

ABOVE: MONACO BOAT SHOW, 2002

Peter Florence from Quantum Hydraulics, with Fred Mayer of Muir US.

RIGHT: VISITING HOBART

*Muir US representative Fred Mayer with John onboard **Westward II** during a visit to Hobart in 2005.*

"Eventually we called it the 'Crackberry' as John was addicted to emails on it, communicating all day long and all night sometimes, during road trips. I would be driving and Johnny would be fingering away. This once went on for four hours as I drove from Seattle to Portland."

Grit, guts and determination. Focus, drive and an urge to do whatever it takes, no matter what.

John Muir: "Fred and Kimmy Mayer remain good friends of mine and are always very hospitable, more often than not I stayed at their home when in Fort Lauderdale. I thoroughly enjoyed their company and being in their home. They had several dogs, I think three, one of them would put his nose in the door when I was asleep and on occasions jump up on the bed with me.

"I first met Kimmy when she and Fred had their own business, representing Italian pumps as well as marine and technical products, which Kimmy sold and on occasions serviced. Kimmy had a mechanical aptitude for servicing and a really good memory for parts and numbers.

"Fred came from an electronics background, and this was a big plus when we were commissioning variable speed drives on many different boats throughout our time together. Fred is a very tall, strong feller, and was a big asset when on occasion we had to remove drive gear for servicing. He could manhandle it himself,

where I would have needed an extra hand. For his size, he got into some very tight compartments, doing inspections, but on one day he got stuck in a chain locker while on board a motor yacht at Trinity Yachts' boatyard in New Orleans, and it was a hell of a job to ease him out.

"In 2007-8 we had 22 projects either on order, in production, or on the water for Trinity Yachts, for vessels ranging from 40 to 74 metres. We lost some of this business as the GFC took hold.

"When we were setting up boat shows, Fred on his own could manage to push around the large vertical and horizontal winch displays effortlessly. He's a fine bloke, a straight shooter and got on extremely well with our customers, and he also knew a lot of crews and owners whose vessels annually docked in Fort Lauderdale.

"There was always someone new to meet when I was with Fred. Almost every medium to large motor yacht in the world, at some time in its cruising life, passes through Fort Lauderdale in Florida for slipping, servicing and providoring, or just en-route to the Caribbean.

"Having the Muir shingle (that's the Muir banner) hanging proud in Fort Lauderdale, showed locals and visitors Muir had arrived.

"Fred undertook the majority of commissioning, travelling from Fort Lauderdale to New Orleans and other places by plane or car. On occasions we would both undertake commissioning, more so myself when we had technical or installation difficulties with things such as inadequate chain locker sizing, or anchor chain spurling pipe designs."

Harking back to those leadership qualities that are outlined at the beginning of this chapter, we know that John Muir and members of his staff were always seeking new ways of doing things, trying to find innovative solutions to problems clients were having, but John Muir is also good at solving complex issues, especially when it comes to the design of intricate winch gear for very large boats.

1. Effective leaders manage complexity. Leaders who know how to manage complexity are skilled at solving problems and making decisions under fast-changing systems.

Ilja van Ketel, one of the joint owners of the European based naval architects firm, Ginton Naval Architects, recognises in John Muir a unique capacity to nut out a complex installation, whilst at the same time, understanding what the client needs.

Ilja van Ketel: "I have always enjoyed working with Muir and with John in particular. We greatly appreciate the professional approach, the personal attention to detail and his technical knowledge. It is very nice that when we call with a question John and his colleagues will try to give you the needed information as quickly as possible, but more than that, they will think with you. If they think for example that the anchor lay-out can be improved with some minor changes that make a great difference they won't hesitate to tell you."

John Muir: "We provided intricate design drawings to facilitate the installation of the Muir anchoring and mooring equipment for Ginton Design. This ensures the shipyard can pre-cut and drill the foundation plates for components in advance of receiving the equipment.

This saves time on the installation and makes the overall task easier. I've thoroughly enjoyed working with Mr. Ginton, Ilja and the team on a variety of projects, large and small, for the past 25 years."

It's called honesty and being upfront, giving advice that can be trusted and when the rubber hits the road, as it did with *Adix* in the Chilean Archipelago, and the yacht has to survive a huge storm, relying for their survival on the Muir anchoring equipment, that's when reputations are made or lost.

MUIR 'MEGA' CATALOGUE
VRC20000 anchor winches. Various products in the catalogue have been manufactured by Muir for nearly 20 years.

> 66 *It is very nice that when we call with a question John and his colleagues will try to give you the needed information as quickly as possible, but more than that, they will think with you.* 99

– ILJA VAN KETEL, GINTON NAVAL ARCHITECTS

TASMANIA
the
POWERHOUSE

Tasmania has a small population; it hangs around the 500,000 mark, sometimes a bit more, sometimes a bit less. Yet it is an island state riven by dissension. We argue constantly and have done for decades about what to do with the vast areas of natural forest that exist in this remarkable place. Should we continue to log them, particularly for paper and woodchip products, to produce immediate jobs and wealth, as we have for decades, or should we protect them and keep them as carbon sinks, tourist drawcards and as unique and valued regions of the planet that have remained virtually untouched for millions of years?

Tasmania has an enormous land area (almost 40%) already secured in National Parks and reserves. It's more than any other Australian state and probably more than any other comparable area of land in the world. These parks and reserves include a diverse range of unspoiled habitats and unique ecosystems found nowhere else in the world. Most of these National Parks are stunningly beautiful, remote, unique, wilderness areas that have not been much trodden, except by indigenous Australians, who learnt to live from and with this amazing landscape. Over half of these National Parks has also been given World Heritage status.

What has all of this got to do with Muir Engineering? It helps set the scene for this chapter, providing the background fodder to explain why and how John Muir managed to do what he did from this isolated island, lying south of the Australian mainland.

In addition to its natural resources, Tasmania is blessed with large mineral resources, particularly copper, zinc and lead. The state is home to the second biggest zinc refinery in the world, with its ore coming from mines on the west coast and elsewhere, the output is almost all shipped to Melbourne and then onto the buyers who are mostly in Asia.

So it is for Muir Engineering, yet, despite its isolation the state has historically and continues to spur some remarkably successful people and businesses.

Tasmania's maritime industry, for example, was established in the decades that followed the arrival of the first Europeans in the early 1800s, driven by isolation and the need to build vessels to furnish growing local, intercolonial and international trade routes. At Battery Point, where John's father Jock established his boatyard in 1948 and where John went on to start his business in 1968, the first commercial shipyard was established in 1835, the output being barques and schooners to ply between Hobart and the mainland. A decade later Peter Degraves, the patriarch of the Cascade Brewery empire, established a shipyard at Battery Point. One of Tasmania's wealthiest and more powerful businessmen, his determination and resolve culminated in the building of the largest vessel yet built in Australia, the 562t *Tasman* launched in March 1847. Remember earlier we mentioned John Muir's convict great-great grandfather working as a shipwright on the vessel. So why did Peter Degraves build such a large vessel and others that followed? Because he could! Not only did the vessel allow him to have greater control over his supply chain, particularly the international import and export trade, but the ship was intended to eclipse all others built in Australia with the notion of showing "the good people of England what we colonists can do." This mindset is indicative of 'Taswegians' and still exists today!

Historically Tasmania has also punched well above its weight in agriculture, wheat and wool supporting the economy in the early to mid-19th century. Still today, the state enjoys an enviable reputation internationally for being one of, if not the cleanest, greenest production areas in the world. Premiums are paid for products such as cherries, apples, hops, barley, medicinal poppies, salmon, branded beef, pork and sheep meats, the list goes on and on. It also includes walnuts, chocolate, olives, wine, whisky and cheeses. What more could any discerning buyer want? We also have the only sustainable wild abalone fishery in the world and well-managed cray fishing and scallop fishing industries.

As any visitor to the island state within the past few decades knows, when you come to Hobart, there is one restaurant and fish and chips outlet that plays host to almost every traveller, not to mention the locals. It is housed in a building uniquely designed on the theme of Fisherman's Wharf in San Francisco. Mures Seafood Centre sits between Constitution and Victoria Docks at the Hobart wharf, where competitors in the famous Sydney to Hobart Yacht Race moor after the race is over. A stunning spot to visit, to wander around and soak up the waterfront atmosphere. The water glitters at night, basks in the early morning light and reflects golden sunsets as the sun drops behind Mount Wellington to the west.

Mostly surrounded by heritage sandstone buildings, constructed during the early decades of Hobart's European settlement, the location was also a place where the indigenous first peoples of Australia used to camp, hunt and fish.

There are sandstone shelters on the flanks of Mount Wellington that were home to the Muwinina people, for the area had a plentiful supply of shellfish, wildlife to hunt and birds eggs to collect.

The Mure family (not a direct descendant of the Muir family, but somehow in the distant Scottish past the two families could be related) also trace their roots back to Scotland but to the other end of the social scale, to the landed gentry.

According to Burke's Landed Gentry, the Mure family in Tasmania is directly descended from Sir Reginald More, or Mure, of Abercorn and Cowdams who, as far as is known, was Chamberlain of Scotland as early as 1329. It was Sir Reginald's younger son, Gilchrist More, who acquired the estate of Caldwell in Ayrshire and Renfrewshire through marriage with the heir of Caldwell, of that ilk. The family pedigree also shows descent from the Mures (or variously Moores, Mores or Muirs) of Rowallan (or Rouallan).

Historically Tasmania has also punched well above its weight in agriculture, wheat and wool supporting the economy in the early to mid-19th century.

The Mures were involved in much feudal fighting. It's worth noting that they had a reputation as 'fighting men' (much like a certain modern day John Muir!).

In 1543, an unnamed Mure and his son John, took part in "the bloody battle called the Field of the Muir of Glasgow." Six years later he was indicted for having "with his five brothers and twenty-six others, armed in warlike manner, invaded Robert Master of Sempill and his servands for their slauchter, near the place and tour of Cauldwell, and put them to flight."

Returning to the more modern day Mure line, a man named David Mure had a son, George, who became the man behind the restaurant and fish outlet at Constitution Dock. George was born in London in 1939 and during the war years lived on his great uncle's estate in Norfolk where he learned to row and fish. George moved to Kenya at the age of eight when his mother remarried. While boarding school life in England was tough, holidays in Kenya, he recalls, were wonderful and fishing became his passion.

"Most school holidays were spent at Shimoni where I had the use of a 20ft gaff-rigged boat, ideal for getting out to the many coral islands and reefs. I swam, fished and goggled, taking my catch back to the East African Fisheries factory managed by a family friend."

His parents, perhaps understandably, had other aspirations for their son. George Mure was sent back to London to matriculate and then embarked on a university-based medical career. However, he failed his exams at the end of the first year, 'and left for Australia under a slight cloud' (at least he wasn't in convict chains.) For two years George worked in a variety of jobs, ranging from a year spent as a jackeroo in northern New South Wales and a period taking tourists big game fishing in the Seychelles, to a stint as a fish filleter on Tasmania's east coast.

There were other adventures too, but bad weather, maritime rescues and a huge financial loss, led to George Mure returning to Tasmania where he and his wife Jill bought a Victorian cottage at Battery Point and opened it as Mures Fish House – a restaurant that was a huge success from the moment it opened in 1973. In fact, in 1986 this restaurant won the Remy Martin/Bulletin award for Best Seafood Restaurant in Australia.

Mures Fish House was both the catalyst for the Mures's entry into the restaurant business and for their re-entry into commercial fishing. Discovering how difficult it was to ensure a regular supply and good variety of fresh fish, they started Australia's first commercial mussel farm at Margate.

In 1985 George and Jill Mure were part of a venture to develop a waterfront fish centre on the dockside of Hobart's Sullivans Cove. It included a 200 seat, licensed à la carte seafood restaurant, a self-service licensed bistro, a licensed sushi bar and a factory selling wholesale fish. The operation is now wholly owned by the couple's son, Will and his wife.

GEORGE MURE

John first met George Muir (left, in the photo above) when he relocated from Western Australia. Together they collaborated on the creation of Muir hydraulic line haulers for the deep sea trevalla fishing industry. George and Don Hazell started Channel Craft, which opened another door for Muir Engineering in the supply of anchor winches, hydraulic steering and line haulers. These Muir products were all fitted to George's first Hobart-based fishing vessel, **Melicent***, which was built by Channel Craft.*
Photo: The Mure Family

The Mures bought a 54ft fishing boat and started to catch fish commercially, at first for their new retail outlets but eventually for the wholesale market. The Mures are now one of the largest owners of fishing quotas in the state of Tasmania.

As George (who died in July 2003) rather modestly put it: "The Scottish influence is alive and well in Tasmania…While relishing such fine dishes as oyster soup, sashimi mille feuille, Tasmanian salmon in Boronia oils, or warm seafood salad, tuned-in diners hearing the creak of rigging, lapping of water and keening of seagulls on the dockside will surely gain some inkling into the Mures long love affair with the sea."

As you have probably worked out by now a close working relationship developed between the Mures and John Muir's business, Muir Engineering.

John Muir: "I got to know George and Jill Mure when they first relocated to Hobart from Western Australia in 1973. George was a Muir customer for many years, and Muir Engineering developed some specialised fishing equipment for their drop lining venture. In close collaboration with George, we also manufactured line storage drums (cotton reels) that were 'quick fit' to locate on top of the line hauler head.

"From a Tasmanian perspective, this was at the forefront in developing the Trevalla long line fishing. (Trevalla or 'Blue Eye' are a deep sea fish caught off the continental shelf to Tasmania's east.) Other equipment we developed and built included bulwark rollers, anchor winches, boom winches, and horizontal storage drums for hook and line handling.

"Back in the mid-1970s George Mure and Don Hazell established a fibreglass boat production business called Channel Craft down in Margate. Muir supplied one of their first vertical anchor winches to *Melicent*, which was George and Jill's first Hobart based commercial crayfish and Trevalla vessel. For the life of Channel Craft, Muir Engineering supplied the winch and hauling gear.

"George Mure pioneered the first semi-displacement and planning hulls for fishing and work boats in Tasmania. Their speed was quite extraordinary for their size and they could reach up to 25 knots. At that time planning hulls were also being manufactured in Western Australia to a design by Len Randall, a well-known Perth naval architect.

> 66 *I remember when the Mures established Tasmania's first licensed seafood restaurant, Mures Fish House, in Battery Point. We used to get quite a few phone calls from people mixing up the names and wanting to book a table.* 99

– JOHN MUIR

"These new boats meant fishermen could reach their fishing destinations in a third of the time of a conventional displacement hull, subject to sea conditions. Channel Craft went on to build many fast work and fishing boats over the years.

"I know George had done some investigation into our joint family histories to see if there was a link. After a couple of visits back to the UK he told me that our families were very likely cousins."

Mures is something of an institution in Hobart and has received many accolades over the past 40 plus years of continuous operation. The waterfront complex was originally managed by George and Jill, and is now owned and managed by their son Will and his wife Judy. Coincidentally, Alex Muir (John's daughter) worked at Mures Upperdeck in the early 1990s when she was studying at university.

Like their namesakes the Muirs, the Mure family have always had an affinity for the sea and fishing. Over the years they have operated a number of vessels, the first was a 42ft rock lobster boat named *Aquanita*, then came the larger 70ft Tully.

In 1976, the Mure family built the *Melicent*, a 50ft double diagonal planked fast fishing vessel named after George's "very tough" grandmother. The *Melicent* developed the Blue Eye Trevalla fishery in Tasmania from a part time industry to a year round operation. The catches were abundant enough to not only supply Mures Fish House with local fresh fish but to warrant the establishment of a wholesale market in Tasmania supplying fish to restaurants and hotels.

ABOVE: MURES FISHING BOAT
Will got his start working for his father, George.
Photo: The Mure Family

OPPOSITE: *DIANA*
Will Mure with the haul at Macquarie Wharf in Hobart, 2016.

The *Kiella* came next, a 54ft steel fishing boat purchased in 1993, with Muir winches already installed and skippered by Will Mure. In 2004 they purpose built the long-line vessel *Diana*, this time named after Will's grandmother. Today the Mure family continues to operate the fishing vessel *Diana*, along with Mures Upper and Lower Deck restaurants, as well as the newly opened Pearl + Co, a five star restaurant and bar, all located on Hobart's waterfront, and a processing factory outlet in Cambridge near Hobart Airport.

John Muir: "I remember when the Mures established Tasmania's first licensed seafood restaurant, Mures Fish House, in Battery Point. We used to get quite a few phone calls from people mixing up the names and wanting to book a table. We had the Mures Fish House phone number on the wall near the phone so we could redirect callers, but they became so frequent near Christmas one year, when things were very busy for us, that our staff were being driven to distraction. (That's a distinct understatement.)

> 66 *There are a number of reasons why I really like Muir winch and anchor gear. When we were cray fishing, then drop lining, the Muir gear is simple to operate, no matter what the sea conditions are.* 99

– WILL MURE, MURES

"Totally frustrated, one of our guys took a booking for ten people for dinner between Christmas and New Year and didn't pass it on. I'm not sure what would have happened when those people turned up at Mures expecting a reservation. However, our office manager at the time, my wife Wendy, found out about it and rang the restaurant to let them know, so all was well in the end."

Will Mure: "There are a number of reasons why I really like Muir winch and anchor gear. When we were cray fishing, then drop lining, the Muir gear is simple to operate, no matter what the sea conditions are. Out where we fish, it can get rough. Next is the reliability of the gear. It gets a lot of hard use on our boats and John's gear just keeps on going. It makes you breathe easy when you know that in the middle of a big haul of say six long droplines, the drum winches are not going to fail, no matter how much weight of fish might be on those lines.

"I remember one trip, it wasn't a fishing trip, it was a holiday. I was with the family and we went right up the Queensland coast and then out to sea. One evening we decided to anchor in a lagoon, surrounded by reefs, it wasn't an inhabited island, just coral reefs and a central lagoon with one narrow entry.

"That night it blew up and the wind got very strong. I was asleep and I don't know what woke me, but when I got into the wheelhouse I realised we were being blown onto the reef. We were dragging the anchor because the wind was so strong. I got

ABOVE AND TOP: MOTHER AND SON
Jill and Will Mure, at their Hobart waterfront restaurant in 2016.

MUIR
HYDRAULIC LINE HAULERS

Model Overside
Tubular Aluminium, Stainless or Galvanised M. Steel construction. Foot operated swivel base, minimises manual handling of gear, stows fore & aft when not in use.

Model Pedestal
Aluminium construction incorporates reservoir above deck, supplied with line storage drums for efficient rope handling and hauling.

LINE PULL 250 - 3000 K.G.

"MUIR FISHING WINCHES PACK MORE POWER"

MUIR HYDRAULIC LINE HAULERS, 1970S

Developed for the drop line trevalla industry, in conjunction with George Mure.

everybody up and we started the motor, hauled up the anchor and moved into the best lee position we could find, then let the anchor go again with all the chain out we had.

"You know the scary thing is that if I hadn't woken up we would have ended up on the reef and we were about 100 miles off the coast of Queensland. Knowing that you can rely on your anchor gear, knowing that it is easy to use even when the weather is rough, knowing that you can rely on the chain and the motors is such a relief, it really can make the difference between survival and disaster."

One of the Mure family's deep sea fishing boats also had a deep water winch mounted on its bow. It meant they could safely anchor in very deep water and not have to run back to the coast to shelter when they wanted to take a break from drop lining. It saved them a lot of time and money.

Will Mure: "When we were drop lining off the continental shelf we might have 20 lines out, each one with 360 fathoms of line, into very deep water, sometimes with hundreds of kilos of fish hooked, dragging them in steadily. It is very tough on the gear and made worse when there is a big swell that puts huge pressure on the drum rollers, the motors and gearboxes. The Muir gear is wonderfully reliable, day after day after day."

In addition to supporting local businesses like the Mure's, there are a number of people who have worked for the Muir family over the years, who left to set up their own very successful businesses. Some of those businesses now export product across the world. Many of these individuals say their time at Muir Engineering or Muir Boatyard made them realise what opportunities there were just waiting for someone to take them on. One such individual is Mike Grainger.

John Muir: "Michael Grainger worked for us, then left to take on Liferaft Systems Australia. He is Chairman of Tasmania's TT Line and Managing Director of Liferaft Systems Australia located at Derwent Park, next door to Incat.

"It's a large international business manufacturing ship-sized liferaft systems. The first liferaft was built in Muir's sail loft with input and support from Incat's Robert Clifford on a trial basis and it turned out to be very successful.

"Liferaft Systems relocated to Prince of Wales Bay, adjacent to Incat, and has continued to expand ever since."

Liferaft Systems Australia (LSA) is a privately owned company formed specifically for the design and manufacture of high quality Marine Evacuation Systems (MES) and large capacity liferafts. They began developing the system in 1992 and pioneered a simple sloping inflatable slide, delivering passengers safely and quickly into a large inflatable liferaft.

The company website says: "The LSA objective then, as it still remains to this day, is to develop and produce a product that is synonymous with quality and reliability, which is of paramount importance in the marine safety industry. LSA constantly develops this objective through a continual program of unrivalled design enhancements, utilising the latest technology while constantly striving to maintain and improve our quality systems and providing excellent service to our ever growing number of valued and satisfied customers. LSA operates a quality management system to ISO: 9001 and are continually improving quality practices."

These days the product can be found on all sizes and types of passenger and defence vessels, including high speed ferries (like the vessels built at nearby Incat), conventional ferries, high-speed craft, military vessels and large private yachts. The company head office is in Hobart, with two commercial and technical offices in Europe and North America. The company is also involved in another unique marine product, the Cormorant Lift Bag, designed to raise underwater mines safely and securely.

From the LSA website: "To this day, 20 years later, we believe the LSA brand is still the world's premier MES providing safe yet rapid evacuation every time. LSA is the simplest MES to use; provides the greatest flexibility to ship operators and ship designers and is cost effective to own."

So what sort of background did Mike Grainger have that saw him starting work with Ross Muir at 2 Napoleon Street at Mick and Sam Purdon's Boatyard, then move onto developing and building an internationally successful marine business? Why don't we let him tell his story.

Mike Grainger: "I began working for Ross Muir in about 1977. We decided to establish a sail making business at Battery Point. At the time Ross had a ships chandlery and a rigging business but he didn't have a sail maker. So we decided to establish a sail making business which we did under the name of Muir Sailmakers.

"We established the business at number 2 Napoleon Street where Ross had his original chandlery, on Sam and Mick Purdon's boatyard, then moved to 44 Napoleon Street where Jock Muir and eldest son John had the boatyard and two busy slipways. The shipyard main building was converted to have a second floor to accommodate a large

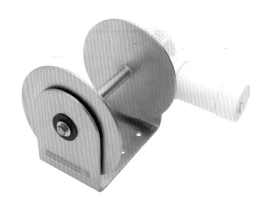

ABOVE: MICHAEL GRAINGER
Now Managing Director of Liferaft Systems Australia, Michael got his start with Ross Muir at No. 2 Napoleon Street, in his chandlery at Purdon Brothers' yard.

TOP: AUTOMATIC FREEFALL DRUM WINCH
Liferaft Systems Australia purchase the Muir DWF freefall drum winch for remote release of their liferafts.

ABOVE: REUNION

Some original Muir's Boatyard sail loft staff in 2016, at the boatyard's revival party. From left: David Rees, Edward Fader, John Muir, Greg Muir (back), Lyn Denehey (née Muir, front), Nick Dineen, Brian Moroney, Richard Goodfellow, Michael Cooper, Michael Grainger.

> 66 *All three brothers are driven, they're very hard working and very, very intense about what they do but they are also good yachtsmen in their own right...* 99

— MIKE GRAINGER, LIFERAFT SYSTEMS AUSTRALIA

chandlery, and alongside a second building was built with a second floor which became the Muir sail loft and underneath on the ground floor incorporated a good size yacht rigging facility.

"Under the chandlery on Taylor Bros' side the Muirs fitted out a new workshop for Yacht Distributors (owned by Greg Muir).

"We expanded our operations there and took on an international franchise, Fraser Sails. A few years later I purchased the Fraser Sails business from Muirs when Ross moved to Queensland."

With the new arrangement in place, Jock, John and Ross owned Muir Boatyard and its operations until Ross relocated to Brisbane. Following, Jock and John resumed ownership of the operation. Jock retired in the mid-1980s and John and Wendy Muir took over all of the Muir's Boatyard existing and slipping operations.

Mike Grainger: "I sold the Fraser Sails business in 1994 after we had established this business (Liferaft Systems Australia). We spent the best part of twenty years down there on the waterfront with the Muir family. It was a wonderful working environment, being on the waterfront and being a part of that local marine industry for such a long period of time.

"All three brothers are driven, they're very hard working and very, very intense about what they do but they are also good yachtsmen in their own right, very good sailors. But their work ethic is second to none. John in particular has an incredible work ethic and even in those early days he was always working 18 hours a day, travelling interstate and overseas every other month, and just working incredibly hard. They're all very good businessmen who like their pound of flesh, and work incredibly hard to achieve what they set out to do."

There is another fellow by the name of Michael Cooper who will tell his story in this chapter and who worked at Muirs at the same time as Mike Grainger.

"Mike Cooper worked for me in the sail loft and was a very loyal, dedicated worker and champion yachtsman who ended up becoming a very successful businessman. We both enjoyed our time surrounded by the Muir family with some colourful memories still etched in our minds. We still discuss those early days over a beer at the Shipwright's Arms Hotel, located a stone's throw from the Muir Boatyard."

Mike Grainger discovered in later years that working with the Muir family not only instilled a strong work ethic that he retains to this day, but he also noticed that to a large extent you don't find that strong work ethic when mixing in academia. The Muirs, he says, just roll their sleeves up and get the job done, all of them, from father Jock down to the three boys, John, Ross and Greg.

"They've got a never-say-die attitude and are very driven. Sometimes that drive was to the detriment of John's health, but they're certainly a business committed family.

"It was a good part of my life down there. There was never a dull moment with those Muirs. On occasion there was tension between John and Ross. Greg sort of removed himself a bit, it was mainly Ross and John who at times would fire up.

"So that's where it all started from, and I'm sure you'll appreciate, at times it was an education down there. But again, the main thing that sticks in my mind was the drive and enthusiasm that John in particular had. I mean it's not, certainly not the way we would be allowed to run a business today, by any stretch. But his drive and his enthusiasm and his dedication was quite extraordinary. John was more or less the glue that held it all together!

"True entrepreneurs are just like that. (Reflecting on the similarities between Robert Clifford and John Muir and the single-minded focus on 'getting it done'.) They haven't got time to worry about the periphery, they don't sweat the small stuff, they've just gotta get on with it and get it done. I really admire people like that."

So when Mike started building Liferaft Systems Australia, as you would expect it was full on and flat out from day one.

"It was no holds barred when we started, we did exactly the same thing, we had to forge ahead no matter what and we got kicked about in particular from other parts of the world, but we never – not once – thought about not ploughing ahead. Because we had to, there was no choice. The first LRS system was built in the sail loft at the Muir boatyard.

"In the early days, when we started this business, we were behind the eight ball, for a number of reasons, but I still had the sail making van and we had about 20 people working for us, and we'd work all through the night, and I'd take them home so they could have a shower, and then pick them back up gain, drop them back at work, I'd go and have a shower and then come back to work again. We did that for, like, ten days in a row. So everyone was like a zombie, but you know, we had no other choice."

John Muir: "From the outset I could see Mike Grainger had 'the gift of the gab' and a real sense of urgency to get things done. In both cases with Ross at number 2 Napoleon Street and when he came across to the Boatyard I knew Mike was a leader!

"He had tenacity, a sense of urgency, tough negotiating skills along with what I call 'the growl' and as required 'the snapping at the heels.' He's a straight shooter, no holding back and gets straight to the point and gets his stuff done. Michael Grainger is Chairman of the TT Line that operates two good size passenger and vehicle ferries between Melbourne and Devonport."

Mike Grainger is now a member of Det Norske Veritas' International Ferry Committee. This committee is active in the implementation of improved regulations for the International Maritime Organization (IMO), an affiliation of the United Nations, regarding international ferry safety standards.

Mike is also a Director of the Board of Interferry, an international shipping association representing the ferry industry world-wide. The current membership consists of over 180 member organisations representing 25 countries. Interferry has consultative status at the IMO.

Michael Cooper became the Managing Director and half owner of Juicy Isle, a well-known and long established family owned business operating in the Tasmanian drink and beverage business. Juicy Isle also exports its products interstate and has a big share of the market. Mike Cooper started his working life as an apprentice sail maker in the Muir sail loft and no doubt, as with Mike Grainger and others, a lot rubbed off and stuck with him as he entered his parents business then moved up to run it himself.

ABOVE: MUIR'S BOATYARD

Taylor Brothers' slipyard on the left and Muir's boatyard on the right. Watercolour painting: Roger Murphy.

Michael Cooper: "I turned up on day one, and obviously the boatyard was very busy in those days because there were people everywhere, there was the slip way, the engineering shop next door, and Ross was there running the chandlery at that stage.

"Wendy (John's wife) was working very hard over at the engineering shop, Ross's wife Judy was running the payroll, and Jock was still around at that stage. Greg Muir had Yacht Distributors underneath. John and Wendy's daughters, Alex and Shona were young then, because there's a few years difference between myself and Alex, and obviously more with Shona.

"John used to come in like a whirlwind. He was a bit of a cyclone. Ross was very similar in a way, he'd probably deny it but they (John and Ross) are nearly identical. They'd leave sticky notes absolutely everywhere. You'd come in on a Monday morning and there'd be sticky notes around the whole building, downstairs, upstairs, in the toilets, just everywhere, with notes about things that needed doing.

"That would be Ross, he was a big sticky note person. John was more of a notepad person. They were just all over every detail, John especially, he would probably write more notes than Ross."

According to Mike Cooper, in those days everyone used to work pretty long hours in the sail loft, but he can remember many times looking down into the engineering workshop and seeing the lights on.

"You'd go down there at 9 o'clock at night if you wanted to have a bit of a tea break or something, and Wendy would be down there just absolutely working her butt off. I remember one time Wendy pulling up and her car boot was just packed full of papers and invoices and book work. It was just so much work for her, more than a full time job.

"I think the success of John is one thing, but Wendy – she was behind him all the way, because she's as hard a worker as he is. She doesn't complain, she just gets in a does it. She's really savvy and she's really smart, but in those days they hadn't embraced emerging technology. I think for previous generations in business it was a trust thing. So John and Wendy would check everything themselves and it was all done by hand. Technology and computers weren't really their forté. Wendy would hand write every invoice, hand write every statement, and she'd check and double check everything.

"What John and Wendy created was a fantastic work ethic within their team and their family, especially with the staff. We knew that if you start at 8, you start at 8. You don't turn up at three minutes past, or you were in the shit. You finish when your job is done, and if that's 9 o'clock at night then so be it. They were always very generous and looked after you – if they didn't pay you overtime, they'd give you a new lifejacket or something. There was always reward for the hard work, and there was always a feeling that they appreciated what you did. Jock was very much like that too, he was a very hard working, salt of the earth kind of guy. I guess all that tradition sort of started from Jock and Mollie – the hardworking man and the self-sacrificing woman behind him."

John Muir: "Michael Cooper has a lot of similarities to Michael Grainger and Ross Muir, he has the bite and determination in him when he needs it. He's tenacious, adventurous and a go-getter, a first class sailor, as proven with all the three generations of the

MICHAEL COOPER

Worked in the sail loft at Muir's boatyard and is now Managing Director at Juicy Isle.

> 66 *You'd go down there at 9 o'clock at night if you wanted to have a bit of a tea break or something, and Wendy would be down there just absolutely working her butt off. I remember one time Wendy pulling up and her car boot was just packed full of papers and invoices and book work. It was just so much work for her, more than a full time job.* 99

– MIKE COOPER, JUICY ISLE

SB20 World Championship 2016 © Neuza Pereira | Clube Naval de Cascais

SAILING ACCOLADES

Michael Cooper, skipper, Matthew Johnston, forward hand, and David Chapman, mainsheet and tactician, sailing Export Roo in Portugal, 2016. They finished 10th in a previous world championship, 5th in 2016 and if they improve again they have a good chance of winning the series next year in Cowes, August 2017, or when it is sailed in Hobart in 2018. Photos: Neuza Pereira, Clube Naval de Cascais

Cooper family. Mike and Bill had what it takes to start a business and drive it upwards as they very successfully did! Michael and his crew on *Export Roo* are a world class outfit and no doubt they will be doing more SB20 racing around Australia and all over the world."

Mike Cooper left Muirs to work with his parents, Bill and Diane Cooper, who had started a small apple and fruit juice bottling business called Juicy Isle. From day one, the business never looked back and in 2015 it was bought by the Myer family.

In November 2015 Damon Kitney, the business writer for The Australian newspaper, wrote the story thus:

"One of Australia's richest families, the Myers, has made its first foray into the booming organic foods industry, buying the nation's largest supplier of organic chilled juice to Woolworths and Coles supermarkets.

"The move came after the deeply private Myer Family Company, now known as Myer Family Investments, recently staged its 90th annual general meeting, which saw a historic changing of the guard on its board with the retirement of former chairman Carrillo Gantner after 27 years of service.

"MFI, the holding company for the Myer family's investment portfolio, purchased Tasmanian juice producer Juicy Isle to add to its portfolio of operating businesses spread across the retail, aged-care and building materials sectors.

"Founded in 1971 by the Cooper family, Juicy Isle is the largest non-alcoholic beverage producer in Tasmania. Its products are stocked in supermarket shelves across the nation.

"We feel that food is one of the key sectors for the country. The organic and better-for-you style of food production is important as a coming trend and Tasmania has a great image in that space,'' MFI chief executive Peter Hodgson told The Australian."

Juicy Isle's 2013 annual report revealed consolidated revenue of $40.5 million and the employment of 69 people. Juicy Isle also owns Hartz bottled mineral water.

Michael Cooper: "Our secret are our people, we look after them and support our teams. We split our profits among the management team. I have mentors and learnt the value of hard work from the Muir family. Over the years we have invested in new technology, like the Muirs."

INCAT GAS TURBINE FAST FERRY

Sold to Buquebus in South America.

There are a number of others who worked for the Muir family, started young, learnt by being 'thrown in at the deep end' (another slang phrase meaning put to work straight away without training), soaked up the atmosphere, then left to start or run family businesses.

It is an appropriate moment in this narrative to once again quote from the Alistair Mant's unauthorised biography of the life and times of Robert Clifford, 'The Bastard's a Genius.'

"Some businessmen (of the kind that banks are comfortable with) start to contemplate their retirement pension-pots when they get into their fifties. Nobody ever thought that Robert Clifford (read Muir) was that sort of businessman. This biographer decided early on that Clifford is a businessman only because getting into business was the basic requirement for pursuing his creative life's work. That work consists of inventing, making and doing in the context of water. He does share an intense competitiveness with most business people, so he dislikes losing a contest just as much now as he did when sailing competitively on the River Derwent. There are two aspects to this, mastery of technique and winning, too many people (not John Muir) are obsessed with winning at any cost.

"Robert Clifford loves to win, but he is also engaged in a higher order contest with the elements, water, wind and physics.

"Every country needs its engineers and manufacturers, but there is a drought of able young entrants to the making and doing trades, like John Muir and many

of his ex-employees, who went on to build big and successful businesses.'

As Alistair Mant points out, there is no shortage of aspirant spin doctors, lawyers, bankers and management consultants. There might be nothing better than to take many young people for a trip on an Incat fast ferry, or for Muir Engineering to take young people out on boats fitted with Muir gear and see it in action.

Of course there is no bigger member of the Tasmanian Marine Industry Powerhouse than Robert Clifford's International Catamarans.

The history behind Robert's amazing success (from the company's website) is worth including. "The Incat group evolved from local Hobart boat building companies, including the Sullivans Cove Ferry Company (SCFC), formed by Robert in 1972. SCFC built conventional steel mono-hull vessels, and operated small ferries across Hobart's River Derwent. The business rocketed into public view after the collapse of the bridge over the Derwent. SCFC transported more than 9 million passengers in the two years following the 1975 Tasman Bridge collapse, the sole bridge link between the eastern and western shores of Hobart.

"After the bridge re-opened, International Catamarans specialised in the construction of aluminium fast ferries. In 1983 the Wave Piercing design was conceived, the 8.7 metre prototype craft *Little Devil* (hull 13) first undergoing sea trials in 1984. The current range of Wave Piercing Catamarans still reflects the characteristics of that early craft.

"The fast ferry design is in a state of constant evolution. With each incremental increase in waterline length comes a myriad of modifications to the hull and structure, however the vessels within each generation are far from identical with a range of configuration, fit-out, and performance variations evident."

In deadweight terms according to research by the writer, 'Incat has built approximately 60% of the world's high speed ferries with capacities of over 750 tonnes.' While the ferries initially revolutionised transport links around the UK, Incat-built ships now operate in North and South America, Australasia, the Mediterranean, Asia and throughout greater Europe.

The Incat group of companies is privately owned, with shares held by the founder and chairman of the board Robert Clifford, the Clifford family, company directors and employees.

It's no wonder that Alistair Mant describes Robert Clifford as one of the world's greatest global shipping entrepreneurs. "After all, if you go into business you might as well experience a financial meltdown, and bank receivership. If you take up yachting you might as well win the Sydney to Hobart race in a near photo finish. If you invent then dominate the world's fast ferry market, you might as well win the Hales Trophy for the fastest Atlantic Crossing, not once, but three times."

Alistair Mant: "Robert Clifford is a man quite unlike the standard issue 'businessman' and much more like those distinguished artists and scientists who are impelled by some inner voice to do the work they do."

John Muir is another Tasmanian who is a driven man. He, like Clifford, wants to and dreams of building things. In John's case it's anchor and mooring winches and the related marine gear that every vessel needs.

Another individual's story worth including is Dave Webb, who started his working life at Muir Engineering in 1997. Dave had just finished his tech college training and was taken on as a fitter and turner.

Dave Webb: "When I finished Tech College I sent the resumes around and I got a call from Muir Engineering Factory Manager Don Di Martino and he said, 'We're looking for a CNC machinist' and I said, 'Okay, well other than what I've done at Tech,' which I said was fairly little, I said, 'I'll be quite honest with you, I've done very little' and he said, 'That's fine'. He said, 'We can train you, no problem at all. Come down and see me and we'll discuss it.'

"So I went down and saw Don and went over a few things and he said, 'That's alright, we can do the training and get you running the machine, no problem. When would you like to start?' So I started the next day and I spent about the first week on a manual lathe.

"At the end of my first week, the bloke who was operating the CNC machine said, 'I'm leaving in a week, so we better get you up to speed on this machine.'

CUT FROM THE SAME CLOTH
Robert Clifford, above, and Robert 'John' Muir, below in 2016 at the Muir's Boatyard Revival.

DAVE WEBB

Above: At his home engineering workshop, 2016.
Opposite: Dave's hobby in his 'spare time' is miniature rail.

"I thought, geez, this is something that I've basically never done before and I got dropped right in the deep end. It was learn or sink. I learnt! Yeah, we nutted it out. At the time I thought it was a bit overwhelming, but looking back, it was probably the best thing that could happen to me."

Dave quickly learnt how to operate the machine and was soon promoted and was running that area of the workshop. Asked what he put that capacity to learn quickly and to accept responsibility at an early age down to, he said, "I found it was more than just a job. It became an interest. Not only was I doing stuff at work that I found interesting, I also found that I could use the machine occasionally to do a job for myself. I'd often go home of a night and I'd sit down and I'd write out a program for something that I wanted to make for myself. The next day I could finish up at work and provided the machine was finished doing what it was doing, Don used to let me to use the machine to make a little bit here or a bit there or a bit for my train or something for my car.

"I found I really enjoyed it to the point where I started saying to people, 'I'm going to buy one of these machines one day.' Never probably really believing that I ever would, but as time went by it turned out I would."

Dave remembers at the time he started, some of the traditional machining they were doing was slow, then it ramped up, in both quality and production volume.

"At the time, the machine tools computer programming we were doing was all done basically with a hand drawing and a calculator, not like what we do today with everything done on the computer, then sent directly to the individual computer controlled machines. We were drilling and tapping holes and keyways in the first instance but as time progressed the programs and the work became more complicated and particularly when the CAD computer program came along."

The anchor and mooring winches got bigger year by year and more complicated, there was more machining to do and less and less by work done by hand.

"When I started that first week I was machining the bases and we were running 10 at a time. When I left we were doing 100 at a time."

Dave Webb stayed at Muir for around nine years then left to try something new, working for the engineering company, Saunders and Ward on locomotives and carriages for the Abt West Coast Wilderness Railway. There he met his future wife, who was a fireman/boiler attendant and learning to be a locomotive driver. At the back of his mind for the two years he was there, was always the thought, maybe a dream to one day own his own business and buy his own CNC machine. Positive thoughts always eventually lead somewhere. A strong willed wife who won't put up with constant 'I wish I could start my own business' also helps.

66 *There's no better person to talk to about starting a business as far as I'm concerned so I went and saw John.* **99**

– DAVE WEBB, WEBBS METALCRAFT

Dave Webb: "I'd spoken to my wife about it often enough and she basically said, 'Look David, go and do it or stop talking about it. Go and do it or shut up about it!' So, I thought, 'I'll go and speak to John Muir.' There's no better person to talk to about starting a business as far as I'm concerned so I went and saw John.

"I wasn't there just to see what work I could get from John but that's how it turned out. John wrote me a letter that I took to the bank basically saying he would give me as much work as I could handle. I went to the bank and said this what I want to do, this is the machine I want to buy, how much I need, and here is the letter that says I have the work and they said, no problem. So I went and bought my first machine, it was a big one. I intentionally bought that machine

because at the time Muirs were starting to get quite a bit of work done elsewhere and that came to me."

For Dave Webb, the decision to invest in his own business in close collaboration and with the assistance of his old employer made a lot of sense. He knew the standard of work that was required, he knew the products required and he knew that he could put in the hard yards and make it pay off.

John Muir: "Dave could see what we needed, and he knew he had to meet deadlines and he did. He worked bloody hard and when people want to make a go of it, you've got to help them get up and going. We've all got to start one way or the other and get a hand up and some good luck."

Being able to put yourself into someone else's shoes is what John did for Dave. John realised that for Dave to get started he needed surety and he gave that surety to Dave in the letter Dave took to the bank. It was a selfless act by John, but it meant a great deal to Dave.

Henry Ford is once quoted as saying that 'If there is any one secret of success it lies in the ability to get the other person's point of view and see things from that person's angle as well as your own.'

Giving someone a hand up to get started was a critical part of how John Muir got started, he had advice and help from his father and from others. He was helped along the way by all manner of people who saw him get stuck in, doing the hard work, putting in the hours that were needed. John Muir is quick to recognise those qualities in someone else and more than happy to lend a helping hand when he can.

Paul Hollingsworth: "In the first couple of years I was running my own business, working as a consultant with John and another company. Within two days of one another, both businesses wanted me to come and work full time for them. I chose Muir Engineering. I said, 'Alright I'll come and work with you for a few years. We'll straighten a few things out.'"

Paul remembers that when he started John Muir was having trouble concentrating on the business as his wife, Wendy was undergoing a number of operations and wasn't able to get about much at all.

Paul Hollingsworth: "I think business was getting on top of John, but I knew I could straighten a lot of that out.

"We had a few arguments along the way, but we also straightened a lot out. One that I remember was with one of the senior workshop staff, Don Di Martino who didn't like the changes I was suggesting."

Being able to put yourself into someone else's shoes is what John did for Dave. John realised that for Dave to get started he needed surety and he gave that surety to Dave in the letter Dave took to the bank. It was a selfless act by John, but it meant a great deal to Dave.

John Muir: "To this day Dave still subcontracts to Muir and also does a variety of other engineering work including manufacturing his own ride-on trains and miniature railway parts."

Dave Webb: "I do a bit every now and then for the Antarctic Division and also CSIRO. Those two with Muir and Cadbury, they'd be my four biggest customers by far."

These many recollections and anecdotes about the business powerhouse that is Tasmania would be incomplete without sharing the Paul Hollingsworth story. Paul Hollingsworth is a man who needs no introduction if you are into Lightning Protection, but that's a story we are to reveal soon. First we need to tell the tale of how Paul came to Muirs and what became of his time spent there as a change management consultant.

John Muir: "Don Di Martino was one of my right hand people for a long time, but Don, with the greatest of respect, didn't like change, and wasn't keen on people coming in suggesting there might be another way of doing things. I can still remember the day Don came to my office and said he was resigning.

"I said, 'You sure about this Don?' I didn't try and talk him out of it. He'd been with me 28 years. He said he didn't like the changes that were going on! It's sad when it has to end like that."

Paul Hollingsworth: "A lot of the changes we did suggest were bordering on revolutionary, well maybe not quite that, but close. My work was mostly about streamlining the processes and procedures of the business. I saw that there needed to be a much closer working relationship between different sections of the business."

This was not an easy time for John Muir, losing one of his stalwarts from the factory and still having to travel around the world selling, selling, selling and he realised that change was coming his way as well when he appointed Paul Hollingsworth as the new General Manager of Muir Engineering at Kingston.

John Muir: "I needed to settle down the management side of the business and handball some of the stuff I was always handling. I had never had or needed to work with a General Manager before.

"It was tough when Don told me he was leaving, he was a good man, a reliable bloke. You wouldn't get any better because he'd be in the workshop sweeping up — he'd run the place on the smell of an oily rag, he was invaluable. I seem to have been able to predict things that might happen with the workforce. Fortunately I had Ian Stocks working with Brett Ross at Battery Point engineering shop. He had been an understudy to Don and knew the run of the workshop and work involved. Ian started as workshop production manager the day after Don departed."

> 66 *I liked working with him because he is a strong family man. That value was important to me and I'm not just talking about close family, I include the employee family.* 99
>
> – PAUL HOLLINGSWORTH, LIGHTNING PROTECTION INTERNATIONAL

Paul Hollingsworth: "I liked working with John and let's be honest, it wasn't for the money. I liked working with him because he is a strong family man. That value was important to me and I'm not just talking about close family, I include the employee family. We share the same set of values. You look after your people, I look after mine. I guess the thing that really stuck out for me, was that John is incredibly tenacious. It doesn't matter what's going right or wrong you just stick with it and keep beavering through."

Paul, like most engineers, is a systematic sort of individual, he is used to doing things in a systematic fashion.

"I was always amazed at the grip John had on his business with not much other than what he observed with his eyes and wrote in his pocket note book. He could tell me what was going to go through the books next month without notes or spread sheets. Whereas I'm thinking to myself, how do you sit down and work that out? I would sit down and work it out and guess what? I came up with the same answer as John. Amazing. Maybe it was fluke I thought. Next month, same thing and I thought, he's got a pretty good grip on things."

PAUL HOLLINGSWORTH

John brought Paul on as General Manager after Don Di Martino left. Paul is now CEO of local Tasmanian export company Lightning Protection International, and credits some of his leadership philosophy to John's example.

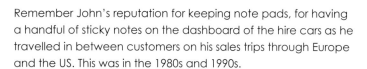

TOP NOTCH: Muir Engineering general manager Paul Hollingsworth shows off the company's capstan winch.

By DANNY ROSE

Marine engineers winch in an elite export award

A TASMANIAN company which has some of world's richest people as its customers has won a national export award.

Kingston-based Muir Engineering, which makes winches and other bolt-on devices for luxury yachts, received the award at a gala event in Queensland on Thursday night.

The company clinched the top honour in the Small to Medium Manufacturer Exporter of the Year category at the Australian Export Awards.

It comes after Muir Engineering was named Tasmanian Exporter of the Year 2004.

General manager Paul Hollingsworth said the latest accolade had recognised a "continued improvement in export performance" for the family-owned company, which started in Battery Point in 1968.

"Our exports have grown past 50 per cent of our business turnover," he said yesterday.

"The sort of market we sell into is the mega-yachts — the sorts of boats that Bill Gates and Tiger Woods have.

"There's been a huge growth in that market over the years, and we've picked up quite a substantial part of it."

The company employs about 60 Tasmanians in design and manufacturing roles and it exports to about 40 countries.

You can buy a Muir Engineering winch for a pleasure craft for about $1000, but a complete fit-out for a mega-yacht can set you back $700,000.

Economic Development Minister Lara Giddings said the Tasmanian-made products could be seen in ports around the world.

"Last year, the company supplied anchoring systems for the largest yacht made in the USA since the 1930s, and its order book is brimming with contracts," she said.

"Recently, participation in trade shows in Monaco and Fort Lauderdale in the USA have generated exceptional interest and a number of high-profile orders have been secured."

Remember John's reputation for keeping note pads, for having a handful of sticky notes on the dashboard of the hire cars as he travelled in between customers on his sales trips through Europe and the US. This was in the 1980s and 1990s.

John's nickname was 'Faxman.' It originated from his overseas and interstate trips when he would send back to the business in Kingston, reams of faxes. (There weren't any single sheet fax pages in those days, they were on a roll and John had to remember to number each section where one project finished and another one started.) They were metres long, sent late at night from hotels across the world, to the frustration of late night hotel staff, not to mention employees back in Hobart who would arrive at work to find reams of fax paper in a heap on the floor, resembling an unravelled toilet roll, and then have to decipher John's notes and drawings and relate each section to a particular project. More important to John were the contents of his faxes, they were full of design specifications, drawings, ideas for new products or any new idea he had whilst on the road.

John Muir: "I've never spent a lot of time on a computer. I've managed by being mobile and not seat bound, keeping track of what I glean by writing in my shirt pocket size note books and then passing them on to one of my personal assistants in Kingston to decode and send emails or faxes as required. In the mid to late 1990s I upgraded to a Blackberry, then an iPhone, then an iPad. This gave me more mobility to keep abreast of everything while I was travelling.

EXPORT AWARD

Top left: Paul Hollingsworth, then General Manager of Muir Engineering, in a local newspaper article after Muir won the Small to Medium Manufacturer Exporter of the Year in 2004. This award came shortly after Muir was awarded Tasmanian Exporter of the Year.
Article: The Mercury

*Above: John and daughter Alex receive the 2004 Australian Export Award on the Gold Coast, presented by Lara Giddings. This is where John and Alex were when they received the phone call from David McQueen asking them to inspect **Ilona** in Sydney.*

> **" *I was always amazed at the grip John had on his business with not much other than what he observed with his eyes and wrote in his pocket note book.* "**

– PAUL HOLLINGSWORTH

"When we installed a full blown computer system and a stock control system everything could be easily costed and charged or included in quotes. That's why in the early days I would write everything down that I couldn't retain in my head."

Paul Hollingsworth: "Well, I guess my style has changed a bit as a result of that. I still do it all, facts and figure systems are tickety boo, but every time I sit down with the production guys I think you need to buy more of these, more of these, less of that. And I keep that information in my head as well as on computers. It keeps you in touch with reality."

John Muir: "I was brought up with a 'hands on' father and uncles. Hands on, making it, building it, walking past it, where is it? That's not right, where's this? So after a while that's the way your head works and it's hard to change the way you think. I must say I have always been meticulous with writing things down along with keeping notes and sketches and drawings. I ran a diary when in my office and when I travel and have ensured management did the same, be it on their bench or later on desks.

"My father Jock Muir could have been an accountant; he was very particular about keeping track of costs and made sure his employees did the same when it came to booking time and materials out to a job or a particular customer. In fact Jock did his own accounts and costings for every single boat he built.

"We still have some of his large size hard cover note books with the details of various projects. One in particular that comes to mind was the yacht *Balandra*, built for Robert Crichton-Brown of Sydney in 1965. The notebook showed that it took 21,000 hours to build. And recorded all the materials used on the vessel. Jock told me he later discovered that her sister ship in the UK took a lot longer to build."

* Source: The Sydney Morning Herald, August, 2013.

Robert Crichton-Brown was a champion yachtsman who competed in the Sydney-Hobart race on 11 occasions. He won it in 1970 in his yacht *Pacha* and in 1967 was part of Australia's winning Admiral's Cup team in his famous ocean racer *Balandra*.*

John Muir: "When I've written things down I can virtually 'feel' the project, it's how I keep in touch. I've always been in touch with everybody, it's part of how I manage things. From the floor sweeper to the money side, the ladies in the office, the whole ruddy thing and you get a good idea of where you are with the business and how well it is working. When signing cheques for suppliers I wanted every invoice that went with that payment to look over all of it. That way you keep track of both sides of the ledger. You can go broke very quickly if you don't do your sums.

"That's me, that's how you keep control of your pennies."

To round this chapter off, it would be remiss not to include a tale or two about modern day seafarers who have left the island shores of Tasmania to seek adventure on the high seas, any which way they can. There are too many individual stories to record here, but enough to give you a sense that Tasmanians who go to sea, who learnt to sail in little boats, have a huge international reputation.

Anyone who can say, 'Yep, been in a few Sydney to Hobart races,' is almost instantly accepted as a 'good hand' to have on board, someone who knows what it's like to tackle really rough conditions, someone who is not afraid of big seas.

Robert Vaughan is one such individual who epitomises this rare breed of 'gypsy' like sailors.

"I left Australia in 1971. Commodore Les Gabriel of the Royal Yacht Club of Tasmania organised for me to meet an American sailor, a fellow named Donald Cohan who was representing the USA in the 1972

Olympics in Dragons and went on to win a bronze medal. I'd never sailed on a Dragon. I'd sailed in International Cadets over in Lindisfarne and I sailed on Commodore Gabriel's yacht *Carousel* for three or four years.

"Donald Cohan had said to Commodore Gabriel can you find me someone who'll come over and work on the boats, prepare them for the regattas and sail with us and Gabriel put my name in the hat. He also mentioned it, probably offered it to a mate of mine, Jap Head Lamprill, but Jap Head couldn't go, that's how I got a ticket out of here and I left."

There it is in black and white, evidence of this network of interconnecting sailors from around the world materialising before your eyes. Why does a new and budding sailor from the USA look to the commodore of a yacht club many thousands of kilometres away for crew? Why? Because Tasmanians have an international reputation as good hands and Robert Vaughan was one of them.

VAN DIEMEN III
*Robert Vaughan's 20m cruising yacht **Van Diemen III**, designed by Warren Muir and fitted with a Muir VRC3500 anchor winch. Photos: Robert Vaughan*

Robert Vaughan: "I only intended to be gone for six months, maybe a year and that was 45 years ago. But for 45 years I also knew I was coming back and maybe one day I will."

Locals, watch this space!

Donald Cohan started his sailing career when he was 37. Five years later he won a bronze medal in the Munich Olympics. He was a member of the US team at the World Sailing Championships in 1969, 1970, and 1971. Cohan then won the 1972 US Olympic trials, becoming the first Jew to be a member of the US Olympic Team in sailing.

His story is one of courage, resilience, focus, grit and determination. Sound familiar? It is also worth a brief mention in passing.

Bob Ford, a staff writer for the Philadelphia News Network, publishers of the Inquirer and Daily Newspapers described Donald Cohan as an 'old yachtsman with resolve' when he was describing the sailors latest tilt at Olympic representation, trialling for the Soling class of boats, one of 10 classes contested at the 2016 Olympic Games in Rio.

"At the age of 66, listing slightly to portly, Cohan doesn't appear much of a threat to younger competitor's ambitions. He won an Olympic bronze medal in 1972, but the crop of young sailors regards that as the age of Viking ships."

"There's a certain fondness toward me," Cohan says. "As if I don't belong out here."

Ford says Cohan has survived Hodgkin's disease, endured intensive chemotherapy and is back on the water after giving up sailing for four years while he recovered. As a result of the chemotherapy, Cohan lost 20% of his lungs, his legs aren't always as sure as they once were, and his arms and hands are usually so swollen that the lines on his boat must be thicker than usual so he can grasp them.

Competitive sailing, as the Muir family can attest is a risky business, ask John, Ross or Greg. For Donald Cohan the recent 2016 Olympic trials were also life threatening.

During the US championships off the west coast of Florida, Cohan and his crew were rushing along with a 20kt wind when another skipper lost control of his boat and rammed them.

MISTRAL V
Photo: The Guy Rex Collection courtesy Suzanne Rex.

"Put a huge hole in the boat, and their bow went right up through my mainsail," Cohan says. "A foot either way and my middle man or I would have been killed. The spinnaker pole snapped off the boom, hit me in the head, and if I hadn't been strapped in, I would have been knocked out of the boat."

Donald Cohan unfortunately didn't make it into the US sailing team for Rio, but it wasn't for the lack of trying.

Robert Vaughan: "Anyway, back to history. I left in 1971 and sailed with Cohan. We went to Europe and had a good time with the Dragons. In winter I switched to sailing the yacht that replaced Dragons in the Olympics, the Solings.

"Then I knew a bloke who knew another bloke who ran North Sails and I got a ride on a big boat for SORC. (The Solo Offshore Racing Club based at Southhampton in the UK.) Once you get in a big boat,

you don't go back to Dragons I can tell you. It just led from one thing to another, to Commuter races and then Trans-Atlantic racing. The plan was to head home to Tasmania. Never happened. I'd sailed with Dennis Connor before and he contacted me and made me an offer I couldn't refuse. He said, 'Come to San Diego, stay with us down there and sail' and well, it just kept going."

It was when Robert first arrived in the USA to begin his sailing and racing career, that he became aware of how well thought of Tasmanians were at an international level and how many ex-Taswegians there were messing about in boats and in competitive yacht racing in America.

Robert Vaughan: "When I first got over there, there was Nick Wells and Dick Neville. Dick Neville was originally from Burnie on Tassie's northwest coast, but went to uni in Hobart and sailed a little bit down there.

"Dick was over there, there was Tripper Crisp and there were a couple of other guys involved with the America's Cup that Bondy won for Australia. Toby Richardson, who set up Richardson Devine was also over there for a while, but came back to Tassie, he didn't stick around. Andrew Hagar, Gramps Hagar, he was over there. There were, at that time I think there were six or eight Tasmanians in the top end ocean racing circuit and you know, it was like, where are you from? Tasmania. Oh, come sail with me. It wasn't a case of how good are you. It was readily accepted that if you came from Tasmania you knew how to sail competitively."

As those who are a part of that sailing world know, it is a relatively small circle and you can run into almost anyone, someone you know at any time.

Tasmanian sailors have a reputation for being versatile, reliable, quick thinking, competitive, but above all, they have that unique Australian quality of 'just getting on with the job.' Many can turn their hand to almost any career, so long as it involves doing something, building something. One of the things you learn very quickly when sailing is how to patch up a bit of gear that nature has shredded or broken, using anything that might be available at the time.

In the 1948 Sydney to Hobart Yacht Race, the Hobart Mercury reported that the crew of the newly launched Hobart yacht, Mistral V had to retire from the race after unsuccessfully trying (for hours and hours) to stop a leak in the bow that was below the waterline. Apparently caulking in a seam had failed. The crew jammed an old sandshoe against the leak trying to stem the flow, as well as pumping the bilges in a race against time. The yacht was being slammed by constant heavy weather, big swells and strong winds. At the moment they decided to abandon the race they were lying fourth with a good chance of winning. Such are the realities of life.

John Muir and his brothers broke a spinnaker pole in a Hamilton Island race one year. Almost everyone else would have retired, not the Muirs. They ripped the legs off the cabin table (it wasn't even their yacht, just a hired one!) and lashed and strapped them to the broken pole, and fixed it. On they went with the race. So it is for Robert or 'Vaughany' as he is fondly known.

Robert Vaughan: "The first boat I sailed on in the US was called Arcadia. Then I joined a boat called Sorcery. Sailed with them for a couple of years, then I was hired by the guy who ran Charisma. We built a new Charisma and did the Admiral's Cup twice, and then I went to the west coast and we built a boat called Brovera and raced that to Tahiti. Then I joined Windward Passage and after Passage I sailed on a couple of boats called High Roller and did, in the process, I think three Admiral's Cups and about six or eight Transvac races and Transatlantic races, and I think eight southern circuits. The Southern Circuit used to be a series in Florida. It was like the grand prix of yacht racing. The Admiral's Cups and a couple of Sydney to Hobart's were next. I've only done two Hobart races but one memorable one was on Kialoa III when we set the race record in 1975, there were three Tasmanians, me and Andrew Crisp and Dick Neville. They had a picture of us in the paper, in The Mercury in Hobart and it was captioned 'The Crew with a Clue.'

"I ended up in California, getting married to a local girl and had kids. Then got into the building business. I sailed a bit out there. I was the skipper of Windward Passage when she made a visit to Tasmania and then took it north to Japan and Hong Kong. Then did a bit of maxi boat sailing and finally went to work for a company building sail boat masts. They hired me to run the company because they knew I was crazy enough to work 24 hours a day and so I ended up getting into the building game full time and became a weekend sailor."

Robert ended up in Newport, California and has been there for nearly 30 years.

"I built 40-50 houses and a couple of them were $US10 million waterfront houses, some of them $US200,000 condominiums. A few shopping centres and a couple of industrial buildings and in the mean time when the building business was slack I did some re-fits on a few boats always as project manager, trying not to get my hands too dirty. Built one 20 metre sail yacht for myself and I have had that for about 10 years now."

As would you expect the conversation with Robert turns to winches and in particular Muir winches and what has been his experience with them?

Robert Vaughan: "From using them personally? I've had 10 years of trouble free use. From what I've observed on other boats they're considered the Rolls Royce of winches. You see these 250 to 400 foot superyachts right out there. They'll be bang, bang on each side and John's laughing all the way to the bank."

John Muir: "It's all about being competitive but also about being the best. Best design, best quality and always reliable. The winch market has always been competitive, so you've got to find a way to sell it, you know. You just don't open the door up."

> ❝ *It's all about being competitive but also about being the best. Best design, best quality and always reliable. The winch market has always been competitive, so you've got to find a way to sell it.* ❞
>
> – JOHN MUIR

If it's big...it's Muir

In business for over 40 years - we're here for the long haul

MUIR SINCE 1968

www.muir.com.au

Try the front door, if that doesn't work go round the back. If that fails find a side door, or an open window, go through those, at worst go down the chimney if you have to, never give up. It may take ten years, but in the end if the product's good enough you will win. (The marketing philosophy of John Muir.)

Robert Vaughan: "I've found, as an Australian there's an advantage and I think that the same probably applies to John's product. They know it's well made. They know it's good quality."

John Muir: "We've got quite a lot of gear on big boats. We've got winches on one of the biggest motor yachts in the world. She was a converted Dutch frigate, built at Royal Schelde Shipyard in Vlissingen in the Netherlands. At about 141m in length, she's the biggest boat I've ever done. We go from equipping small boats to really big ones."

The frigate was sold by the Dutch navy in 1998 to the United Arab Emirates navy, renamed *Al Emarat*. Decommissioned in 2008 she was rebuilt as a luxury gigayacht by ADM Shipyards in Abu Dhabi using the original steel hull with a totally new lightweight composite superstructure.

Muir supplied Austal Ships with the majority of their anchoring and mooring systems for the fast ferries they built (42m to 100m) throughout the 1980s and onwards.

And you know, well maybe you don't know, but it's never too late to learn that there simply isn't anything quite like 'messing about in boats.'

ABOVE: WINCHES FOR MOTOR YACHT *YAS*

The 141m motor yacht started its life as a Dutch Naval frigate. Muir supplied VRC24000s and two sets of VC24000 mooring capstans. All mooring and anchor winch gear controls were frequency (soft) drives. Anchor stud link cable was 38mm U3.

> ❝ *Believe me, my young friend, there is nothing—absolute nothing—half so much worth doing as simply messing about in boats.* ❞

– THE WIND IN THE WILLOWS

Kenneth Graham knew that, when he penned his famous and one of my favourite books, 'The Wind in the Willows.' Ratty knew that when he met Mole when they were two happy little animals who happened upon one another on a warm spring day at the river bank. He soon had Mole entranced. The pair set off on a watery adventure.

"Hullo, Mole!" said the Water Rat.

"Hullo, Rat!" said the Mole.

"Would you like to come over?" enquired the Rat presently.

"Oh, it's all very well to talk," said the Mole rather pettishly, he being new to a river and riverside life and its ways.

The Rat said nothing, but stooped and unfastened a rope and hauled on it; then lightly stepped into a little boat which the Mole had not observed. It was painted blue outside and white within, and was just the size for two animals; and the Mole's whole heart went out to it at once, even though he did not yet fully understand its uses.

The Rat sculled smartly across and made fast. Then he held up his fore-paw as the Mole stepped gingerly down. "Lean on that!" he said. "Now then, step lively!" and the Mole to his surprise and rapture found himself actually seated in the stern of a real boat.

"This has been a wonderful day!" said Mole, as the Rat shoved off and took to the sculls again. "Do you know, I've never been in a boat before in all my life."

"What?" cried the Rat, open-mouthed: "Never been in a—you never—well I—what have you been doing, then?"

"Is it so nice as all that?" asked the Mole shyly, though he was quite prepared to believe it as he leant back in his seat and surveyed the cushions, the oars, the rowlocks, and all the fascinating fittings, and felt the boat sway lightly under him.

"Nice? It's the only thing," said the Water Rat solemnly as he leant forward for his stroke. "Believe me, my young friend, there is nothing—absolute nothing—half so much worth doing as simply messing about in boats. Simply messing," he went on dreamily: "messing—about—in—boats; messing—"

"Look ahead, Rat!" cried the Mole suddenly.

It was too late. The boat struck the bank full tilt. The dreamer, the joyous oarsman, lay on his back at the bottom of the boat, his heels in the air.

"—about in boats—or with boats," the Rat went on composedly, picking himself up with a pleasant laugh. "In or out of 'em, it doesn't matter. Nothing seems really to matter, that's the charm of it. Whether you get away, or whether you don't; whether you arrive at your destination or whether you reach somewhere else, or whether you never get anywhere at all, you're always busy, and you never do anything in particular; and when you've done it there's always something else to do, and you can do it if you like, but you'd much better not. Look here! If you've really nothing else on hand this morning, supposing we drop down the river together, and have a long day of it?"

It's obviously time for us mess about in boats that are a tad bigger than Rat's dinghy and to sail on into the Megayacht Millennium.

THE MEGAYACHT MILLENNIUM

What makes a child do well in school? What makes a young man, like John Muir do well in business? What makes John the man he is? Driven, focussed, some would say bordering on obsessive, certainly honest and not afraid to 'have a go.'

Research suggests that it's not the school a child goes to that decides their future, or how much money their parents have. It's what's inside a young person that counts.

The major influences on young John Muir were his parents. His mother, for her reassurance and support, his father, an internationally renowned yachtsman, boat builder and designer, for his mentoring and both his parents for helping him see the importance of doing his best. His uncles and aunts, his mates in the rough and tumble suburb of Battery Point and his brothers and sister were also an important influence on him on him in one way or the other.

There is growing evidence to suggest that there are six key qualities that contribute to an individual's capacity to do well later in life:

1. Joie de vivre: The ability to love life, to appreciate what others can offer and to be open to ideas and to feel connected.
2. Resilience: Providing the capacity to ward off depression and anxiety. Resilient people never give up, they seem to have an inner capacity to keep on going against the odds.
3. Self-discipline: The capacity to keep going when things don't work, to focus and sort out what is important and what isn't.
4. Honesty: Honesty matters because it's opposite quality, deception, will slow or halt progress and development. Honesty allows you to develop networks of people who trust you, want to do business with you because they know you are not trying to 'rip them off.'
5. Courage: To go where others fear to tread, to take on your inner fears and have a go at the unknown. To try, fail and try again.
6 Kindness: The capacity to empathise, to bolster your own learning by listening to others.

*The German shipyard Nobiskrug built two award-winning superyachts, **Triple Seven** (2007 International Superyacht Society Award) and **Sycara V** (2011 World Superyacht Award). Muir equipment was fitted to these two as well as other Nobiskrug motor yachts.*

In order to succeed, in his chosen business, against the odds, against the tyranny of distance, against a high Australian dollar, against recessions and global financial meltdowns, John has needed virtually all of these characteristics. He has courage in spades, he is resilient, honest as the day is long, has self-discipline that amazes many who know him and he has the capacity to show kindness when it's needed. He also has the capacity, to be as tough as old boots, to dig his heels in when he reckons its time and to be an obstinate coot.

As the new millennium dawns, it's these qualities that see John continuing to grow Muir Engineering as a preferred supplier to the mega and gigayacht and boat building sector. His business' reputation was also growing as the provider of one of the world's best and high end quality anchor and mooring winches. Certainly a good reputation to have. By the time the new millennium dawned, most people within the global yachting and motor yacht construction industry, particularly those who needed to know, knew of Muir Engineering, what they made and sold. The increasing cost of construction of these luxury vessels into the many millions of dollars seemed no obstacle to the ever increasing demand.

The orders flowed in. The work continued apace at Muir's Kingston operation. Muir Engineering suppliers were also benefiting from the new business.

The German shipyard Nobiskrug built two award-winning superyachts, *Triple Seven* (2007 International Superyacht Society Award) and *Sycara V* (2011 World Superyacht Award). Muir equipment was fitted to these two as well as other Nobiskrug motor yachts.

In some cultures the number seven is said to bring good fortune. This was true with the 67m superyacht *Triple Seven*. She brought luck to shipyard, the German designer and the client. *Triple Seven* was the first

yacht to be built completely under Nobiskrug's own team. The construction engineers ensured that the yacht could cruise smoothly and stably. They laid out the 12m wide frigate-like hull to an optimum, thus reducing water resistance and as a consequence, fuel consumption. Nobiskrug managed to include many innovative features during *Triple Seven*'s construction.

John Muir: "*Triple Seven* was to be Muir's first anchor and mooring winches order for Nobiskrug Shipyard back in 2004. *Triple Seven* was delivered in 2006. This order came our way through getting to know the Captain who had a genuine interest in the design and quality of Muir equipment; he had previously used a European competitor's equipment.

"Initially the shipyard could not comprehend why any European shipyard, let alone a German one, should be buying anchor and mooring winch gear from Australia when in their own backyard they already had a well-known winch maker.

"So the next challenge was to convince Nobiskrug of the quality of Muir equipment and that it came with the best back-up and service. I used one of my well versed sayings at the time which was 'You will never know how good Muir equipment is until you buy a ship set,' and reiterating by adding, 'In Australia we buy Mercedes trucks and motor cars along with BMW, and the likes of Dutch DAF commercial vehicles, and throughout Tasmania and the whole of Australia we provide excellent service and warranty, and we can do the same here in Europe via our Muir sales and service.'

"By this time Muir equipment was well known throughout Europe, having been available from the Cramm Group in the Netherlands since 1982. We had support and service in place through Cramm, along with a local service engineer based in Hamburg, Arto Lehtonen."

* Source: Article by Hillary Wilce, in October 2013 for the British online newspaper, The Independent.

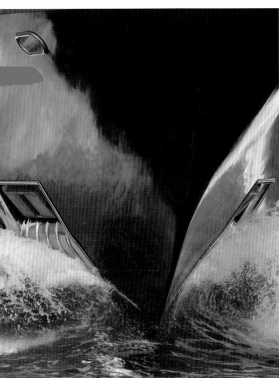

MY *TRIPLE SEVEN*

Muir supplied two VRC20000 anchor winches and two chain compressor anchoring systems, forward, and two VC20000 mooring capstans, aft.

Photos: Nobiskrug

MY *SYCARA V*

Muir supplied two VRC20000 anchor winches and two chain compressor anchoring systems, forward, and two VC20000 mooring winches, aft.

*Top right: John Muir, Matthew Johnston and Richard Chapman of Coursemaster onboard **Sycara V** at the Monaco Boat Show in 2009.*

Vessel and equipment photos: Nobiskrug

John Muir: "Finally, with all of Nobiskrug's concerns addressed, Muir was awarded an order for the now very popular high-end 20000 range which was at the forefront of winch gear available for 60m–75m motor yachts, and sailing yachts up to 85m.

"The order included;

– Electric 400 volt 3-phase drives and dual polished stainless steel VRC20000 anchor winches.
– VC20000 mooring capstans for the aft deck.

Anchoring systems comprised chain compressors, raised bases for chain compressors, four pocket chain rollers and devil claw assemblies to suit 24mm U3 stud link anchor chain."

The owner of Sycara V is an enthusiastic and experienced yachtsman who had a vision of building something different – a ship with a deliberately modern and powerful, yet at the same time, elegant appearance. The 68m superyacht was delivered in 2010.

John Muir: "Although the owner of Sycara V and his highly experienced project manager Steve Narkawicz were insistent on having Muir anchor and mooring winches, the shipyard wanted instead to fit equipment from a local winch maker. For several weeks I continued to negotiate with the shipyard by phone, but by that time I was becoming uneasy about the Sycara V order. So I brought forward my next trip to Europe by a month and arrived in Hamburg 34 hours later.

"Arto Lehtonen met me at Hamburg airport and we drove to Nobiskrug shipyard in Rendsberg — arriving there with maybe only an hour or so to spare before the shipyard people and Steve made the final decision on the purchase of anchor and mooring winches. I knew Steve would be holding his ground on the Muir equipment for Sycara V, and I phoned him from the foyer to let him know I was outside. He came out to meet me. Steve was surprised we made it in time, saying that we would have to give something away right now if we were to get the order. On the spot I agreed to a discount.

"Sycara V was fitted with the same 20000 anchoring and mooring equipment as Triple Seven. Our success was all about timing, and getting a break; we were in the right place at the right time!"

Other well-known shipyards Muir supplied in Europe and the USA were Derecktor, Broward, Halter Marine, Intermarine, Midland, Northern Marine, New England Boatworks, Viking, Flagship, Striker, Swiftships, Rybovich, Spencer and more.

John Muir: "The hardest yards of setting up in new markets are when you are travelling alone and before you know anyone. You have to find your own way around. That's how it was back in the 1970s and 1980s. Once established with a distributor it certainly becomes easier."

Success didn't stop with Europe; it was duplicated in sales to super and megayacht shipyards across the USA. The list included Delta Marine, Trinity Yachts and Christensen and others. Commensurately, there was a growing list of satisfied customers.

Muir's USA agent, Imtra, based in New Bedford and Seattle have supplied Muir equipment to boat builders and the trade across America for more than 30 years, and continue to do so today. The Muir gear includes a range of small, medium and large anchor and mooring winches for sail and motor yachts, work boats, coast guard vessels and ferries. Imtra's product range is one of the most comprehensive in the business and includes the famous, Norwegian made bow and stern thrusters.

Included amongst the new European contracts was one of the world's largest privately-owned two masted schooners and the most technologically sophisticated classic sailing yacht to date, the 62m superyacht Athos, launched in 2010 for Gerry Pepping, who operates a large refrigeration shipping company, with several vessels running between New Zealand and Europe. Athos was designed by award-winning designer Andre Hoek in conjunction with the renowned Dutch builder Holland Jachtbouw. The schooner carries two forward anchors, as is the standard with sailing yachts of her size, and a specially designed stern anchor winch. Athos (according to the yacht's website) is one of the most spectacular and innovative sailing yachts recently launched.

John Muir: "In 1989 we were manufacturing large anchor windlasses and mooring capstans for the likes of the 56 metre SY Adix, for Project Manager and Skipper Paul Goss, on behalf of a European owner. Some of the engineering designs we used on Adix were referred to twenty years later when we were bidding for the SY Athos project.

"On board Athos we installed two polished stainless steel VR18000 low profile hydraulic anchor windlasses, in conjunction with heavy duty chain stoppers for 24mm U3 stud link chain and a lever-action devil claw arrangement, for securing the anchor and chain when travelling.

"The stern anchor windlass was a hydraulic polished stainless steel VR13000 with chain stopper and devil claw arrangement."

Gert Veneen, the Media Manager for the European based Gerry Pepping, is an integral part of this next anecdote that is revealing about business ethics and the standards that John Muir lives up to and is well known for. It's also revealing about how John Muir behaves when he thinks he is being 'dudded.' As you can imagine, he, like most of us, he doesn't like it at all. (Being 'dudded' in Australian slang terms means being ripped off or conned.)

Gert Veenen, Media Manager for Gerry Pepping: "In the building phase of the SY Athos (around 2010) I had the pleasure of meeting Mr John Muir in person. I've no idea if Mr Muir's business was at the time concentrated on superyachts or if Athos was just an extraordinary project. (A one off.)"

John Muir: "I engaged a northern European based sales agent in the 1990s. I travelled with him all over Europe – Holland, Italy, France, Spain - selling mainly mega winches.

*Included amongst the new European contracts was one of the world's largest privately-owned two masted schooners and the most technologically sophisticated classic sailing yacht to date, the 62m superyacht **Athos**.*

OPPOSITE: SY *ATHOS*

*Clockwise from top: On a four week trip along the west coast of Greenland, 2013; Under full sails in a race in Caribbean waters; John in the Kingston factory with one of the winches as installed on the vessel. **Athos** was fitted with two Muir polished stainless steel VR18000 low profile hydraulic anchor winches, suited to 24mm U3 chain, chain stoppers and devil claw assemblies. The stern anchor winch was a VR13000 in polished stainless steel with devil claw assembly.*
Photos: Gert Veenman, Gerry Pepping

SY SHAMOUN

Shamoun *had the first ever VRC8000 polished stainless steel hydraulic anchor winches built by Muir. They beat their Dutch competitor for the order.*
Photos: Gert Veenman, Gerry Pepping

"Things went well for a few years then I heard on my marine industry grapevine that he was working with another company, a competitor of ours, and branding their winches as his own.

"There was a lot of competition for a new superyacht, the 33m SY *Shamoun*, being built for Gerry Pepping. (Well before the construction of *Athos*.) I heard my agent was trying to take this particular order from us and instead supply his re-branded winches. At the time he owed me around $20,000 dollars for an earlier winch sale and when I found out what he was up to, what I call 'back-dooring' Muir, he was terminated! We lost our $20,000 but he paid dearly for his behavior later when he bought an engineering workshop and eventually went out of business."

John Muir: "Muir Engineering were exhibiting at the METS in the late 1990s in Amsterdam and we were talking to Mr Pepping, along with several of his project team members. We were discussing the proposed equipment for the SY *Shamoun*. They were making comparisons between Muir equipment and a competitor. Towards the end of the boat show, Mr Pepping stopped by our display and told me that

"I had Mr Pepping's home fax number in Belgium and I forwarded this fax to him and followed up with a phone call. As far as I can remember he said something like, 'Well John, you have my verbal confirmation of this order, and I'll let your competitor know he's lost the order.'"

Muir Engineering won the *Shamoun* order and some years later were bidding for the 62m two-masted schooner *Athos*, being built for the same owner, Mr Pepping.

John Muir: "Once I had the *Athos* order I made sure I liaised closely with the owner's representative, Jos Scholten. I had worked with Jos previously on the other vessel for Mr Pepping (the 33 metre sailing yacht *Shamoun*, built in 1999) where we supplied a set of VR13000 low profile polished stainless steel anchor winches."

Some basic facts to ponder about *Athos*. She is one of the biggest and technically most complicated superyachts crossing the oceans today. Her size and weight (62m and 425t) is comparable to a Boeing 707 fully loaded, ready for takeoff. Under full sail she carries about the same sail area (3300m²) as a Tea

It made John more aware than ever that there are some people in life and business who cannot be trusted, who do not adhere to the six basic qualities of success.

a competitor had approached him and said, 'Mr Pepping, I thought you should know that the Muir winch equipment on the *Adela*, built by Pendennis shipyards in Cornwall in the UK, was faulty and was replaced with my gear.'

"This came as a hell of a surprise to me, as, to my knowledge, everything had been fine with *Adela*. I told Mr Pepping I thought it was a lie and that I'd be in touch with him soon to confirm that the claim was not true.

"I then spent several days trying to contact Henk Wiekens the Managing Director of Pendennis Shipyard. It took quite a few days and I didn't get through to him until I was in Dubai on the way back to Hobart.

"When I finally caught up with Henk, I told him the story and he confirmed that the competitor's story was incorrect. I asked him to put that in writing and when I got home there was a fax confirming that all the Muir anchoring and mooring equipment was still installed on *Adela* and operating satisfactorily.

Clipper did last century. However the clipper used approximately 35 different sails; *Athos* uses five or six. She can make speeds of up to 18kt when under full sail in the right conditions.

John Muir: "I found Jos good to work with, especially when it came to the complex installation of the anchor windlasses. He has great technical knowledge, knows a lot about yacht construction, and devised creative solutions for some of the more challenging anchor chain routing and stowage situations."

As you have gathered by now, John Muir won the contract to build and supply the superyacht *Shamoun* with anchor windlasses, chain stoppers and aft winch gear, but it was touch and go at times. It made John more aware than ever that there are some people in life and business who cannot be trusted, who do not adhere to the six basic qualities of success. It's a pity his adversary didn't understand how important one of those basic human qualities, honesty, is.

Jos Scholten: "You know, it's interesting that my long relationship with John Muir has been smooth and there is not so much to anecdote. I highly respect the way John has led the company over the years.

"When I think back about why, again and again, I advised my customers to use Muir equipment on their yachts and launches I come to the conclusion that there is one man giving directions. I have a strong aversion against accountant driven companies. They make for a while nice profits but these accountants have no clue about the technical details of the products they sell. Their focus on profit diverts from the need of the customers and R&D usually suffers.

"For me that is where John Muir stands out. Once or twice a year you could receive a call from the director who travelled the globe to give personal advice on chain run, anchor rollers, brake bands or hydraulics, you name it.

"Not only that, but I and my customers always had the chance to comment or suggest changes that would suit the project.

"The fact that Muir always kept the focus on their main business, being anchor systems, gives me the confidence that my customers can rely on that 'shiny thing on the foredeck' which can all of a sudden be the last bit of hope of surviving."

John Muir: "From my perspective, Jos Scholten was one of the best project managers/owner's representatives I've ever worked with.

"He has a thorough understanding of design, engineering, mechanics, hydraulics and overall motor and sail yacht construction. Jos is the sort of person who always is straight to the point and expects things done in a timely manner and good to work with as long as he's kept in the loop. His expertise came to the fore when he supervised the construction of the *Athos*."

Jos Scholten was project manager on the building of two outstanding sailing yachts – *Shamoun* and *Athos*. Both were built for Mr Gerry Pepping and both are fitted with Muir anchor and mooring winches. SY *Athos* participates in regatta and race events in the Caribbean and the Mediterranean and is also available for charter.

Another reason why Muir Engineering has succeeded against the odds is John's immense technical knowledge of winches of all shapes and sizes, how they work, and what makes them tick and the capacity to listen to a client's needs. He talks to ship engineers and project managers and comes up with innovative solutions that suit their needs.

A well-known shipyard had purchased Muir anchor and mooring winches for their first large 70m motor yacht. It's quite normal in

66 *The fact that Muir always kept the focus on their main business, being anchor systems, gives me the confidence that my customers can rely on that 'shiny thing on the foredeck' which can all of a sudden be the last bit of hope of surviving.* 99

– JOS SCHOLTEN

THIS PAGE AND OPPOSITE: SY *ADELA*
Fitted with Muir VRC11000 vertical anchor winches and VC8000 mooring capstans.
Photos: Pendennis Shipyard

these situations, when it's a first design that there will be minor problems and technical issues with the location of the anchor winch, chain locker and spurling pipe.

John Muir: "I received a call from the yard's engineer asking me if I would visit their shipyard and discuss the installation. The vessel had been launched and was on its first charter in the Indian Ocean. There was a second vessel at the shipyard, in the early stages of construction, and he was keen for me to view the installation on the first vessel before they committed to Muir gear equipment on this second yacht.

"Within 24 hours of leaving Sydney, I was on board the yacht where I stayed for a couple of nights. Unfortunately I couldn't get a flight home for another two days, so was invited to stay on board and live the dream of having my own super yacht.

"I evaluated the installation, ran the anchor winches, climbed around in the chain locker and thoroughly examined the anchor chain routing and stowage.

"Some motor yacht designs have a fine forward hull entry. (In layman's terms that means long and skinny.) In some designs, the finer forward hull can create challenges in accommodating an adequately sized and wide enough chain locker. The trick is to install the anchor windlasses in the preferred operational position as far aft as practicable that allows the anchor chain unrestricted vertical fall into the centre of the chain locker below. If the chain falls against a bulkhead or the side of the chain locker, it will pile too high without spreading, restricting the stowing of the anchor chain and potentially jamming the winch gear. When the chain falls into the centre of an adequately sized chain locker, it will allow the chain to evenly spread out, which conversely works to minimise any restrictions when the chain is being run out.

"By the end of the second day I had prepared a sketch of modifications to improve on the installation for the next vessel. The solution was to increase the angle of the spurling pipe, (that's the large pipe below that carries the chain fall from the anchor chain roller to the chain locker, angled up no less than 45°), to prevent the anchor chain sticking and at the same time dropping the chain closer to the centre of the chain locker. This modification was undertaken by the shipyard and the second vessel incorporated the new design.

"Due to some of the anchor chain stowage challenges arising from such installations, I decided to include the preferred stowage configuration in our new Mega catalogue on page 5. I am pleased to say this is now used by the Muir design team, naval architects and boat builders worldwide.

There comes a time when it's appropriate to reflect on the thought processes and sales techniques that underpin success. They are lessons that everyone who wants to enter the sales game should have at the front of their training manual.

Let's join in a conversation at the John Muir Sales School of Essential Learnings.

1. It's far, far less costly to keep a customer than it is to lose one! Sometimes it's called 'going the extra mile,' at least it was when Dale Carnegie was writing his book, 'How to Win Friends and Influence people.' His suggestion was to avoid arguments. This would seem to be almost a 'given,' but far too many salespeople, perhaps in their zeal, engage in arguments with a customer who shows resistance or says he or she likes another brand. Carnegie said, "The only way to get the best of an argument is to avoid it." Be respectful of the customer's opinion. Do not argue, criticize, or condemn. You will have an opportunity to brag about your offering soon enough.

2. Part of the John Muir selling strategy is to get on board as many boats at shows as you can and swap business cards with one or all of the boat builders, sales representatives, and the importers. While looking around the vessels, write down the anchor winch make that is installed, the anchor chain size and the kilowatt (kW) of the winch motor. If you can, ask about the price for the existing winch gear. Importantly ask everyone, "Does the winch gear meet your expectations?"

It is particularly important to do this at all the boat shows where boats from all over the world are moored. Boat shows like Miami, Fort Lauderdale, Genoa, Paris, London, Dusseldorf, Monaco, and closer to home – Auckland, Sydney and Sanctuary Cove.

John Muir: "These are the times when smaller power boats, motor cruisers, sail yachts and megayachts are together in the show vicinity. It is a wonderful opportunity to look for new customer prospects. Always ask if it's OK, it may not be a good time, they may say, 'Come back later' that day or early in the morning when less people are around!

Dale Carnegie rolls this advice into two tips, smile and listen. Smile. Carnegie called it "a simple way to make a good first impression." Every business encounter — across the desk, at the customer's front door, and even on the telephone — should begin with a smile. 'Actions,' Carnegie noted, 'speak louder than words.' And a smile says, 'I like you.' Listen. Customers and clients want to hear what you have to say, but they want you to hear what they have to say first. Beyond that, consider this: How can you, as a sales rep, know what customers need if you don't give them chance to tell you?

3. Get to know your competitor's equipment and accessories as well as you know your own. Keep abreast of what the competition have so you can answer every question from a client. Again, Dale Carnegie says arouse an "eager want." It almost sounds poetic. Carnegie cited Harry A. Overstreet as the originator of this idea. Overstreet said, "Action springs from what we fundamentally desire." If you own a bait store, understand that customers do not desire night crawlers; they desire catching fish. Capisce?

4. Remember customers and everyone you can by their first names. There are Australian politicians who got re-elected every term simply because they had the remarkable capacity to remember their constituents' names and a bit about their lives. Done deal every election. Bill Clinton has a reputation for being able to remember virtually everyone he has met and people tell you that when he is talking to you he is actively listening, even if you are being boring. Carnegie agrees. Use names. Learn the names of your employees, your customers, and your prospects as they enter your sphere of business. After you learn those names, use them. Carnegie's principle here is simple: A person's name is, to that person, the sweetest and most important sound in any language.

5. Get to know as many people in the customer's business as you can, from the top down and don't overlook the person in reception. It's all about learning the customer's business, showing an interest and eventually they might well buy your gear and not realise that you have sold it to them. Carnegie calls it "Letting customers sell to themselves". In general, people do not like to be told what to do or what to buy. Provide information and be helpful, but let customers make the decision. You do this by asking questions and steering the conversation until customers realize that your product or service is the solution they've been looking for.

> ## *From the moment I met John I was struck by the investigative, curious and vivid nature of his gaze. He looked me in the eye from the moment we met.*

— LUCA SIGNORINI, TBS MARINE

Carnegie's strategy was simple: 'Take a genuine interest in the lives of others.' He also suggests that if you get it wrong, apologise then fix it. Do you remember the *Adix* construction story? John and his competitor had underquoted the size of the winch gear needed on a boat of that size. John realised his mistake, went home, designed and built new and bigger winches and equipment. Once it was built and shipped, he rang the Project Manager Paul Goss. He told Paul that the winch and mooring gear he originally quoted was too small, as was the competitors. He told him that Muir has shipped larger sized anchor and mooring winches and chains and to let John know what Paul thinks of the gear when it arrives.

Muir Engineering had the order and were paid for the larger equipment.

Dale Carnegie says, "You can make more friends in two months by becoming interested in other people than you can in two years by trying to get other people interested in you." Never a truer word was spoken!

According to the John Muir School of Essential Learnings there is another somewhat light hearted saying that sums it all up.

" P___ Poor Planning equals P___ Poor Performance!"

Success is also about building a product that lasts, that even when some think it's worn out or in need of replacement, as George Gershwin penned, 'it ain't necessarily so!'

Now it's time to relate a story that springs straight from the Dale Carnegie School of Business and the John Muir Sales School of Essential Learnings. This is how John Muir appointed a new sales representative in a foreign country.

Let me introduce Luca Signorini, a young and energetic Italian salesman from TBS Marine. The company's website describes itself as: 'a young and dynamic company, a new name for the distribution and representation, specialising in yachts and mega-yachts.'

Luca Signorini: "My memories of John Muir start when we met for the first time in Monaco Yacht Show in 2010. My former business partner and I were introduced to John by a common friend who was aware that Muir was looking for an Italian distributor.

ABOVE: TRAVELLING WITH LUCA
Top: John and Luca Signorini doing sales calls throughout Italy, then on their way via rail from Pisa to Amsterdam for METS 2010. Middle and bottom: John and Wendy caught up with Luca on a more social basis in 2015 while sightseeing in Italy.

"From the moment I met John I was struck by the investigative, curious and vivid nature of his gaze. He looked me in the eye from the moment we met. I got the impression that he was wondering if it would be wise to trust two young, relatively unknown but highly motivated Italians, to be his new Italian sales representatives.

"I couldn't believe my ears when, after only three minutes of chatting he said, 'I judge people from the way they look me in the eyes – you did it – so I propose to you a gentleman's agreement, to make you Muir's Italian sales representatives. If you agree and we shake hands, this is far more important than a signed contract black on white. Do you agree?' The nodding of our heads and our smiling faces were the most appropriate replies. We were speechless."

For John Muir, his word is his bond. It doesn't come more straightforward than that.

John Muir: "I thoroughly enjoyed working with Luca on our trips throughout Italy. When Luca got really excited he would talk very fast like a racehorse caller, and you really had to listen to make out the words. So fast in fact, I couldn't tell which words were Italian and which were English!

"Luca worked long hours and was a partner in TBS and managed the marine sales office in Viareggio along with two other employees. All up, four people with the partnership.

"Viareggio is one of a handful of yachting hubs along the Italian coast where major boat building and servicing takes place. It's what I would call a romantic place to visit, most of the hotels are along the main street and face the Mediterranean. At night very tall yacht masts stand proud with red navigation lights atop, and seeing up to ten large Perini motor yachts moored stern to the main wharf, is really a sight to behold on a beautiful warm night."

John travelled a lot through Italy with Luca, on occasions from Viareggio to La Spezia, on to Genoa, then travelling at night all the way across to Ancona on the opposite coast. They would bed down for the night, rise early, have a quick breakfast, and visit several of the local shipyards in one day.

John Muir: "Most of the time when we visited Ancona, we drove back to Rome. On one occasion, Luca's then business partner drove us from Viareggio to Naples to visit several shipyards, and we returned home that night. I must say most Italian drivers scare me a bit, because the foot is right down, and I'm sure they think they're driving racing cars."

John gets a bit misty-eyed thinking about people like Luca, as many have strong family ties.

John Muir: "Luca has a lovely wife and two young children, and like most of us endeavours to spend more time at home, which is difficult because he works such long hours and travels so much.

"Having travelled so much myself for the past 40 years, throughout Asia, North America, Europe and Scandinavia, throughout all seasons, I relish getting home to spend time with my family. I've often been asked, of all the places I've visited, where the best place is to have a holiday. My answer is always, 'Tasmania, down the D'Entrecasteaux Channel on our yacht, catching up with family and friends.'"

According to John anyone who travels extensively for work really feels the pressure of being away from home and family. You miss family birthdays, anniversaries, special events, whole stages of your childrens' development. According to John sales people, living out of suitcases for weeks on end, who do well, who don't sell gear below the profit margin, should be paid at least the same or more than the CEO.

John Muir: "I was fortunate that Wendy didn't need to travel and in reality brought up our two girls mainly on her own, with some help from her parents. In the early 1990s in the 'recession we had to have,' I was travelling a lot, and at one point Wendy tracked the time I was away, and it was almost half the year.

"From where we are based in Hobart, we are on the opposite side of the world to our major customers in the northern hemisphere. Some of our customers generally don't like the long travel south from the northern hemisphere to Australia, so we don't see them very often. Unless someone jumped on a plane and went to visit them, we would hardly see them. Added to this was the tyranny of distance to ship a large order to Europe or the US, which could take up to 60 days, whereas a European supplier doesn't have that added cost or delay."

There are great sacrifices to make if you decide to build a global business when you are based in Tasmania. The manufacturer (Muir Engineering) has to bring the business to the customer. (Whether they be in Europe, the USA or Asia.) Several factors combine to ensure you win an order: price, quality, service and relationships.

John Muir: "On occasions these four factors would rank equally. In discussions with shipyards in the early days of exporting, they would ask why they should buy Australian made winches for their European yachts. There are several responses, but one of my favourites is, 'You won't know how reliable a Muir winch is until you buy one.' Or I'd try this one, 'Australians buy a lot of European cars, because they are considered the best in the world, so why wouldn't you want the best winches in the world, no matter where they came from?'"

John Muir built up a network of strong local service and sales representatives over the years. He says every customer, no matter where they are situated around the globe, expects the very best service response in the same time zone as they are operating.

Maintaining global representation is vital to business success. And it's a must having a local sales and service agent.

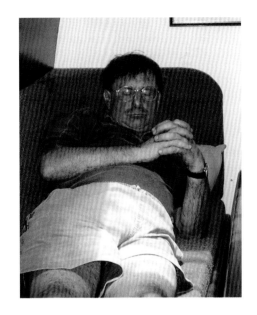

REST AND RELAXATION
Above and below, John has always used the water to unwind from long periods travelling for work. It also helped in his recovery from acute pancreatitis.

> **❝** *Having travelled so much myself for the past 40 years… I relish getting home to spend time with my family. I've often been asked, of all the places I've visited, where the best place is to have a holiday. My answer is always, 'Tasmania, down the D'Entrecasteaux Channel on our yacht, catching up with family and friends.'* **❞**

John Muir: "Of all the countries I have visited overseas, Italy stands out as one of my favourites. I love the culture, the ancient history, the cuisine, the lovely friendly people, and in particular the beautiful Italian coastline and coastal towns.

"Ever since I began in business, selling and travelling overseas, I have had a passion to succeed, and that includes to do my utmost to go back home with the orders. Being away, jumping from one plane to another, visiting shipyards, factories and suppliers, exploring new possibilities, accepting new challenges everyday. For me it became the model I would follow.

"One way to measure the performance of a sales person, is with results. It doesn't matter what time they go to bed or get up in the morning, or how many hours or days they work, the only way to measure sales performance is by what they sell and what profit or margin they make. No more, no less."

For Luca Signorini the vision of John Muir, doing what he does, year after year, travelling endlessly, building his global business was a strong role model.

Luca Signorini: "The example John set wasn't only important for the successes achieved in a whole life of hard work, but more for the man that was behind the entrepreneur. He taught me the real value of relationships in business.

"His attachment to traditional values based on hard work, family, and mutual help made me proud to be part of Muir's 'circle of trust.'

"I also have many other good recollections of small episodes which consolidate my career and my life with John, Matthew, Ian, Jason and all the other guys at Muir.

"For example when several years ago we visited the Muir factory along with an engineer from an important Italian yard, Mr Mirko Mammarella, we had the opportunity to see the people at work, the tests in the facilities, all the milling CNC machines at work, the design departments with the amazing 3D prototyping, and meet all the people behind this great brand we are so proud to represent."

Mr Mammarella was the project engineer responsible for all machinery and deck equipment on a new 74m motor yacht project being built by CRN at their Ancona shipyard, for a Middle Eastern owner. Luca, his then business partner Cristian and Mr Mammarella came to Hobart to look over the Muir facilities and to witness the interstate surveyor testing the anchoring and mooring equipment being built for the project. They were all impressed with the Muir facility and the testing of the equipment.

For the comparatively young Luca there are countless tales, some tall, some true, about the adventure lived by John Muir. He wasn't just thinking about time spent together at endless boat shows, but about the seemingly tireless working capacity of a man old enough to be his father, who really knew what he was on about when it came time to fixing a problem or servicing a charter yacht's gear.

Luca Signorini: "It wasn't only the amazing times we spent together in Monaco, Amsterdam, Viareggio, Cannes, and countless others, but also the big challenges posed by the strict time schedule of the charter yachts we had to service, to let them continue their trips.

"Customer satisfaction was top of the priority list and the will to overcome every logistical difficulty, lifting, overhauling and servicing the heavy stainless steel 'Muir babies' in few hours, without the owner even noticing our passage on the deck. We serviced yachts in Sardinia, the Red Sea, Singapore, Portofino, the Maldives, jumping on a plane as we saw John doing many times, spares in the trolley and a few tools to do the work.

RIGHT AND OPPOSITE: MY *YALLA*

74m motor yacht project built by CRN at their Ancona yard and installation of the winch gear was overseen by Luca. The vessel was fitted with Muir two VRC22000 anchor winches, two chain compressor anchoring systems and two VC20000 mooring capstans., all in polished stainless steel. Photos: TBS Marine

"It was mission accomplished every time, report done, factory in Hobart informed, where Matthew and Ian awaited the outcome of our efforts. The sensation that prevails is the satisfaction to be walking the same track outlined by John Muir over so many years and to be part of something bigger that I dare to call Family."

When trying to compress their visits to the Italian yards into a few days or at times all week driving thousands of kilometres, John would be constantly attending to his emails, ready for the next meeting, and, Luca vividly remembers John would be fresh as a rose every morning, while a much younger man, may be dead flat tired.

Luca Signiori: "I do remember once when we first travelled by train with John, then onto an airline, in and out of airports, into Holland, loaded with six bags and trolleys full of brand new brochures. We moved all that to Ancona and Venice from Florence with that burden to load and unload all the time.

"I also remember when the first time John taught me the meaning of some 'rude' Aussie slang, like when he said... 'You Luca, you know how to speak with people, you silly bugger!' I thought I had done something wrong at the beginning, lost as I was in the translation!

"Our conversation in Viareggio's local pub, with a beer in front of us after 14 hours of work, were illuminating for me. Listening to the tales of travels around the world, meeting with the most influential and important owners' representatives, yard owners and so on in an endless flow of memories which I avidly stored in my head."

Another much younger man who John engaged as his Dutch and Western Europe technical and service representative is Philippus (Philip) Feenstra. Philip is a graduate mechanical engineer from NHL Hogeschool in Holland. He has been a project manager and project engineer for Cramm Yachting Systems and is fluent in Dutch, Northern Frisian, German and English. Just the sort of individual you need to do the tasks John needs done and done well. These days Philip runs his own business: FEEBE Boarding Equipment for the megayacht industry, and still works with Muir on sales and service.

Philip Feenstra: "I consider John a close friend these days and I've learned a lot from him. Our relationship is still strong.

"We met in Monaco, around 2007, at the Monaco Boat Show. I had just started my own company [PSI Feenstra, now FEEBE Boarding Equipment] and

John gave me the opportunity to travel around Holland with him. We chatted a lot on our travels. He taught me a lot about the importance of quality, service and customer relationships, and it was very helpful for me."

John Muir: "Philip is qualified as a mechanical engineer, he served his early days as a junior engineer with well-known hydraulic equipment manufacturer, Cramm, located in Berlikum not far from his own new workshop. He's a hydraulic specialist, and the FEEBE equipment is mainly hydraulic, which he combines with Muir hydraulic and electric winching systems and undertakes the complete installation design, and in cases, the installation of the products."

John's first meeting with Philip came about when John was kneeling down putting brochures in the stand on the Muir display at the Monaco Boat Show. He looked up and saw this really tall guy looking down at him.

John Muir: "I asked if I could help him, he replied, 'Yes I'm interested in representing you and doing some service work.'

"Philip explained he'd just set up his new business, and he was working from home at that time. Towards the end of the show we met again, and I informed him we could commence working together.

"Following Monaco, he travelled with me through the German and Dutch yards I was visiting regarding new projects. I introduced Philip to key people within the servicing and procurement aspects of the industry. Subsequently, when I was back in Europe, often four or five times a year, I would meet up with Philip and he would drive us around continuing to learn more about Muir and our winching products.

> ❝ *I consider John a close friend these days and I've learned a lot from him…He taught me a lot about the importance of quality, service and customer relationships, and it was very helpful for me.* ❞

– PHILIP FEENSTRA, PSI

"On several occasions I engaged Philip to service winching equipment on 60 to 70m motor yachts, some in the south of France. It was work that he and his tradesmen did well.

"On several occasions Philip talked about a new business name, and we discussed this over several months. The name he landed on was FEEBE, which was used for his new range of cranes, hoists, and boarding ramps and ladders.

"On subsequent get togethers we discussed a new workshop, which he proposed to build in Arum, close to his home in the north of the Netherlands. Philip sub-contracted the construction out and undertook most of the fit-out himself.

ABOVE: PHILIPPUS FEENSTRA
Philippus Feenstra in his workshop in the Netherlands.

"From there he has progressed and made in-roads to a good lot of the northern European shipyards."

Philip Feenstra: "I helped John Muir a lot in the Netherlands – and to expand the servicing. It was all the way on the other side of the planet from where Muir was based, but for me it was just a few hours' drive away.

"FEEBE endeavour to supply our clients with a complete package. It's better for everyone, and for after sales there's only one company for the customer to deal with. We appreciate our clients spending their money with us, and it's important to us that they get a nice holiday on their boats with their families, knowing they are safe and comfortable.

"It really makes sense to combine the technical items that we do, plus Muir products into one package."

Muir provides detailed installation drawings with dimensions for location and size of all foundation holes for the winching equipment. These detailed drawings are passed on to the shipyard to use when constructing the fore and aft deck. This process is vital due to Muirs' distance from northern Europe, and the time it takes to ship or air-freight the gear to Europe. (Six weeks shipping time or seven to ten days by air.)

The main advantage in doing it this way is that the fore and aft decks have been completed by the time the winches arrive from Australia. Then it's simply a matter of dropping the winches into place and bolting them down. This is how Muir manages to sell and service its products so effectively throughout Europe.

John Muir: "Philip would often call me for information, at odd times when he was on a service or installation project. Being on the opposite side of the world, his calls came either very early in the morning or very late at night for me."

Philip Feenstra: "If there are any issues, John's on it right away. His approach is, 'Do it properly, and do it fast.' One of the most important lessons John taught me is that it's crucial to action requests immediately, and make sure everything's ok so the owner can enjoy their holiday."

John Muir: "When it comes to spare parts and servicing our customers, it's often up to us to work any required hours through the day or night to meet the deadline. You can't say no to an owner or captain who wants to go away on their motor or sailing yacht at short notice. They've spent a lot of money on buying Muir equipment in the first place and they expect it to work every day of its life."

Philip Feenstra: "The after sales service is 'a very special thing,' as John says. On occasions for customers we knew well, we would send new parts first, regardless of who is at fault, and sort the financial part out later. There is nothing worse than an owner having his boat out of operation, particularly during the charter season."

John Muir: "Be it either FEEBE or Muir equipment, Philip is involved hands-on in overseeing the technical, installation and commissioning processes of all the equipment. The FEEBE business today is flourishing and continues to expand."

Let's revisit the Muir School of Essential Learnings and the input from Dale Carnegie. Lesson one from John Muir was, "It's far, far less costly to keep a customer than it is to lose one!" Dale Carnegie said, "The only way to get the best of an argument is to avoid it." It seems that Philip Feenstra has passed at the very least that section of John's course with flying colours.

Another of John's long term friends and business partners, Ian Pettitt formed Muir UK in the mid 1980s. It was a joint venture between the two families. It was indeed sad that Ian passed away in 2001. In normal circumstances that would have probably been the end of that business relationship. John would have had to find someone to take over.

ABOVE: HANDING OVER THE BATON
Left to right: Muir UK representative Ian Pettitt, John, and Ian's son Simon Pettitt at METS, 1998.

BELOW: MONACO BOAT SHOW 2009
From left, Simon Pettitt, Fred Mayer, Matthew Johnston and Christoff Quesnel.

OPPOSITE: FILLING HIS FATHER'S SHOES
Simon with John and Chris Michael at METS in 2001.

> ❝ *The whole time I've known him, John has probably only ever missed one or two of the annual METS trade shows in Amsterdam. He'd be there helping to set the displays up before the show, and breaking them down at the end of it.* ❞
>
> – SIMON PETTITT, MUIR UK

As chance would have it, there was someone waiting in the wings. It was Ian's son, Simon, who took over the business and continued the partnership with John. Simon at the time was crewing on a large sailing yacht and welcomed the opportunity to be involved.

Simon Pettitt: "Muir UK was a joint venture between John Muir and my father Ian. I started working for Muir in 1999, but after my father passed away in 2001, I was handed the baton. I've been involved with John ever since."

John Muir: "Simon took over the Muir UK business after his Dad, Ian died. I visited his father in hospital and we discussed the future of the business. He asked me if I would work with Simon to get him on track because he'd been primarily sailing for years and would need some guidance and support. I have worked closely and mentored Simon ever since."

Ian Pettitt was a trail blazer and in his early days worked tirelessly for the American firm, Cummins Diesel. When Simon and his sisters were young, the family travelled the length and breadth of the Middle East for several years, while Ian was setting up distribution, sales and service networks for the company. In later discussions Simon told John that they lived in a variety of hotels, attending schools scattered across the region. Ian was totally supported in his business endeavors by his wife Jan, as was John by his wife Wendy.

The new relationship between John and Simon, one older and worldly wise, the other less experienced in business but with years of experience sailing on a variety of large racing and sailing yachts, would prove to be a business relationship made in heaven.

Simon Pettitt: "My background is working as crew on megayachts, so I was able to offer an insight into how the gear our company was producing would be treated by the end user. The gear wasn't always necessarily used the way it should be as crews were often hard on things. They didn't want to know too much about it, it just needed to work.

"John approached things from an engineering perspective whereas I was approaching it more from a usage standpoint. I'd go to boat shows, talk to captains, and pass their feedback onto John – 'John, this is how the crew is going to look after it, they just want it to work.'

"The whole time I've known him, John has probably only ever missed one or two of the annual METS trade shows in Amsterdam. He'd be there helping to set the displays up before the show, and breaking them down at the end of it. Back in the hey-day, around the mid-2000s, the show would start at 10 am and there'd be people lined up waiting to talk to us from 9:30.

"John has a tendency to overwork (somewhat of an understatement) so I'd keep an eye on him to make sure he was taking his insulin shots. Being a type 1 diabetic and needing to inject his insulin several times a day and of course eating properly, but looking back, he was probably also keeping an eye on us [laughs].

"John is well known for his faxing abilities. At one show, I was in my hotel room and one of John's business cards appeared under the door. It had written on it: 'Been on fax since 4am, I'll be late to the show.' Everywhere we went, there had to be a fax machine. I would often think, 'God John, how do you organise all of this?' We'd be driving somewhere and there'd be faxes all over the dashboard of the car."

John Muir: "While we were travelling, I'd make the most of every free moment and write out my faxes and notes, then clip them together and leave them on the dash board of the car. It was just like having a mobile office."

Simon Pettitt: "If you had a problem, you could always pick up the phone and speak to John. If he didn't answer, you'd be guaranteed he'd call you back within a few minutes. If you had a problem, instead of having to wait a day for the factory guys you'd get an email response from John. He always had time for you. I mean, you always have your disagreements, [with anyone] but it was all positive really."

According to Simon, John's product knowledge about his competitors was extensive. At boat shows, Simon says John was always keeping a close eye on what they were doing.

Simon Pettitt: "Whenever we travelled together I was always having to carry windlasses in my hand luggage. I'd be going to Holland and held up at Customs having to explain what these mysterious items in my case were and why I had them. They'd never believe you, so they'd have to run it through the x-ray several times. John regularly carried up to 70kg of luggage without having to pay extra. No doubt all the airlines knew him. He travelled so much and was a frequent flyer member with several airlines that membership allowed him to take 72kg of luggage."

> ❝ *If you had a problem, instead of having to wait a day for the factory guys you'd get an email response from John.* ❞

– SIMON PETTITT

For Simon there is one trip with John that is stuck forever in his memory, it was to Russia and neither of them had been there before. It was all new and at times quite scary.

Simon Pettitt: "John and I went to Russia on a trip to work on a new 73 metre motor yacht project which John needed to close, as he and one of his sales guys had been working away at it for more than 18 months .We weren't sure what to expect. The owner told us there'd be someone to pick us up at the airport, so we were expecting a private car or limousine, but no, it was a grubby cab.

ABOVE: MUIR UK
Simon Pettitt at the Monaco Boat Show, 2002.

OPPOSITE: MUIR UK OFFICE
Simon, back in 2001, outside Muir's Southampton office.

"We felt rather uncomfortable for the whole ride to our hotel but the driver knew where we were to go! We arranged to meet the owner of the megayacht at the hotel, but as we were checking in the owner who John had met before appeared out of the hotel lift, to take us up to his hotel suite. We thought this was rather odd but it was our first time in Moscow. Turns out he was staying there and had a very large suite he was using as his office and meeting place. Actually John thought he may have even owned the hotel."

John Muir: "Not long after we moved into our rooms at this hotel, I had a knock on my door. When I opened it I found an attractive woman standing there and she asked me if I would like a lady? I was quite taken aback, and all I could manage to say was, 'No, I don't, but there is a bloke up the hall who might' and sent her off on a wild goose chase.

"A few minutes later, Simon turned up at my door and we had a good laugh about it, then ventured out for a meal. Moscow is not a good place to walk around at night, it can be a very scary place."

The shipyard they were visiting had just been declassified, as in its former life it built submarines for the Russian Navy. After two days of working things out,

in John's inimitable style, they got the order. Muir was paid the balance owing less 10%, until the vessel was commissioned and accepted by the owner.

The project involved two 74m motor yachts, both for one owner. Muir received a deposit on the work for both yachts and progressive payments followed. However there was a 12 month time lag between the boats. The balance owing was due to be paid when the yachts were commissioned. There was a long delay at the shipyard so the first vessel was launched, made seaworthy and began a long tow behind an ocean going tug destined for a German shipyard to finish the work. On the western side of the Norwegian coast the tow-line broke and the yacht was wrecked. The project was covered by insurance and the owner negotiated with the German yard to replace the hull, lengthen it by another 6m to nearly 80m and within two years had a new and larger motor yacht ready for launching.

John Muir: "The second yacht was transported from Moscow to an Italian shipyard for completion. We lost track of what was happening and the Italian yard finished the project without our assistance, installing our equipment, without us commissioning it. The final upshot saw us losing about 10% of the sale price.

MY SHEMARA
Above and opposite photos: Boat International
Left photo: Simon Pettitt, Muir UK

"The Russian shipyard had taken nearly two years to get one vessel half completed. The German yard designed and built a new and larger vessel and had it ready to launch almost in the same time frame. It's German expertise at its best."

John and Simon were then due to visit DML Plymouth (in England). Just before they were due to arrive were the terrorist bombings in London. The city, the docks and boat building yards were locked down.

Simon Pettitt: "The DML shipyard was located on a British Naval base, so we had to give the yard 24 hours notice of our visit to arrange the proper security clearances. There was a communications cock up, and they thought it was just John who was visiting. We both turned up at security but they would only let John in, so he had to go into this meeting alone and without me and for once in his life he was semi-unprepared."

Another of these seemingly endless stories involves a large and quite old motor yacht from the 1930s, *Shemara*. Originally it was a classic 65m luxury motor

the yacht to its former glory. *Shemara* was one of the most involved and intriguing classic yacht projects I have ever been involved with.

"It was a huge and complex project that involved cutting and removing the keel and part of the hull, then re-engineering a new keel and hull up to the water line — work that was undertaken by a team of highly experienced shipbuilders. The project also included new propulsion and generating equipment.

The work on the yacht was carried out to the highest possible standards which meant when it came time to install the ten Muir winches, the design and rigidity of the fore, aft, and mid-ship deck foundations were easily strong enough to hold everything in place, particularly when under full load when the yacht was undergoing sea trials.

All the Muir winch equipment was 400Volt, 3 phase, 50hz. Up forward were installed dual polished stainless steel VRC18000 vertical electric anchor winches with variable speed frequency 'soft' drives. Mid forward

> **❝ In much the same way as classic cars are restored, the owner was more interested in restoring the yacht to its former glory. Shemara was one of the most involved and intriguing classic yacht projects I have ever been involved with. ❞**
>
> – JOHN MUIR

yacht that had been abandoned up a creek for a long, long time. It was a traditional old style motor yacht without a bulwark. (In layman's terms a bulwark is an extension of a ship's sides above the level of the deck.) The new owner, an Englishman, arranged his own shipbuilding company for the restoration project.

Simon Pettitt: "As the Muir representative on the project I remember we negotiated for some months and were genuinely interested in supplying the best Muir vertical anchor and mooring winches we could. Looking back I am sure *Shemara*'s Captain and the shipyards project management appreciated John's advice that *Shemara* was going to be fitted with the best suited anchor and mooring winches and accessories money could buy."

John Muir: "In much the same way as classic cars are restored, the owner was more interested in restoring

were dual VC11000 electric mooring capstans, aft mid-ship there was another set of dual VC11000 mooring capstans and on the aft deck dual VC13000 mooring capstans.

John Muir: "The completed vessel, the renovations, engineering, the highest quality custom made furniture, internal and external finishes are a credit to the design and rebuild team. The shipyard management, contractors and especially the owner deserve the highest accolades for this remarkable restoration project that took several years to complete.

"*Shemara* was re-christened in 2014 and successfully sea trialled, easily fulfilling the expectations of the shipyard, captain, owner and Muir."

Muir equipment is made to last a lifetime and can be more expensive, but it's reliable and it works. Muir's also offers a worldwide service to clients.

ICE-CLASS EXPEDITION YACHT MY *STEEL*

VRC20000 anchor winches and VC18000 mooring capstans finished in polished aluminium-bronze.
Photos: Pendennis Shipyard

> ❝ *John told the boat show management in no uncertain terms that his winch was going to be exhibited one way or the other, as he didn't want Maxwell stealing the limelight.* ❞

— SIMON PETTITT, MUIR UK

Another really interesting project during this time period was the motor yacht *Steel*, being built at Pendennis yards in Cornwall.

The surveyors wouldn't accept the proposed anchor weight on that particular sized anchor chain, suggesting a larger chain size. This does happen from time to time, it's just part and parcel of the anchor and chain package.

John Muir: "About a month after the order was placed, it was decided the vessel was too short and need a longer hull. So the boat was cut in half and had 5 extra metres added to its length to become a 50m motor yacht. Because it was now larger, we could more readily provide and install the larger windlasses. During the construction process the bottom of the vessel from the waterline down was replaced, together with replacement propulsion systems and all equipment located below decks.

"*Steel* started off as a 45m build. The forward anchor winches we thought were oversized, were a matched pair of VRC20000 vertical windlasses, aft mooring capstans were VC18000, all customised aluminium-bronze and stainless steel anchoring systems. Aluminium-bronze retains its traditional gold-like appearance, occasionally requiring a surface polishing to maintain its sheen. It's also a more traditional look."

Some time later during the re-build process the stern was lengthened adding another 5m to the overall length. Now *Steel* was a 55m motor yacht. Fortunately for all concerned Muir didn't need to change the anchor chain, anchor or windlasses.

MY *Steel* is an impressive ice-class expedition yacht, it really is a "go anywhere motor yacht."

Simon Pettitt: "At the Monaco Boat Show, 2005, we displayed our first large vertical 20000 Windlass. The display weighed nearly a ton, and it was flown in from Australia. We had to let the organisers know in advance so they could reinforce the floor, but once there we were told, 'It's too heavy, you've got to leave it outside.'"

John was not a happy man, he had air freighted the roughly 1,000kg 'huge winch' to Monaco and arranged with several shipyards to meet him on our

stand. His New Zealand competitors Maxwell had a big winch (about the same size) on their stand. John told the boat show management in no uncertain terms that his winch was going to be exhibited one way or the other, as he didn't want Maxwell stealing the limelight.

Simon Pettitt: "John didn't accept 'no' for an answer and always says, 'it can be done.' In the exhibition building, we were positioned next to Quantum, right near the fire exit. We had to put this windlass on our display, but the floor manager was adamant that it was too heavy and it would cause damage to the floor. Of course, we thought he was just being over cautious.

"As a compromise with the show's organisers, we were allowed to put the windlass on the Quantum stand."

John Muir: "We put the big winch on the Quantum stand for the night, just to get it in the door. Quantum weren't on their stand at the time so I called John Allen later that evening and told him what we'd done. John was the owner of Quantum and he agreed but told me to make sure it was gone by morning."

Simon Pettitt: "We paid the pallet truck man a couple of hundred Euros to leave the truck for us to use. We moved the windlass to our display, and immediately the floor starts creaking and then cracked. The Floor Manager comes over and he's raving mad, he threatens to turn the lights off on our display."

John Muir: "We found some structural ply outside and built a support and distributed the weight more evenly so the winch stayed there for the entire show. The floor Manager came back and said, 'Yes, you can leave it here for this show but next time you will be outside on the concrete under one of those tents!'

"The next year we set up outside as the Floor Manager had said, but we were inside what was called the designers' tent. As luck would have it, it was by far the best location as we were surrounded by a lot of the European shipbuilders' displays."

All's well that ends well.

ABOVE AND TOP: MY *SILVERFAST*

Built by Silveryachts in Henderson, Western Australia. Muir supplied two polished stainless steel VRC15000s anchoring systems, forward, and VC13000 capstans, aft. Muir equipment has been supplied as standard on all Silveryacht vessels.

RIGHT: MEGA GEAR

*VC13000 mooring capstan and VRC15000 anchor winch, similar to those fitted on MY **Silverfast**. The particular anchor winch assembly shown here has a chain compressor, raised base and chain roller.*

ABOVE: MANUFACTURING THE VRC20000 WINCHES FOR MY STEEL

The Muir team in the Kingston workshop.

Back row left to right: Ian Stocks, Leigh Salter, Paul Rodgers, Cian Carey, Unknown, Gilbert McCalister, Andrew Bylet, Chris Harris.

Front left to right: John Flynn, Lyndon Potter, Joe Didocha, James Wells, Greg Goodwin, Matthew Herron.

LEFT: GETTING READY TO SHIP

David Oates packing up the Pendennis Shipyard order for MY **Steel**, ready to leave Hobart for Cornwall, UK.

SURVIVING
the
GLOBAL SUPERSTORM

"It was the year the neo-liberal economic orthodoxy that ran the world for 30 years suffered a heart attack of epic proportions. Not since 1929 has the financial community witnessed 12 months like it. Lehman Brothers went bankrupt. Merrill Lynch, AIG, Freddie Mac, Fannie Mae, HBOS, Royal Bank of Scotland, Bradford & Bingley, Fortis, Hypo and Alliance & Leicester all came within a whisker of doing so and had to be rescued.

"Western leaders, who for years boasted about the self-evident benefits of light-touch regulation, had to sink trillions of dollars to prevent the world banking system collapsing."*

This is the reality of a massive economic storm breaking, the Global Financial Crisis (GFC). For Muir Engineering, a small export business by global standards, based in isolated Tasmania, the warning signs of the impending storm hardly ever made it into the local press. Those sort of economic problems usually happen 'somewhere else,' not in Tasmania and certainly not in Australia, the so called 'lucky country.' But not this one, this storm struck with unabated fury and took a terrible toll.

The people who were immediately affected were not members of the political classes, the captains of industry, the upper echelon of the banks, board members or the CEOs of huge finance and insurance companies. The people who had led us into this super storm were, to a large extent, immune from total personal economic disaster. It was those down the ranks, in middle management and particularly currency and investment portfolio traders who paid a terrible price. Their stories would echo around the world, but apparently no-one was listening. Globally everyone was struggling to come to terms with the catastrophic changes that were unfolding.

This is the anonymous reality of the GFC, sourced from the Australian mental health support organisation Beyond Blue: "I'm a victim of the global financial crisis (GFC). Fifteen years of high-pressured, well paid, intellectually challenging and demanding work destroyed in 2008. I was in property investment banking. As the GFC took grip, money disappeared. I was quickly discarded by a decimated industry. This was an ugly insight into humanity. It was survival, it was brutal, and I can tell you no-one cared."

* Source: Nick Mathiason, The Guardian, Sunday 28 December 2008

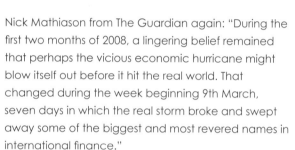

LEFT: 'BUILT CATERPILLAR TOUGH'

Two VRC7000s installed on a motor yacht in the late 1980s, the first megayacht built by John Dane and Billy Smith, who went on to found Trinity Yachts. These are the winches that Fred Mayer mentioned 'did him out of a sale' – the new owners wanted to replace the existing winches but John said Muir could refurbish them instead.

ABOVE: BULL MARKET

John poses with the Wall Street Bull in the 2000s.

Nick Mathiason from The Guardian again: "During the first two months of 2008, a lingering belief remained that perhaps the vicious economic hurricane might blow itself out before it hit the real world. That changed during the week beginning 9th March, seven days in which the real storm broke and swept away some of the biggest and most revered names in international finance."

For Muir Engineering coming up to the GFC they were flat out. Order books were full to overflowing and they were going to be hard pressed to get the work done on time.

John Muir: "We knew there were rumblings but we had no idea of what was to come. We had 22 ship sets on order from Trinity Yachts, from really big jobs to much smaller ones, all worth a lot of money. Our order books were full to overflowing.

"When the storm hit we were lucky really. We lost four orders, others did not pay in full and a couple we shipped gear and didn't get paid at all.

"We didn't really feel it until 2010."

That in itself is amazing, but as Benjamin Franklin said in 1789, 'Nothing can be said to be certain except death and taxes.' Through the 2000s Muir Engineering and New Zealand based Maxwell Winches had between them a significant part of the world's winch market.

Nick Mathiason from The Guardian: "It took a year for the financial crisis to come to a head but it did in September 2008 when the US government allowed the investment bank Lehman Brothers to go bankrupt. Up to that point, it had been assumed that governments would always step in to bail out any bank that got into serious trouble: the US had done so by finding a buyer for Bear Stearns while the UK had nationalised Northern Rock.

"When Lehman Brothers went down, the notion that all banks were 'too big to fail' no longer held true, with the result that every bank was deemed to be risky. Within a month, the threat of a domino effect through the global financial system forced western governments to inject vast sums of capital into their banks to prevent them collapsing. The banks were rescued in the nick of time, but it was too late to prevent the global economy from going into freefall.

"Credit flows to the private sector were choked off, consumer and business confidence collapsed. The winter of 2008-09 saw co-ordinated action by the newly formed G20 group of developed and developing nations in an attempt to prevent recession turning into a slump. Interest rates were cut to the bone, fiscal stimulus packages of varying sizes announced, and electronic money created through quantitative easing.

"There was a rush of fiscal expansion projects around the globe as individual countries pursued their own agendas."

Our anonymous storyteller continues his harrowing tale: "I completely broke down in late 2009. Every day I'd shower in our upstairs bathroom, sit on the shower floor, water pouring over me, and burst into tears. I was at the depths of despair, could see no future and money was running out. I hid the breakdown from everyone and cried alone so my wife and children didn't hear. Two years of mild depression and anxiety turned into Major Depression and Generalised Anxiety Disorder (GAD)."

Nick Mathiason from The Guardian: "The 9th May, 2010 marked the point at which the focus of concern switched from the private sector to the public sector. By the time the IMF and the European Union announced they would provide financial help to Greece, the issue was no longer the solvency of banks but the solvency of governments. Budget deficits had ballooned. Greece had unique problems. Austerity became the new watchword."

The Australian Psychologists Association says that following disaster, people frequently feel stunned, disoriented or unable to integrate distressing information. Once these initial reactions subside, people can experience a variety of thoughts and behaviours.

Fortunately, research shows that most people are resilient and over time are able to bounce back. It is common for people to experience stress in the immediate aftermath, but within a few months most people are able to resume functioning as they did prior to the disaster. It is important to remember that resilience and recovery are the norm, not prolonged distress.

John Muir tends to bunker down, look at what has to be done, make a decision and then get on with it, almost no matter what situation threatened his business. He's never had to face financial disaster, but he has had moments when debts piled up,

> 66 *Credit flows to the private sector were choked off, consumer and business confidence collapsed....Interest rates were cut to the bone, fiscal stimulus packages of varying sizes announced, and electronic money created through quantitative easing.* 99

The anonymous story concludes: "My state was as overwhelming as the worst hangover or migraine. I was on autopilot; two to three hours sleep a night, angry, irritable, demanding, needy, clingy and couldn't concentrate or hold coherent conversations. It was horrible. I knew something was wrong. After six months I'd had enough and snapped out of the morass. I lashed out at those around me. This took its toll. I lashed out at a friend who I'd placed a ridiculous amount of reliance on while ill, and knew I had to do something.

"I was fully diagnosed by a clinical psychologist who has been invaluable. I am recovering, but this has been slow, difficult and with its setbacks. I've learned who those are who really care about me. This has been wonderful. I have about 10 people who truly care, and in this day and age, that's pretty good. My wife is truly fabulous and the most tolerant and caring person I could hope for. I love her dearly. The unconditional love of my young children's smiles and hugs helps tremendously."

The reality of his new life, inside out and upside down, was almost too much for the former currency trader. It's interesting to compare different responses to calamity and personal or business disasters.

payments didn't come and loans and mortgages had to be negotiated. Through it, Wendy and John have survived and the business did too.

It's interesting that John says the 'recession we had to have,' in the 1990s, hurt Muir Engineering more than the GFC.

On 17 January 2014 News Limited (Australia) carried a story tracking the impact of the GFC in Australia. It's not pretty reading, so it's pretty remarkable when you think that Muir Engineering managed to survive the economic onslaught.

News Ltd: "A quarter of a million Australian jobs have vanished since the start of the global financial crisis. Australia has 722,000 people out of work — 45 per cent more than at the start of the global financial crisis."

Australian Bureau of Statistics data shows that 223,900 workers have joined the unemployment queue since December 2008, when the unemployment rate was 4.5%.

John Muir: "In 2008 we employed 70 people, we had so many orders to hand plus more in the pipeline we didn't really start to feel the brunt of the crisis till 2010. One of the very big projects we had on order in 2010 was for a 141m motor yacht for a Middle East shipyard. The shipyard was doing a conversion on a former Dutch frigate.

"Before we got so busy I was contemplating a larger model anchor winch because the shipyard's naval architect had contacted me several times telling me he wanted Muir winches and mooring gear and asked me to put a price on the package.

"At this time Jason Page (one of our employees) said to me that future orders looked like they were losing momentum so we should be able to take on this really big job. When you include spare parts, it ended up as one of the biggest projects Muir had ever undertaken.

"The project required a set of bigger winches than we had ever made, our new VRC24000 and the order was for six sets, all to be controlled with variable frequency drives. The motors, drive gears and the components were two steps up on the previous slightly smaller model and there was a hell of a lot of work, both design and production, to do in the ensuing six months, given that we were starting from scratch."

It's not surprising that Middle Eastern buyers were still in the megayacht market, the price of crude oil plummeted from US$135/barrel to US$40/barrel in late 2008, by early 2009 it was on the way back up again. The latest price drop only started in late 2014.

Because of the existing business workload, the task of managing the new Middle Eastern project was to fall on John's shoulders. This was a huge project. The shipbuilders had a former Dutch frigate that they were to convert to a new and sparkling motor megayacht.

John Muir: "Not long before this big project came on the horizon we were approached by a fellow with production background, Andrew Dickinson. We took him on and fortunately it turned out that he was a good man to have on board.

"Once we had the order confirmed, and the deposit paid and banked, we put the wheels in motion. I held a meeting at work with our Production Manager, Ian Stocks and several other key employees, including Andrew and briefed them on the project. It turned out to be a really good project and what's more came out ahead of budget."

This project got underway at ADM Shipyards, formerly Abu Dhabi MAR, in the midst of the chaos of the GFC and was a godsend for Muir. *Swift141* when finished was projected to become the sixth largest yacht in the world. It certainly didn't hurt the Muir Engineering business reputation to have scored this job.

This project got underway at ADM Shipyards, formerly Abu Dhabi MAR, in the midst of the chaos of the GFC...

ABOVE: THE BIGGEST WINCHES TO DATE
The new VRC24000 anchor winches manufactured for Yas.

OPPOSITE: EXTENSIVE REFIT
MY **Yas** *started life as a Royal Dutch Navy frigate. Photo: © Jacinto Cinto, etc.*

The 'megayachtsconcepts' website says, "The vessel was styled by Paris-based Pierrejean Design Studio, with the super sleek yacht's futuristic exterior featuring curved green glass sweeping through a pure white hull and superstructure. The stunning yacht's distinctive narrow profile has been built on the steel hull of a former Royal Dutch Navy Frigate, originally built by Koninklijke Schelde Groep BV in 1978.

"The hull conversion involved a tailored renewal of the electrical, automation, navigation and communication installations. The converted, narrow frigate hull was then paired with a lightweight composite superstructure to create a spectacular megayacht unlike any other.

"To give you a brief insight into the features of this luxury yacht, its key features include a swimming pool, heli-pad and space for tenders. She can accommodate up to 60 guests and a 56-strong crew.

"*Swift141* will be the first yacht to launch from ADM Shipyard's state-of-the-art facilities in Port Zayed. With futuristic styling and an impressive speed of 26 knots, *Swift141* is sure to make a big impact among the world's finest yachts on the water."

Andrew Dickinson: "*Swift141* initially came through as a request from a well-known Dutch naval architect. He had been chasing John for over 18 months to supply

Muir equipment for this project. This was a large Dutch frigate conversion into a 141m motor yacht. We knew it needed high strength chain and we realised it would need a vertical windlass that was larger than our current vertical models. We were asked to also design the deck arrangement for the anchor handling gear. The chain compressor, also a new design, was positioned up forward at the chain roller, the winch was further aft and a series of large chain roller guides spaced between the two.

"A mock-up of the design was created on computer using scaled up versions of our VRC22000 anchor winch. This design was sent to the Abu Dhabi MAR ship project manager and was immediately accepted. It was clear that the pace of build for this project was going to be rapid, at least that's what we thought at the time.

"The project also called for four enormous custom made capstan winches with custom built flared bases to allow mooring lines to lead onto them from the deck. These were quickly designed and a local pattern maker was commissioned to build the wooden patterns required for the enormous castings. The large chain compressor capacity required for the project was so big that we needed to use new techniques of computer stress analysis to ensure the design was structurally sound before risking potentially destructive testing.

"*Swift141* was a top-secret project, however concept renderings were available to be viewed on the shipyard's website. This ambitious project involved the conversion of a Dutch frigate into one of the world's most audacious megayachts. When we saw the design concept for the yacht we couldn't believe our eyes. If you get the chance to see an image of the finished yacht you will see what we mean."

> **" *This ambitious project involved the conversion of a Dutch frigate into one of the world's most audacious megayachts. When we saw the design concept for the yacht we couldn't believe our eyes. "***
>
> – ANDREW DICKINSON

ALLOY YACHTS, *SY KOKOMO*

58 metre fly bridge sailing sloop.

Muir supplied dual hydraulic VR15000 anchor winches, combination chain stopper and devil claw assemblies in polished stainless steel.

*John was on a business trip in Auckland in 2012 when **Kokomo** was undergoing commissioning there. Pictured at left is the enormous mast with John in front for scale.*

OPPOSITE PAGE

TOP: FEADSHIP PROJECT

Lyndon Potter with anchoring systems ready to pack and ship. These anchoring systems were supplied for a 98m motor yacht in Europe.

BOTTOM: MY *TRIDENT*

*John with the VRC20000 anchor winches and anchoring systems on Feasdhip MY **Trident** at Monaco Boat Show in 2009.*

John Muir knew what was needed up front and already had prepared sketches of the shape and size of the equipment.

Launch images showed the finished yacht named simply 'A' on its lifting ship. Even when viewed from hundreds of metres away, the Muir anchor gear is clearly visible on the foredeck. A fitting position for what was up to that time Muir's largest yacht project.

In fact in pure economic terms, Australia, as it turned out, was one of, if not the best country in the world for Muir Engineering to call home. Rich in natural resources, with a mild and largely productive climate, far enough away from most of the world's trouble spots, it's no wonder it has the global reputation as 'the lucky country.'

A former bank economist, journalist for the Australian Financial Review and economic advisor to Prime Minister Julia Gillard, Stephen Koukoulas, quoted on the ABC Rear View program in May of 2014 said about the Australian economy: "I was having a look at 42-odd

Ken Henry as treasury secretary and Glenn Stevens as RBA governor, decided to spend money to try to limit the fallout from what was obviously just horrendous global economic conditions. It was just a miserable time for the world economy. What they did was of course very costly in terms of dollars but obviously very beneficial in terms of economic growth and jobs. A couple of percent of GDP was pumped into the economy and it caused the Budget deficit to blow out to the highest deficit that Australia has ever seen."

In the meantime while all this frenetic activity is going on, John Muir was travelling again, keeping sales up, visiting clients, hoping that boat building, (which for both large and small vessels sits largely at the luxury end of the economic spectrum) doesn't get hit too hard by the impact of the global storm.

It took John Muir almost a decade to finally sell anchor and mooring winches to the Royal de Vries shipyard. The following year, Royal Van Lent also started to order Muir equipment.

According to John, Dutch shipbuilders are amongst the best in the world for design and construction of mega motor yachts.

years of budget history, and in that time, roughly half of those years we've had a surplus, roughly half we've had a deficit and when we compare ourselves to many of the G7 countries, our fiscal position is outstanding. I don't think there is any other way to describe it.

"For example, our level of net debt is 10 percent of GDP. In countries like the US, Germany, UK, it's about 80 percent to 90 percent of GDP, so it's about eight or nine times larger. In today's Australian dollar terms that's about $1.5 trillion difference, which is a huge amount of money. Compared to America and other countries, Australia's track record balancing surpluses and deficits over the past 40 years has been good.

"The election of the Rudd government in 2007 in Australia coincided with the GFC and the worst recession since the 1930s.

"It was obvious that the world economy was going into a very nasty slump, the banking sector was grinding to a halt, banks were failing around the world and Mr Rudd, (the Australian Prime Minister) with advice from

According to John, Dutch shipbuilders are amongst the best in the world for design and construction of mega motor yachts. The ownership and management of their businesses stretches back generations, always with an emphasis on quality, service and excellence. The next-door German yards that build even larger vessels also have an enviable reputation, again with strong family links going back decades.

The acquisition of large shipbuilders as clients in these two European countries was important to Muir Engineering during the GFC and in the years that followed. Yet sealing an international equipment deal is not an easy task.

John Muir: "I can tell you that a big order doesn't come easily. There's the owner, the captain, the owner's rep, the shipyard, the price, the quality, the service, and of course, the relationships to work through and maintain. I was approached by a good friend at the Fort Lauderdale Boat Show in the late 1990s. He was the owner's representative on several motor yachts built by Austal Ships in Perth. He was also

FORT LAUDERDALE BOAT SHOW, 2000

Above: Jerry Truax with Delta Shipyard management.
Right: The Muir display.

the skipper of several American-owned motor yachts built by Oceanfast, and another vessel built for the descendants of Henry Ford. All up Buddy Haack had skippered around 10 motor yachts, all fitted with Muir winches. (He was an important strategic alliance partner.)

"We were trying to secure an order for three ship sets of Muir anchor and mooring winches for 64m vessels that were going to be built In Europe in the early 2000s."

"The Fort Lauderdale Boat Show was coming up. Buddy was familiar with the reliability of Muir deck machinery, I knew he was coming to the show with the owner, so we decided to have on our Muir display the particular equipment he and the owner were looking for.

"These anchoring and mooring systems were destined for the Delta Shipyard in Seattle for the 73m motor yacht *Laurel*. Coincidentally, the captain of this vessel was an Australian."

Before the Fort Lauderdale Show, John visited the shipyard and discussed the possibility of Muir winning the business for the three vessels. He met and talked with two of the yard's senior personnel. It was still early days for the project, but John had his toe in the door and did his best to keep it there.

The Fort Lauderdale Boat Show soon followed (the last week of November). All the displays looked great and on the second night of the show, Australian exhibitors put on a party. There was some fine food, Australian beer, wine and music.

John Muir: "Representatives from the shipyard and the owner's rep were present and everybody was having a good time. It was so good, that one of the directors of the yard was seen speaking lovingly to a VRC20000 winch. He thought it was a beautiful thing, and I knew I was in with a good chance.

"At the time, the shipyard was negotiating new business, and price was king. From Fort Lauderdale I travelled to METS where I had further discussions with the owner's rep. A week later I was in the shipyard working towards securing the order.

"I was accompanied by our Europe Representative Sergei Postal from Belgium. There were around eight personnel from the yard covering technical, legal, financial and commercial matters, plus myself and Sergei. It was a prolonged meeting starting early. I did my best to hold my ground on the price, which was ultimately going to be the key to doing the deal, as all other boxes had been ticked. For some time I resisted a discount and as time went on, people present were becoming irritated, including me."

The day ground on, as did the discussions about price. It was midday when Sergei went outside for a breather. He was told in no uncertain terms that unless John gave them a bigger discount off a large package (having kicked off negotiations with a small discount offer), Muir would not get the order.

John Muir: "While we were having lunch and coffee, Sergei whispered to me, 'John you don't want to lose this order, do you?' I responded, 'No, but I don't want this discount to go much higher.' The meeting commenced again, and the first thing raised was a bigger discount.

"We continued on for 30 minutes or so, and everyone was becoming stressed, so I asked management, 'If I was to give you the higher discount, would you give me the order today?' The answer was 'Yes', so we all shook hands, and Sergei and myself were left in the room alone. Sergei had a dry sense of humour and he looked at me and said, 'John that will be the most expensive sandwich you ever have in your life. It cost you an arm and a leg.' Nevertheless, we were happy with the order confirmation.

"Not long after we received the three ship set order, metal prices around the world almost doubled, putting the pressure on shipyards as well as Muir and its suppliers who work on fixed price negotiations."

Some metal prices almost doubled and made it even harder to negotiate a discount from Muir's suppliers. At the time, some of the Australian foundries and component suppliers were doing it tough. John took it upon himself to do the negotiations and successfully leveraged an almost identical discount from all the suppliers. It was a really big order, in some cases the biggest they had ever had from Muir, so like John they were happy with the outcome.

Given that the world was in a state of some economic chaos, you would expect the super and megayacht business to have been hard hit. Hit it was, but it wasn't a knockout punch. The industry survived and eventually recovered, keen to tell the world that this type of shipbuilding was a critical part of every economy in which it operated.

On a global scale, the superyacht industry had grown by 26% a year over the past five years. The growth is being led by the traditional markets, the US and Europe, with rapid new appetite for large craft from Russia, Eastern Europe and the Middle East with the rise of affluent, acquisitive classes.

METS EARLY 2000S

Above: Muir Europe representative Sergei Postal from Belgium;
Opposite: Simon Pettitt on the Muir stand with a VRC18000 anchor winch.

Jeni Bone, writing for Marine Business in early 2008, detailed the knock on effects from the construction and operation of superyachts in Australia and overseas.

"Much has been spoken, written and forecast for the superyacht industry, and the superlatives are not unfounded. This segment of the marine industry is big business in Australia, promising an economic flow-on to communities in the realms of millions of dollars and infrastructure totalling $1bn."

"One of the common fallacies about the super-yacht industry is that 'it's the domain of the wealthy," explains Lance Cushion, Gold Coast based President of the International Super-yacht Society (ISS).

"We have spent many years educating governments on the benefits of the superyacht industry and the value of investing in its infrastructure. It's not just for the rich and famous. It's about flow on to the communities who host these superyachts."

Cushion recalls the biggest boat to visit Australian waters, the 127m *Octopus*, which moored off Darwin. 'It took on $690,000 in fuel, $320,000 in provisions and had a crew of 60 in Darwin for seven days. God only knows what they spent while they were here, but it does flow on 'right down to the local florist!'"

* Source: http://www.marinebusiness.com.au/archive/super-superyachts

There are as many as 3,000 people engaged in work on superyachts in Australia and tens of thousands more around the world. It's a massive growth industry. Defined as boats above 24m, power or sail, there are around 777 superyachts under construction, 719 of them powered.

There are an estimated 7,000 in the world and they are getting bigger and bigger, 65m is the new mean. (That was back in 2008, these days it's 100m or bigger.)

On a global scale, the superyacht industry had grown by 26% a year over the past five years. The growth is being led by the traditional markets, the US and Europe, with rapid new appetite for large craft from Russia, Eastern Europe and the Middle East with the rise of affluent, acquisitive classes. But so great is the demand, that if you ordered a superyacht right now, (2008) the earliest you'd be able to take delivery is 2010 or 2013.*

In the first quarter of 2015 the French Ship builder Piriou, based in Concarneau, announced the launching of the 77m expedition motor yacht *Yersin*. This was Piriou's first superyacht project. She is more complex than many other similar sized vessels because of its multi-purpose design, combining the comfort of a superyacht with the go-anywhere capabilities of an explorer and the scientific facilities of a research ship.

The motor yacht is named after Alexandre Yersin, the Swiss physician and bacteriologist who is perhaps most famous for the late 19th century discovery of the bacterium that causes bubonic plague, a discovery that led to an understanding of the disease and the development of treatments and vaccines. Yersin was also a great explorer and is honoured by this modern day explorer, his namesake the MV *Yersin*.

The MV *Yersin* is a true expedition motor yacht able to accommodate up to about 18 passengers plus crew, with facilities suitable for scientists, technicians, engineers and surveyors. She has two laboratories, a media room, an infirmary, a scuba-diving room, landing craft and various winterised tenders — and is also designed to carry a seaplane. *Yersin* can operate safely and comfortably in extreme ambient temperatures down to minus 20°C or up to plus 50°C. The ice-strengthened "Ice 1C" class hull has a relatively shallow draft for navigating shoal waters, with a pump jet instead of a bow thruster.

Designed for sailing the more remote shores and extended transoceanic voyages, *Yersin* has impressive green credentials. She features diesel-electric propulsion with two 1500 kW Schottel azipods allowing the 2169 GRT displacement boat to cruise at about 11 knots. At this speed she consumes only about half of what a standard diesel engine set-up would. At a speed of 9 knots the total consumption (electricity, heating/air conditioning included) falls to about 180 litres per hour, resulting in a range of 12,000 nautical miles and 50 days at sea with 40 people on board. Furthermore, all grey and black water is recycled for wash downs.

Construction of *Yersin* began in 2012. She features a steel hull and aluminium superstructure. All the wood on board is sustainable and decks are Bolidt artificial teak — greener, cooler, lighter and hardier than the real thing. Muir anchoring and mooring winches are installed and the equipment is electrically driven at 400V 50Hz via variable frequency (soft) drives to all anchor winches and mooring capstans.

Forward anchoring equipment comprises two Muir variable electric drive VRC20000 stainless steel, vertical reversing anchor winches with capstans. Cable lifter (chain gypsy — wild cat) and 32mm grade U3 stud link chain. The two anchors each weigh 1305kg.

Aft anchoring equipment, starboard side, comprises a vertical electric VRC15000 stainless steel, vertical reversing stern anchor winch with cable lifter, variable frequency drive, and a combination of 26mm U3 stud link chain and 855kg anchor. The drive motor, gear and cable lifter were located below deck and an extended deck main drive shaft passed through the aft deck to drive the capstan warping drum; the winch drive can be engaged and disengaged from on deck. On the port side of the aft deck, a VC15000 mooring capstan and a variable frequency drive. At mid-ship there are two vertical electric VC15000 mooring capstans.

MV YERSIN

The expedition yacht **Yersin** is an ice-class expedition yacht featuring Mu. VRC20000 anchor winches forward and VC15000 mooring capstans mid and aft. Both in a machined satin finish, in contrast to the usual high polish required on luxury yachts.
Top and middle photos: Matthew Johnston
Below photos: © Erwin Willemse (via www.marinetraffic.com)
Opposite page photo: © Ameller

John Muir: "I first met Jean Dumarais in Cantieri di Pisa, Italy, where as her Captain he was following the construction of a 38m *Akhir* for the crown of Qatar back in 2003. The second time I met Jean was in November 2011. At the time Muir Engineering were one of a group of around twenty five Australian exporters exhibiting their respective marine equipment at the METS in Amsterdam (Marine equipment trade show) and the largest of its kind in the world.

"On the first morning I was approached by Jean Dumarais who bought along with him the specifications and drawings of his new upcoming project, a 77m expedition motor yacht that he had designed. I was surprised to see in the specifications one of our competitor's names. So I said to myself there and then, there must be a good reason for Jean to come to see us within the first 5 minutes of the doors opening at the METS! At this time Simon Pettitt of Muir UK, and Fred Mayer of Muir USA were working on the Muir stand.

"After the METS closed we visited the impressive Belship (our Dutch distributor) displays which pretty well represented all the Belship International suppliers. From memory there were around 20 other Belship supplier companies all lined up on both sides of walk way!

"It was normal practice after the show ended to pass by the Belship displays to meet up with the various other exhibitors who we knew well. And the other reason was to have a can or two of popular Heineken beer!

"Following Belship the three of us walked several hundred metres along to Fred Mayer's hotel to have dinner and a chat about the first day of the METS. While we were having our third Heineken we noticed Jean Dumarais was over the way, and so the four of us had dinner together. Jean asked when he could expect the offer and he was informed the next morning. Jean was staying in the same hotel as Fred, and Simon and I were in another hotel 15 minutes away by taxi.

"The next morning Jean arrived once again on our stand first off. I said to myself at the time I think we have a good chance here, knowing the offer I intended to give him was competitive as by now we were having all our Europe winch controls, including variable speed controls, made in the vicinity of Amsterdam. There was another big plus here in that we were able to engage the same electrical controls supplier for the commissioning of all the 6 sets of winch gear if so required. The boat show was very busy with a lot of genuine enquires.

ABOVE: JFA SHIPYARD, FRANCE

*18m sailing yacht, left, with a 44m expedition yacht at
JFA Shipyard in France, 2003.*

*The sailing yacht had a VRC3500 installed by the shipyard,
and the expedition yacht had two VRC11000 anchor winches,
two VC8000 mooring capstans, chain compressor and
anchoring system, finished in polished stainless steel.*

BELOW: MY *KOGO*

*74m motor yacht built by Alstom Yachts France, 2005. Fitted with dual VRC20000
anchor winches with soft (variable frequency) drives, and dual VC20000 mooring
capstans with frequency drives.*

*At the same time in the huge Alstom shipyard, there were four of the largest cruise ships
in the world at that time under construction.*

Another huge project on its own was the new **Queen Mary II***, nearing completion at Alstom.*

**ABOVE AND LEFT:
PALM BEACH MOTOR YACHTS**

One of Australia's premium motor cruiser brands. Shown at left and above is the last PB55 launched in 2016 with a Muir VRC2500 installed.

ABOVE: MUIR HORIZONTAL 11000

*Installed on the 22.5m schooner, **Astor**. Twin 16mm chain gypsies, independent warping capstans, and hydraulic drive. Muir installed the windlass during one of the early Wooden Boat Festivals in Hobart.*

RIGHT: M3 HYDRAULIC ANCHOR WINCH

Installed on a 23m motor cruiser, Fort Lauderdale Boat Show 2000.

"Like all the big international trade shows in Europe and USA there are a lot of costs to attend to and every year, however, we always had something new for the particular boat show markets, be that mega or pleasure markets, and we were fortunate to have all the 20000 anchoring and mooring equipment on display for *Yersin* and Jean.

"The next day Jean came by early with some technical questions, and later that day he came back again affectionately rubbed his hand over the top of the VRC20000 anchor winch capstan and mentioned he was definitely interested. Of course it generally takes a few months to have all the i's dotted and the t's crossed with the usual to- and fro-ing.

"After several months the shipyard called to say the order was agreed, and after that it was only a matter of weeks until we had the order in hand.

"I must say, back in Australia we really had a great group of people. While I was overseas, whenever it came to lending a hand with just about anything to do with sales or service I could call on either Matthew Johnston (a year later to become Managing Director) and two very knowledgeable and capable sales and support personnel, Chris Evans based in the Hobart works and Jason Page based in the Queensland Gold Coast office. The same goes for the design office; if there was something I needed in a hurry there was always someone willing to stay back at work to lend a hand."

Working for Muir Engineering, across Australia and the globe, were a select bunch of sales representatives. Some had been asked to join the team after one brief meeting, others taking longer periods to come on board. Michael Trickey took over from John's long-time friend and Queensland representative, Ken Padgett.

> ❝ *I've always said it's a bit like the Australian Cricket Team – it's harder to get out than to get in!* ❞
>
> – MICHAEL TRICKEY, MUIR QLD

Michael Trickey: "I got to know John through Ken Padgett (my father-in-law), and obviously got to know more about him as Ken was talking about winding up with Muir and retiring. I took over from him in 2002 after an informal chat with John, we shook hands and that was it. I've been working with Muir for over 14 years now, and I'm the Manager in Queensland. I've always said it's a bit like the Australian Cricket Team – it's harder to get out than to get in!

John's one of those guys who doesn't take no for an answer. He's a super tenacious man, and a good fellow to work for. If he trusts you, he gives you full autonomy to do what you need to do.

ABOVE: MICHAEL TRICKEY
Sanctuary Cove 2002, Michael's first ever boat show – two weeks after joining the company.

BELOW: THE CHARMING JOHN MUIR
A caricature of John drawn by his friend Paul 'China' Hurd for John's 50th birthday.

MAA! ME WINCH WON'T FIT ME BOAT

OPPOSITE: SANCTUARY COVE 2008

The Muir team enjoying a well earned dinner after another successful day. Left to right: Craig McNaughton, Muir NSW manager; Don Haber Canada agent, since retired; Chris Evans, Muir sales Kingston; Steve Mullins, Muir QLD, since moved on ("a great salesman, went into his own business" — John); Michael Trickey, Muir QLD manager; John Muir.

"One of the funniest things about John is that he can never make up his mind about taking flights. He has tickets he's purchased just in case, but sometimes doesn't decide whether he's going or not until half an hour beforehand, and then of course it's a mad dash to get him to the airport on time, running red lights and taking shortcuts. The result of that is he's always running late and gets there with minutes to spare, sometimes just as they're closing check-in.

"When talking to John, he's always got another idea in his head. One of the things he often says is, 'Yeah, yeah, yeah you're right... but...' and goes into his idea.

"He's a bit of an enigma. He's always done it his way, and it's worked for him. He's very sharp and he has a memory like an elephant.

"Two of his favourite sayings are, 'You only get out of life what you negotiate' and 'Push them 'til they show their teeth.'

"The GFC really was earth shattering for our industry. Pleasure craft are one of the first things to go when things get tough, they're a toy. It was a time when many businesses went from very prosperous to being cut in half. There were tough decisions to be made, but John stepped in early and put his head down, and made the difficult decisions that had to be made, and that helped us stay afloat.

"I remember back in the fallout from the GFC, boat builders were closing down left, right and centre. There was one that owed us a bit of money, and John came up to Queensland to see what could be done as they were pretty much closing their gates. He told us to go over there and rattle their cage about what they owed us. That was his way, he'd never give up."

John Muir: "Michael is a tenacious individual. He's like a dog with a bone when he gets onto something. Excellent with customers, a real people person. He runs a tight ship, doesn't waste money, and looks after business assets like they're his own. He's a great family man, a deep thinker and a good listener.

"Michael served his apprenticeship in the marine industry and outboard business. His wide technical knowledge was a big plus when kicking off with Muir, as the winch business is primarily mechanical.

"Michael has picked up most of his father-in-law's traits, which can only be positive for managing a business like Muir. He has managed the Muir Queensland operations well through the boom times and also the hard times."

One of Ken Padgett's sayings was, 'John, customers will love you for 10%, but not for 20%.' (What he means is that customers will stick with you if your prices are 10% higher, but not more).

APOISE
visits
HOBART

John Muir: "*Apoise* was in Australian waters during a round-the-world voyage in 2008 when we received a surprise call from one of the two full time captains onboard. She was bound for Hobart, intending to stay for two weeks, and the crew needed to know who to speak to regarding a berth in one of Hobart's ports. Muir's Matthew Johnston contacted Tas Ports and arranged this for them.

"The captain also mentioned the anchor winches and their frequency controls required servicing. We said Muir could certainly have a look at this. A week later when she docked, Hobart electrical engineer Gary Smith, who manufactured the Muir winch controls, went onboard for the inspection.

"*Apoise*'s owner was a Canadian engineer, and the family company he started was one of the world's largest buyers and auctioneers of used and surplus industrial equipment. The Australian arm of his company buys equipment and machinery locally and refurbishes it ready for sale overseas if necessary.

"Over several days, Muir's engineers took care of the mechanical servicing of the vessel's winches, and were treated afterwards to a tour of the spectacular vessel. The owner even enjoyed a beer with them!

"The news spread quickly back at Muir's factory, and another eight staff members expressed interest in going onboard. The captain was very obliging and the group were shown over the vessel the following day, also enjoying a beer and a chat with the owner.

"We invited the owner and his partner down to the Muir factory in Kingston for a tour of our premises, and we discussed our collective concerns about the financial system troubles, which of course later became a full-blown global crisis.

"Wendy, Alex, Matthew and myself were invited to a lovely dinner onboard the night before she departed on the next leg of her long voyage.

> ## 66 *The Apoise visit to Hobart is one we will never forget!* 99

SHEEN: John Muir, left, and ship captain Delos Gurney, of Seattle, admire the Tasmanian-made stainless steel anchor winch on the super yacht Apoise yesterday at Princes Wharf in Hobart.
Pictures: KIM EISZELE

Ahoy, rich boy's toy arrives

DANIELLE McKAY

THE Tasmanian-made anchor windlass system aboard super yacht Apoise is a sleek engineering marvel that is sought-after the world over.

The rest of the 66m, 1600 tonne, vessel — which docked in Hobart yesterday — is just as spectacular.

Owned by a Canadian businessman, the motor-yacht draws four metres.

She boasts six decks accessed with a glass elevator, a pool with a bar, five speed boats and a helipad.

Apoise is the largest vessel of its type to dock in Tasmania.

It has two chefs, five stewards, five deckhands, three engineers, two captains and its guests will spend up to a month in the state.

An entire day will be spent filling up the 220,000 litre fuel tank which gives the yacht a range of over 8000 nautical miles.

Also while in the docks, John Muir, the owner of Muir Engineering, will service his Tasmanian-made polished stainless steel fittings that were added while the vessel was built at the Lurssen factory in Germany.

Mr Muir said that the hair on the back of his neck was standing up with the excitement of seeing his work on a boat like Apoise.

"It took us about 10 years to get a major upmarket company like Lurssen and since then it has really given us a boost," said Mr Muir.

"We really had to work hard and being onboard a big yacht like this today really fulfils our passion. It's incredible."

Celebrating 40 years in the business, Mr Muir said that over 60 per cent in the international super yacht market.

With over 500 super-yachts being built at any one time, there was plenty more work ahead, he said.

By next year, Mr Muir estimated that more than 70 per cent of his production would be for superyachts.

Growing up around his boat-building father, Mr Muir said that he was living his childhood dream.

He would look at his father's magazines filled with pictures of 18m yachts and hope to be a part of the industry.

Now he is fitting out yachts bigger than 130m with his products and exports to more than 40 countries.

He said that in the past five years the market had expanded dramatically with the average size yacht going from 50m to a whopping 70m.

He predicted that given another five years they would be up to 80m.

By adapting to industry demand, Muir's had remained buoyant and at the top of their industry. But Mr Muir remained grounded.

"We talk quite often about how fortunate we are that people are building yachts," said Mr Muir.

"They're paying our wages and they're fulfilling our passion."

LUXURY: Six decks, five stewards and two captains.

ABOVE AND OPPOSITE:
APOISE VISITS HOBART

*In 2008, the 67m Lurssen-built motor yacht **Apoise** (formerly known as **Marlin**) visited Hobart. It's Canadian owner allowed John and some of the Muir team onboard to view the boat – a rare opportunity considering most of the luxury yachts Muir winches are built for are based in Europe and the Americas. **Apoise** was fitted with two VRC20000 frequency drive (soft control) anchor winches, two chain compressor anchoring systems and two VC20000 two-speed mooring capstans. John, pictured opposite with ship captain Delos Gurney, of Seattle, inspected and serviced the polished stainless steel anchoring and windlass equipment while the yacht was docked. It was the largest vessel of its type to ever have docked in Hobart.*

Photos and article: The Mercury

Michael Trickey: "Service is 90% of the sales in our business. It's that commitment to after sales service and looking after the customer that has been John's biggest asset. That combined with his natural ability to sell, and of course his technical background, means he can be hands on in dealing with customers. He'll go look at boats, crawl into chain lockers, look at winches, just do whatever he needs to do. People really appreciate his desire to go the extra mile."

Meanwhile the GFC was having a big impact on shipbuilding in European countries like Holland.

"The financial crisis affected the Dutch economy through three channels: plummeting global demand, problems with bank balance sheets, and the decline in producer and consumer confidence. To each of these channels the Dutch economy seems to be relatively vulnerable, compared to other European countries. It severely hit the shipbuilding industry, which resulted in big excess capacity problems."*

As the crisis rolled on, traditional industries, like car manufacturers and others were quick to point out their value to the Dutch economy. Superyacht construction had always 'hid its light under a bushel' and shipbuilders found themselves having to publicly justify support from government.

with a further €10.24bn generated indirectly including €4.3bn spent ashore and more than €1.6bn on crew jobs.

"The London School of Economics has also noted that employment in the superyacht industry has risen 10% in the past five years.

"Ken Hickling, president of the International Superyacht Society, which represents the large yachts industry worldwide, insists no other segment of the luxury market has the capacity to redistribute wealth in this way.

"When compared to art, property, jewels and [different forms of] luxury transport such as cars and planes, super-yachts are the most ethical. Buying boats supports jobs. Buying big boats supports more jobs."

So where does the money go? Wealthy buyers who want a custom-built superyacht usually spend 5-10% of the building costs on top-name design studios and naval architects. Specialist law firms are engaged to guide the client through the design and new-build contract process. For new-build and second-hand purchases, yacht brokers and the houses they work under are brought in to handle arrangements, introductions and negotiations, typically charging about 5% of the sale price.

It shows how building a strong business relationship at this level takes time and perseverance. It had already taken almost ten years for John to win the order for **Rasselas***.*

"Five years after the GFC took the wind from the sails of the luxury yacht market, shipyards and brokers have begun to promote their industry with a broader message: superyachts are economic drivers."**

"Industries such as automobiles and aviation often report on the economic value of their work. But the superyacht industry's largely private and independent nature has meant that until recently, few outsiders have needed to be persuaded of its economic impact.

"A report last year by the Superyacht Intelligence Agency, which tracks the superyacht market, found that in 2010 — by all accounts a quiet year — €13.76bn was generated in the super-yacht industry supply chain through sales, wages, expenditure and charter revenue

Once commissioned, the shipyard will receive an upfront payment to begin work. Before 2007, some yards would begin work with no money up front, but today, yards expect to see upwards of a third of the building cost before hull work begins. In 2012, 169 superyachts were delivered with an estimated total price of £3bn.

Superyachts require registration with classification societies, surveys, insurance and regular visits from technical specialists to maintain everything from the air conditioning to the satellite communication systems. Not forgetting crew, food and fuel. Operational and management costs for a typical superyacht are roughly 10% of its build price per year. That is another £3m for a £30m yacht.

* Source: Economic analysis from the European Commission's Directorate-General for Economic and Financial Affairs, December 2009
** Source: The Financial Times, September 2013, by Don Hoyt Gorman

> **❝** *He has never forgotten what the true fundamentals are…and what it takes to drive sales particularly in a competitive global market place. He is the consummate networker and no one is left out when he is around.* **❞**

MARYANNE EDWARDS
CEO of AIMEX (Australian International Marine Export Group).

Once launched, superyachts — like cruise ships — often inject large sums of money into the destinations they visit. Data collected by the US Superyacht Association, a trade body, show that on average, a 55m superyacht will annually spend about £70,000 on provisioning, £220,000 on dockage fees and £250,000 on fuel in the ports it visits.

Then there is the charter industry. There are more than 1,200 superyachts available worldwide to rent for an average rate of about £200,000 a week (the most lavish can cost more than £1m a week). Guests on board can be profligate, spending money on anything from helicopter flights and security to food, drink and lavish nights out in town. Tips (usually 10% of the charter fee and shared among the crew) are often spent within walking distance of the marina.

"A superyacht can contain 30-40 times the value of a passenger vessel, freighter or other commercial ship," says Henk de Vries, chief executive of Royal de Vries, part of the Dutch Feadship yard. "There is economic value in what we do."

John Muir wouldn't argue with that claim, because a perusal of the list of megayachts built by the large Dutch based shipbuilding firm de Vries and its sister ship builder Van Lent, equipped with Muir winch and mooring gear is revealing. It shows how building a strong business relationship at this level takes time and perseverance. It had already taken almost ten years for John to win the order for *Rasselas*.

Since then Muir have supplied the majority of the anchoring and mooring systems for the Feadship group.

That's two of the world's best yards both based in Holland. It does not count the large number of other super and megayacht builders that Muir was supplying across the globe, in Germany, the UK and the USA.

So now we know the number of people in the global marine shipbuilding industry who hold John Muir in high regard, who have seen and experienced first-hand his determination, perseverance and focus.

The Australian International Marine Export Group (AIMEX) is the peak body representing the Australian marine export and superyacht industries, its CEO is MaryAnne Edwards.

MaryAnne Edwards: "John is a stalwart in the industry and an example of what so many businesses should be like but simply are not.

"He has never forgotten what the true fundamentals are re: running a successful business and what it takes to drive sales particularly in a competitive global market place. He is the consummate networker and no one is left out when he is around. He has a friendly greeting and smile for everyone and very rarely forgets a name.

"He is great to do a boat show with, he never stops but walks the show to ensure he leaves no stone unturned and no customer is left unsatisfied. His commitment, energy, sense of humour (he likes to text you jokes when we are all getting bored on the stand) and his professionalism has meant he is truly a global personality, well known and admired by many in the industry.

"I would like to clone his experience, skills and can-do attitude. He is someone who makes things happen and does not stand around saying what happened! Unfortunately too many people see opportunities pass them by because they take easy roads and go to shows unprepared and unplanned."

As we now know all too well, not John Muir.

MY *HAMPSHIRE II*

78m yacht delivered in 2012. Commissioning the Muir VRC22000 anchor winches with two combination chain stopper and four pocket chain roller assemblies. Aft were two VC20000 mooring capstans.

Top left: Assistant Project Manager Henk Glasburgen with John.

Above: Philip Feenstra from PSI Feenstra.

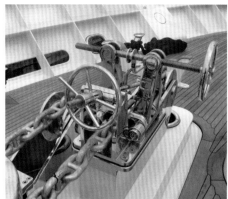

MY SEA OWL

John Muir in 2015, with Muir VRC20000 anchor winches with raised bases, chain compressors and four pocket chain roller assemblies, and VC20000 aft mooring capstans. Above, Robert Eekman, Muir Europe representative.

FEADSHIP BUILDS

Since the early 2000s Muir have been supplying anchor and mooring winches to Feadship for some of the world's finest luxury motor yachts..

Photos: Feadship

*MY **Vanish***

*MY **Go***

*MY **Tango***

*MY **Kathleen Anne***

*MY **Moon Sand***

*MY **Trident***

*MY **Moon Sand Too***

*MY **Sea Owl***

*MY **Savannah***

*MY **Halo***

*MY **Como***

*MY **Kiss***

*MY **Ocean Mercury***

*MY **Avatar***

*MY **Larisa***

*MY **ROCK IT***

*MY **Air***

John Muir: "I have travelled to many boat shows in conjunction with MaryAnne and other AIMEX members. She is a great networker and every year, with MaryAnne at the helm, we saw an expansion of our capacity to meet and talk to prospective customers with their support.

"MaryAnne would set up meetings with prospective customers and suppliers at boat shows like Fort Lauderdale, Monaco and METS. She also set up a large area at METS for daily functions, inviting European customers to be involved in on-site discussions with AIMEX members like Muir and others."

MaryAnne Edwards: "John is also someone who lends a willing hand to set up stands, to make introductions and to help new businesses trying to make their mark. He certainly is someone businesses should emulate if they want to be successful. The fundamentals are always the same; hard work, proactive nature, positive attitude and a strong customer focus while always keeping your eye on the bottom line."

Don't think for one moment that attending boat shows and other trade events is all about social outings, tea and biscuits and later on, beverages of a different nature, consumed in large quantities. These shows are about economic survival, they are also about making sure that the Australian stand looks bigger and brighter and more inviting than its counterpart from New Zealand across the ditch. (The Tasman Sea.)

There is fierce rivalry between these two countries, stuck as they are in the isolated southern oceans, many thousands of kilometres from the big US, Asian and European population centres and markets. The rivalry is in every sport or area of human endeavor that is known to man. It includes rugby union, cricket, sailing, basketball, netball, equestrian events and of course the manufacture of anchor and mooring winches.

In fact if you ever tell a Kiwi (a New Zealander) that you love their Australian accent, it will not go well for you at all. In fact your life and liberty may be in danger. Seriously. Likewise if you say to an Australian that they sound like a Kiwi, look out!

John Muir: "As one of the three founders of AIMEX, I had experienced the force of the New Zealand Marine Group (MAREX) which was established by Peter Rachtman to promote their local marine industry products, which Peter did extremely well. I arranged for Peter to visit Australia and talk to our AIMEX group in the mid-late 1990s, and subsequently a strategy was put in place by the AIMEX board. We aimed to counter the New Zealander's efforts, which were dominating Australasian markets as well as having significant success elsewhere overseas.

"I admire the hard-fought efforts of MaryAnne in expanding the AIMEX membership, getting its members into new markets, and encouraging overseas customers and suppliers to visit AIMEX members in their workplaces around Australia."

> **"** *I admire the hard-fought efforts of MaryAnne in expanding the AIMEX membership, getting its members into new markets, and encouraging overseas customers and suppliers to visit AIMEX members in their workplaces around Australia.* **"**
>
> – JOHN MUIR

THIS PAGE: THE PACK UP

An enormous amount of work goes into preparing and setting up a trade show. Often the team would work well into the night to pack up a show after it's finished. Above: Muir's European representative Sergei Postal and Muir UK's Simon Pettitt; Left: Muir's Duncan Norton with John, Sergei and Simon.

OPPOSITE: THE AUSSIE CONTIGENT

A typical Australian section at METS in 2001 shows the great work AIMEX do for Australian marine exporters.

Given that MaryAnne Edwards and many others admire John Muir's toughness, drive and determination, you should not be surprised to learn that he sets high standards for himself, his employees and his suppliers, just like his customers also set high standards.

Andrew and Alan Perkins have been suppliers of Muir Engineering from the very early days, first as Skeels and Perkins, then later as Apco. Apart from a brief hiccup, when there was some argy bargy over payment of an outstanding account, Apco have been and still are Tasmania's sole suppliers of stainless steel castings to Muir.

John Muir: "Some time back in the mid-2000s Apco were having casting problems with 316 grade stainless steel, resulting in castings which wouldn't polish well. The material would come out with spots through it that couldn't be polished out. Andrew came down to Kingston and told me and the production manager [Ian Stocks] that Muir didn't know what they were doing with the polishing. Muir Engineering did more polishing than most manufacturers and we prided ourselves in our ability to obtain a mirror-like shine on metal substrates. The outcome of this conversation was that Apco reluctantly replaced some of the castings, as Muir Engineering only had one standard and would not compromise."

Andrew Perkins: "Apco are the only company casting stainless steel in Tasmania and about ten years ago began producing the large superyacht winch castings which were very demanding because they needed to be machined and polished to a mirror finish, without any blemishes which is very difficult with large castings.

"We've been Apco Engineering since September 2001, and we're still making castings for Muir. Over the years the economy has changed and in order to remain competitive it became necessary for Muir to get more of their castings from overseas. But the Asian foundries are not so good at making small quantities of castings or special one-offs. Muir still come to us for the special items and larger stainless steel castings."

John Muir: "Muir were later pushed to purchasing components from overseas for some of our products because of the larger volumes required, especially in 316 stainless steel. Throughout the 2000s, the strong Australian dollar meant we had some of the highest wages and overheads in the world marine market. That was bad enough, but purchasing Australian made castings, with the inclusive higher wages and costs, meant there was no longer a margin for us."

Andrew Perkins: "Working for Muir has improved our quality, as John has very exacting standards. Muir is always after ever-better quality. They helped drag us kicking and screaming out of the 'she'll be right' mindset."

> 66 *Working for Muir has improved our quality, as John has very exacting standards. Muir is always after ever-better quality.* 99
>
> —ANDREW PERKINS, APCO ENGINEERING

HIGHLY POLISHED

Muir has always prided itself in being able to achieve a high level of polish on its stainless steel products.
Above: Low Profile VR4500; Left: VC4000 Tall Drum mooring capstans.

THE MODERN MUIR FAMILY

The modern Muir family, consisting of John, Wendy, the girls Alex and Shona, brothers Ross and Greg, sister Lyn and the extended family of wives, husbands, children, aunts, uncles and cousins are a complex lot. On the surface they are close and supportive. They are all proud of what each individual has achieved, whether it be in business, employment, sport or just being seen as a 'good family' person.

Scratch the surface, well, maybe dig a little deeper and you find, as with almost every family, tensions and undercurrents running, some that began their movement back in the days of growing up. For those hoping to find the details of those undercurrents, you will be disappointed.

Lyn Denehey: "I remember once when Mum and Dad went to a function at the Royal Yacht Club, I was looking after the boys and quite early in the evening I had to phone them to say that Ross had hit John with a glass milk bottle following a wrestle on the back lawn and broke his nose. There was blood everywhere. Mum and Dad had to leave the dinner and come home early to sort it out.

"On another occasion, Mum and Dad went to the Motor Yacht Club in Victoria Street in the city but when they decided to leave early they discovered Dad's car was missing. The Police were called, but as it turned out John and his friends had 'borrowed' the car."

The modern Muir family are generally outspoken and driven. Collectively, they are a bunch of strong individuals, some of whom have gone on to achieve great things, while others have chosen a less obvious and publicly displayed procession through life, playing a more supportive and encouraging role. While others still have just quietly got on with their lives.

What you will also discover as you read on, are people with the courage to bare their souls, to reveal who they are as human beings and what the core human emotions that drive them are. To share with every reader the joys and heartaches of being part of the Muir family and also being a passenger to John's business journey. The two are inextricably intertwined.

These are people with the courage to say to the world, 'This is who I am, who I have been, doing what I do. This is what I think and why.' You can read, mark, learn and inwardly digest the stories, but remember that these individuals are people who have, to a degree, openly and honestly bared their souls for public inspection.

Why?

Because we have asked them to contribute. Nothing more, nothing less. Some have been more forthcoming than others, that doesn't matter. What you will discover as you read on are insights into some fascinating human journeys, into the decisions we all make from day to day that can have a remarkable impact on those we are closest to. Sometimes we are so focussed on what we ourselves are doing that we don't see the bigger picture or the impact of what we may be doing to others.

One of the most revealing insights into the Muir family of John, Wendy, Alex and Shona is this tale. Personally, I don't think that I would have done what John Muir did, but don't think for one moment that I am making a value judgement about his decision.

The day dawns, today is Alex's big day. She is to be married to her life partner, Matthew Johnston, who in 2005 would start work at Muir as the General Manager. In 2012, he would take over from John and become the Managing Director of Muir Engineering. He would leave that role and the Muir Engineering business to pursue other challenges. Like the Muirs he is also from a family with a sailing background. In fact, as this chapter is being compiled Matthew has just returned from Portugal where he was sailing on *Export Roo* with Michael Cooper and David Chapman in the World SB20 Championships.

ABOVE: ALEX AND MATTHEW
On their wedding day.

BELOW: ALEX AND JOHN
Wooden Boat Festival, Hobart, 2013.

> 66 *So I just threw my arms up in the air and said to John, 'Well go. If you're here, you're here. If you're not, you're not!'* 99

– WENDY MUIR

John Muir: "On the morning of our daughter Alex and son-in-law-to-be Matthew Johnston's wedding I accepted an invitation from the Australian Navy to fly from Hobart airport and land on an American aircraft carrier that was somewhere off the Tasmanian coast, heading towards Hobart, to tour all five decks of the huge carrier, have lunch with the Captain and then return to Hobart. My daughter Shona was in the navy at the time and thought it would be an amazing experience.

"The carrier was on its return from the Middle East and its position could not be disclosed for security reasons. When I accepted the invitation all I knew was that the trip would take about two to three hours just to get to the vessel. We were instructed to report to Hobart Airport at 0730 for departure at 0800."

This is the morning of John's eldest daughter's wedding. The day John should really be with the family doing what bride's fathers do: getting stressed, getting dressed, watching his beautiful daughter get ready for her big moment. The moment when she would officially cut the umbilical cord binding her to John and Wendy. Not John.

Wendy Muir: "Shona was in the Navy and it was her second year. She was at the Australian Defence Force Academy in Canberra and she was coming down for the wedding. We told her about John's opportunity to go on the flight and she thought it sounded great.

"So I just threw my arms up in the air and said to John, 'Well go. If you're here, you're here. If you're not, you're not!'"

John Muir: "I really wanted to go on this trip, so there was a lot of discussion and jockeying within the family for two weeks while I worked out how I could possibly do both. The wedding ceremony was to be at 6pm at St. David's Cathedral, and once I knew I was going, I was given strict instructions to be home by 5pm. So I accepted the invitation and confirmed with the US Navy that I would take up the offer."

What did John's eldest daughter Alex think about her father's decision? We shall never know because Alex chose not to share those feelings with us. It may be just as well that she wants to let sleeping dogs lie. Wendy, however, gives us a mother's insight into what her eldest daughter probably thought at the time.

Question: "How did Alex feel about that?"

Wendy: "I'm not really sure actually. I suppose we did tell her. She probably thought the same as me: 'I've got more to worry about than whether my father's going to be there or not.' We just went along with it."

John Muir: "There were others on the flight, including Robert Clifford, and business, government and maritime industry people. I had a few minutes to spare before take-off and called Jerry Truax in the USA. He asked me where I was and if everything was coming along alright for the wedding. I said everything was going to plan, but I was just about to get on a mail plane to fly out to a US Navy aircraft carrier. He yelled at me, 'John you've gotta be ******* kidding me!' 'No Jerry, I've gotta go soon, we're about to leave.'

"Jerry instantly called a mutual friend Jim Studley, who was an American fighter pilot in the Vietnam War, and asked him what he thought of this idea? Jim is never short of words, he was alarmed, and asked

Jerry if I realised how dangerous landing and taking off from aircraft carriers could be? Particularly in rough weather, and even more so on the day of my daughter's wedding."

In case John did not get back for the nuptials, Wendy asked her father if he would stand in for John and walk Alex down the aisle and give her away. She also told the priest what was going on.

It had been blowing hard from the west overnight and around the time John took off from Hobart airport, Wendy received a phone call from the Moorilla vineyard (now a part of David Walsh's MONA), where the reception was to be held, to tell her that gale force winds had flattened the large marquee installed for the wedding reception.

John Muir: "This caused a bit of a melt-down — me on the plane, wedding calamity underway, so Wendy rang her friend Margot Scales for help, hastily picked her up, and they headed out to see what they could do."

Wendy Muir: "When my girlfriend and I arrived at the reception location, the guy in charge was running around like a blue-arsed fly, he had a very red face, hot and flustered, and he said, 'It'll be okay, it'll be okay.' Apparently they erected the marquee the night before and the wind had blown it down. They'd only just re-erected it, but without any of the fancy stuff in it, so I'm thinking oh my God, you know, are they going to be ready on time?"

This is a revealing moment, Wendy Muir is the sort of individual who just gets on and does what is needed to be done. For Wendy it's a case of 'no point crying over spilt milk,' just ask, will everything be ready? Yes it will. What John is doing is now an afterthought, even if it's a question of 'will he get back in time?' That thought probably didn't even cross her mind while she was watching the organisers running around like cut cats.

John Muir: "Meanwhile I was on the mail plane, on another adventure of my life and recalling something else my Dad used to say when he was on his way somewhere, be it by car, boat or plane — 'You are aware of how things are as you depart on a trip somewhere — but what you don't know is how it will end up.' Never a truer word spoken; here we are — heading into a stiff westerly, flying for around two hours when a female voice came over the speaker (it was the pilot) letting us know she was still searching for the ship and would let us know once it was sighted, also telling us we only had one chance to land on the deck and if any errors were made we'd be promptly heading back to Hobart Airport.

"Within 15 minutes or so the pilot reported they had sighted the USS *Carl Vinson* and she was going to attempt a landing. This could have been a dangerous feat but the hook on the plane picked up the stop wire on the deck and we all felt a hell of a jolt as we landed. The carrier was travelling at 20 knots with a beam roll."

John and the other adventurers enjoyed lunch with the Captain and officers. By 2pm the visit was over and it was all aboard the mail plane for a catapult launch take-off. The strong tail wind proved to be a plus on the return flight.

John Muir: "In preparation for take-off, we were sitting facing the tail of the plane, strapped in tightly, arms crossed, chin on chest, and we were anticipating the jolt from the high-speed catapult used to launch us from the very short runway. We knew the ship was pitching, and we only had one chance to get it right.

John Muir: "I arrived back at Hobart Airport at about 4pm, drove home and amongst all the fuss of wedding preparations, managed to jump in the shower and dress in my tuxedo with all the trimmings. By 4:45pm on the dot I was ready to go, waiting for the car. The bride had been delayed and the car did not arrive to pick me up until around 5:30pm. So off to St. David's Cathedral we went, Matthew and his groomsmen arriving not long after, and — with Alex on my arm — we entered the church right on time at 6pm.

"Once assembled, the priest told the congregation where I'd been and that Wendy's Dad had been standing by in case I didn't make it. After the ceremony we went out to the vineyard, had our toasts, speeches, meals and then the rock band fired up. We danced all night. After that, all I can remember is me climbing up the stairs at home with Wendy prodding me from behind. This had to be, to date, the best day of my life, apart from my own wedding day."

> 66 *I can't speak highly enough of my Mum, she's amazing. Mum let Dad go and do all the Sydney to Hobart races, and the Hamilton Island races and the trip to the US aircraft carrier; Mum's an extremely tolerant person.* 99

– SHONA PRIOR (NÉE MUIR)

The catapult is the biggest jolt I've ever experienced – it's instant acceleration and you're pushed hard into your harness. Your chin hits hard into your windpipe, it takes your breath away."

The USS *Carl Vinson* continued its journey onto Hobart where she anchored well south of the port of Hobart, in the River Derwent, between Taroona and Howrah. She was a nuclear powered warship and those were the rules. It was a controversial visit, bringing out many protesters concerned about the ship's nuclear capability, the safety of the city and the people of Hobart. It also saw many remotely controlled garage doors in the nearby river suburbs not responding to hand held controls. Once shut they stayed shut. The very strong wireless network used by the carrier was on the same frequency as remotely controlled garage doors!

The carrier had a crew of 5,000 spread over four decks. It was so large that personnel from one deck didn't even know everyone they worked with, let alone the crew on the other decks.

Shona Prior (née Muir): "I can't speak highly enough of my Mum, she's amazing. Mum let Dad go and do all the Sydney to Hobart races, and the Hamilton Island races and the trip to the US aircraft carrier; Mum's an extremely tolerant person.

"Dad can be self-centered, that's part of what makes him who he is. It's necessary to have that drive to do as well as he has.

"My relationship with Dad has stayed strong. We've got mutual interests about being fit and healthy, we often go walking together. Dad has five grandchildren and loves them all to bits, as well as his young Labrador dog Gus who is on loan from Alex and Matthew while their house is being renovated.

John Muir: "Alex and Matthew had another beaut black Labrador, named Jack. He used to spend a lot of time with me and we were real buddies. When Jack was about 10 he had cancer in his liver and needed to go to Sydney at short notice for an operation.

"I brought forward one of my trips to Northern Europe and arranged with Qantas to fly Jack to Sydney on the same flight as me. Jack had to be fed regularly because of the effects of his diabetic type illness, so one of my good friends, Winston Bevis, kept the food up to Jack until my departure from the airport. Like Gus, who is now two years old, Jack was a big Lab by build. On arrival at Sydney airport I picked up my luggage and Jack and waved down a taxi. The first driver was not going to have a dog in the boot of his cab. It was fortunate another driver wanted the fare so off we went to the veterinary hospital on the north shore. Jack had his operation the following day and I stayed with him for another day before heading off to Hamburg.

"A week later Jack was made ready for the flight back to Hobart and was delivered back home this time by a veterinary travel service. From then on we referred to him as 'Flying Jack!'"

"FLYING JACK"

*The much-loved black Labrador was a regular crew member on boating adventures. Right: Onboard **Shonandra** with Shona in 1998; Below: Onboard **Shonandra**, left to right Stewart Griggs, Wendy Muir, John Griggs, Margot Scales, Jack the Lab.*

> ❝ *I worked with Dad for 18 years and I learned a great deal about the marine industry, exports and manufacturing, as well as the need for perseverance and hard work associated with working with your family.* ❞

– ALEX JOHNSTON (NÉE MUIR)

On arrival in Hamburg after a 30 hour flight, John's mobile phone battery was dead and he had no way of contacting his German agent, Conrad Sthoemer who was coming to pick him up. John was getting more and more stressed, as he was concerned about Conrad who he knew would be trying to find him. (Stress is not good for a diabetic.) He bought a phone charger and set it up on top of his bags. He left the gear for what seemed like 15 seconds to walk to the exit door to see if he could find Conrad. When he turned around, the bags and his phone were gone.

In his bags were all the contracts needed for the trip, his cash and, more importantly, his insulin. Finally John found a police officer who could understand English and explained his plight and the urgent need to check his blood sugar levels. (There was nothing anyone could do about the stolen bags.) Eventually John was taken to the police station at the airport where there were frantic phone calls to Hobart and eventually Simon Pettitt in the UK, who gave John Conrad's number. It was four hours after his arrival in Hamburg that John and Conrad met and John was taken to a 24 hour chemist to get supplies of insulin and glucose.

THIS PAGE: MUIR IN ALEX'S DAY

Alex stayed with the company for 18 years before moving on to pursue her own business interests.

OPPOSITE: FAMILY TIES

A photo from Sanctuary Cove Boat Show in 2002 with the Muir team, from left: Michael Trickey, Matthew Johnston, John, Ken Padgett, Eddie Hidding, Alex Johnston. It was a big show and a very successful business opportunity for Muir.

When Alex completed her university degree in commerce and marketing, she mentioned to her father that she was contemplating a marketing position. Up until this time John had maintained an overview of all sales and marketing at Muir Engineering. Within two weeks Alex was appointed as Marketing Manager for Muir Engineering.

Alex Johnston (née Muir): "I worked with Dad for 18 years and I learned a great deal about the marine industry, exports and manufacturing, as well as the need for perseverance and hard work associated with working with your family.

"Not sure how I did it! It was certainly a long and arduous apprenticeship but with many valuable lessons learned and knowledge gained."

Soon after Alex started at Muir Engineering at Kingston she was right into her work and had a quarterly newsletter underway, along with several new marine equipment catalogues. During her time there she

worked in various sections of the business including invoicing, accounts and debtors, reception and sales. She also travelled to mainland and international boat shows and worked the Muir stand making a point, like her father, of visiting every prospective customer's stands and going on board as many of the motor and sail yachts on display at the show. It's all about reinforcing relationships and looking at both Muir and their competitors' equipment.

John Muir: "Alex travelled a lot for the business throughout the 1990s and early 2000s. Alex went to the USA and attended the Fort Lauderdale and Miami boat shows on several occasions with me and managed the Muir stand, allowing Fred Mayer and myself to spend time visiting customers. These two boat shows are huge by comparison to most of the European shows, with around 300,000 visitors arriving at the Miami Boat Show alone. However, the Genoa International Boat Show in Italy has about 400,000 visitors in good times, making it the largest in the world."

MUIR LEGACY

Both John's daughters have been involved in the business at some stage. Left, Alex on the Muir stand at Sanctuary Cove in the early 2000s. Right, from left: Sergei Postal, Shona Prior, Anneka Deaton, Simon Pettitt, Monaco Boat Show 2004.

There is a story that does the rounds that the first time Alex attended a weekly management meeting at Muir's Head Office John had to remind her that she wasn't at home at the dinner table (where most things were discussed). The story goes that Alex let fly at John and he had to remind her she was at work and not at home. John and Alex could both be blunt and forthright at times. If this is true, it's quite probable that John would have told Alex, somewhat colourfully, to keep home away from work and work away from home.

Shona Prior (née Muir): "Dad has always been a strong role model for me. Growing up, he instilled in me a lot of values. The values of perseverance and hard work, and the importance of having passions and a vision in life.

"Alex and I were prefects at St. Michaels Collegiate school. Both Mum and Dad encouraged Alex and I to do our best and always go the extra mile.

"For me, Dad's been a strong role model but Mum's really the matriarch. They both supported me when I decided to join the Navy and go to the Defence Force Academy in Canberra. I always felt I could come home, and I had such a strong base to come back to. Most of that is Mum but also Dad, no matter how busy he's been, Dad's always been at the end of the phone if I've ever needed advice or needed to talk to someone."

Shona had four years at the Defence Academy in Canberra, then went into Navy Logistics, spending time with the Submarine Squadron and Clearance Diving teams. She also undertook Antarctic-related research in the United Kingdom following the death of

a marine biologist from a leopard seal attack. Shona is now back in Hobart working in the public sector and continuing in the Navy Reserves.

What is it that sets the relationship between children and parents, what builds emotional ties and bonds, and what can just as easily tear them apart? There are strong forces at work within the Muir family. We know John is driven, passionate and determined to succeed in life and his business. He knows his father Jock participated in 19 Sydney to Hobart yacht races and didn't think there was anything wrong with being away from the family at Christmas. John himself sailed in 16 Sydney to Hobart races. (He was 15 when he sailed in his first race on board *Lass O'Luss* in 1959.) That was the way life was, that's what he saw, that's what he did.

Wendy, on the other hand, is one critical person John has relied on and who has supported him all the way through.

Alex Johnston (née Muir): "While Dad inspired many of his staff with his drive and passion, he would chase a sale to the end of the earth to get it, and he rarely gave up til he got it. He was very much an absent father at times. We never seemed to suffer much because Mum was always there for us and Dad certainly put us and our family in good shape."

The family had great boating holidays, more often than not sailing in groups with friends on other boats all around the coast of Tasmania and its many islands. There were also a couple of trips to the USA that were a mix of pleasure and work.

Alex Johnston (née Muir): "Dad travelled extensively for over 40 years and many times in the early days for 6-8 weeks at a time, so growing up we rarely had family holidays, apart from almost every year time away in the family's boats."

"An industry colleague once told me that they had never met anyone more determined, hardworking and passionate than John Muir! He was rewarded by his industry a few years later by being named the Australian Marine Industry Export Champion in 2009."

Two years later (in 2011) John won the Australian Institute of Export's Hero Award following in the footsteps of Robert Clifford of Incat and John Rothwell of Austal Ships from Western Australia. For John Muir it was a humbling experience, because he held both of these men in the highest regard and to be awarded the same honour as they had achieved was an amazing experience. Two years later Alistair Murray won the same Export Hero Award.

Alex Johnston (née Muir): "Dad loved his work so much that when we visited Disney World in Florida I can remember Mum saying to us as we were lining up for a ride, 'God, where's your father gone?' Looking around, we found him sitting on the side of a garden bed writing notes ready to fax back to the office!" (He was known internationally as Fax Man in those days!)

Wendy Muir: "John's Dad, Jock did lots of sailing. Well, John was gone for 16 Christmases for Sydney to Hobart yacht races. He'd either be gone before Christmas for the Southern Cross Series or he'd fly to Sydney on Christmas afternoon or night. He followed in his father's footsteps.

"He did the Hamilton Island yacht race for about ten years running, but the truth of it is I used to encourage him to do that. The Hamilton Island races he almost always did with his brothers. A couple of times he'd say, 'I'm too busy at work' and I'd say to him, 'Well look if you can't have a couple of weeks off work to go and do something you want to do, well then it's time you gave it away' so I'd pack him up and send him off.

"On most occasions I would pack his luggage. I would have it all ready so all he had to do was just grab it as he ran out the door. I did encourage him to do it. I didn't travel with him myself because I had the children."

> ❝ *Dad has always been a strong role model for me. Growing up, he instilled in me a lot of values. The values of perseverance and hard work, and the importance of having passions and a vision in life.* ❞

– SHONA PRIOR (NÉE MUIR)

MARITIME GENES
Above: Shona has served full time in the Royal Australian Navy and continues as a Lieutenant in the Navy Reserves.
Top: Shona and husband Anthony Prior wed in 2009.

ABOVE: CHRISTENING THE FMAILY YACHT

Wendy christens **Shonandra** *at Muir's boatyard in 1982.* **Waubs Bay** *shown in the background.*

RIGHT: THREE GENERATIONS OF SAILORS

John, Alex and Jock took part in the Sydney-Southport Race in 1990, becoming the first three-generation team to compete.

Wind, water and an almost irresistible urge to succeed are part and parcel of the extended Muir family. It's in the family's genes and it is certainly embedded in the day to day life of John, sister Lyn, brothers Greg and Ross and their extended families.

When you realise that all three boys began their business careers near or at their father's boatyard and all loved sport including hockey, tennis, cricket and football and particularly competitive sailing, it's no wonder the children of the next generation have been encouraged to mirror their parents' activities.

Ross Muir started his working life as an apprentice shipwright, employed by his father at the family's Battery Point boatyard. He remembers building small racing dinghies, as well as helping with the construction of a range of racing yachts and working boats, like the 34ft Van der Staat yacht, *Bindaree*, for Graham Blackwood, a local sailor who became Commodore of the Derwent Sailing Squadron, the fishing boat *Dorothy Fay*, for Arnold White a fisherman from Bicheno and the 46ft racing yacht *Balandra* that sailed in the Admirals Cup and many Sydney to Hobart

races. After that it was a 'top hat' design *Chindrina* for Herbie Frey and in 1969, the 34ft canoe stern Jock Muir-designed *Lady Nelson*, built for New York-born Robert Robe.

John Muir: "When *Lady Nelson* was christened, it wasn't the usual run of the mill of event. It was one hell of a big party, the Boatyard was all lit up and streamers were flowing in the breeze. There were several waiters running around filling up glasses and plates of the very best food, along with pretty well any drink you could imagine, and there must have been at least 200 people present. This was the only time I can remember our father Jock being so exuberant and thirsty. In fact, he was so exuberant he had to be driven home that night which was well after midnight!"

During this period Ross built *Venom* and then raced other 12ft cadet dinghies, including *Venom* in which he won the Stonehaven Cup (the Australian championship series) held in Hobart in January 1964 at the age of 17. Ross was helmsman, John Griggs and Adrian Gorringe were his crew. These boys had all grown up together and lived around or near Battery Point.

BEHIND EVERY SUCCESSFUL MAN...

Wendy has been an invaluable support to John over the years, keeping things running at home with the family and the business, while he travelled extensively for work. By John's own admission, he 'wouldn't have been able to do it without her.' Left Wendy with her mum, Betty Harwood, in 2009 at Shona and Anthony's wedding. Above: Wendy steering **Westward II**.

PLAYS TOGETHER, STAYS TOGETHER

John, Wendy and the girls enjoyed many family boating holidays over the decades. Below, on **Shonandra** *in 1987.*

Shonandra on Opening Day, October 1984. Mollie Muir standing in centre, Cliff Harwood at back in tan jacket, next to wife Betty Harwood, with friends and children.

Beach party on a sailing trip in Mickey's Bay, Bruny Island Tasmania, Easter 1993. John (in white hat) and Bob Cowle nearest to camera.

One of many yachting trips over the years with a big group of John and Wendy's friends.

Shona with a VM500H manual anchor windlass, c. 1990.

John with a young Alex and his friend Tooby (Kerry McNiece), bound for Nubeena in 1983. Cray pots were set near Wedge Island along the way.

FAMILY SAILING

Boats and the water have always played an important role in family life, with his own children, and now with the grandchildren.

John and Shona sailing a sabot dinghy in Sykes Cove, Bruny Island, 1982.

'Easter catch.' Shona with a catch of Atlantic Salmon in Sykes Cove, Bruny Island Tasmania, 2003.

A raft-up in the 1990s of John and Wendy's yacht **Shonandra** (far left) with friends' yachts, down the D'Entrecasteaux Channel, Tasmania.

Shona, Wendy and Alex, c. 2011.

Wendy and John, mid-1989 at the Tasmanian Small Business Awards.

JOHN'S FAMILY ALBUM

John says, "Although my girls say we never had many family holidays, we had a couple of trips to the USA, and Alex and Shona have had a couple of trips to Europe with Wendy. We had many trips away on the family yacht with other family and friends, plenty of good times rafted up somewhere down the D'Entrecasteaux Channel. Wendy and I both enjoyed these opportunities to get away from work.

"Now that the family has two shacks at Triabunna, Tasmania, we don't spend as much time away on the yacht. As anyone will tell you, it's much easier to jump in the car and drive an hour and half than it is to pack up gear and take the boat somewhere. It's a lot less work for Wendy – less packing, less organising and less cleaning. She also likes to get away from me sometimes! She's always been a busy woman, and she enjoys her own space these days, as she's entitled to do."

*2.5 year old Gus the Labrador – John's new 'first mate' – waits patiently on the marina next to **Westward II**.*

John with Shona at Cambridge University, England, c. 2007. Shona was studying there at the time and John stopped by to visit during an overseas business trip.

Wendy and John with Shona's daughter Grace, at Government House, Tasmania, 2015.

Anthony Prior with son Lachie, 2015.

Alex and Matthew's children Claudia, back left, and Scarlett, and Oliver, front left, with Shona's son Lachlan as a baby. around 2012.

Shona and Anthony's children Lachlan, 4, and Grace, 18 months, in 2015.

Oliver on John and Matthew's 23ft Haynes Hunter, 2013.

Claudia fishing for crays with Matthew, 2013.

Scarlett fishing, 2015.

EPIREZ

Epoxy Concretes and Adhesives for the CIVIL ENGINEER

LEFT: SHARING THE INDUSTRIOUS GENE

Greg also possessed a strong desire to run his own business. Left, Greg on the Tasman Bridge repair and widening job using epoxy products, 1976. An entire span of the bridge fell in 1975 when the freighter **Lake Illawarra** *collided with it. The freighter's wreck now sits at the bottom of the River Derwent underneath this bridge section.*

OPPOSITE: YACHT DISTRIBUTORS AND LATER YD WATER SPORTS

Above: Greg built the successful business Yacht Distributors, which started in Ross's chandlery at Purdon's Boatyard. When it became larger it morphed into YD Water Sports which was one of the first importers of windsurfers into Tasmania. Article: The Mercury.

Right: Greg riding his windsurfer on the River Derwent, off Battery Point, in the 1970s.

Greg Muir always had some form of business from a young age, driven by a desire to be creative and to make money, just like his older brothers. During his school days he was always hanging around Jock's boatyard, working where he could, certainly watching and learning from the men who worked there. After matriculating he was accepted as a cadet engineer with the Tasmanian Hydro Electric Commission (a mix of working for the Hydro and attending college lectures) which provided a combination of practical and theoretical training. He graduated with a diploma in Engineering in 1974 and became a member of the Institution of Engineers, Australia in 1977.

Soon after graduation Greg moved into the world of private enterprise, starting as a design and contract engineer for a firm called Frigrite, a national company specialising in commercial air conditioning, plumbing, electrical and building services. He was part of a local 300 strong team and said, for him, it was a steep learning curve.

Both Ross and Greg were always on the lookout for commercial opportunities and together in 1975 they started Yacht Distributors, setting up just down the way from their Dad's boatyard, selling production yachts,

catamarans and sailing dinghies from Ross's chandlery business at Purdon's Boatyard.

The business grew quickly and when the Tasman bridge disaster happened (sections of the bridge collapsed after the freighter *Lake Illawarra* collided with a bridge pylon in 1975), Greg left Frigrite and bought brother Ross out. Greg expanded the business with a distributorship for epoxy resins that were used in large quantities as the bridge was being repaired and widened.

(This work laid the foundation for further business expansion as Greg set up two specialist companies in 1989 that he later sold to staff: Maintenance Systems Pty Ltd and Build Tech Supplies Pty Ltd.)

In 1979 Greg re-joined the family boatyard operation, moving Yacht Distributors to a retailing area under the Muir's Battery Point Boatyard. Ross had also moved his ship chandlery business onto the same site. The family was re-united, all in business together, but running distinct business entities. John by then had bought into his father Jock's boatbuilding operations and owned a 25% share of the boatyard, slipway and associated buildings. He also built the adjacent sheds where he established Muir Engineering and Diesel Services.

SURFING
By
MARTIN
JENKIN

The 'wounded seagull' rides again. Four-times world champion, Mark Richards (once affectionately known as the 'wounded seagull') drives down the face of a eight-metre Waimea monster on the way to winning the Billabong Hawaiian Pro this week. Australians Gary Elkerton and Glen Winton were second and third respectively.

HOBART'S most successful surf and sailboard manufacturer and retailer, Yacht Distributor manager Greg Muir, says he is in the business because he wants to be, not just for the profits.

With the poor financial track record of other Tasmanian board manufacturers during the past two decades, Muir's statement is not just a throwaway line.

YD's product, Island Energy Surfboards, may be on a par with present and previous products (that's for the individual surfer to decide), but it's Muir's marketing expertise and family background that has seen the Sandy Bay YD showroom grow and prosper, when many previous surf outlets have failed to take off.

"We are genuinely interested in surfboards and sailboards, and we like to get really involved with these sports," Muir said.

"Yacht Distributors prides itself on giving people what they want, and we are proud of our credibility.

"My accountant is spinning out about the heavy amount of stock we continue to carry, but we want to give Hobart surfers a choice," he said.

"We try to employ local hot surfers such as Arturs Innes and recently-returned traveller Martin Keil for shop floor expertise and advice.

"Island Energy shaper, Nick Stranger, probably is the hardest-worked surfboard and sailboard shaper in Australia — he is very versatile and keen to be innovative."

Muir, who is a member of the well-known Hobart yachting and ship-building family, has been involved with water sports from a young age, including racing and building dinghys, surfing, water skiing and skindiving.

Muir is now mostly into sailboards and regularly makes the pilgrimage to Hawaii to sail and to get the latest on the design of hulls and other equipment.

"Yacht Distributors' first board was a sailboard made by Mike Skeels about five years ago."

"Our extensive research has led us into a new surfboard manufacturing technique where we use a tighter-weave fibreglass cloth with epoxy resin and then spray finish the boards with a white eurethane.

"We also have used a carbon-fibre and Kevlar construction method with sailboards, which although expensive, makes them almost bullet-proof."

Muir said YD was successful because it was prepared to operate on low margins and offer a big selection.

"If we looked at the business critically, we should be charging $500 and up for a custom surfboard instead of the present basic $450 for an Island Energy shape, but we want to be involved in this business so we charge what the Tasmanian market is prepared to pay," he said.

"Our trading figures might be down a little, but we figure that's only a temporary lull.

"We started to stock some general sporting goods for a while but felt that that cost us credibility in the surfing market."

Credibility obviously is an important facet of the business to Muir, who mentions helping to start the teams boardriding concept in Tasmania with a little pride.

"We helped start the teams contest concept in the State about three years ago as a means of encouraging the more average surfer to come along and have fun in their sport," Muir said.

"We saw ourselves as late starters in the surfing scene, and with a name like ours, we wanted to be recognised as supporting the sport.

"Surfing in Tasmania has opened up a bit from its underground image but it is still a bit parochial.

"However, we will continue to support the State titles and we still want to bring hot interstate surfers down here so Tasmanians can benefit from watching different styles.

"Surf board riding still is regarded as the pinnacle of activity in the water and, that's the sport YD wants to continue to be involved in," he said.

★★ ★★ ★★

AFTER weeks of silence about Tasmania's proposed first professional contest, apparently scheduled for early March, 1987, promoter Ian Weir last week said he was confident the event would go ahead.

Weir, a partner in the Frankston (Victoria) surfshop, Koalabunga, and "The Promotion People" said he had employed an experienced baseball promoter, Rick Lewis and Associates, to try to tie up sponsorship for the Tasmanian event.

"We're still trying to get sponsors for the Tassie Pro," Weir said this week. "We're still hopeful the event will go ahead, and we have a few things up our sleeves."

He said that if a commitment from a major sponsor could not be obtained by mid-January, the contest could lapse.

● The windsurfing column, previously printed in The Sunday Tasmanian, is now incorporated in the On The Water column in Thursday's Mercury.

GREG MUIR

The site was literally humming with activity, the slipway was always full, boats moored nearby waiting to go on the slips or have work done by Muir Engineering or the boatyard. Ross was selling associated yachting gear and Greg was flat out with dinghy and pleasure boat sales and other activities.

Greg's business, Yacht Distributors, morphed into a larger business called YD Water Sports and was soon selling the majority of sailboards, windsurfers and other water toys for the Tasmanian market, until 1993.

Greg Muir: "I have had some big wins commercially, but I have also had some big losses, including land and warehouse developments. For me, losses almost always mean future wins, as long as you learn the lessons you should from each experience."

Greg and his wife Sue have three children (Tim, Ben and Lucy), who, like their father but unlike their grandfather and great grandfather, have gone on to university-based careers. But all, like their many forebears, have strong links to wind and water, they have raced and done well in sailing dinghies in both national and world titles. They also love snow sports.

GREG'S FAMILY

Greg and his wife Sue have three children –
Tim, Ben and Lucy.

Top: Greg enjoying the tuna fishing at the edge of the continental shelf off Tasmania's east coast, 2016.

Middle: Tim Muir with wife Jo, and sons from left, Jack , Max and Nick.

Bottom left: Lucy Klein (née Muir) with husband Martin and son William.

Below: Ben Muir with wife Meegan, and children Gabby and Elliot.

MAINTAINING THE FAMILY LEGACY

Greg's son Tim and Ben have maintained the family's maritime legacy. Both have sailed competitively in dinghy classes. Shown below leading the field in heat 5 of the Sharpie Nationals in 2010 is Tim.

Left, as a kid Ben sailed sabot dinghies, and both boys enjoyed accompanying John, Greg and Ross on sailing adventures as Tim above, on a Port Davey trip in 1998.

In 1987 Ross and his family moved to Brisbane and established a traditional ship chandlery business at Manly, an area that is home to several thousand pleasure boats. His son Jason runs the business now, but when younger had great yachting success himself. Jason started sailing Optimists in Hobart in 1983 and joined Paul Wyatt for his first world title in Spain in 1986, in International Cadets. At the age of 14, in 1987, Jason won the Australian Sabot Sailing Championships, as well as other national dinghy titles. His father Ross was a tower of strength, passing on from one generation to another, everything he knew about competitive sailing.

In 1990 Jason was crowned Australian Youth Yachtsman of the Year after finished third in the Laser II World Youth Championship held in Holland. His stellar sailing career continues. In 2009 he teamed up with three friends, including his ex-Tasmanian childhood mate Paul Wyatt, to win the Etchell National Title, then the World Etchell Yachting Championship at Royal Brighton Yacht Club in Melbourne.

Jason has three children who, following in the family tradition, sail in Optimists and Sabot class dinghies at Manly near Brisbane.

The Etchell website reported Jason's win:

A Queensland crew skippered by Jason Muir out-sailed their 84 opponents to claim their first world title, winning the 2009 Audi Etchells World Championship.

ETCHELLS WORLD CHAMPIONSHIPS

Above: From left, Buck Smith, Matthew Chew, Paul Wyatt, Jason Muir, Etchell World Titles in Melbourne, 2009.
Below: Ross, Jason, John and Greg at the Etchell World Championships in 2009.

OPPOSITE: ROSS'S FAMILY

Adults from left: Jake Coulter, Danielle Coulter (née Muir), Ross Muir, his wife Judy, Jason Muir, his wife Sue Muir. Children from left: Thomas Coulter, William Coulter, Jessica Muir, Oliver Muir, Sam Muir.

"They were competing against some of the megastars of the sport, including America's Cup and Olympic sailors. Jason's crew included his long-time sailing partner Paul Wyatt, along with Matthew Chew and Bucky Smith.

"They beat the pre-event favourites, referred to as 'the Olympic crew' of John Bertrand, British Olympic great Ben Ainslie and Andrew Palfrey, an Australian Olympian, who has coached three Australian crews to world title wins in three classes."*

If you wonder where this competitive spirit comes from, wonder no more. It is embedded in virtually every Muir. It is no more publicly on show for the yachting world to see than in the annual Hamilton Island Yacht Races held in Queensland.

It was during the historic America's Cup match in Newport, Rhode Island, in 1983 that Hamilton Island's developer, Keith Williams, hit on the idea of staging a major annual yacht regatta out of the island.

He discussed it at length with a friend, Rob Mundle, who was reporting on the America's Cup in Newport at that time, then, on his return to Hamilton Island he approached a Melbourne yachtsman, David Hutchen, who was living in the Whitsunday region and detailed his idea for the event. Hutchen seized on the concept and was subsequently commissioned by Williams to get it organised.

A few weeks later a small group, including Hutchen, Mundle and Australia's original America's Cup challenge skipper, Jock Sturrock, were at Hamilton Island with a view to formulating the parameters for what would become the now famous Hamilton Island Race Week. With that done, Hutchen headed the organising committee that included two of his sailing mates out of Victoria, Warwick Hoban and Leon O'Donoghue.

* Source: www.etchells.org.au/news/news.asp?newsID=11

LYN'S FAMILY

Left to right: Jock Denehey, Mark Rasmussen (back), John Muir (front), Wayne Denehey (back), Lynette Denehey (front), Michael Denehey, Richard Curtis, Lisa Curtis née Denehey, Louise Rasmussen (née Denehey). Kids in pool: William Curtis, Tom Rasmussen, Lily Rasmussen, Max Denehey.

Mark and Molly Rasmussen at the National Heron Cla Championship, 2007. There was no wind, the race was abandoned, and they needed an outboard motor!

*Mark, Lilly and Molly Rasmussen at the wheel of Mottle 33, **Southerly**.*

Mark and Molly Rasmussen, prize winners, National Heron Class Championship 2007.

LYN DENEHEY
Onboard **Westward II**, *February 2016, off Recherche Bay, Tasmania.*

Tom Rasmussen sails Optimist class **Jackhammer**.

William Curtis climbs aboard the family powerboat.

Rasmussen family aboard Mottle 33, **Southerly** *which was also owned by Lyn and Wayne Denehey.*

The inaugural Hamilton Island Race Week was staged in April 1984, immediately after Easter. The response for the week-long series was way beyond expectations: 93 yachts travelled from as far afield as Perth to participate. Unfortunately the weather was not what anyone had envisioned when it came to sailing in the tropics. The 'wet season' lived up to its name: rain poured down for almost the entire week. This led to the series being referred to light-heartedly as Hamilton Island Rain Week in the 'Wetsundays'. The harbour-front Mardi Gras party that was staged mid-week became known as the 'Muddy Gras'.

For the first eight years, Race Week was held in April, but the impact of the wet season eventually took its toll (Cyclone Aivu visited Race Week in 1989). After much consideration the organisers rescheduled Hamilton Island Race Week for August, a time of year that promised warm weather and trade winds sailing.

For many years, prominent sailor and famous Australian vigneron, Bob Oatley and family members, were regular competitors at Race Week. In 2003 – the year that Bob's son, Sandy, won the Grand Prix Division with his yacht, *Another Duchess* – Bob was asked if he might be interested in buying the island. His positive response was almost immediate and within weeks the family owned the island. Since then the Oatley family has taken Hamilton Island, and Race Week, to the position where both stand as icons in their respective fields in Australia and internationally.

The 30th staging of what is now Audi Hamilton Island Race Week in 2013 was a huge success. A fleet of more than 200 yachts from Australia and overseas participated.

Every year Hamilton Island Race Week is recognised for setting new standards in the world of sailboat racing. In doing so, it remains as Australia's premier regatta for offshore yachts.*

The Muir's boats competing in the Hamilton Island Yacht Race Series have been skippered by John, Ross, Greg and their sailing friends from both Tasmania and Queensland. The competition on the water between the brothers has been fierce. It obviously harks back to the cadet dinghy and lightweight sharpie days and racing against one another on the River Derwent. In fact there has always been a competitive, some would harshly say combative, spirit, between John and Ross. One of the many crew on those boats was a close friend and sailor, Greg Williams.

Greg Williams: "The brothers are wonderful guys and supported each other off the water, but on the water was a different kettle of fish. In 2005, the year before they joined forces, John turned up to the Sunsail Marina to find his hired boat tied up side by side with Ross's. Not surprisingly, before John had arrived, Ross had added a bow sprit and two telescopic spinnaker poles to his boat and had bought a new headsail, reacher, MPS, and a couple of new kites one of which was enormous. (For the uninitiated, a kite is another term for a spinnaker.)

"I sailed with Ross that year and despite the crew struggling with the new gear we spanked John's boat over the first two races.

"John was not happy. Next thing, the spinnakers from Stephen Keal's 50ft *Cyclone*, as well as the two long spinnaker poles (and a new bowsprit) and no. 1 headsail from John's yacht *Shonandra*, turned up at the marina, flown in directly from Hobart. The racing was a lot closer after that but Ross at the finish had just trumped John and beat him on the score sheet in the first two of three races. However, John and his crew eventually won the overall prize."

In those early years of racing at Hamilton Island, John was joined by a mate and employee, Michael Cooper.

Michael Cooper: "We were sailing along, we had the spinnaker up, and the spinnaker pole broke. Normally this would be the end of the race or you'd at least have to take the spinnaker down and retreat to port for some repairs. Not the Muir's, they looked for ways to fix it so they could not only keep competing, but keep the spinnaker up. They took the legs off the table (from a boat that didn't belong to them) and ended up using the timber as a splint in order to fix the spinnaker pole.

"I remember it was all covered in rope and tape and all sorts of stuff, and there were these table legs – beautiful turned timber table legs mind you, part of the boat's permanent furniture. They just ripped them off and got the job done and worried about the consequences later. They got the spinnaker up again and finished the race.

"I think the organisers just accepted this was what they were like — do first and worry about paying for it later. I'm sure John had to pay for quite a lot of things over the years."

* Source: www.hamiltonislandraceweek.com.au/about/race-week-history

73FT SCHOONER ASTOR
During Hamilton Island Race Week, 2004.

MUIR TEAM LEADING THE RACE

Fired up and in the lead on their Jeanneau 49.1, 2012.

These yachts were chartered for the races. Everyone flew to Hamilton Island and would be given a yacht to compete with. The Team Muir yacht would always be decked out in stickers and flags and branded sails with Muir all over them, literally covered in Muir marketing stuff.

Michael Cooper: "A whole container of stuff would be shipped up a week or so before the competition started. The Muir's would retro-fit the yachts for their own purposes, they'd rip excess weight off the boat and take all unnecessary items out. One year they even freighted up their own propeller, a special kind they wanted to use, and replaced the propeller on the yacht they were racing in. I remember there was this dinghy at the marina full of stuff they'd taken off the boat — pots and pans, chairs, anything that they didn't need to race. This dinghy was just full to the top, barely floating. It was really serious competitive business."

Greg Williams first started racing at Hamilton Island around 1994 with a bunch of Tassie sailors mostly mates from the Bellerive Yacht Club who had a common interest in escaping the Tasmanian winters for 10 days of warm water sailing in the Northern Tropics. The Muir brothers entered in 1998 and 1999 with Timmy Watts as navigator sailing a chartered Beneteau 46.6. They have won, either as individuals or as a combined crew, more than their fair share of races.

Greg Williams: "Around that time John and Ross saw reason and joined forces and with younger brother Greg became a formidable force. The next year they retained a 47.6m Beneteau yacht called Rainbow and fitted all their own gear to the boat and renamed it 'Muirs.' (Obviously to promote the Muir Engineering business.) The Muir boys have never been shy with the signage, it usually took Greg a full day with help to apply and then remove the Muir 4m long blue decals from the boat's sides.

HAMILTON ISLAND RACE WEEK

Top left: Robert Clifford in September 1999, celebrating his win.
Top right: John with Wayne Banks-Smith.
Above: Matthew Johnston, Michael Cooper, Brett Cooper and Ross Muir, 1998.
Right: A whale breeches in the Whitsundays.

"During the next few years (2006-2009) the Muir boys suffered at the hands of the handicapper and often had crews of mixed experience. The helming was always shared between Ross, John and Greg, sharing two races each which created a competition within the competition; however they remained wonderfully supportive of each other with not a terse word between them." (Can you believe that?)

The Muir boys saw off a number of serious Tasmanian challengers. One year prominent Hobart yachties, Hughey Lewis, Wayne Banks-Smith (Banger) and Stephen Keal (Kealey) decided to mount a challenge. They flew north taking with them all of the gear they could strip from their various boats to improve the performance of the boat they chartered.

Greg Williams: "I still recall the look on their faces when they drove around the corner to see the Muir boat on the slip with the crew changing the prop and wet and drying the bottom. The Muir boat soundly beat them despite protests to the handicapper and it was not until the next year when they bought the 50ft racing yacht *Cyclone* to Hamilton Island and entered her in the cruising division that they were able to beat the Muir Boys.

"Around this time Ross had a brain wave and had a zip-on additional 1.5m added to the bottom of the large spinnaker that was already enormous, and this required an 8m telescopic spinnaker pole to set. The crew christened it 'the prawn net' and we had some fun retrieving it from under the boat on a number of occasions."

The Muir boys were hard to beat and often the fleet had to rely on them beating themselves. This usually occurred when they had far too much sail on for the

COLOURFUL FLEET

The Muir's yacht (red and blue spinnaker with winch logo), under full sail.

conditions. Ross bought a 1970s Blooper off *Trevassa* to Hamilton Island one year. Most of the other crews and sailors had never seen a Blooper let alone knew how to set one.

Greg Williams: "We were winning the Lindeman Island race in 20 knots of breeze by a mile until Ross said 'Set the Blooper.' We had it up for about 10 minutes before we Chinese-jibed and all hell broke loose. It took close to 20 minutes to get the boat upright and the race was lost for us, however the Blooper was the main talking point among all the crews on the marina when we arrived back.

"From time to time we had some casualties and men overboard. In 2005 Ross's brother-in-law Mike Wilson sailed with us in the South Molle race just after he'd had a serious operation. Ross put him up on the main sheet traveller and the only way he could get comfortable was to sit astride the traveller. Ross crash tacked the boat which forced the main sheet traveller up between Mike's legs. We can laugh now but poor old Mike ended up in a bad way in an ambulance back on Hamilton Island with damaged family jewels. John was running a close second at the time with wind peaking at 30 knots, and went on to take line honours, and to win overall."

In 2011 and 2012 they chartered a cruising version Jeanneau 49.1. The Muir boys had this yacht really well rigged and tuned and she outsailed the Jeanneau

49.1 racing version. Finally in 2012, after winning many individual races over many years, the Muir boys won the series. That year they had Tasmanian yachting legend and orchardist Ian Smith on board, Greg thinks Ian's tactical input helped them to finally claim the series trophy after many years of competing.

Michael Cooper: "One time during a Hamilton Island race they got the headsail wrapped around the furler. This would mean usually you'd have to stop and go back to the marina to untangle it, it was just a mess and sails would need to be cut out and ropes and rigging redone. It was the end of the race for most people, as it was just too hard to rig some sort of fix on the go in order to remain in the race.

"Not the Muirs. They turned the yacht and kept going in a really tight circle in the opposite direction the sail was wound on, and figured they'd unwrap it. This caused the yacht to be right over on its side, you could barely stand up, everyone who was watching from the other boats wondered what the hell these crazy guys were doing. But it worked, the sail unravelled and they were able to keep racing."

John Muir: "Michael Cooper has the bite and determination in him when he needs it. He's tenacious, adventurous and a go-getter as proven with all the three generations of the Cooper family. Mike and Bill (his father) had what it takes to start a business and drive it upwards as they very successfully did!"

ASTOR, HAMILTON ISLAND, 2004

*Greg, John and Ross celebrating winning one of the races of the series, crewing on **Astor**.*

The tale of Michael Cooper, his parents and the Juicy Isle business is told in an earlier chapter. Now it's back in time to the late 1960s and early 1970s, to the days when John was getting started in business but also deeply involved in competitive sailing, lightweight sharpies in particular on the River Derwent.

Chris Fuglsang, physically the exact opposite of John Muir, coming in at 6 foot 5 inches, built like a beanpole, was just what the doctor ordered for a forward hand and was asked to sail with John as crew on his lightweight sharpie. It was all about being as competitive as was humanely possible. Having a really tall, skinny forward hand was a big plus, especially when it blew hard, and he was out on the trapeze.

John Muir: "We were in our element."

Chris Fuglsang: "I grew up from my early teen years around John's brothers, Ross and Greg and I knew his parents Jock and Mollie very well. I was really excited at the age of about 19 to be asked by John, who I didn't know really well, to sail in his new Lightweight Sharpie, which he had named Stratus. This boat had been built by his brother Ross and at that stage was

to be launched in the coming season. The main hand Bob Laing (known as Pix), and John (known to me and his close friends as Sam) and myself as forward hand quickly became very close friends."

The first time the three young men sailed *Stratus* together was in a Bellerive Yacht Club race. They were running late and had only just that very morning finished getting the boat ready to race for the first time.

Chris Fuglsang: "We got to the starting line and more or less had to start straight away. I had never been on a trapeze before and on the way across the Derwent, Pix had had to push me out on the wire and hold me for a few moments, as I was pretty hesitant for a while. I'll never forget the excitement of my first experience on a trapeze in a hard reach.

"After about an hour of exhilarating slog in hard northerly up to 30 knots, we found ourselves in front. Most of the fleet were either spending a lot of time trying to re-right their boats or had retired. Towards the end of the race, however, on a spinnaker run, we were hit by a huge gust and lost our mast, so found ourselves floating in the water, retrieving bits of the mast and rigging.

CHARGING ALONG IN THE LEAD

The Muir charter yacht with a borrowed spinnaker from the yacht **Cyclone**, *Hamilton Island, c. 2005.*

"The skipper of the Bellerive pick-up boat had devised a new technique of getting the line to the crew — he threw the line, which had attached to it, a buoy (which happened to be a considerably solid heavy fibreglass buoy). We tried to catch it and missed, and it disappeared straight through the beautiful brand new ash deck. The expletives that Sam consequently uttered cannot be repeated here. However, I can say that after this, the skipper of the pickup boat became known to us as the Dog Catcher."

From that day on it became obvious to Chris that Sam (John Muir) was determined to make sure the boat was always seaworthy for racing and to lessen the possibility of anything breaking. By the very nature of his meticulous eye for detail and his strategic thinking, Chris said Sam made sure that things were in the best shape possible before a race.

But there is a side to John Muir that reveals a fellow who loves to play a practical joke on his mates. His father was just the same.

John Muir: "On most occasions myself or Chris (the forward hand) would pick up Bob Laing (Pix), who was our main sheet hand, from his nearby home. It meant he didn't have to drive home after racing and could partake of more than just a few beers. It also meant there was no way he would wear out his very first car, a high performance Mini Cooper. I remember once we were running late to rig the boat ready for racing, so I called a taxi to pick the Pix up. I told the driver he would have to reverse down the steep drive as the customer was 'incapacitated.'

"We were tired of carting him everywhere. The driver knocked on the door of the house and asked for the 'incapacitated' passenger, Pix instantly responded, 'What the******* do you mean?' The driver said, 'Well that's what they told me!' Pix wasn't happy so he told the cabbie 'I will come with you but I'm not paying the ****** fare.' The trip had cost the princely sum of $1, so reluctantly Pix paid up. He walked straight up to me and said, 'That cost me a ***** dollar Sam,' so I gave him a dollar and said, 'Now we are quits.'"

LEFT AND TOP: SYDNEY-SOUTHPORT RACE, MID-1980s

Top: The crew, back row from left: Steve Masters, Kerry McNiece (Tooby), John Cole-Cook, Edgar Roe, 'Kibbie', Wayne Denehey. Front, left to right: John Muir, Jock Muir, Bob 'Pix' Laing.

Left: North Sydney Head, bound for Southport, Tasmania. **Shonandra** *sailed in three Syney-Southpost races.*

ABOVE: 'SOMETHING'S JAMMED!'

John's friend, Paul 'China' Hurd did this excellent caricature of him sailing in the Hamilton Island races, 1990s.

MUIR'S BOATYARD, C. 1978
Waubs Bay on the slip nearing completion of major fit-out and machinery works. On the right, a Jock Muir 25ft auxiliary motorboat with fishing well. *Painting by Tim Fish.*

Chris Fuglsang: "Pix and I would often go to the club and play snooker, satisfied things had been finalised ready for the days racing, whilst Sam would stay on before we launched the boat, paying careful attention to every detail of the rigging and sails, and checking fastidiously the shrouds, shackles and blocks etc.

Pix and I both learned through him that we had to get better as a crew and tack the boat faster. One of the most valuable bits of advice Sam ever gave me, was to go to bed and reflect on a race and think about how I could have helped make things better. It had never occurred to me to do this before and this was typical of John's attitude to sailing and life in general – always seeking to improve and progress things as best he and his team could."

This is an early sign of the focus, drive and grim determination that was to fully surface within John Muir as the years went by. This is the utterly determined John Muir that so many of his sales representatives and clients all talk and marvel about. It's what got John to be recognised as a business leader and success story, just as his father before him had been recognised as a 'Great Tasmanian.' Like his father Jock, John is happiest or most energised when he's "up against it". Like his father he also likes wild weather the best when sailing.

Chris Fuglsang: "As time went on, he became busier with the rapid growth of his business and there was the odd occasion where he was distracted from the race by what was going through his mind with his work. I do remember one example at the starting line manoeuvres: he said, 'We're going about' but instead he jibed and we ended up in the drink. 'Oh shit I've got things on my mind,' he said (or words to that effect) and Pix or I either said, 'You don't have to tell us that!'

"It came as no surprise to me and my family that Sam won top honours in the 2009 Tasmania Telstra Business Awards – Muir Engineering being named as Tasmanian Business of the Year. In the words of Brett Riley, then Telstra Country Wide Group Managing Director, he 'turned his love of boats into a world-class engineering business.

"Sailing with Sam on two different lightweight sharpies (*Stratus* and later *Shilo*) were the best years of my sailing life and I put that down to the close friendship and the knowledge and skills gained in those years. Nothing ever came close to the enjoyment and exhilaration I felt when sailing with Sam – not even a Sydney to Hobart could go close. You know, when I think about it, a lot of the details of the races were a blur to me as we worked so hard and had to concentrate on what we were doing all the time."

John Muir: "I used to always look towards the foreshore as we were near the starting line in any race, and if we were under the pump at work I could easily be distracted. Throughout the hectic 1970s and 80s the two Muir businesses at Battery Point employed almost 50 people and being involved with both businesses, there was a lot going on there all the time.

"The weeks ahead were always challenging coming into the busy boating and yachting seasons; cray fishing, drop lining and scallop seasons all on the go at the same time. Back then the Muir Boatyard slipped more than 200 boats a year and there were always boats tied to the jetty or on the 10 moorings waiting to be hauled out.

"However, once the starting gun went and we were under way everything always settled down!"

When John is talking about how hectic things were at the boatyard, particularly when the yachting and cray seasons were approaching, what he doesn't mention is just how dangerous these boatyards could

the slipping anyway. At the time, our manager Brett Ross, told this bloke there was insufficient water and it needed another six inches or so of depth."

As you have no doubt gathered that warning was ignored.

When coming in and approaching the cradle, the owner drove the boat up on the cross beam, pushed on further, then the deep keel dropped through the cradle and fell hard on the sea bottom. Disaster. John got a phone call from a panicked Brett telling him there had been a mishap with the slipping and the owner was going to call shortly.

I'm not sure about the accuracy of the content of that call, I think it would have been a helluva lot more agitated.

John Muir: "It was around six o'clock that evening when I received a heated call from the owner. He was very unhappy and inferred it was the boatyard's fault and demanded I immediately meet him at the yard to try and rectify the situation. I told him outright, from

Sure enough next morning there is the owner's insurance assessor. The situation ends in John being sued, the owner claiming the keel had been bent in the process and it's all John's fault.

be to work in with so much going on at the same time. Yet despite this outlook there have historically been, in the 180 years that the location has been used for ship and boat building and slipping activities, very few workplace serious accidents. There are, however, several stories told over the years of slip wires breaking and good sized boats going roaring down the slip rails.

John Muir: "Back in the 1990s I had a particularly bad experience with slipping at our boatyard in Battery Point. An acquaintance phoned me several times about slipping his yacht, as the Yacht Club was at that time overbooked. The type of yacht he owned, a deep and narrow keel design, is not easily slipped. I gave in and agreed he could rig the slip himself, as long as he accepted sole responsibility. I warned him that I thought it would be tricky with the depth of the keel, and that the tide was on the low side and the slipping cradle was out as far as it could go, but he proceeded with

what Brett had told me, there wasn't enough water and he'd been advised not to proceed."

Next morning, after the yacht had been carefully extricated and was safe above high water mark (the result of four hours of hard slog the night before), Brett and John are standing around at the boatyard, scratching heads, looking at the yacht. It's the end of a busy week and John was trying hard to restrain himself. Just what you need, the wisdom of hindsight is taking effect.

John Muir: "Here's a case for not implicitly trusting other people's judgement. I should have had that bolshie owner sign a waiver or other legal documentation before proceeding, to make sure he was liable for his own stuff up."

Sure enough next morning there is the owner's insurance assessor. The situation ends in John being sued, the owner claiming the keel had been bent in the process and it's all John's fault.

WAUBS BAY

Above: The White's boat, **Waubs Bay**, *on the slip for repairs in 1996. The bow section was removed and an underwater bulb fabricated and fitted, designed to increase the boat's speed. Brett Ross hard at it.*

Opposite: Moored off the beach at Bicheno, in **Waubs Bay** *(the boat's namesake) 2015. Waubs Bay at Bicheno is named after Wauba Debar, a Tasmanian Aboriginal woman who rescued two sealers from drowning after their boat was wrecked offshore.*

John Muir: "I heard on the grapevine from two of my mates who sailed with this bloke that the boat had previously run aground on rocks near Wedge Island and bent the keel. Subsequently, the keel had to be straightened, which involved a hell of a lot of work and cost. I claimed that on my insurance but the exercise cost me a $5,000 insurance excess so I wiped my hands of the guy after this.

"Some time later on Opening Day, I was on the bow of *Shonandra* in its berth at the Yacht Club, and I heard a familiar voice shouting my name. I looked up and here's this same bloke decked out in his best gear, standing on the jetty 30 metres away talking to several Yacht Club officers. As he raised his hand to wave at me, he shouted, 'Hi John!' My immediate response was, 'I don't talk to a _____ !' He was indeed surprised at my response, as were the others who were associates of mine, and made a gesture of ducking for cover. I was reprimanded by the Club for my behaviour, however when management were made aware of the events leading to my outburst they were somewhat sympathetic but did warn me there were rules and I needed to better compose myself in future."

The moral of this story is that when hanging about with yacht club officials it's not a good idea to verbally harass or abuse someone (even when they might richly deserve it). Do it when no-one is listening or looking on. Trouble is, if no-one else hears about how you have managed to get even, then it's hardly worth the effort.

The Muir boatyard at Battery Point was one of the busiest slipway operations in Hobart.

John Muir: "We were slipping *Waubs Bay* for Arnold White at peak pre-crayfish season. The tide was high and she was a large 60ft plus steel fishing boat and we had her on two big cradles. It was late afternoon when she was halfway up the rails and several of the cradle wheels jumped off the rails.

"The cradles holding the boat would have to be jacked (by hand) back onto the slip rails.

"We were working in water up to our thighs. We had hydraulic jacks under the cradle beams on blocks, plus jacks to the side wall pushing her over. It was close to midnight when we finally had her back on the rails, out of the water and chocked up. We were all exhausted and everyone came back to my house to crash for the night."

It's important to remember when slipping boats that the 'you know what' can hit the proverbial fan and almost always happens at the worst possible time. You can't plan for it, you just do what you have to do to fix it. The

next day they found a couple of the axle wheels on the cradle were misaligned and a join between two rails required repair. Back then, *Waubs Bay* was the largest commercial boat the Muir yard had ever slipped.

One Saturday morning, in the mid 1990s, Brett Ross and two divers were re-aligning the main slip rails using a bogey cradle, as well as two vertical and one horizontal planks clamped on to the cradle, to check the horizontal level of the slip rails.

John Muir: "They started early in the morning and just prior to midday called it quits. Brett, before leaving, asked me if I could pull the cradle up clear of the water. Wendy's brother Chris was visiting from interstate and staying with us for a few days, helping out. We had a line from the cradle up to a winch block. Further up the slipway, happily sitting in its cradle was a beautiful 50ft timber fishing boat. I was operating the winch drum, Chris was standing down the slope below the large fishing boat. The bogey cradle wasn't budging, the tension on the wire tightened, suddenly, the fishing boat was somehow dislodged and the boat roared down the rails like a runaway locomotive.

"Chris was a big bloke and I've never seen anybody jump out of the way so fast. If he had been hit by that boat, he could easily have been killed or at least seriously injured. But 'Safety Dad' was on our side because we had a safety cable chained to the winch and hooked up to the front of the dislodged cradle. It stretched a helluva lot when it took the full weight of the out of control cradle and boat, but it held.

"So here we are, both alive but I could bloody near hear Chris's heart hammering. He was standing just to the side of the fishing boat and breathing hard. Chris sat down ashen faced, and had a smoke. I went for a much needed visit to the toilet."

Luck was on their side, the weight of the boat rushing downhill had seen it jammed into the lowest cradle arms, with just a bit of new paint removed. That was fixed, the owners had no idea just how close it was to a complete disaster.

John Muir: "Towards dusk, still rattled, we headed home. Chris would have been mowed down had he not reacted so quickly, and the damage to the boat could have been much worse. On Sunday morning we returned to the yard and touched up the hull with

WESTWARD II'S FISHING DINGHY

Winston Bevis, inside Cape Queen Elizabeth on Bruny Island, pulling and tipping cray pots with a Muir VC600 cray pot winch, c. 2008. This cray pot winch was fitted up at Battery Point by Brett Ross and Ian Stocks. There aren't many 12ft dinghies around with a battery driven pot hauler and tipper – it's easy enough for one person to do it on their own.

a final coat, pushed in the vertical cradle arms. The owner was due to arrive Monday morning at 8am to have a final look underneath before she was launched. I was up on the deck when he arrived, on the stern. He jumped out of his car, made a bee-line for the aft of the boat, and put his hand on the propeller to make sure everything was aligned. Looked around at the anti-fouling, looked up to me and said, 'Looks good John, we'll put her in. To be honest with you, I don't understand why you're still stuffing around slipping boats.' My response was, 'Mate, if you only knew.'"

On another occasion, at the slipway when John's two children were young, there was a serious incident involving Alex.

John Muir: "Alex was probably seven or eight. We had *Shonandra* on the slip getting her ready to launch. We didn't have any safety rails around the edge of the deck at that stage and Alex was up on the yacht wandering around, having a look at everything.

"One second she is standing up on the deck and the next second she has gone, she took a step back into space. She did 180 degree flip and landed on her feet. Scared the living bloody daylights out of me. She had somehow, like a cat, managed to land on her feet. All around her were slip rails, beams of timber and steel. How she didn't kill herself I don't know, it was a three or four metre fall.

"I really got into strife with Wendy for letting her up on deck. That's probably one of the worst family accidents I've ever seen because she could have fallen on her head and killed herself, she could have been paralysed for life. She just stood there and screamed, then came right after a while.

"I was on the other side of the deck and I saw her vanish. It was very scary. It was a thump when she went down and it does scare the hell out of you, out of any parent. When something goes wrong you start to think about all the things you should have done to make the place safe."

All the Muir children, of every generation, have grown up running around the Battery Point boatyard and exploring the nearby rocks and water's edge. So as you would expect, boys being boys, from time to time they got up to mischief. Greg Muir, the youngest of the Muir clan, copped more than his fair share of grief from his two older and very competitive brothers.

Greg Muir: "I remember when I learnt a hard lesson about the basic laws of physics. I'm sure that surviving that escapade gave me a much better grasp of technical matters later in life. I think it helped me to stop and think about things before making a decision or taking action.

"There were many old wooden barrels stored in a warehouse belonging to Jones and Co. at the top of the boatyard. One day I climbed into a barrel and my mate (unnamed) started rolling me down the bumpy gravel road towards the water. (It was a steep slope from the top to the water's edge below.)

"As I progressed the barrel picked up speed and with me inside adding weight, simply added to the momentum. Eventually the barrel crashed into the brick wall of Burnett's shed.

"Peter Creese was working at his family's boatyard next door and heard the noise. Coming over to investigate he found me and dragged me out of the barrel. My mate who started me rolling was no-where to be seen. I was like a stunned mullet, he gave me a big serve and asked me why I was trying to kill myself?

"Not sure why I did it to this day, trying life's adventures I suppose. While I'm thinking and reflecting I want to say that I had enormous respect for John and Ross as they were both tough buggers and I was a bit lightly built in the early days.

"I started gymnastics and weight training at about 16, and by 18 I was in good shape and the runt of the litter became the biggest. One day I recall John challenged me to a fight in our backyard at home. I took him on but in a flash he threw me on the ground and badly winded me. Oops, I had overlooked his wrestling training and experience."

Like all negative things that happened in Greg's life, he had the good sense to sit back and evaluate what had happened and why. He discovered that there was always something positive that came out of each negative. The minor defeat by John led to Greg improving his self-defence skills and more importantly, subsequently improving his capacity to always assess the competition later in life, in both business and sport.

Shona, John's youngest daughter, also has vivid memories of life at school, at the boatyard and at home at the time when her father and mother were both focused on building the business at Battery Point. John was working long hours, always at the boatyard or starting to travel interstate, hardly ever home for dinner. Wendy was also deeply involved in the business, as a qualified book-keeper she managed all the finances and accounts, payroll and tax matters.

Alex would often prepare dinner for Shona and herself and put aside John and Wendy's dinner. Alex would take care of Shona, help with her homework, do her own, wash up and do any housework that was needed before going to bed. It's the motherly instinct that a lot of girls have, especially when there is a younger sibling to take care of.

Yet despite the long hours and hard work, throughout the girls' school years at Collegiate, Wendy was totally involved in various parents and sports committees. On occasions John took the girls to their sports, but Wendy did most of the running around. Wendy also

HOW THINGS HAVE CHANGED

Above: Glenn Gleeson, foreman, testing a SD250 drum winch at Battery Point, consisting of gearbox, mild steel fabricated winch drum and brake, and galvanised base, in 1996.

Below: Lyndon Potter, supervisor of the fabrication workshop at Kingston, 2015, with two polished stainless steel anchoring systems. Each 650kg anchoring system comprised a raised base, chain compressors, four pocket chain rollers and devil claw assembly, and were manufactured for a 98m motor yacht in Europe.

> **❝ *Mum would get home about 9pm, Dad would get home much later. Mum would probably have preferred being at home. Instead she was working in a noisy engineering workshop.* ❞**

SHONA PRIOR

tutored the girls with their homework and exams. But there was a lot of stress coming from the expanding business, keeping up with the work, chasing money and never enough time.

Shona Prior (née Muir): "I was in about grade 6 and Alex was about grade 10, and often Alex would cook dinner. Mum would have organised meals like pre-made stir-fry, and I can remember sitting at home with Alex having dinner. Mum would get home about 9pm, Dad would get home much later. Mum would probably have preferred being at home. Instead she was working in a noisy engineering workshop. It was a small business and really busy, I do recall the down turn in the early 1990s and the recession we had to have, it was a real slump and I remember how stressful that was for both my parents."

While the girls were young the business was continually growing and with about 20 people on the payroll John decided to hire a salesman at Battery Point. Wayne Carter took over sales and his wife Lyn took over the day to day paper work.

Shona Prior (née Muir): "I grew up around all sorts of interesting people. Dad's brothers are just as driven and passionate as Dad. That's the way they were brought up.

"Dad is about always negotiating the best possible price for the business and he really looks after his customers, that's what it takes to get there. Some people who used to work for Dad were critical of him, but they also acknowledge that his demand for best of service and quality is what made them who they are now.

"In some ways Dad's extraordinary in his obsession and focus, and the whole aesthetics of the winches, the way they are and his forward thinking, vision and risk taking. Mum agreed the need to finance their very first

Japanese computerised machine tools not long after Dad was back on track after being very sick... I'm amazed Mum never came down seriously ill and thank our lucky stars she didn't!"

John Muir: "I do reiterate how fortunate I was to have Wendy all through these challenging but interesting days.

Richard Fader: "We certainly had some interesting times at the boatyard, because we were a tenant there for four or five years. The business we bought in the mid-1990s was Muir's Chandlery. When we first bought it, there were a lot of fishing boats and yachts that would come up on the slip at Muir's, so they [the customers] would come and buy their bits and pieces. There was the sail loft next door, but really that business was a business where people wanted stuff, they didn't need it. They wanted a new sail, or they wanted a new block or they wanted a new engine.

"Working around the Muirs has shaped my approach to business, and probably shown me what I shouldn't be doing as well. John takes his work very seriously, hopefully he's relaxed a bit now but he probably nearly killed himself there for a while. It was probably a bit ridiculous and it's made me think, well, it's not all about success at any cost. You probably need to have a happy balance. If work can afford you the toys, then it's no use having the toys when you can't use them."

John Muir: "Richard and his younger brother Edward certainly are switched on business and boat wise, I could see that when they first commenced working with us at Battery Point. They have done incredibly well since working for themselves, including operating their own fleet of commercial offshore and inshore vessels. Owning and operating the long established Purdon and Featherstone providoring business, suppliers of foods and beverages to the majority of cruise and Antarctic ships that come via Hobart."

HERE
for the
LONG HAUL

Tom Koulopoulos is one of the USA's leading authorities on innovation. The author of ten books, the founder of the Delphi think tank, a columnist for Inc Magazine, adjunct professor at Boston University Graduate School of Management and Executive in Residence at Bentley University. He has studied many of America's most successful business operators to glean what it is that sets them apart from mere mortals.

According to Tom, if you measure success in dollars alone, John Muir never needed to play that game. Amassing wealth wasn't one of his early driving forces. After 48 years of winching John Muir is the only original global anchor winch manufacturer of high end pleasure and mega winching equipment. Both John as an individual and Muir Engineering as a business are long term corporate survivors. John likes making things and he likes to make sure they are really well made. He has, by all accounts, done extremely well and has achieved, he says, what he set out to do, to be recognised as one of the very best.

In the international anchor and winch business, several competitors, including close to home Maxwell of New Zealand and Lewmar in the UK, have been sold and re-sold several times, with varying degrees of corporate success. On the other hand John Muir has been there for the long haul, as managing director of one of the world's most successful global marine businesses.

He is a driven man, determined, focussed, commercially and financially successful, against the odds. A true 'Battery Point Boy' according to Robert Clifford. Boys who learnt at an early age, crying doesn't fix anything. Boys who learnt to look after themselves.

"Hey four eyes I hear you can look after yourself!" Said a big fella to a much smaller, bespectacled John Muir on his first day of high school. It was not a good opening move!

"Who's askin'?" said John.

"Me" he replied.

"The big bloke put his head down and rushed straight at me. In a matter of seconds I had him in a headlock and I charged him head first into a nearby telegraph pole. It knocked him out flat and shut him up."

In some situations size doesn't matter! Decisions made under pressure do. John Muir, his brothers, sister and mates around Battery Point all learnt the same lessons. They are all competitive to different degrees, most sail, most race, so do many of the following generations.

We all have our own definition of what success means or looks like. For some it's money. For others it's about being good parents. It varies from person to person. For the extended Muir family it is almost certainly doing well at whatever it is you do. Be it at home, at work or at play. Putting in 100% effort. In our society, unfortunately, success is most often measured in terms of money and wealth. Some, however, are different. Some people value the freedom to spend their time as they want, to be as 'free as a bird.' Others value the ability to help those in need. Yet, according to Koulopoulos, there is a core set of personality traits common to all successful people, and it's not just about money and wealth.

Koulopoulos thinks that the most critical trait is refusing to be defined by failure. John's business has been hit by economic tidal waves, recessions, deals gone bad, serious illness and the GFC. Faced with these hurdles, John not only hung on, but endured, re-tweaked, readjusted his business to market forces, and prospered.

Some of the other critical personality traits common to successful people, according to Koulopoulos include:

A Need to Compete. John Muir has this in spades. His will to win is legendary, as is his competitive drive. Successful people obsess over creative ways to get a leg up on their competition. They hate losing with an abiding passion.

Chris Fuglsang: "One of the most valuable bits of advice Sam (John Muir's nickname when sailing as a young man) ever gave me, was to go to bed and reflect on a race and think about how I could have helped make things better. It had never occurred to me to do this before and this was typical of John's attitude to sailing and life in general – always seeking to improve and progress things as best he and his team could."

The Capacity to Let Go. Successful people are not anchored by the past. They learn from it. According to Robert Clifford, the shaft and stern bearings of his second catamaran were not up to his exacting

standards, the bearing was so tight that the shaft would not revolve. It never happened again. Commensurately, the standards set at Muir became second to none, at least as good as your competitors, and if possible, even higher.

A Passion for Improvement. This trait is evidenced by John Muir's constant investment in new technology, constantly evaluating his competitors' gear. Always striving to be better.

Obsessive Attention to Detail. The more you read the stories of those who knew and worked with John Muir, the more you realise he isn't satisfied with mediocrity. His equipment has to be the best, no matter what. This trait has the capacity to drive others crazy. It also has the capacity to inspire.

Andrew Perkins from the foundry business Apco, formerly Skeels and Perkins: "Working for Muir has improved our quality, as John has very exacting standards. Muir are always after ever-better quality. We've worked hard to improve our quality to meet Muir's demand. They helped drag us kicking and screaming out of the 'She'll be right' mindset."

Compulsively Working their Network. John Muir is the most successful networker many of the people he works with have ever come across. He is relentless. He is also empathetic, he can see what his customers need and he's more than happy to work harder to get them what they need.

MaryAnne Edwards, the CEO of AIMEX: "John Muir has never forgotten what the true fundamentals of running a successful business are and what it takes to drive sales particularly in a competitive global market place. He is the consummate networker and no one is left out when he is around. He has a friendly greeting and smile for everyone and very rarely forgets a name."

All success is built on a network of human connections that need to be nurtured and reinforced.

Not Wavering in a Crisis. One of the greatest determinants of success is the ability to keep your head in a firestorm. The Muir family have learnt this lesson the hard way, all of them in life threatening situations, all while ocean sailing. Young John, his father Jock, the boat owner Russell Duffield and three other crew were on board the 15m sailing yacht *Trevassa* on her delivery trip to Sydney. They were running before a strong south westerly, reaching at 9 plus knots and were abeam of Green Point off the south coast of Victoria, when suddenly and unexpectedly the yacht was slammed from astern by two huge colliding rogue waves. The boat was sent surfing down the front of the 20m wave, then capsized as the huge sea crashed on the port side. John screamed the magic four letter word, but his father Jock calmly said, "Looks like we are going are down to 'Davey Jones' Locker!" Fortunately they all survived.

On separate occasions two years apart, John's brothers Ross and Greg were both thrown overboard in wild seas. Ross went into the water at night when another rouge wave crashed under the stern, lifting the boat and hurtling him into the air and over the side. Luckily the lights were on below deck and the glow from the porthole allowed Ross to grab the trailing main sheet (rope). He was hauled back on board by his father Jock and Adam Brinton.

It started when he was a youngster, seeing his father become a boat builder and designer with an international reputation as one of the best. It continued when he was an apprentice diesel fitter at Webster Woolgrowers, whilst in his spare time, continuing to watch and learn from his father, uncles and others in the boatyards of Battery Point. He went to the school of hard knocks all his life. He was always asking questions about how business works, about lifestyle and about what it took to be the best in his game. He learnt his trade by getting his hands dirty and by not being daunted or cowed by 'brick walls' as he likes to call them. Brick walls are simply something you climb over, knock down or go around to get where you want to be.

It's nearly impossible to achieve any degree of success without being trustworthy.

Greg had a life jacket and a safety harness on and the combination saved his life. He was the skipper on the yacht *Farr Fetched*, trying to make headway up a breaking 10m sea and labouring under storm sails. In the wild conditions there wasn't enough sail or lift from the small rig to keep the yachts speed up and as she neared the crest of the wave she fell backwards stern first into the trough, partly swamping the yacht below deck. At the same time as the sea washed into the cabin it smashed the starboard cabin windows. Greg was thrown overboard and under the yacht. 'It seemed like a hell of a long time,' said Greg, 'before the boat finally righted and I was pulled back on board.'

Striving for Authenticity. It's nearly impossible to achieve any degree of success without being trustworthy. For successful people, being authentic means that they are clear in expressing their opinions and consistently truthful and transparent. You don't have to agree with them but you'll never be confused about where they stand. Michael Trickey, who ran the Muir Queensland operation after his father-in-law Ken Padgett retired, said: "John's one of those guys who doesn't take no for an answer. He's a super tenacious man, and a good fellow to work for. If he trusts you, he gives you full autonomy to do what you need to do."

John Muir didn't go to university to study business, to learn about the principles of business or success. Instead, he watched others and learnt from them.

As you gain a deeper insight into John Muir and the way he built his business there remains a lingering question. Why has he, over so many years, given so many young people 'a go,' or a start in their working life? There is a caring side to John Muir that doesn't surface very often, but he does like to give people a start in life, or as he calls it 'a break,' because he is thankful for all the breaks he's had. On John's 70th birthday, his brother Greg said, "John, you spend a lot of time giving and not taking and in particular supporting and spending time with older family members." He was also an example for others who were working next door to the Muir Engineering business at Battery Point in the early days, people like Mike Grainger and Michael Cooper and more.

Mike Grainger: "We spent probably the best part of twenty years on the waterfront with the Muir family in Napoleon Street. It was a wonderful working environment, being on the waterfront and being a part of that local marine industry for such a long period of time.

"All three brothers are driven, they're very hard working and very, very intense about what they do but they also are good yachtsmen in their own right, good sailors. Their work ethic is second to none, John in particular, he has an incredible work ethic and even in those early days he was always working 18 hours a day, travelling every other month, and just working incredibly hard. They're all very good businessmen who like their pound of flesh, and work incredibly hard to achieve what they set out to do."

Successful exporters to be honoured

THE 1996 Tasmanian Export Awards and Australian Export Awards pay tribute to the outstanding achievement of local companies and organisations who have expanded into overseas markets and continue to provide superior products or services.

The awards seek to celebrate those quiet achievers who create growth and new employment opportunities which contribute so vitally to the prosperity of our State, says organiser Charles Scarafiotti, Tasmanian Development and Resources marketing manager.

Award categories are:

● New Exporter — for outstanding export achievement by an organisation which has been exporting manufactured goods or services for three years or less.

● Small to Medium Manufacturer — for outstanding export achievement by a manufacturer with total annual sales of $20 million or less.

● Large Manufacturer — for sales over

$20 million.

● Mineral Products — For outstanding export achievement by an organisation exporting mineral products.

● Agricultural Products — for an organisation exporting agricultural products.

● Services — for outstanding achievement by a recognised Australian service industry the achievement must be quantifiable with specific export earning which are verifiable).

Applications must be lodged with the TDR by Friday, August 2 and the Tasmanian winners will be announced at a presentation ceremony in Hobart on Friday, October 18.

The winning entries will be forwarded to Canberra for national finals which will culminate in the presentation of the Australian Export Awards at Parliament House, Canberra on Tuesday, November 19.

TDR marketing manager Charles Scarafiotti (left), Muir Engineering MD John Muir (1995 small/medium manufacturers award winner), Jenny Stalker of Aquasmart, and Global Lightning CEO Stephen Gumley (1994 winner).

Stylish haven opens on Channel

Muir Winches managing director John Muir with a set of 700Okg winches ready for Dorbyll Shipyards in South Africa.

Muir winches up a winner

By ANNE BARBELIUK

A TASMANIAN engineering company has developed a revolutionary boat winch, which allows the anchor and chain to free fall at the flick of a switch and be stopped at any stage in the fall.

Muir Engineering's automatic free-falling winches are the result of a $242,000 research and development grant from AusIndustry.

Federal Science, Industry and Resources minister Nick Minchin visited the Kingston engineering firm yesterday to congratulate the 60-strong workforce on its success.

Senator Minchin said boating was one of the few activities he enjoyed outside of politics.

"I have a five-metre half-cabin runabout and I get sick of

BREAKTHROUGH: Senator Minchin, left, with Muir's Chris Michael, Ian Stocks and John Muir yesterday.

pulling up the anchor up, so I'll take pleasure in having a good look at this," he said. Senator Minchin said Tasmania was a

pany had been developing the idea for years but the research and development grant helped put it into action.

The winch provides single-handed capabilities for yachting, fishing and ease of anchoring.

Senator Minchin said: "It will be a boon for sailors facing danger from a sudden weather change, because it enables them to get away from the danger zone a lot quicker"

He said the company, which already exports about 45 per cent of its production, would significantly increase its earnings by targeting niche overseas markets.

Mr Muir said the small winches would retail at about $1500 each and the larger ones $3000.

good example of the "inventiveness" of regional Australia. Muir Engineering managing director John Muir said the com-

Marine company lifts $1m order for winches

MERYL NAIDOO

A TASMANIAN company has been working feverishly to manufacture three gleaming ship winches worth $1.2 million for international mega-yachts.

The winch sets will leave Muir Engineering's factory at Kingston next week for clients in Britain, Germany and Holland.

The polished stainless steel and aluminium bronze winches were built for a 54m ocean-going motor yacht at the Pendennis shipyard in the UK, a 70m yacht for Germany's Lurssen shipyard and a 35.6m vessel at Holland's Oceanco all world leaders in mega-yacht construction.

Managing director John Muir said, while the windlasses were used on the decks of yachts worldwide, it was unusual to ship three orders of such a size from the Kingston factory in a short time.

"It has been a busy time, there has been unlimited overtime in the workshop," he said.

The shipment, which will

take 10 days to pack, will be loaded by eight to 10 employees from Muir Engineering.

"It's a big job to pack them and get them into containers," he said.

The company has also secured a $500,000 order for windlasses from a Russian shipyard, which represents a new and expanding market.

Mr Muir expects another order from the Russians of the same value in a few months.

The company, employing 65 people in design and manufacturing roles, exports to about 40 countries.

Muir Engineering designs and makes anchoring systems and windlasses for pleasure craft, commercial vessels and super yachts from five to 120m.

Its exports double every five to six years with the mega-yacht sector experiencing the fastest growth.

In 2004, after winning the Tasmanian Exporter of the Year Award, Muir Engineering went on to be named Australia's top-performing exporter.

BUSY: John Muir with his million-dollar shipment of winches for foreign mega-yachts. Picture: LEIGH WINBURN

Exports a source of pride

Tasmanian engineers a success story

MINISTER'S EXPORTER OF THE YEAR AWARD

LARA GIDDINGS
Minister for Economic Development

Congratulations to the winners of the
Tasmanian Export Awards 2004

FORESTRY TASMANIA Tasmanian Chamber of Commerce and Industry Agribusiness Award	**MCLACHLAN STUDIO** Austrade Arts and Creative Industry Award	**THE FRIENDS' SCHOOL** Australia Post Education Award	**QMS CERTIFICATION SERVICES PTY LTD** WIN Television Services Award
AUTECH SOFTWARE Telstra Country Wide Information and Communications Technology Award	**CATERPILLAR ELPHINSTONE PTY LTD** Airsafus Large Advanced Manufacturer Award	**EASY-FIT FENCING COMPONENTS PTY LTD** The Examiner Newspaper Regional Exporter of the Year Award	
MUIR ENGINEERING PTY LTD Aurora Energy Small to Medium Manufacturer Award	**UNDER DOWN UNDER TOURS** Hotel Grand Chancellor Tourism Award	**HANSEN ORCHARDS PTY LTD** AusIndustry Emerging Exporter Award	

MY BUSINESS

John Muir, 61, managing director of Kingston-based Muir Engineering

MEGA BUSINESS: John Muir with winches destined for European mega yachts.

With MERYL NAIDOO

Muir rides a tidal wave

TIM MARTAIN

BUSINESS is booming for Tasmanian marine fittings manufacturer Muir Engineering, which is also celebrating its 40th birthday this year.

Muir now exports windlasses, winches, anchoring and mooring systems to more than 40 countries.

The company is planning to expand its Kingston operation to keep up with demand.

"Business is busy, it's been doubling every five or six years and it's been a handful trying to keep up with that," founder and managing director John Muir said.

"Our biggest export market is Europe, where we are selling a lot of big winch equipment for the booming mega-yacht market and some commercial markets."

In 40 years, the company has grown from a one-man refitting operation into a thriving manufacturing business which employs 65 people in Kingston.

It has warehouses and distribution offices in New South Wales, Queensland, Western Australia, Victoria, the USA and port city Southampton in England.

Mr Muir said the interna-

HAPPY BIRTHDAY: John Muir at Kingston with a consignment of winches for the busy export market. Picture: LEIGH WINBURN

tional boat-building market was thriving, which guaranteed a healthy trade for his business.

"We're fortunate that people are building boats, they're paying our wages and fulfilling our passion," he said.

"Russia, at the moment, is building these big private mega-yachts 180m long with 100 crew and they are overtak-

ing the American market."

Mr Muir said exports accounted for 45 per cent of sales and the coming financial year was looking so prosperous he would need to expand the

manufacturing operation, hire more staff and add an extra shift to meet demand.

"We're working on double the projects we had this time last year," he said.

Award further anchors success

LOCALLY based international success story Muir Windlasses Australia has been given another award marking its global achievements – this time within the large super-yacht industry.

Muirs, with its head office at Kingston, manufactures a range of anchor windlasses, anchoring systems and deck equipment exported from Tasmania to more than 40 countries.

It caters for recreational and commercial vessels from five

metres to 159m and has steadily built a reputation within the burgeoning super-yacht market.

This was recognised last month at the 2013 Club Marine Australian International Marine Export Group conference in Queensland.

Muir Windlasses Australia won the prestigious Superyacht Industry Business of the Year Manufacturer award.

As well, company director and founder John Muir was recognised as the Marine Ex-

port and Superyacht Industry champion and inducted into the Australian Marine Export and Superyacht Industry hall of fame.

Mr Muir was overseas and could not attend the awards ceremony, but Muir managing director Matthew Johnston said he had been delighted to be recognised.

Mr Johnston said Muirs had been working with Europe's most reputable and prestigious super-yacht yards for many years.

RECOGNISED: John Muir.

Articles: The Mercury

STOCK TAKE 2002

Right: Ian Stocks, Adrian Neville and Chris Stennard. Above: Chain gypsies by the score!

Michael Cooper: "I turned up on day one, it was full on, there was the slip way, the engineering shop next door, and Ross Muir was running the chandlery. Wendy (John's wife) was working very hard over at the engineering shop, Ross's wife Judy was running the payroll, and Jock was still around at that stage. Greg Muir had Yacht Distributors underneath. Alex and Shona were only young then, because there's a few years' difference between myself and Alex, and obviously even more with Shona.

"John used to come in like a whirlwind, as he does. He was a bit of a cyclone. Ross was very similar in a way, he'd probably deny it but they (John and Ross) are nearly identical. They'd leave sticky notes absolutely everywhere. You'd come in on a Monday morning and there'd be sticky notes around the whole building, downstairs, upstairs, in the toilets, just everywhere, with notes about things that needed doing. That would be Ross, he was a big sticky note person. John was more of a notepad person. They were just all over every detail, John especially, he would probably write more notes than Ross.

"What John and Wendy created was a fantastic work ethic within their team and their family. Especially with the staff, we knew that if you start at 8, you start at 8. You don't turn up at three minutes past, or you were in the shit. You finish when your job is done, and if that's 9 o'clock at night then so be it. But they were always very generous and looked after you – if they didn't pay you overtime, they'd give you a new life jacket or something. There was always reward for the hard work, and there was always a feeling that they appreciated what you did. Jock was very much like that too, he was a very hard working, salt of the earth kind of guy. I guess all that tradition sort of started from Jock and Mollie – the hardworking man and the self-sacrificing woman behind him."

A handful of other young men worked for a few years at the Muir boatyard, learnt the ropes the hard way, then left and set up their own businesses. Many of these men have gone onto be extremely successful in their own right.

Dave Webb was one who stayed at Muir Engineering for nine years then left to try something new, working for the engineering company, Saunders and Ward on locomotives and carriages for the Abt West Coast Wilderness Railway. At the back of his mind for the two years he was there, was always the thought, maybe a dream to one day own his own business and buy his own CNC machine. Positive thoughts always eventually lead somewhere.

Dave Webb: "I'd spoken to my wife about it often enough and she basically said, 'Look David, go and do it or stop talking about it. Go and do it or shut up about it!' So, I thought, I'll go and speak to John Muir. There's no better person to talk to about starting a business as far as I'm concerned so I went and saw John.

"I wasn't there just to see what work I could get from John but that's how it turned out. John wrote me a letter that I took to the bank basically saying he would give me as much work as I could handle. I went to the bank and said this is what I want to do, this is the machine I want to buy, this is how much I need, and here is the letter that says I have the work and they said, 'No problem'. So I went and bought my first machine, it was a big one. I intentionally bought that machine because at the time Muir's were starting to get quite a bit of work done elsewhere and that came to me."

For Dave Webb, the decision to invest in his own business in close collaboration and with the assistance of his old employer made a lot of sense. He knew the standard of work that was required, he knew the products required and he knew that he could put in the hard yards and make it pay off.

John Muir: "Dave could see what we needed, and he knew he had to meet deadlines and he did. He worked bloody hard and when people want to make a go of it, you've got to help them get up and going. We've all got to start one way or the other and get a hand up and some good luck."

There isn't a law anywhere that says, "You have to give people a hand up." It doesn't exist, except that there are, thankfully, many people like John Muir who not only think it's a good idea but put their money where their mouth is, so to speak. Dave Webb can attest to that.

Mathew Hale is another young man who was given a remarkable opportunity by John Muir. He was, for a few years, the marketing manager for Muir. Remarkably he was fresh out of university with no business experience at all, yet he caught John's eye as someone with potential. Mathew's degree was unusual; it was a mix of engineering and economics. Two weeks after starting work with Muir Engineering at Kingston, John literally threw Mathew in at the deep end, the very deep end!

Mathew Hale: "My first trip representing Muir was two weeks after I started working there in 1993. I was headed to the Osaka Boat Show in Japan. I was in my early twenties, this was my first full-time job out of University, and this was a sink or swim experience.

"I got lost. I'd never been overseas before in my life and I found the whole experience quite daunting."

John Muir: "At that time Mathew didn't have a passport, had never been overseas, hardly travelled in fact, and he looked at me in amazement when I made this suggestion. I told him that, having worked with him for a short time, I was convinced he was the best person to send because I could rely on him to pursue a sale to the end."

> ❝ *John used to load me up with winches in my suitcase. This was back in the days when I think you were allowed to carry maybe 25 kilos of carry-on luggage…this suitcase I reckon was 40 kilos plus. Then I had to try and get it in as hand luggage.* ❞
>
> – MATTHEW HALE

Mathew Hale: "I was conscious of the money it was costing the company to send me there. I was quite frugal because I knew these things were expensive. While visiting a shipyard in Thailand on the way home, the guy I was liaising with left the room momentarily – and left a competitor's quote on the desk. I was able to get us the job because I knew what we were competing with. Afterwards, at the hotel, I decided to reward myself with the full hotel experience – a long, hot shower, full dinner, the works."

BOULDER CREEK TRAMWAY

Former Muir employee Dave Webb went on to run his own engineering business… and develop his passion for miniature rail. Dave and his wife Caroline have both worked on the Abt West Coast Wilderness Railway and decided to construct their own rail track and custom built locos. It features approximately 1,200m of tracks with tunnels, bridges and stations.

ABOVE: MEGAYACHT BROCHURE, 1993

Matthew Hale designed this brochure and its contents in his second year with Muir. He proudly appears alongside John inside the front cover.

LEFT: MATTHEW HALE 2016

Matt, like many other former Muir employees, has gone on to own his own successful businesses and now works with the Faders at Offshore Unlimited.

Mathew's first successful sale was a substantial order. It included two ship sets of VRC11000 windlasses, anchoring systems and mooring capstans. It was a marketing coup for both Mathew and Muir because it was the first big order for a shipyard in Thailand. John was impressed by what he called Mathew's grit, determination and negotiating skills.

John knew very early in Mathew's time with Muir that there could be no better person to be selling Muir gear than young Mathew. John's capacity to identify Mathew's selling abilities and work ethic had been proven.

For the relatively young Mathew Hale, this job and the opportunities it brought with it were exciting. He could not have asked for more. Just out of university and being able to travel internationally, working for what he called a 'dynamic business' must have made him the envy of his recently graduated mates. He went on to score sales in Korea for a high speed ferry and many others.

Mathew Hale: "I learned heaps from John, he's a great mentor. Most important was his absolute commitment to customer service – making sure we delivered and the customer received their order on time. They were good, growth times. They were exciting times with new markets.

"John used to load me up with winches in my suitcase. This was back in the days when I think you were allowed to carry maybe 25 kilos of carry-on luggage. Anyway, I was packing up my gear, and John kept telling me I could fit more stuff in, and here was a new design – I had to take on those - and before I knew it, this suitcase I reckon was 40 kilos plus. Then I had to try and get it in as hand luggage. They don't weigh hand luggage, but I had to march up to the check-in counter at the airport making out what I was carrying wasn't that heavy. I remember getting it up over my head into the overhead locker on the plane, and I remember thinking to myself that if we had some turbulence, it's more than likely going to come out on top of me or someone else.

"Wherever I went I was just constantly lugging winches. I'd be going through security scans in airports and have a hell of a time explaining what they were and why I had a suitcase full of them."

John Muir: "As a sales and marketing manager Mathew was one of the very best people I've ever worked with. Straight out of university, he had the smell of a dollar, he had business smarts, a real sense of urgency and he had long legs. (Not sure what long legs have to do with successful selling, but John was impressed.) He could stride down the end of the workshop and leave me behind – he could really do anything, whatever you put to him, he did it. That's exceptional."

But if you scratched the surface, you would discover there was a lot more to Mathew Hale than first thought. He too, like John, had grown up getting his hands dirty, learning the intricacies of truck and tractor motors, how to pull them apart and fix them when things went wrong. John describes Mathew's father, Harry Hale, as a gentle giant and an industrious construction guy. Harry Hale had several trucks and tractors and did his own servicing and maintenance. During school and university holidays Mathew would work with his Dad,

servicing engines and hydraulics. Even though Mathew came to Muir with a degree in engineering, plus finance, sales and marketing, he brought with him as a bonus a wide range of knowledge about mechanics and machinery. That core knowledge is critical to successful selling when dealing with a specialised product like Muir's windlasses, winches, mooring and anchoring capstans and the motors that drive them.

Yet there is more, as the ad's say, much more to the relationship between the Hale and Muir families. In true Tasmanian style, John already knew Mathew's father well before he'd applied for the job as marketing manager at Muir.

John Muir: "I served my apprenticeship with Harry Hale at Webster Woolgrowers, and we became good mates. Me, a short bloke, and Harry, almost two metres tall! I looked up to the Hale family. I have a great deal of admiration for them. On one occasion, I went to the Hale's for dinner, at their farming property overlooking the River Derwent at Tinderbox. (Tinderbox is south of Hobart.) All the family were tall and I discovered they all had a hell of an appetite. On this particular evening we had a large stew with vegetables, stew is my favourite meal, and Harry was very surprised that

I'd finished mine before he did. It was one of those windy and rough winter nights, and I ended up sleeping overnight.

The Hale family was, like the Muirs, very competitive. Harry Hale was state and national rowing representative and has a rowing boat named after him at Hutchins School, the same school Robert Clifford attended.

Mathew Hale: "John always said everyone had to be able to sell. No matter who you were are where you were, everyone was a salesman. At some point the client's going to speak to the factory manager, or he's going to speak to someone in spare parts. You've gotta be able to sell the product, from the person at reception, all the way through the team to the guys on the floor."

John Muir: "Mathew's right. When you visit a shipyard, it's good to get to know and show respect for everyone. You might meet the receptionist, the guy that sweeps the floor, the lady that pays the bills, it's all good because sometimes you might not be able to get in with one person or another, but you can get around them and get a foot in the door through someone else and if they know you have treated them with respect, you are more likely to make a sale."

Mathew Hale's first successful sale into Korea was when he sold two ship sets for high speed ferries. John and Mathew had decided to extend one of Mathew's trips to south-east Asia, to visit South Korea, on the off chance of getting new customers.

Mathew Hale's first successful sale into Korea was when he sold two ship sets for high speed ferries. John and Mathew had decided to extend one of Mathew's trips to south-east Asia, to visit South Korea, on the off chance of getting new customers.

Mathew Hale: "We'd had a couple of inquiries but nothing certain, and to be honest I really didn't have a lot of faith in what was going to happen, but we ended up with a sale, and we even got a second one after that. I had quite a few overseas trips in the time I was with Muir's, to Asia, the USA. Two or three trips to Europe, to the UK. The trip I most remember lasted six weeks and was very exhausting."

'Nothing ventured, nothing gained,' isn't that the saying? As my mother used to say, 'Knock and the door shall be opened,' even though for her it had mostly religious connotations, it still applies to the techniques used by John Muir and his team.

John Muir tends to polarize people; some respect him, some admire him, some love working both for him and with him. Others find him difficult to deal with, particularly if they have him on the 'back foot.' It's probably the same for anyone with drive, determination and a real sense of passion for his business and what he does.

ABOVE: FIRST OF A KIND, 1969

Muir's first ever pot hauler, manufactured under the 'Hydnautic' brand. It was designed around a car differential with a v-belt drive which offered a neutral and a drive gear.

OPPOSITE: GETTING THE 'AOK'

Matthew Hale towers over the Korean test certificate supervisor during testing for the three SD300 drum winches in 1993 at Battery Point.

John is always full of praise for his father and his mother. Mollie was the quintessential self-sacrificing wife and mother. It's hard to know what kind of man Jock really was, but he could be difficult like John. Yet everywhere you go when you mix with the Battery Point lot, no-one has a bad word to say about Jock Muir. In fact he is one of the most respected and revered boat builders and international sailors of his time.

One of John's favourite sayings, and there are a few, is this one: "Just remember, your parents gave you the breath of life, so get on with it."

Matthew Johnston asked John in his early days at Muir, "What drives you?" Some people can't answer this question but John always thumps his chest and says, "The Muir Passion." Is it passion for his products or passion for his chosen industry? Is it passion for his family? It's probably all of those things combined.

John is physically unable to leave anything unfinished, particularly if it's getting close to a deadline. Those that know him well will tell you that even at this stage of his life, he can be so focussed on a project and have weeks where he gets less sleep than a university student before their exams. It doesn't seem to bother him.

Simon Pettitt (Muir UK): "John has a tendency to overwork, (somewhat of an understatement) so I'd keep an eye on him to make sure he was taking his insulin shots. Being a type 1 diabetic and needing to inject his insulin several times a day and of course eating properly, but looking back, he was probably also keeping an eye on us [laughs]."

66 *Just remember, your parents gave you the breath of life...* 99

Luca Signorini (Muir agent in Italy and Europe): "It wasn't only the amazing times we spent together in Monaco, Amsterdam, Viareggio, Cannes, and countless others, but also the big challenges posed by the strict time schedule of the charter yachts we had to service, to let them continue their trips.

"Customer satisfaction was top of the priority list and the will to overcome every logistical difficulty, lifting, overhauling and servicing the heavy stainless steel "Muir babies" in a few hours, without the owner even noticing our passage on the deck. We serviced yachts in Sardinia, the Red Sea, Singapore, Portofino, the Maldives, jumping on a plane as we saw John doing many times, spares in the trolley and a few tools to do the work."

When trying to compress their visits to the Italian yards into a few days or at times all week driving thousands of kilometres, John would be constantly attending to his emails, ready for the next meeting, and,

MONACO BOAT SHOW

Always an amazing spectacle, the show attracts some of the world's most luxurious yachts. Muir has been exhibiting at these shows since their inception in 1991. Top: Monaco Boat Show in 2010, John with Matthew Johnston, left, and Richard Chapman, right. Bottom: The Muir sales team enjoying dinner during the Moncao Boat Show, 2009. Left to right: Simon Pettitt, Matthew Johnston, John, Christophe Quesnel, Dan Thain, Don Haber, Andrew Pedlingham.

Luca vividly remembers John would be fresh as a rose every morning while he, a much younger man, was dead flat and tired.

In the Foreword to this book Robert Clifford, the man behind the amazingly successful business, International Catamarans, another 'Boy from Battery Point' recalled an incident that he says he will never forget, one of those defining moments in the relationship between two men and their businesses.

"When the bailiffs knocked on our Battery Point door one day in 1979, Kerry was not amused to say the least when the burly gentlemen wanted to know who owned the fridge.

"John Muir, or at least his bookkeeper, had sent the bailiffs in to collect. Did we owe Muirs money, yes, but I was not a happy customer. The shaft and stern bearings of my second catamaran were not up to my exacting standards, the bearing was so tight that the shaft would not revolve, even with the help of a long lever… and besides I was skint. My international customer had let me down, his deposit cheque had bounced, and times were tough.

"I made sure that John's invoice never got into the payment hat for a month or two because of that but eventually we settled. We still do business with one another."

John recalls that he fixed the propeller shaft bearings that were at the heart of that incident. John Muir can also be a tough bugger to deal with as well. Just like Robert, John didn't like it when a supplier, the foundry firm Apco Engineering, (formerly Skeels and Perkins) suggested he should pay his account, as it was overdue.

John Muir: "In the mid to late 1980s Muir, Incat and Apco were expanding. Incat established their large complex at Prince of Wales Bay. The Perkins brothers, with their business Apco Engineering, purchased land and built a modern foundry and comprehensive machine shop nearby. Muir Engineering were approached by Robert Clifford to build a workshop at Prince of Wales Bay and be a sub-contractor to Incat, supplying fabricated components. Until this time, Muir had been supplying Incat with winch gear and machined items such as propeller shafts and bearings. Instead, we opted not to interfere with Apco's proposed relationship with Incat.

"Incat had many other locally based suppliers, and we didn't want to create competition with our own, or conflicts of interest with our customers."

Another one of John's favourite sayings that is relevant to this story is, 'Don't bite the hand that feeds you!'

Some years later John Muir was approached by the Tasmanian Development Authority and asked if he would guarantee ongoing casting work to Apco for three years. Apco were further expanding around Incat's business.

John Muir: "We'd always maintained an excellent working relationship with Apco, and it suited Muir Engineering because it would give both Muir and Apco a larger reach with cast products, so we agreed to the proposal. Apco were also a valuable outsourcing option for machining when Muir was too busy."

However, it wasn't long before John Muir was upset and embarrassed by an incident that happened a while later.

John Muir: "We had an overdue invoice with Apco which we'd overlooked paying. The cheque was ready in our office, but for some reason it didn't end up going with the driver. When he arrived at Apco, Andrew Perkins must have been having a bad day because he said to the driver, "Go back and tell John to sell his new yacht so he can pay his bills."

The young driver went back without the castings and told John what Andrew had said. It was a red rag to a bull.

John got on the phone to Andrew, told him the cheque was coming back with the driver. He also instructed Andrew to keep the patterns for the castings that were still on order, but to load up every other single pattern so the driver could bring them back to Kingston.

According to John, Andrew spluttered back, "John you can't do that!" John's response was, "Yes I can, and from now on, all my bronze casting work is going to Retlas Bronze." It took another visit to Apco to get all the patterns, but within a couple of days they were all delivered to Apco's competitors, Retlas.

It obviously doesn't pay to upset the Blue Heeler from Battery Point. Happily, as is the case between Muir and Incat, the business relationship between Apco and Muir is repaired.

John Muir sometimes describes himself as 'a moody bugger,' his diabetes may have something to do with that as evidently diabetics can suffer 'mood swings.' Others who've provided anecdotes for this publication claim John could be a moody bugger back 30 years ago, pre-diabetes, if things weren't going to plan or if someone surprised him!

ABOVE: BOYS AT THE BEACH
John, far left, with friends c. 1960.

RIGHT: FOOTBALL TEAM
John, third from back, in a football team photo from Albuera Street School.

John also, on occasions, says he can be an emotional person. He may well struggle with that concept, as he tries to reconcile the emotions he actually feels with the 'strong old school head of the family' he's supposed to be.

Remember, Dr Gail Goss, Ph.D., Pd.D., M.Ed., speaker, author and a specialist in Human Behaviour, Parenting and an Education Expert said parental role models have a huge impact on boys.

"Boys will model themselves after their fathers. They will look for their father's approval in everything they do and copy those behaviours that they recognize as both successful and familiar.

"Human beings are social animals and we learn by modelling behaviour. In fact, all primates learn how to survive and function successfully in the world through social imitation. Those early patterns of interaction are all children know and it is those patterns that affect how they feel about themselves, and how they develop.

The late Professor of Sociology and long time faculty member at the University of Houston, Janet Saltzman Chafetz wrote extensively about the seven characteristics of man saying:

"No matter what geographic location or social situation, men work primarily to feed and create an environment of comfort for their wife and family. This is the commonly accepted role of the man within the social system and proves a formidable challenge that almost every man must accept.

"The denial of ones emotions is ingrained in men from a very early age. The phrase 'boys don't cry' about sums it up. Whatever his position, a man must manage without regard to the emotional effect that issues have on him. Among some of the characteristics commonly attributed to me are ambition, pride, honour, competitiveness and a sense of adventure."

John Muir isn't concerned with flashy 'things'. He's pretty basic, although he's always been a Range Rover man, it's not a status symbol, it's because he considers the Range Rover the world's best 'off road' 4 wheel drive, and not unlike his renowned Muir winches. Reliable equipment lasts for years, be it Muir winches or Range Rovers, they don't need replacing every two years. John has been driven by a personal yearning and a passion for success and the rewards have followed. Success for John Muir also includes being able to sleep soundly at night.

John and Wendy have had sailing and cruising boats, large and small, still do, but boats have been a part of his life since he could crawl, but he's not out there to impress others. His boats are beautifully crafted, a marine work of art. *Trevassa*, built by his father has strong emotional ties for the entire family. It's jointly owned by John, Ross and Greg and often sail her with family and friends during the warmer Tasmanian months.

John and Wendy also own a 15.5m Pilothouse cruising yacht, built by Buizen Yachts in Sydney. All large Buizen yachts are fitted as standard equipment with an HR 2500 Cheetah horizontal anchor winch. Shorter yachts, 13.5m are fitted with a VR 1250 vertical anchor winch.

For John Muir, family doesn't just mean those who are blood relatives, his wife, children, brothers and sisters. It includes his staff at Muir Engineering and the many people who work with and for Muir Engineering across the globe.

A lot of men from his generation consider providing for their family to be the highest achievement of a man. They don't comprehend emotional involvement beyond that, 'That's Mum's job'. Yet John Muir does have a soft spot, particularly for someone he knows is in trouble through no fault of their own. He extends the hand of friendship and offers of help quietly, with no fuss or fanfare.

There is another and deeper insight into the way John Muir works with people, particularly those who have a visible capacity to focus and work hard. Take another young man who, like Mathew Hale, also started at Muir Engineering when he was attending university. Jeff Taylor first discovered Muir's when as a third and fourth year mechanical engineering student, he was offered work experience at the Kingston factory, a necessary part of his degree's requirement.

Jeff Taylor: "As part of the course all students had to complete a 12 week paid placement at a Tasmanian business in that area of expertise. I was very happy to be placed at Muir for a number of reasons. The first was due to the possibility of seeing a side of these impressive yachts, of which I didn't know a huge amount about, that is rarely seen or known about. Secondly it was something different compared to the majority of other placements that were with the bigger traditional businesses like Hydro Tasmania, Pasminco's zinc works or the paper mill of Norske Skog. The other reason was that it was only 15 minutes from my doorstep to the doorstep of Muir."

Jeff started on the workshop floor helping assemble the smaller pleasure boat winches with a very colourful character by the name of Rodger Dixon. Roger's been at Muir for almost 30 years. Working with Roger was in itself an experience, but also informative and helpful to the young student.

Jeff Taylor: "Building the pleasure boat winches helped me not only understand how these products were put together but I also gained a better understanding of how John Muir initially started his business. After a few weeks of this I went and helped out with the production of the larger megayacht winches. The general principles are the same as the smaller pleasure winches, however on a larger scale. After a few weeks of this along with the occasional time spent on the CNC machines I moved into the design office.

WESTWARD II

The 48 Buizen has been the Muir family's pleasure yacht for the past 14 years.

Above: The crew during a navigation trial in 2003, left to right: Nick Griggs, 'Honda', Matthew's father Rowan Johnston on the wheel, Matthew Johnston, unknown, Rodney Banks-Smith (Wayne Banks-Smith's son).

"I worked under Alastair Currie and the quality assurance manager, Brett, for the remaining time of my work placement doing a variety of small jobs that ranged from assembling manuals to updating drawings. I also managed to play around with some of the 3D models of the megayacht winches that Alastair had begun to assemble in Autodesk Inventor. The 3D models were the most interesting to me and where I wanted to advance my skills further. It was also where I saw the biggest chance of improving how the products at Muir were assembled."

Already, Jeff is seeing ways to improve products and processes at Muir, he's got his eyes wide open, sucking up the atmosphere and learning where he could. Other undergraduate students might have got their knickers in a knot over working on a factory floor. Not Jeff, for him there was valuable experience available and lessons to be learnt where he could.

Jeff Taylor: "One major advantage that I believed I had gained from my unique start at Muir was the experience I obtained from starting out on the shop floor. By first building the windlasses of varying sizes before working on their design gave me a better understanding of the way the winches worked, the construction methods used, and the varying issues in production specific to each product. When I began designing windlasses I was able to recall from this previous experience and put it into place on new unique builds. It also helped with improvements through R&D."

The right attitude can reap large rewards, not thinking that the world owes you a living also helps around John Muir and his team.

Jeff Taylor: "After my 12 week placement had finished I was lucky enough to get casual/part time work at Muir Engineering during my final year of university. After graduating at the end of 2005 with a Bachelor of Engineering (mechanical) and after dealing with a couple of speed bumps I began full time work at Muir in January 2006 at the age of 22 as a designer and draftsman.

"Being already familiar with the lay of the land at Muir, transitioning into full time work was quite simple. After six months or so of working with a couple of experienced engineers I was well and truly thrown into the deep end when both Alastair Currie moved interstate and Brett moved back to Canberra. It left me on my own for a short while, however there was always support and technical help available from the others in the workshop.

"With the support and guidance of Ian Stocks and John Muir and when Andrew Dickinson came on board, everything settled down. I managed to survive and went from graduate engineer when I began full time work to managing the design office before I left in 2012 at the age of 28.

"I left Muir to further my career and head overseas to Nice, France. After spending many years on designing and producing the winches and equipment for yachts, I had a desire to work on board these vessels and see the equipment first hand. I felt the need to

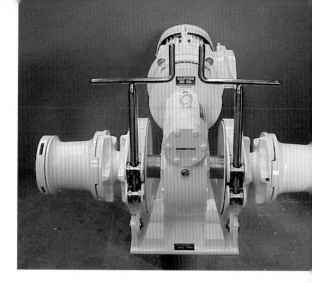

THIS PAGE: SINGLE GYPSY CAPSTANS
Commercial work boat winches. Top: SGC1; Middle: SD3. Bottom: Jeff Taylor working on some renders of a vertical VRC11000, 2011.

KINGSTON FACTORY, C. 2011
From left, Muir employees Asher Post, Zane Wooley, Joel Britton and Ian Stocks preparing a shipment of VRC24000s for the motor yacht **Yas**.

see and witness the many years of hard work and dedication in action. The winches we developed at Muir weren't just a winch they were a work of art.

Unfortunately for Jeff the impact of the GFC was still being felt and the luxury ship building and charter yacht industries were hit hard. No-one was expanding and looking to take on new, young engineers, so after a brief tour around Europe he came back to Australia. Back home it didn't take long for his time at Muir to pay dividends. He found work in a similar position in a Victorian business.

Jeff Taylor: "It appears my knowledge and skills had impressed them. Ironically I am yet to step foot onto a megayacht that has Muir equipment on board, but hopefully I will get the chance to do that sometime in the future.

"There is one project that sticks in my mind the most and the one I am the proudest of. It was the anchor and windlass equipment I helped design for an ex-Dutch Navy frigate to become a 141m gigayacht. Built as *Swift141* then named *Yas* at launch. It is quite mind boggling when you think about it.

"The luxury megayacht project required the largest vertical anchor windlass, the VRC24000, anchoring system and mooring capstans that Muir had ever manufactured for luxury motor yachts. It necessitated

new designs and tooling prior to manufacture. The international classification workshop testing rules required of the anchor windlass and chain compressor (clamp) system were successfully met. From a design and lift perspective this project tested our imagination and posed a few headaches for myself and Andrew to overcome.

"Working at Muir Engineering will always hold a special place in my heart. It was my first full time employment as a graduate engineer and was my first introduction into the manufacturing sector. It allowed me to expand and hone my skills and knowledge within an intriguing sector that not many people know about. I worked with Ian Stocks and John Muir. Ian was the workshop production manager and in charge of the day to day operations. He had a wealth of knowledge, not only with winches and equipment, but also machining methods and practices. Ian was hard but fair and knew how to get the most out of people."

According to Jeff Taylor, John Muir was an incredible person to work with. Jeff was impressed with John's knowledge of projects and products, of vessels, past and present. He says John was able to recall previous builds off the top of his head and also the issues that came with them. Jeff also recalled John as a smart and capable business man and was impressed by what he had achieved over the years building the Muir business.

Jeff Taylor: "John knew where he wanted his business to be heading and what was required to get it there. He was extremely passionate about the large and very large motor and sailing yacht industry, and the perception of Muir within its various parts.

"John's passion rubbed off onto others around him and I became proud of the Muir brand, and more especially when the Muir equipment was sitting proudly on the fore and aft decks of so many amazing luxury motor and sailing yachts.

"I remain proud to see the Muir equipment in photos and images on these impressive yachts and to know I have been part of its design. It gives me a great sense of joy to know such reliable and well known equipment is being manufactured in my home state of Tasmania. I will be forever grateful to John, for the experiences and opportunities he gave me. For his unconditional support and understanding he showed not only to myself but to his whole company."

Jeff Taylor's time with Muir, at that critical and formative part of his working life has obviously left an indelible impression on him. It will almost certainly remain with him for the rest of his working life.

Jeff worked for Muir Engineering between 2006 and 2012. He was there at a time when the business endured and the got back on track (relatively quickly) after the impact of the GFC, particularly when compared to the impact of the 1990 recession 'we had to have'. The world's luxury super and mega sailing and motor yacht markets were once again picking up speed and Muir were riding the same wave of recovery. It wasn't an easy ride, however. John Muir, Matthew Johnston and other Muir representatives retained a watchful eye on industry developments while in the process navigating changes internally and in the marine industry in general.

Matthew Johnston is John Muir's son-in-law, married to his eldest daughter Alex. In 2005 he was appointed sales and business development manager and spent a number of years working closely with John. In 2012 he was to replace John as the managing director following John's decision to sell part of the business.

Matthew Johnston: "I have been lucky enough to do quite a bit of overseas travel with John, particularly in my early days. There is one trip in particular that I will never forget. It was 2005 and we headed off to the Monaco Boat Show. After the show we hired a car and set off on the traditional post boat show visits to yacht and motor boat builders, to drum up business.

"We had been on the road around the Amsterdam area and our first appointment for the next day was in Oss, (southeast of Amsterdam) so we decided to head down that way and stay at a hotel close by in readiness for the client visit next morning.

The trip was before GPS navigation was available, John was navigating, using maps and Matthew was driving. They arrived at

SHANGHAI BOAT SHOW 2005
Muir's Hong Kong agent, Holy Light, displaying Muir equipment.

MONACO BOAT SHOW 2009
John and Matthew checking out the marinas.

> ❝ *I was amazed at how many mega motor and sailing yachts had Muir winches fitted to them, but I was also amazed that the brand was so well known in the global superyacht industry.* ❞

– MATTHEW JOHNSTON

a town near Oss, around 7pm. John popped into a small pub to see if they would recommend a place where the two men could stay. The publican said the town's accommodation was full because of a conference but he gave John directions to a 'nearby' hotel.

"It's only 15 minutes drive up the road," he said.

Then followed 30 minutes of turning, stopping, checking directions, all to no avail. It was dark and not easy to work out where they were. A phone call to the hotel saw the owner, who in broken English, provided more directions that were not easy to follow.

Matthew Johnston: "For the next three hours we continued to get hopelessly lost. The hotel owner was being called a lot and he would try and assist and we slowly got closer and closer to the hotel. By the end

of trip the owner had walked out of the pub and was down the road with a torch looking for us and we were finally found.

"It was about 11:30pm and we were both stuffed. The hotel owner helped us with all our travel bags, opened up the kitchen (that had been closed for some hours) and the bar and made us a meal and gave us a beer. It also happened to be my birthday so we enjoyed a nice pint of ale over a feed in this obscure pub in the middle of nowhere. Somewhere near Oss."

Matthew Johnston: "I had six years working with John before I took over as general manager. During the early part of that time (2005 – 2011), Muir Engineering enjoyed our best years (financially) as part of the global boom prior to the GFC.

FORT LAUDERDALE BOAT SHOW, MID-2000s

Left, John with Eddie Hidding of Muir and Federico Verona, from Cantalupi. Right, John with Dick Davidson from Imtra.

"I remember my very first Monaco Boat Show in 2005 (which is the biggest and best superyacht show in the world). I was amazed at how many mega motor and sailing yachts had Muir winches fitted to them, but I was also amazed that the brand was so well known in the global superyacht industry. I think that fact gets lost on a lot of people particularly in Tasmania. (And to a lesser degree Australia.)

"You have to admire how John (and Wendy) had worked extremely hard to grow the business over the years from humble beginnings in Battery Point to a world leader in anchoring equipment. I am the first to admit that John has taught me a few valuable lessons along the way."

The first lesson for Matthew was the importance of persistence. He realises that it is the key to winning any business but particularly when dealing with the bigger superyacht orders. It is also important to offer a quality product at a competitive price and back it up with the very best of service.

Matthew Johnston:

"It also helps to know who the following people are:

- The owner's representative.
- The Purchasing Manager for the yard (he/she is the one that will make the purchasing decision).
- The Naval Architect who may have specified Muir equipment.
- The Captain.

"John would always say you need to go through the front door (to the shipyard), in the side door (might be talking to the naval architect/owners rep/captain) and through the window (anyone else who could assist with Muir being chosen for an order) in order to get the business.

"There are really two sides to John Muir. There is John the salesman and John the business owner. John the salesman is the ultimate gentleman and is known throughout the industry as an icon and someone that others aspire to be like.

"John the business owner is the very driven individual who will stop at nothing to achieve his desired outcomes. It's fair to say that I have never met a more business driven individual in my life! (I have met a lot of people.)

"John also had a very tight grip on the business and knew everything about it from the bolts in the store to the price of the metals we used in production to the amount of labour required to turn out a large job. Most if not all of this information was in John's head!

That's exactly what impressed Paul Hollingsworth when he began working with Muir Engineering as a consultant. He had never seen anyone like it before. Tell John Muir 'It can't be done' and he most likely will do it anyway.

Paul Hollingsworth: "I was always amazed at the grip John had on his business with nothing other than what he observed through his eyes. He could tell me what was going to go through the books next month with no other information in front of him. Whereas I'm thinking to myself, how do you sit down and work that out. I can work it out and I came up with some similar figures and okay, well that's pretty good. Maybe it was a fluke I thought, but no, next month, same thing and I thought, he's got a pretty good grip on things."

Matthew Johnston: "I remember one of my first METS shows (METS is the biggest marine trade show in the world with over 1,500 exhibitors and is conducted in Amsterdam), John and I had a meeting with one of the best known German superyacht builders in the world – about a large motor yacht project. This was a repeat

" This guy had his calculator out and did some sums and then sat back for a minute, he then spoke to his colleagues and they agreed on the order. I think he was gobsmacked. "

– MATTHEW JOHNSTON

specification for some work that Muir had already built for the company. The original order was for three ship sets and this was for a single set. However, since the first job prices had gone up for some of our raw material such as stainless steel castings. We were aggressively negotiating this order, there was John and I and about five people from shipyard. They were throwing all sorts of curly questions about the increase in pricing at us.

"Their head of purchasing turned to John and asked what the raw material increase in stainless steel had been per kilogram since the last order. John quick as a flash said 'about $x per kg'. The purchasing guy then asked John what was the weight of the stainless steel that was in the proposed anchoring equipment we had included in our offer. Again, John as quick as a flash said 'Approximately .x of kg.'

"This guy had his calculator out and did some sums and then sat back for a minute, he then spoke to his colleagues and they agreed on the order. I think he was gobsmacked.

"Bear in mind John did not have the old price in front of him but needless to say John's working, multiplying the increased price of the metal by the weight of the metal component worked out to be exactly equal to the cost increase of the new order. It was within a few dollars on a really big ship set."

In late 2011, while the business was doing well, John Muir decided to sell a majority shareholding in Muir Engineering Pty Ltd. He took a place on the board but found it different and difficult, particularly only having one vote. It was a world apart from the wholly owned family business it had been and where he was the managing director for 44 years.

After John stepped back from the managing director role and handed the baton to Matthew Johnston, he was asked to return to Muir almost full time in March 2012 to travel and sell. Muir's sales manager had departed suddenly and it's not easy to find a suitable person to do that task successfully and live out of a suitcase for weeks on end.

Over the next 18 months John travelled to Europe every couple of months and secured many orders for Muir. Just because the business had been successful for the past few years, selling large winch and anchoring systems to large motor and yacht building firms didn't mean that the orders would automatically continue to flow in the door. As Jeroen Jeltes, one of John Muir's many friends and company representative in Europe for over 30 years, says — grunt work is needed to keep orders flowing:

Jeroen Jeltes: "You have to work hard to keep these customers; you can't just assume that because you got one order that you'll be the first choice next time. There might be a different purchasing or project manager next time. Relationships are very important. People move about in this industry, they leave shipyards and go elsewhere, or they retire or whatever, and then it's somebody else who likes to be respected as well so it's important that they change things and then the loyalty is gone. If you're lucky the old contact shows up at a different shipyard, so you manage to get a foot in the door there."

Sage advice for those who have followed in John Muir's footsteps, because, as with all things, there comes a time for change, for handing on the baton, for letting go, even though that would be one of, if not the most difficult decisions that John Muir has ever had to make.

Richard Fader (who worked with and for Ross and John Muir back in the mid to late 1980s at the Battery Point boatyard): "When I started working there John, Jock and Ross owned Muir's Boatyard. I worked for them for about a year, and then bought the chandlery and brokerage side of the business from John, and at the same time Mike Grainger bought the sail loft.

"Early on, I used to go and help John with a few boat shows, mainly the ones in Sydney. I'd go with him and help set up the stands and sell the winches. It was an amazing experience that will stay with me for the rest of my life. John's passionate about what he does, and his heart is always in the right place."

MATTHEW JOHNSTON

Checking in with work while out sailing.

John had managed the business profitably for over 44 years. The change in corporate structure from a wholly family owned and operated business to a corporate entity, with a remote chairman and director was going to test John's nerve and grit to the limit.

By June 2016, after four years, the majority shareholder decided to sell and move on. Prior to this, John had been given an opportunity to buy the business back, lock stock and barrel, meaning he would have total ownership and once again carry full responsibility. For several reasons he decided against it.

This was to be one of the few occasions when John decided, like Falstaff in Shakespeare's King Henry the Fourth that, 'Discretion is the better part of valour.' Caution was far preferable to rash acts of so called bravery.

Any way you look at it, letting go is tough. Here is John's business that he started and spent blood sweat and guts building over many decades, overcoming all manner of obstacles, surviving economic recessions and the GFC. But, in a moment of reflection and caution, deciding not to launch himself head first back into the business he says 'I've got more important things to do with my time these days.'

Matthew Johnston: "Since John sold the majority shareholding and relinquished the role of managing director, it has not been an easy transition for him. Because prior to this change he had never had to answer to anyone. (Still doesn't really, maybe Wendy on occasions!) Then suddenly he is part of a board structure setting strategy and not in the business day to day at a micro level as he had been all his life.

"Through this period we have also experienced a GFC and in recent years have had a very high Australian dollar and shrinkage of the marine business generally which has brought with it many challenges.

"Pleasingly the currency fluctuations have settled down and the international climate continues to improve as does the business but I know that John would rather be more hands on than hands off."

Under a corporate structure (as opposed to private family ownership) there are a lot more reporting and compliance issues for the business to address, it is a necessity in today's corporate world.

Matthew Johnston: "Being his son-in-law and running the company John founded has had its challenges and I always said when I took this on that I would run the place differently. However, I have also used a lot of things that John has taught me along the way.

"It's fair to say John and I have had a few strong verbal discussions along the way (not many) and at the end of it I would be wound up like a clock and stewing over it. For John, he is pretty thick skinned so would simply brush it off and move on to the next task as the though the disagreement never happened, quite amazing.

"John (and his team prior to me starting) have done a fantastic job in the national and international branding of Muir Engineering. I know that everyone who has ever worked (and still works) for Muir is enormously proud of what it stands for and that it is a global brand that epitomises quality and reliability. For my small part I have tried to follow that mantra during my 11 years or so at Muir Engineering. But it's time for me to leave and begin a new corporate life doing something else."*

There are, as this book has attested, many people from around the world who echo those sentiments. As Jeff Taylor said, it is amazing how many small, medium and large motor and sail yachts have Muir's reliable anchor and mooring winches, on their fore and aft decks!

It's no wonder that accolades like these appear in the anecdotes and stories of some of the many people who worked with or for John Muir:

> *"John Muir is a legend of the Australian marine industry...and a good mate!"*

> *"John is a great believer in established quality, but also a champion of innovation."*

> *"I have never heard John whinge or complain."*

> *"The Muir Brand has a stellar reputation globally and I cannot remember the last time we had a warranty issue."*

> *"John is a lovely likable man. At every boat show that we've been to, John is always a thorough gentleman, always knowledgeable and always supportive."*

> *"He's just so tenacious, but he can be difficult."*

Strength, assertiveness, reliability and action are all core parts of what makes a man's man. This doesn't mean that you're failing if you aren't achieving some of these aspects, but rather, they're goals to keep in mind as you forge through life's journey seeking to become better in your chosen profession or field. Any

way you slice it, men are still going to compete in all aspects of life -- and you need to be ready for what gets thrown your way.

John and Wendy still own the original Muir Boatyard. John knew one day he would not be running the Muir Engineering business and has been revitalising the Battery Point business. There are two original cottages above the slipway that have been leased to the Wooden Boat Guild of Tasmania, who will be undertaking refurbishment work. Next door Taylor Bros are proposing a face lift and historical renovation.

The location is undergoing a very welcome renaissance. Max Creese's boatyard has a new owner in Robert Vaughan. He left Hobart in his late teens to race in the international big yacht circuit and has been living in the USA ever since. He intends to bring his own 20m sailing boat back early in 2017.

Doyle Sails and Chandlery and Boat Sales Tasmania have re-located to Muir's Boatyard. The new owners bring new life to the old boatyard. John remembers his father, Jock often said 'surround yourself with young people, because it will keep you young.'

These brief, personal and anonymous paragraphs below sum up John Muir, his mission, his drive, his passion, his commitment to family and his extraordinary level of success.

"I have enjoyed travelling and working with you John. The passion you have for your work is inspirational. Thank you for all the valuable lessons I learned, not just about work, but about family and life in general. Thanks for the stories and the laughter we shared.

"I am not just very lucky, but I am also proud and thankful to have worked with you! Thankful for all the doors you opened, and more importantly, the great people I got to know through you.

"Most of the people we met and worked with have moved on, retired or are not working where we would meet again, but I am continually running into others who constantly ask after you. They are genuine in their enquiry, they want to know how you are getting on.

"I don't miss working for Muir, but I do miss working with John, as I feel I could have learned much more. Thanks so much John, enjoy sailing with family and doing things at the Muir Boatyard."

* August 2016

> *It's been a remarkable journey that has come about by the hard fought efforts of my entire family.*
>
> — JOHN MUIR

As this chapter closes, and so with it the biography of a remarkable man, a Tasmanian, a man who started from scratch, defied the odds and built an internationally successful business in spite of the obstacles, John's life has come full circle. The Blue Heeler remains tied to Battery Point particularly through the continuing ownership of the Muir Boatyard (started by his father Jock and his mother Mollie 70 years ago) and Muir Engineering workshops where he started in 1968. Those buildings are leased to several highly skilled metal workers, Metal Manipulation and Wellington Steelworks.

Jock also started small, with a boat building business in Sydney, was struck down by Polio, recovered and went on to design and build remarkable sailing boats like 42ft *Westward*, that won handicap honours in both the 1947 and 1948 Sydney to Hobart races.

It is worth recording that when *Westward* was first reported as coming to Sydney to compete in the race, she was described as a 'fishing smack.' The reporter at the time obviously knew little about boat design, because *Westward*, for its time, was a revolutionary design. Jock Muir had built her with a long keel and an aft hung rudder. She would outclass and outperform all the similar rated yachts, particularly when she had her spinnaker up in a 40kt northerly crossing Bass Strait. Her crew was a Muir family affair; the eight man crew in 1947 included brothers Jock, Wally, Don and their father Ernie, while in 1948 it was Jock and Wally in a seven man crew.

Jock Muir went on to build an enviable reputation as a boat designer, builder and blue water yachtsman of international acclaim. Equally deserved, through innovation, ingenuity, perseverance, sheer bloody mindedness and some might argue combative competitiveness, John Muir has followed in his father's professional footsteps. Since its establishment at that same Battery Point boatyard in 1968, Muir Engineering has grown to become one of, if not now the best winch, windlass and anchoring system manufacturer in the world.

MUIR'S BOATYARD IN 2016

Still owned by John and Wendy, the boatyard and engineering workshops are now home to three metal workers, a sail making shop & chandlery, a boat broker, two jewellery makers, and boat builder. It also houses historical machinery and memorabilia belonging to the family.

TOP: SAILMAKERS

Doyle are now occupying the old chandlery and sail loft, having removed the wall between the two sheds to share the top floors. Left to right: Lucy Rees, Brian Moroney, Nathan McMillan, Elson Kiddle, Nick Dineen.

ABOVE: SALES RETURN TO THE BOATYARD

Boat Sales Tasmania. John, left, and Paul Nanscawen.

John Muir: "It's been a remarkable journey that has come about by the hard fought efforts of my entire family. Never to forget the combined efforts of all Muir Engineering employees, past and present and the hard yards over 48 years by the tradesmen and factory workers who were and remain the lifeblood of Muir's. From Wendy's and my perspective, these people are all members of our extended family."

In the process, through the efforts of John, Wendy and their family, the Muir name has continued its long and successful association not only with Tasmania's maritime industry, but in the bigger national and international arenas.

Jock Muir: "Make sure the winch you design and build is stronger than the deck it's bolted down to. Make sure that if anything fails it's the deck or the anchor chain and not the winch!"

And he did just that.

The global Muir legend lives on.

> 66 *I am not just very lucky, but I am also proud and thankful to have worked with you! Thankful for all the doors you opened, and more importantly, the great people I got to know through you.* 99
>
> – MATTHEW JOHNSTON

BELOW: AFTER THE WIN
Westward on the slip, 24 January 1948, at Perce Coverdale's boatyard after winning her second Sydney to Hobart Yacht Race in a row. The fishing vessel in background is thought to be the Casilda. Photo: Bert Johnson, Jonothan and Diane Davis Collection.

APPENDIX

DESCENDENTS
of
ERNEST JACK "JOCK" MUIR

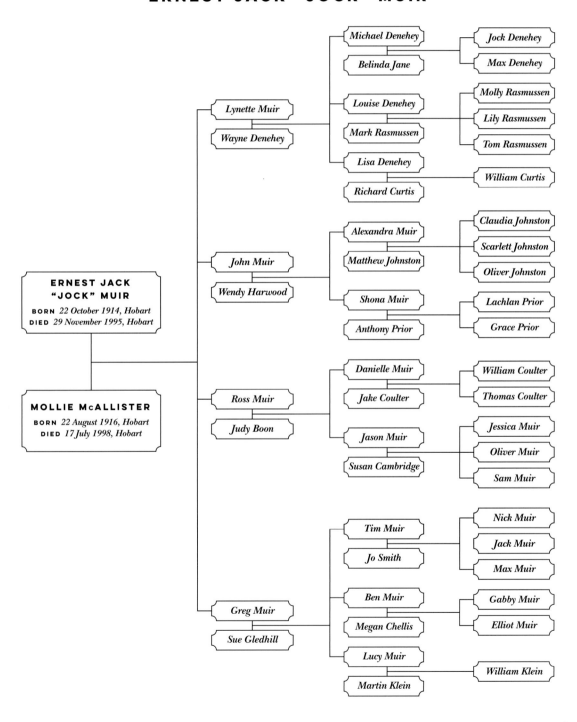

ERNEST JACK "JOCK" MUIR
BORN *22 October 1914, Hobart*
DIED *29 November 1995, Hobart*

MOLLIE McALLISTER
BORN *22 August 1916, Hobart*
DIED *17 July 1998, Hobart*

Lynette Muir
Wayne Denehey

Michael Denehey
Belinda Jane
Louise Denehey
Mark Rasmussen
Lisa Denehey
Richard Curtis

Jock Denehey
Max Denehey
Molly Rasmussen
Lily Rasmussen
Tom Rasmussen
William Curtis

John Muir
Wendy Harwood

Alexandra Muir
Matthew Johnston
Shona Muir
Anthony Prior

Claudia Johnston
Scarlett Johnston
Oliver Johnston
Lachlan Prior
Grace Prior

Ross Muir
Judy Boon

Danielle Muir
Jake Coulter
Jason Muir
Susan Cambridge

William Coulter
Thomas Coulter
Jessica Muir
Oliver Muir
Sam Muir

Greg Muir
Sue Gledhill

Tim Muir
Jo Smith
Ben Muir
Megan Chellis
Lucy Muir
Martin Klein

Nick Muir
Jack Muir
Max Muir
Gabby Muir
Elliot Muir
William Klein

MAX MUIR

Jock's brother and much loved uncle of John. Above, with Jock in 1994, watching the Sydney to Hobart Yacht race from Jock's home in Sandy Bay. Left, Max in 1990.

MAX MUIR

and

FAMILY

Much has been written about John's father Jock Muir, particularly in Jock's own book Maritime Reflections. In contrast, little has been written about Jock's younger brother and work mate Max Muir. This short biography highlights Max's career and personal life, and deserved inclusion in the Muir maritime legend.

Arthur Maxwell (Max) Muir was born 3 April 1916 at his parents' home, 39 Colville Street, Battery Point. He was the second son of Ernie and Elsie Muir. His older brother Ernest Jack "Jock" Muir was born on 22 October 1914. Three more children were born in the years succeeding Max's birth: Wallace born 1918, Bessie born 1922 and Donald born 1925.

Through his teenage years Max became a keen and accomplished sailor. The start of the 1931/32 yachting season saw Max first competing in the cadet dinghy *Mayfly*. Proving himself an accomplished sailor, Max was selected to represent Tasmania in the 1934 Stonehaven Cup, held in Sydney in January of that year. At the event Max helmed *Kittiwake* to equal third with a crew comprising D. McAllister and A. Mills. The following year saw Max, again in *Kittiwake*, selected as Tasmania's sole representative to compete for the 1935 Stonehaven Cup, held in Melbourne. Here Max and crew finished first, successfully returning the cup to Tasmania. Interestingly, of the 12 years in which the Stonehaven Cup had been sailed up until 1935, Tasmania won seven and drew one. Max's win in Melbourne followed in the footsteps of Jock who had won the 1933 Stonehaven Cup in Adelaide, also sailing in *Kittiwake*.

By the early 1940's Max was undertaking an apprenticeship with Percy Coverdale at his Battery Point boatyard. While with Percy, Max helped build the 52 ft auxiliary cruising yacht *Winston Churchill*, launched on 29 October 1941. The vessel was sadly lost in the disastrous 1998 Sydney to Hobart Yacht Race.

Following the launch of *Winston Churchill*, Max began work as a shipwright at Purdon and Featherstone, further along the Battery Point shore. It was World War II and the yard was busy with the construction of a new type of vessel: HDML, harbour defence motor launches. Three such launches were built by Purdon and Featherstone between 1943 and 1944 specifically for use as patrol vessels by the Royal Australian Navy. These were the *HMAS HDML* 1321, commissioned on 11 November 1943; the *HMAS HDML* 1322, commissioned on 17 January 1944; and the *HMAS HDML* 1327, commissioned on 19 May 1944.

On 1 February 1945 Purdon and Featherstone launched the sea ambulance *Koorakee*, one of the first vessels of its kind to be built in Australia. Measuring 80ft in length, the AH1730 *Koorakee* was capable of carrying a crew of 13, a staff of 10, with room for 33 patients. She was built to the order of Australian Army Medical Service and intended for service in the Pacific.

In 1948 Max joined his brother Jock at Muir's Battery Point Boatyard where the first boat to come off the slip, the 41ft *Lass O'Luss*, was launched on 4 December 1948, built to the order of John Colquhoun, a yachtsman of Sydney. Max remained working at the yard until his retirement in 1984. Two more vessels were completed in 1949 and 1950: the 47ft *Waltzing Matilda*, built to the order of Phil Davenport and launched on 2 July 1949, and the 47ft *Patsy*, built to the order of A. C. Cooper, vice-commodore of the Cruising Yacht Club of Australia, and launched on 4 April 1950. In the succeeding years Max was intimately involved with the many more well-known vessels built at Muir's Boatyard.

Working conditions at Muir's Boatyard, as well as other boatyards along the Battery Point shore, must often have been difficult in those early years. A photo of *Patsy* under construction in early 1950 provides a good example, showing how exposed working conditions were, and that the only protection from the elements was a tarpaulin or two pulled over the top of the large wooden frame. It is astounding to realise now that high quality boats and even ships were built under such difficult conditions, and had been for over a century at Battery Point. It is testament to the skill, perseverance and work ethic of people like Max and Jock Muir that they were.

Max Muir was not "just" a shipwright; he was also a true and skilled craftsman when it came to working with wood. More often than not he preferred to use hand tools where he could, rather than

LEFT

Max at work with hand plane, October 1958 – pencil sketch on marine plywood.

ABOVE

Unknown yacht near Piersons Point, travelling abeam of Max, Easter 1974 holidays.

OPPOSITE PAGE

Top: Young Max (on Ernie's shoulders) and Jock.
Middle: Max in his Jock Muir designed cray dinghy, 1960s.
Bottom: Purdon and Featherstone staff 1944. Max is front row, second from right. The original photo was presented to H.I. (Henry) Featherstone by staff on 26th July to commemorate his 74th birthday. Photo: Copy of original courtesy of Bill Foster.

power tools, as they gave him a much better feel for the material he was working on. Max's workmanship can still be seen today on boats such as *Trevassa* which is now owned by Jock's family and berthed at the Royal Yacht Club of Tasmania. A fitting memento that captures the essence of Max working with wood is a pencil sketch of him using a hand plane; the sketch was drawn by a customer at Muir's Boatyard in October 1958 on an "A4" sized piece of marine ply off-cut.

On a personal level, Max married Phyllis (Phyl) May Armstrong on 4 December 1943 at Holy Trinity Church in Hobart. Phyl was born 5 May 1918 in Greenford Village, now a part of Greater London. Her father, Charles Armstrong, served with Australia's 15th Battalion during World War 1. Charles returned to Australia in February 1919. Phyl's mother Mabel Thorpe was a War Bride, one of about 13,000 mostly English women who married WW1 Australian servicemen. Brides typically first met their future husbands while the servicemen were on leave or during training stints in England. Mabel and Charles had married in England; she was finally able to emigrate in 1921 and bring daughter Phyl out to Tasmania, settling with Charles at Cygnet.

Max and Phyl had two sons; Philip born in 1955 and Stephen ("Steve") born in 1959. Even before the kids arrived Max and Phyl holidayed on Bruny Island at Christmas and Easter. Some of the kids' earliest and most precious memories are of holidays spent on Bruny Island. The family would depart from Battery Point and head south in a little boat, come rain, hail or shine. In the early 1960s Max owned one of the Jock-designed cray dinghies with an open cabin at the front.

A little bad weather never discouraged Max; his sou'wester and wet weather gear were always ready to be donned. By the mid-1960s Max had sold the cray dinghy and in following years would head off to Bruny in a boat borrowed from friends such as Sonny Clark, Lindsay Masters and Alan Hume. Unlike the cray dinghy these boats were more suited to the family – especially in the wilder weather that sometimes hits the Derwent Estuary and D'Entrecasteaux Channel. The Easter 1974 holiday trip to Barnes Bay had Philip and Stephen a little worried as they watched a much larger yacht travelling abeam of them making very heavy weather of it while Max and the family thumped up and down in their little boat. Max of course was unflustered as he ducked the sheets of spray, and so mum and the boys soon regained their confidence.

Philip Muir's earliest recollections of those Bruny holidays are from when mum and dad would stay in dear old Mrs Lipscombe's house at Barnes Bay in the early 1960s. Every Easter Mrs Lipscombe would have a jar of clear pink home-made quince jelly for them to enjoy. Her house was located just above where the old jetty used to be near the northern end of Simmonds Bay; the house was demolished many years ago and replaced by the A-frame house that can be found there today.

There were some interesting characters in and around the Barnes Bay settlement in the 1960s. Nigel Denne was one. He lived "on the hill" about 300m up Church Road from the old jetty and Mrs Lipscombe's house. In the very early 1960s Nigel operated the local "petrol station," for want of a better description, which simply consisted of an old-type bowser topped by a large glass cylinder; a lever was manually operated to pump petrol up into the cylinder, and when the required volume had been pumped the glass cylinder was drained by gravity into the car's tank. Nigel also operated the local "shop," again for want of a better description, which was a tiny shed/outhouse stacked with wooden crates and shelves. Max or Phyl would occasionally take the kids for a walk up past the old community hall (now demolished) to Nigel's to buy something, usually a small handful of biscuits from the large biscuit tin. Philip's vague recollection is that the shop had rather limited supplies comprising not much more than biscuits, sugar, and tea! A shopping trip was more often an excuse for Max or Phyllis to socialise.

Brian Denne and his family, including several daughters, lived in the house next to Mrs Lipscombe. The ladies of the household would prepare various tasty goodies for the Barnes Bay regatta, and Philip especially remembers the coconut ice! A few years later the family moved up to the house on the hill, about 300m further north. Philip remembers Brian bringing a hessian sack of oysters to show Max one day; those oysters were the forerunners of what you can harvest from the shores of Simmonds Bay today if you want to have a feed.

Many a sailor or fisherman or other "boatie" would call into Barnes Bay and visit Max while the Muir family were there. Philip can recall one time in the early 1960s when about five or six fishing boats were tied together in a raft off the side of the old jetty, including Rupert Denne's Lyndenne, Clydie and Winnie Clayton's boat, and several more. Many cups of tea, or more likely glasses of beer, would have been consumed on that occasion!

Cyril Wisby, who lived off Killora Road above Quarantine Bay, was a good friend of Max. Cyril would deliver a bottle or two of farm milk to Max and Phyl at Mrs Lipscombe's house every couple of days. By the late 1960s Max and Phyl had changed their holiday lodgings and began to stay at Alan and Betty Clark's shack located at the end of Power Road, on the opposite side of Simmonds Bay just inside The Narrows. Cyril continued to deliver the milk. The new shack location was also convenient for Max because on a Saturday he could take Philip and Stephen for "a bit of a walk" up to Cyril's house and listen to the horse races with Cyril.

THIS PAGE

Left: Phyl, Max and Philip playing cards (euchre) in Fazackerley's shack, 1982; Right: Stephen's model yacht, Barnes Bay, early 1970's.

OPPOSITE PAGE

Top to bottom: Mrs Lipscombe's house, Barnes Bay, 1960s, site of today's A-frame house; Philip and Max, with Cyril Wisby and (?)grandson delivering milk to Clark's shack, Jan 1967; Bruny ferry Melba in Simmonds Bay, Jan 1967 with the boat Max had for the holidays at bottom left; Stephen and Philip on the Bruny ferry Mangana, Jan 1967; Max, Stephen and Philip, D'Entrecasteaux Channel day trip, Jan 1967.

Compared to today, Barnes Bay was a much busier settlement in the 1960s and 1970s, a time when the Bruny Island ferries ran from Kettering all the way into Barnes Bay. The *Melba* ran the service up until 1961, and from then until 1983 the *Mangana* was the main ferry with the *Melba* kept as a backup. Max knew the ferry captains and crew well. When a day's fishing had caught plenty of salmon Max would come alongside the *Mangana* when it docked at Barnes Bay and give the crew a feed of fish. Occasionally, for something a little different to do, Max and the kids would take a ride on the ferry over to Kettering, sometimes grabbing a snack from the shop to eat on the way back.

Almost invariably Max would trail salmon lines behind the boat as the family ventured out on day trips, ranging as far afield as the Iron Pot on some occasions. Couta were also on the catch list sometimes, particularly in earlier days. One time when trawling for salmon, a couta was caught because it was too greedy and had bitten into a salmon already hooked on a salmon line. The couta held onto the salmon tenaciously, never letting go as the line was pulled in, so in the end one fresh couta and one partly filleted salmon were landed in one hit!

Another memorable day saw Max and his guests catching couta by the dozen out in Storm Bay off Kelly's Point. Couta are large and messy so Max decided that those caught had to be thrown back into the dinghy; the dinghy could easily be washed out later. The couta "went mad" and Max ended up with half a dinghy full of them; there were so many that the dinghy didn't have much freeboard left. On the way home most of the couta were thrown up onto the Dennes Point jetty for locals and visitors to take home; the jetty was busy and many people had delicious couta for dinner for weeks to come!

Fishing with hand lines was also a favourite pastime, and favoured locations included places such as the north shore of Woodcutters Point, Cyril Wisby's "secret perch bank" off the end of Speculator Point, the south side of Bligh Point at Killora Bay, as well as less frequently visited locations like Rosebanks near Alexanders Bay and other places.

Max used to make his own lures for catching salmon, and people would often shake their heads in disbelief when he told them what the lure was, sometimes thinking that he was pulling their leg. The idea may have originated from seeing Phyllis "do her hair," we don't really know, but one type of ladies hair curler comprised a small perforated aluminium cylinder (about the size of a small cigarette) with a clip that swung over it and latched at the end. Max would remove the aluminium cylinder and slip it over the stem of the hook; it was as simple as that. On many an occasion Max's boat would be pulling in salmon left right and centre (literally! Because he'd trail three lines), while another boat nearby may be having no luck at all.

Kids start to grow up and do their own thing in their teens. By the 1980s Max and Phyl were still holidaying at Barnes Bay, as they did for almost the rest of their lives together, but most often Philip and Stephen were elsewhere. Philip, who was working interstate, and Stephen would sometimes join the pair for a few days when they could. Playing cards was a common evening pastime, with euchre being the favourite game. At this stage Max and Phyl began to stay at some of the other lodgings at Barnes Bay; Linda Graham's shack just below Clark's shack; Fazackerley's shack opposite Mrs Lipscombe's old house site; the former shop for ferry patrons which backs onto that shack; and the little shack out on the end of the point immediately north of where the old jetty used to be.

Some small event can often head people off in various unexpected directions. It must have been around 1968, soon after Greg Muir had finished sailing cadet dinghies, that Max said Jock was offering to let Philip sail the cadet dinghy *Kittiwake II* if he was interested. For some reason that Philip can't remember he declined the offer. It was a small decision which, in hindsight, was quite significant because it probably marked the start of Philip heading down a more academic path, through university, and into a career in geology. Had his decision gone the other way Philip might also have followed the more traditional Muir direction and become an accomplished sailor. As it is now though, he still loves being under sail but looks to his brother and cousins when experience counts!

By contrast Steve followed in the Muir tradition much more closely. During the early 1970s Jock taught Stephen the skills for designing and drawing boat plans. Initially he prepared drawings for model yachts, carved and built them in the "bread and butter" method, and sailed them on the Derwent and Channel – much the same as Jock and Max had done in the 1920s and 1930s.

Later Stephen completed a small number of plans for commercial fishing vessels and assisted Jock with the plans for the Snook 22 fibreglass yachts produced at the boatyards. One of the first of these, a bright green yacht named *Chento*, was used by Max during his holidays on Bruny Island and provided an opportunity for Stephen and Max to do some sailing together.

In 1973 Jock asked Max to join him on opening day of the sailing season. Being somewhat busy, Max suggested Stephen may like to go, which he did. From then on ocean racing became an integral part of life for Stephen. Jock had *Patsy* (by now known as *Patsy of Island Bay*) at the time and Stephen became the mainsheet hand on the vessel. This gave him strong exposure to offshore racing with a number of highly regarded crew such as Bill Watson, Adrian Gorringe, John Griggs and others.

Between 1975 and 1978 Stephen sailed on a number of offshore yachts including *Mirrabooka* (John Bennetto) and *Anaconda* (Guy Ellis). In 1979 he competed in his first Sydney to Hobart Yacht Race on board *Puss 'n Boots* (Hank Boot). Since then, between 1980 and 2004, Stephen competed in another 14 Sydney-Hobart races, crewing on board *Puss 'n Boots, Scorpio II* (John Fuglsang), *Roller Coaster* (John Fuglsang), *Margaret Rintoul II* (Roger Jackman), *Inch by Winch* (Joe Goddard), *Doctor Who* (Roger Jackman), and the later *Mirrabooka* (John Bennetto).

Over the years since starting with Jock on *Patsy*, Stephen has competed in most of the major local offshore races such as the Maria Island and Bruny Island races. He has had a long association with Roger Jackman and son Rod since 1985, and today he continues to sail on their yacht *Doctor Who*.

Brothers Max and Jock remained close throughout their retirement years, still sharing the love of boats. A photograph taken of the two of them in Jock's house on Churchill Avenue, Sandy Bay, while watching yachts approach the finish of the 1994 Sydney to Hobart seems to capture some of the essence of their close relationship. Max passed away on 4 April 1995, and Jock later the same year on 29 November; the close timing of their passing is a little uncanny when you recall that they both started their very close working relationship when Jock established the Muir Boatyard in 1948 and Max joined him that same year.

Max was survived by Phyllis who lived to see her two grandchildren grow up (Steve's kids, Katrina, born 1994, and Justin, born 1997). One of the last photos of Phyllis was taken on her 90th birthday at the Royal Tasmanian Botanical Gardens in Hobart with her sons and grandchildren. She passed away on 9 September 2009. ⚓

PATSY OF ISLAND BAY
Back in Jock's hands, with Stephen crewing, 1973-4.

ARNOLD

and

MICHAEL WHITE

Men and women who choose to earn a living from the sea, take on an inherently dangerous occupation. It is in fact, one of the most dangerous in the world, up there with underground miners and riggers on high rise construction projects. The industries where you are more likely to be seriously injured or killed than any other.

That reality does not seem to have been a factor in the chosen occupation of Tasmanian cray, giant crab and scallop fishing family, Arnold White and his son, Michael.

Arnold White decided to become a fisherman when he was 18 years old. He invested everything he had in his first boat, the *Mavis Anne*. It was not by any means what you would call 'flash.' It was a 21ft classic Huon pine and Tasmanian hardwood boat, built to last and to withstand rough seas. The motor was small, an 8hp Stuart Turner two stroke petrol engine. Not much bigger than a large ride-on lawn mower engine. The boat was built in Devonport on Tasmania's north west coast by Rozema Brothers. (The brothers were in the boat building business from 1949 until 1960.)

Arnold White: "I was a young bloke when I first started fishing at 18. I started on my own, on the *Mavis Anne*. I used to pull the cray pots up by hand and if they were full they would be really heavy. Some years later I went real modern and got a bit of a winch made up, out of a hand grinder, you know those hand ones with the emery wheel on it?

"After that it got really modern with hand made pot pulling motors and winches made from a steering box and worm gear out of a truck, until eventually we bought a manufactured pot puller from Phillip Island Engineering."

What Arnold doesn't tell you is that cray fishermen work in a risky business, they are at the mercy of wind and weather and unpredictable markets for their catch. (A Tasmanian cray fish is a local name for the Southern Rock Lobster.)

The fishermen usually set the pots close inshore, in and around rocky and inherently dangerous coastlines. They do set pots in deeper and more open water and use GPS technology to locate them, whether it be daylight or dark.

When the prices for crays are high, the cray boats can be seen heading out to sea in what some would describe as stormy and dangerous weather, risking life and limb to score a valuable catch.

Arnold white: "Just after we fitted our cray boat up with the latest in hydraulics, running the steering and pot hauling gear, I almost got wrecked on a rocky area called 'The Nuggets.' "

The Nuggets are three very small islands, lying east and a bit north of the internationally famous Freycinet National Park and its stunning beach at Wineglass Bay.

Arnold White: "Coming to terms with these new fangled hydraulics was a nightmare to start, until I got used to 'em. I know on my first trip, [using hydraulics, on a new boat called *Waubs Bay*] I was going to set our pots, just near the Nuggets. I was going to go between the islands where the passage is pretty narrow and suddenly, no bloody steering, none at all.

"Bloody oath. I didn't know whether to jump over the side, or what to do. I had no emergency steering in those days and I am out on my own as usual. There was nothing I could do except lift the hatch and go below to see if I could fix it before I hit the rocks. It turned out one of the taps on the hydraulic lines was turned off when it should have been turned on. So I fixed that, went back up and it was lovely. I thought, gawd... that was close."

66 *In her time **Dorothy Fay** would have to have been one of the fastest 42 footers on the coast. After that we upgraded to the boat we still use, the **Waubs Bay**, built at Rokeby about 1980 by Trevor Hardstaff to a Max Creese design in Steel!* 99

– ARNOLD WHITE, FISHERMAN

In the Tasmanian Seafood Industry News publication of October/ November, 2013, Tim Emery, Klaas Hartmann, Bridget Green, Caleb Gardner and John Tisdell from IMAS and the School of Economics and Finance at the University of Tasmania, published research finding that Australian fishing had the highest occupational fatality rate of any industry, (it was up there with logging and farming) and was six times more dangerous than average occupational hazards in other industries.

That fact didn't stop Arnold White's son Michael from following in his father's footsteps. The White family have had and still do have a close working relationship with the Muirs. Their second fishing boat, the *Dorothy Fay*, was a 42ft Jock Muir designed and built Huon Pine and Blue Gum ribbed fishing boat.

THE WHITE FAMILY

*Arnold (opposite, top) started fishing in the days when everything was done manually. His son Michael (left, above) has now taken over and along with his wife Debbie (above, second from left) runs a successful business catching crayfish, deep sea trevalla, scallops and giant crab off the Tasmanian east coast on their boat **Waubs Bay** (opposite, bottom).*

Arnold White: "In her time *Dorothy Fay* would have to have been one of the fastest 42 footers on the coast. After that we upgraded to the boat we still use, the Waubs Bay, built at Rokeby about 1980 by Trevor Hardstaff to a Max Creese design in Steel!

"I'm still waiting for the account from Max Creese for his design work, and have said on a number of occasions 'you haven't sent that bill yet for the design of the boat.' He generally says, 'I'll get around to it someday. You're not worried about it are you?' I said I wasn't.

"I don't think I will ever forget the fitout for the *Waubs Bay*. It was carried out at Muir's boatyard in Battery Point with the deadline being the opening of the cray season. We had about six weeks to get the boat fitted out, a normally impossible task."

John Muir: "Muir Boatyard shipwrights undertook this big project with a very tight deadline. The work included the timber fitout, a lot of fibre glass work, including freezers, a brine tank, bait freezer and a fit out of the forecastle. The wheelhouse,

accommodation, engine room and freezer room were all fitted out. Muir chandlery undertook the rigging, and supply of the ground tackle and set up the main mast and boom rigging. A. C. Gibson (Al) took care of all the DC electrics for the machinery and all the lighting. There were some really good hands back then working with the boatyard. Some that come to mind were Max Muir, Dave Wardrop, Jim Groves and Adam Brinton. I remember Joe Vaughan installed all the refrigeration."

Arnold White: "I remember being at the boatyard and there were a lot of men working on the boat. There were more jokers running around there than a busy schoolyard! Every other day John's hair was going whiter, Bob Harper's was too, trying to keep up with them all."

The comprehensive work undertaken by Muir Engineering would normally have taken 12 or 14 weeks, not this job. It's another indication of just how hard these men and women working in both the boatyard and support offices were prepared to work. The boats

THE EARLY FISHERMAN GETS THE CRAY

*Crew members of the **Waubs Bay** during a 2015 cray fishing trip off the east coast of Tasmania. Barry Crawford in yellow waders, and Michael White's brother Geoffrey White in orange waders.*

main engine was installed, as well as machining and alignment of the stern gear, installation of plumbing, wiring and exhausts. Installation of a 5LW Gardner auxiliary driving the hydraulics, to operate the anchor winch, pot and line haulers and an overside roller assembly. They installed a complete hydraulic system for the anchor winch, line hauler and power- assisted hydraulic steering. They fitted fuel line couplings and filters, mast and boom winches, customised above deck lifting winches and much more, all in six weeks.

Waubs Bay catches crayfish, deep sea trevalla, scallops and giant crab off the Tasmanian east coast, out over the continental shelf. Arnold says he doesn't go fishing anymore after he was told by his son, Michael, that 'he was a stick in the mud.'

Arnold White: "I said that's easy fixed, no trouble, I won't go out anymore. He only said 'it was only a joke Dad!' When I bought the cray fishing licence for *Waubs Bay*, it was for 38 pots. It cost me about £5000 for the entire licence, one pot now would cost about $50,000."

Michael White: "The bulk of our fishing using *Waubs Bay* are crayfish, giant crab and scallops. I have a crew of two people working full time, and a couple of others when we're scalloping. My brother Jeff also crews for me.

John Muir : "Arnold and now his son Mike and his brother Jeff have always maintained their fishing boats in A1 condition. Freshly painted every season, their boat has the appearance of a very well maintained motor yacht instead of a working fishing vessel.

"Working with the White family for over 40 years has been rewarding for myself, and also Brett Ross who continues to keep in touch with the Whites. Brett Ross managed Muir Engineering and Boatyard operations at Battery Point over a long period and continues to keep in touch with the Whites.

"I have a saying 'how lucky we are as people building boats. Our clients pay our wages and help us to fullfil our passion, it doesn't get any better than that!'" ⚓

INDEX

Abram, Nerilie 92
Abu Dhabi MAR 312-313
Acacia 22
Adela 287, 288, 289
Adelaide Boat Show 120,
Adix 14-16, 92, 121, 141, 143, 216, 218-220, 223-224, 252, 285, 291
ADM Shipyards 277, 312-313
Admiral's Cup 273, 276, 346
Advance Australia Foundation 170, 173
AH1730 Koorakee 402
AIG 309
Ainslie, Ben 357
Air 333
Akka 123
Al Emarat 277
Al Mirqab 236-237
Albatross 19
Alstom Yachts 322
Alec's Marine 133-134
Allen, John 207-208, 306
Alley Cat 244
Alliance & Leicester 309
Ambrosia 236
Amels Yachts 95, 155, 187, 189
America's Cup 150, 161-162, 170, 176, 182, 203, 239-240, 242, 244, 275, 357
American Bureau of Shipping 177
AMI Sales 113-134, 154
Amevi 237
Anaconda 406
Anaconda II 85
Anastasia 231, 236-237
Anastasia 3 237
Anderson AJ 234
Another Duchess 360
Apco Engineering 108-109, 136, 231, 233, 241, 244, 336, 376, 385
Apoise 327
Aquanita 257
Arcadia 276
Armstrong, Phyllis May 403
Armstrong, Charles 403
Astor 323, 361, 365
Astrolabe 98
Athos 284, 285, 287
Aussie Rules 182-183, 190, 208
Austal Ships 95, 132, 140, 156, 182, 208, 241, 277, 316, 345
Austrade 115-116
Australia II 161-162
Australian Army Medical Service 402
Australian Broadcasting Commission (ABC) 3, 7, 18, 51, 91, 203, 209, 316
Australian Bureau of Statistics 128, 311
Australian Defence Force Academy 339
Australian International Marine Export Group (AIMEX) 7, 114, 329, 334-335, 376
Australian Marketing Institute 170, 173
Australian National University 92
Australian Psychologists Association 311
Australian Trade Commission 160, 162, 170
Australian Wooden Boat Festival 115, 323, 338
Avatar 333
Azam Marine 246
Bailey, Tim 59
Balandra 106, 273, 346
Banks Smith, Wayne 363, 387
Bannenberg, Jon 182
Barnes-Keoghan, Ian 91
Barry-Cotter, Bill 197, 212, 224, 226, 227-228
Barwick, Bill 33

Batchelor, Mrs 78
Batt, Kenn 32, 92
Batt, Neall 31
Batt, W. P. "Skipper" 31-32
Bayliner 163, 193, 203
Bear Stearns 310
Belize 197, 200
Bellerive Yacht Club 362, 365
Belship 150, 152-153, 155, 158, 321
Benetti Shipyards 152-153, 182, 237
Benna, Steven 229
Bennetto, John 406
Bertram 147-149, 212
Bertrand, John 161, 357
Bevis, Winston 166, 341, 372
Biddulph, Steve 41, 77
Bindaree 346
Bijoux 154
Blackwood, Graham 346
Blundstone Boots 87
Boat Sales Tasmania 106, 395, 397
Bond, Alan 150, 161, 218, 244
Bonfiglioli 128, 130, 132, 152, 180-181
Bonfiglioli, Sonia 128
Boot, Hank 406
Bone, Jeni 319
Boral Group 211
Box, Richard 176, 239
Bracken and Swanson 225
Bradford & Bingley 309
Bradshaw, Gary 151, 231-233, 235
Brain, Brian 193
Brain (née Muir), Mary 193
Brand Tasmania 246
Bridges, Roy 33
Brinton, Adam 60, 69, 377, 409
Brooker, Alan 132-133
Brovera 276
Brown, Don 145
Brown, Peter 225
Brown, Stan 194
Brown, Trevor 87
Bruv's Bodyworks 78
Buckley, Bruce 92
Build Tech Supplies Pty Ltd 352
Buizen Yachts 94, 387
Buquebus 246, 266
Bureau of Meteorology 91, 92
Burnett family 5, 44, 85, 373
Burridge, Dudley 194
Cadbury's Chocolate Factory 87, 270
Cambria 170
Campbell, Jock 195
Campbell McBride, Elizabeth 20
Captain McKenzie 87
Caribbean Boat Factory 146-147
Caribbean Cruisers 120, 147-149, 228
Carnegie, Dale 290-291, 298
Carousel 273
Carter, Lyn 237
Carter, Wayne 237, 374
Carvey, Ray 229-230
Cascade Brewery 254
Cass, Darryl 134
Cass, Phillip 133, 134
Casy, J. A 201
Catalina Yachts 193
Chambers, Tim 36
Channel Craft 255, 257
Chapman, David 265, 338
Chapman, Richard 282, 384

Charisma 276
Charles Davis 31, 36
Chellis, Megan 399
Chento 406
Chernyaev, Anatoly 201
Chew, Matthew 356-357
Chicago Boat Show 113, 160-161, 193, 204
Chichester, Francis 123
Chindrina 346
Christensen Shipyards 204, 248, 285
Chugg, Phil 61, 62
Clark, Alan 404
Clark, Betty 404
Clark, Robert 54
Clark, Sonny 403
Clark family 405
Clayton, Clyde 404
Clayton, Winnie 404
Clifford, Kerry 5, 6
Clifford, Robert 5-6, 28, 31, 194-195, 197, 211, 241, 244-246, 260, 262, 266-267, 339, 345, 363, 375-376, 383, 385
Clinker Craft 224
Clinton, Bill 290
Clyde Marine 122-123
Cohan, Donald 273-274
Collins, Frank 167
Collins, Pat 87
Collins Marine 167
Colquhoun, John 38, 54, 402
Como 333
Compagnia Italiana Magneti Accessori (CIMA) 7, 160, 178-179, 180, 212
Connor, Dennis 275
Constellation 232-233, 236
Cooper, A. C 402
Cooper, Bill 265
Cooper, Brett 363
Cooper, Diane 265
Cooper, Michael 261-265, 338, 360, 363-365, 377, 379
Cooper family 45, 264, 265, 364, 365
Coulter (née Muir), Danielle 356, 399
Coulter, Jake 356, 399
Coulter, Tom 356, 399
Coulter, William 356, 399
Coverdale, Percy 5, 31, 34, 38, 401
Cramm Hydraulics 152, 155, 169, 216, 235, 280, 295-296
Cramm Yachting Systems 152, 155, 169, 216, 235, 280, 295-296
Cramp Brothers 77
Crawford, Barry 410
Creese, Max 395, 408-409
Creese, Peter 373
Creese family 373
Crichton-Brown, Robert 273
Crisp, Andrew 226, 276
Crisp, Tripper 275
Crowther Design 245
Cruising Yacht Club of Australia 402
Crusader 54
Cummins Diesel 299
Currie, Alastair 388
Curtis (née Denehey), Lisa 69, 358, 399
Curtis, Richard 358, 399
Curtis, William 358-359, 399
Cushion, Lance 319
Cutty Sark 91
Cyclone 360, 363, 366
Damen, Mr 155
Damen family 155
Damen Shipyard 155, 158
Danko, William 128

Darcey, Bruce 54, 167
Darsea 154
Davenport, Phil 402
Davis, Harry 214
De Vries, Henk 329
De Vries, Tom 234
De Vries family 234
Degraves, Peter 19, 254
Delta Marine 248, 285
Delta Shipyard 247, 248, 285, 317
Denehey, Louise 69, 399
Denehey (née Jane), Belinda 399
Denehey, Jock 358, 399
Denehey (née Muir), Lynette 45, 49, 66-69, 84, 261, 337, 346, 358-359, 399
Denehey, Max 358, 399
Denehey, Michael 69, 358, 399
Denehey, Wayne 54, 67-69, 358, 359, 367, 399
Denne, Brian 404
Denne, Nigel 404
Dennis, CJ 6
Derwent Foundry 108, 136
Derwent Sailing Squadron 44, 50, 346
Desiree 232
Det Norske Veritas 177-178, 262
Devine, Ron 244, 246
Diana 247, 258
Didocha, Joe 128, 138-139, 182, 237, 308
Di Martino, Don 123, 138, 170-171, 197, 212, 228, 237, 267, 270-271
Dickinson, Andrew 312-313, 388
Dixon, Rodger 237-238, 387
DML Plymouth 304
Doctor Who 406
Don Hoyt Gorman 328
Dorothy Fay 346, 408-409
Doyle Sails 106, 395, 397
Drager, Danny 212
Duffield, Russell 57, 59-60, 98, 108, 126, 150, 376
Duncan, Elizabeth 19-20, 22, 26
Duncan, James 19
Dwyer, Ma 6, 44, 51-52
Dylan, Bob 18
Edwards, MaryAnne 329, 334, 336, 376
Edwards family 44
Eira 123
EJ Milde and Co. 120
Elizabeth & Henry 20
Electrolytic Zinc Company (Nyrstar) 51, 73, 387
Ellis, Guy 85, 406
Emery, Tim 408
Endeavour Yachts 193
European Council 201
European Union 86, 201, 311
Even 63
Evans, Chris 324-325
Export Roo 264-265, 338
Fadden, Arthur 89
Fader, Edward 261
Fader, Richard 78-79, 112, 374, 393
Fannie Mae 309
Fantasy 194
Farr, Bruce 61
Farr Fetched 61-62, 377
Fazackerley family 405
Feadship 234-235, 314, 329, 332
Federal Reserve Bank of Kansas City 201
FEEBE Boarding Equipment 152, 295-298
Feenstra, Philippus (Philip) 295-298, 330
Field, Michael 172
Fleming, Kevin 160-161, 163, 203, 214
Fleming, Nick 124, 143
Fleming Marine 100
Fleming Wind Vane 161, 163
Flintoff, Malcolm 113, 134
Flintoff, Michael 113
Flintoff, Rob 113, 132-134, 154

Florence, Pete 207-208, 251
Flynn, Errol 33
Fogagnolo, Jocelyn 26, 32, 63
Ford, Bob 274
Ford, Henry 269, 317
Fort Lauderdale Boat Show 144, 168-169, 193, 204, 208, 216, 290, 316-317, 323, 334, 343, 392
Fortis 309
Foster, Bill 38, 44, 57, 66, 403, 415
FR Duffield Manufacturing 98
Franklin, Benjamin 310
Fraser, Malcolm 137
Fraser Sails 261
Freddie Mac 309
Frey, Herbie 346
Frigrite 352
Fromstock Filius 123
Fuglsang, Chris 54, 365, 368, 376
Fuglsang, John 406
Gabriel, Les 273
Gantner, Carrillo 265
Gardner, Caleb 408
Gatty, Harold 33
Gear, Bob 98
Genoa International Boat Show 154-155, 160, 290, 343
Gershwin, George 291
Gibson, A. C 409
Gibson, George 29, 37
Gillard, Julia 316
Ginton, Mr 252
Ginton Naval Architects 252
Go 332
Goddard, Joe 406
Goldberg, Abe 203
Goldilocks 117
Gorbachev, President 201
Gorringe, Adrian 44, 47, 50-51, 54, 80, 84, 346, 406
Gorringe, Reg 50
Gorringe, Trevor 50
Gorringe Bros 50, 53
Gorringe family 50
Goss, Gail 31, 386
Goss, Paul 14-17, 92, 121, 218-220, 223, 285, 291
Goward, Russell 203
Graham, Kenneth 277
Graham, Linda 405
Grainger, Mike 259, 260-262, 264, 377, 393
Gray, Robin 150
Green, Bridget 408
Greene, Tim 57
Griffin 225
Griggs, Bruce 54
Griggs, John 44, 54, 57, 341, 346, 406
Griggs, Nick 387
Griggs, Stewart 341
Grinings family 244
Groom, Harold 67
Groves, Jim 409
Haack, Buddy 317
Hagar, Andrew 275
Haig, Andrew 41
Hale, Harry 382-383
Hale, Mathew 380, 381, 383,
Hale family 382-383
Halo 333
Halvorsen 225
Haigh, William 32
Hamilton Island Race Week 116-117, 276, 340, 345, 357, 360-367
Hampshire II 330
Handa Isle 26
Hardstaff, Trevor 408-409
Hardy, Max 92
Harper, Bob 91, 99, 108, 116, 124-125, 130, 132, 140, 143-145, 218-219, 237, 409
Hartmann, Klaas 408
Harwood, Chris 371

Harwood, Betty 144-145, 169, 347-348
Harwood, Cliff 144-145, 169, 348
Hawke, Bob 137, 150, 203
Haygarth, Bob 225
Hazell, Don 126, 225, 256
Hazell, Rowley 126
Hazell Bros. 126
HBOS 309
Heimstra, Reinhardt 153
Helios 236-237
Hempel Paints 121-122
Henry, Ken 316
Hercus, Phillip 245
Hickey, Peter 120
Hickling, Ken 328
High Roller 150, 276
Hintok 53, 58
Hitachi Seiki 171
HMAS HDML 1321 402
HMAS HDML 1322 402
HMAS HDML 1327 402
Hoban, Warwick 357
Hobart Plating Company 233
Hodgman, Michael 170
Hodgson, Peter 265
Hoek, Andre 285
Hollingsworth, Paul 186, 196, 270-273, 392
Holmes, Florence 26
Horne, Terry 166
Howells, Valentine (Val) 121-123, 190, 211
Howells, Eira 121, 123
Hudson, Chris 26, 32, 63
Hudspeth, Audrey 28, 34, 40
Hume, Alan 403
Hurd, Paul 54, 78, 85, 117, 119, 136, 324, 367
Hutchen, David 357
Ilona 95, 186, 187-192, 196, 272
IMTEC 176, 204
Imtra 162, 168-169, 194, 203, 248, 285, 392
Incat Crowther 245
Incat Designs 245
Inglis Smith 100
Inch by Winch 406
Indian Empress 231, 236-237
Innes-Jones, Evan 176
Innes-Jones, Rex 176
Interferry 262
International Catamarans (Incat) 6, 140, 197, 211, 241-246, 259-260, 266-267, 345, 385
International Marine 114, 119, 148-149, 193
International Maritime Organization 262
International Super-yacht Society 319
Isabella 19
Issue 154
IXL Jam Factory 125
Jachtbouw, Holland 285
Jackman, Angie 94
Jackman, Rodney (Rod) 57, 94, 98-99
Jackman, Roger 406
Janes, Roger 246
Jarrod, Kevin 63
Jeltes, Jeroen 150-153, 393
Jessica 218,
JFA Shipyards 322
Johnston (née Muir), Alexandra (Alex) 53, 58, 76, 114-115, 145-146, 161, 186, 238, 257, 263, 272, 327, 337-340, 342-346, 349-351, 372-374, 379, 390, 399
Johnston, Claudia 351, 399
Johnston, Matthew 114-115, 207, 210, 239-240, 265, 283, 294-295, 298, 324, 327, 338, 340, 342, 351, 363, 384, 387, 390-394, 398-399
Johnston, Oliver 351, 399
Johnston, Scarlott 351, 399
Juicy Isle 262, 264-265, 365
Kathleen Anne 332
Keal, Stephen 360, 363
Keating, Paul 137, 172, 202-203, 209

Kelly, Paul 209
Keogh, John 150
Khashoggi, Adnan 182
Kialoa III 226, 276
Kiella 258
Kilimanjaro VI 244-246
Kilroy, Jim 226
Kirkland, Dr. Tom 167
Kiss 333
Kitney, Damon 265
Kittiwake 31-32, 401
Kittiwake II 406
Kittiwake 3 (K3) 32
Klein (née Muir), Lucy 353-354, 399
Klein, Martin 354, 399
Klein, William 354, 399
Kogo 322
Kokomo 314
Kolstrands 163
Koninklijke Schelde Groep BV 277, 313
Kookaburra 3 244
Koukoulas, Stephen 316
Koulopoulos, Tom 375-376
Kramer, Hans 76
Kurrewa IV 63
Kusnetz, Marc 201
Lady Christine 233, 236-237
Lady Nelson 30, 98, 346
Lake Illawarra 211, 352
Lamprill, Jap Head 273
Laing, Bob "Pix" 55, 84, 365-367,
Larisa 333
Lass O'Luss 38, 54, 344, 402
Laurel 247-249, 317
Lehman Bros. 198
Leitch, William 33
Lewis, Hughey 363
Lewis, Malcolm 128, 130, 132, 180
Lewmar Marine 122
Lewmar Scotland 123, 150, 375
Liferaft Systems Australia 259-262
Lighthouse Marine 176-177, 239
Lipscombe, Mrs 404-405
Little Devil 266
Lloyds 157, 177, 186, 188, 190, 219-220, 233
Lofrans 160, 168
Lofrans family 160
Long Beach Boat Show 160-163, 204
Longhurst, Rodney 198, 200-201
Lusty & Blundell 176-177, 239
Lyndenne 404
Lyons, Enid 33
Macfarlane, Ian 209
Maintenance Systems Pty Ltd 413, 352
Mackel, Chris 171
Malcolm 22
Mammarella, Mirko 294
Mangana 405
Mant, Alistair 28, 194, 266-267
Mara Jane 167,
Margaret Rintoul II 406
Marine Equipment Trade Show (METS) 115, 144,
162-163, 193, 207-208, 218, 234, 287, 291, 298-299,
317, 319, 321, 334-335, 392
Mariner 149, 208, 212, 225-228
Maritimo 149, 226-228
Martin, Roger 63
Marwood, Jim 87
Masters, Lindsay 403
Mathiason, Nick 309-311
Maxwell Winches 122, 132, 173, 176, 218, 238-239,
306, 310, 375
Maxwell Cundy 122
Mavis Anne 407
May Queen 50
Mayer, Fred 247-251, 298, 310, 321, 343
Mayer, Kim 209, 248, 251

Mayfly 31, 32, 401
Mays, Nicole 4, 246, 415, 416
McAllister, D 401
McAllister, Dave 32
McAllister, Don 35, 40, 45, 66
McKee, Robert 194
McLaren, Bob 102, 104,
McNaughton, Craig 112, 123, 189-190, 214, 216, 325
McQueen, David 13, 94-95, 132, 181-184, 186, 188,
190, 272
Melba 51, 405
Melbourne Boat Show 107, 110, 114, 117, 120, 148
Melicent 225, 257
Mena, Lopez 246
Mercedes 132
Merkel, Angela 201
Merrill Lynch 309
Metal Manipulation 396
Miami Boat Show 115-116, 144, 162, 168, 204, 207,
290, 343
Michael, Chris 91, 108, 125, 133, 140, 157, 162, 216,
234, 236-237, 298
Milde, Mr 120
Mills, A 401
Minty's 90
Mirrabooka 406
Mistral V 275-276
Monaco Boat Show 144, 151, 154, 193, 207, 251,
282, 290-291, 294-296, 298, 300, 306, 314, 334, 344,
384, 390-392
Moonen Shipyards 152, 154
Moon Sand 332
Moon Sand Too 332
Morten, Murray 164, 173, 176-177, 239-240
Moxey, Wes 197-200
Muir (née Jenkins), Agnes 20
Muir, Ben 353-355, 399
Muir, Bessie 401
Muir, Don 28, 36, 45, 98, 396, 401
Muir, Elliot 354, 399
Muir, Elsie 401
Muir, Ernie 22, 26, 28-29, 31, 34, 39, 44-45, 84-86, 98,
396, 401, 403
Muir, Gabby 354, 399
Muir, Greg 31, 32-33, 38, 45, 47, 54, 57, 59-62, 82, 84-
85, 93, 98, 116, 208, 261-263, 274, 337, 346, 352-356,
360, 362-363, 365, 372-373, 377, 379, 386, 399, 406
Muir, Jack 354, 399
Muir, Jason 356-357, 399
Muir, Jessica 357, 399
Muir (née Smith), Jo 354, 399
Muir, Jock 16-17, 26, 28-29, 31-40, 45, 47, 49, 52-54,
58-60, 63, 66-70, 75, 79-80, 82-87, 89, 92, 94, 98-100,
102, 104-106, 117, 167, 181, 194-196, 226, 238, 247,
254, 260-264, 273, 339, 344-346, 352, 357, 365,
367-368, 376-377, 379, 384, 393, 395-396, 398-399,
400-404, 406, 408
Muir (née Boon), Judy 356, 379, 399
Muir, Justin 406
Muir, Katrina 406
Muir, Max 17, 34, 167, 400-402, 409
Muir, Max (Junior) 354, 399
Muir (née Chellis), Megan
Muir (née McAllister), Mollie 33, 36-37, 38-39, 45, 47, 53,
58, 66-67, 69, 80, 84, 98, 264, 348, 365, 379, 384, 396, 399
Muir, Nick 354, 399
Muir, Oliver 357, 399
Muir, Philip 4, 69, 403-406, 415
Muir, Phyllis 69, 403-406
Muir, Ross 31, 33-34, 37, 39-40, 42, 45, 47, 51, 54,
56-57, 59-63, 66, 70, 77, 79-80, 82, 84-85, 98, 116, 119,
210, 237, 260-264, 274, 337, 346, 352-353, 355-356,
360, 362-365, 373, 377, 379, 386, 393, 399
Muir, Sam 357, 399
Muir, Stephen (Steve) 69, 403-406
Muir (née Gledhill), Sue 353-354, 357, 399
Muir (née Cambridge), Susan 357, 399
Muir, Tim 353, 354-355, 399
Muir, Wallace 28-29, 47, 51, 83, 98, 396, 401

Muir (née Harwood), Wendy 3, 5, 6, 35-36, 53, 58-59,
76-77, 106, 114, 117, 119, 125-126, 128, 132, 144-
146, 149, 165-166, 168-170, 177-179, 203, 206, 228,
258, 261, 263-264, 270, 291-292, 299, 311, 327, 337,
338-341, 344-351, 353, 371-374, 379, 386-387, 392,
394-395, 397-399,
Muir, William Jenkins 19, 20, 22, 26
Muir Sailmakers 260
Mundle, Rob 357
Mure, David 255
Mure, George 255-257, 259
Mure, Jill 255-258
Mure, Judy 255, 257
Mure, Will 255, 259
Mure family 254-256
Mures Fish House 255, 257-258
Mures Seafood Centre 254
Mures Upperdeck 257
Murray, Alistair 114-117, 170,
Murray, Henry 33
Myer Family Company 265
Myer Family Investments 265
Nabila 182
Natal Queen 26
Neville, Dick 275-276
Newman, "Chooky" 5
New York Yacht Club 150
News Limited 311
NHL Hogeschool 295
Nichols, Doug 78
Nilsson 122
Norman, Greg 132, 182, 190, 208
Norske Skog 387
North West Bay Ships 245
Northern Rock 310
Norton, Duncan 176, 214, 234, 335
NQEA 157, 216
Oatley, Bob 360
Oatley family 360
O'Brien, Kerry 203
O'Donoghue, Leon 357
Oceanco 151, 230, 231-237
Oceanfast 94, 132, 181-184, 190, 216, 317
Ocean Mercury 333
Octopus 319
Okazaki family 116-117
Osaka Boat Show 116, 380
Overstreet, Harry A. 290
Pacha 273
Padgett, Ken 210-212, 215, 227, 228, 324, 325, 342, 377
Padgett, Leonie 212, 215
Page, Jason 312, 324
Pajak, Georgie 3, 18, 415, 416
Palfrey, Andrew 357
Palm Beach Motor Yachts 323
Parry Boat Builders 224
Part VI 182
Pastoor, Ben 76
Patsy (of Island Bay) 49, 98, 402, 406
Pearl + Co 258
Pegasus 236, 237
Pendennis Shipyard 216, 218, 220, 223, 237, 387, 288,
305, 306, 308
Pepping, Gerry 285-288
Perkins, Alan 108, 195, 336,
Perkins, Andrew 90, 108, 109, 135, 136, 232, 233, 336,
376, 385,
Perkins, Bill 90
Perkins, Michael 208, 209
Pettitt, Ian 298, 299,
Pettitt, Simon 234, 298, 299, 300, 302, 304, 306, 318,
321, 335, 342, 344, 384
Philp, Colin 37
Pierrejean Design Studio 313
Plastimo ISA 193
Plymar Sales 132, 133,
Pomati, Giovanni 178
Pomati, Luigi 154, 155, 160, 178, 179, 180,

Postal, Sergei 317, 319, 335, 344
Potter, Lyndon 128, 136, 237, 308, 314, 315, 373
Prior, Anthony 345, 351, 399
Prior, Grace 351, 399
Prior, Lachlan 351, 399
Prior (née Muir), Shona 53, 58, 76, 103, 114, 144-145, 168-169, 263, 337-341, 344-345, 347, 349-350, 373-374, 379, 399
Probin, Paul 77, 78, 44,
Purdon, Mick 260
Purdon, Sam 260
Purdon Engineering 138
Purdon's Boatyard 260, 352
Purdon and Featherstone 79, 374, 401, 402, 403
Puss 'n Boots 406
Quantum Hydraulics 207, 208, 209, 251, 306
Queen Mary II 322
Queen Mavia 236
Quilkey 225
Rachtman, Peter 160, 162-164, 167, 203, 334
Randall family 5, 257,
Rasmussen, Lily 358, 399
Rasmussen (née Denehey), Louise 69, 358, 399
Rasmussen, Mark 358, 399
Rasmussen, Molly 358, 399
Rasmussen, Tom 358-359, 399
Rasselas 234, 328-329
Rebel 54
Reece, Eric 33, 74
Retfort Marine 193
Retlas Bronze 94, 99, 108, 136, 219, 385
Reserve Bank of Australia 137, 203, 209,
Richardson, Toby 244-247, 275
Richardson Devine Marine 244, 246, 275
Riviera 149, 197-201, 212, 225, 227-228, 247,
Robe, Robert 346
Roberts, Patrick 95, 157, 237
Roberts, Richard 201
Robinson, Jim 74
ROCK IT 333
Roller Coaster 406
Ronstan Marine 114-116, 170,
Ross, Brett 143, 237-238, 271, 369, 370, 371, 372, 410
Rothwell, John 345
Royal Bank of Scotland 309
Royal de Vries Shipyard 234, 316, 329
Royal Perth Yacht Club 150
Royal Schelde Shipyard 277, 313
Royal Van Lent 316, 329
Royal Yacht Club of Tasmania 32, 44, 50, 59, 98, 167, 210, 273, 403
Rozema Brothers 407
Rudd, Kevin 316
Ryder-Turner, David 194, 195
Ryman, Ken 59
Sailor's Corner 173, 176, 177, 239
Saltzman Chafetz, Janet 386
Samuel Plimsoll 19, 21
Sanctuary Cove Boat Show 122, 210, 212, 214-215, 228, 290, 324-325, 342, 344
Sandy Bay Sailing Club 218
Sattler, John 170, 237
Saunders and Ward 241, 268, 379
Savannah 333
Scales, Margot 339, 341
Scholten, Jos 287, 288
Scorpio II 406
Sea Falcon 247
Sea Owl 331, 333
Shamoun 286, 287, 288
Shilo 54, 368
Shemara 302, 304
Shipwright's Arms Hotel 44, 49, 78, 262
Shonandra 17, 58, 65, 69, 93, 104, 144-146, 160, 210, 238, 341, 346-349, 360, 367, 370, 372
Signorini, Luca 291, 294, 384
Silk and Textiles 87

Silverfast 307
Simpson Lawrence 100, 114, 122, 123, 150, 162, 170, 215
Singapore Boat Show 107, 117, 124, 128, 130, 132
Single-Handed Trans-Atlantic Race 123
Skase, Christopher 203
Skeels and Perkins 90, 108, 135, 136, 165, 231, 232, 233, 241, 336, 376, 385
Skeels, Selwyn 90
Smith, Bucky 357
Smith, Dick 110
Smith, Ian 364
Sorcery 276
South Pacific Associates (So-Pac) 193, 162, 163, 193, 194, 203, 204
Souter, W.A. and Sons 181
Southern Maid 37
Sparkman & Stephens 60, 226
Spooner, Arch 146
Spooner, Barry 120, 146- 148
Spooner, Richard 147
Stargate I 233, 236
Stargate II 233, 236
Starke, Dick 76
Stanley, Tom 128
Steber, Alan 101, 110
Steber, Bruce 100, 101, 224
Steber, Neville 224
Steber family 101, 228
Steber Group 101
Stebercraft 100, 101, 110, 120, 224, 228
Steel 305-306, 308
Steelfire 138-141, 143
Stevens, Glenn 316
Stocks, Ian 162, 250, 271, 308, 312, 336, 372, 379, 388-389
Sthoemer, Conrad 342
Strathleen 167
Stratus 54, 365, 368
Studley, Jim 169, 339
Sturrock, Jock 357
Sullivans Cove Ferry Company 266
Sunrise 233, 236-237
Swift141 312, 313, 389
Sycara V 151, 280, 282-283
Sydney Boat Show 112, 119, 121, 122, 176, 212, 214, 216
Sydney to Hobart Yacht Race 6, 17, 28-29, 37-39, 54, 61-63, 65, 68-69, 80, 84, 92, 124, 226, 254, 267, 273, 276, 340, 344-346, 368, 396, 398, 400-401, 406
Tabarly, Eric 123
Tango 332
Tasman 19, 246, 254
Tasmanian Archive and Heritage Office 52
Tasmanian Development Authority 244, 385
Tatlow, Mike 51, 52
Tatoosh Marine 162, 163
Taylor, Jeff 238, 387, 388, 389, 390, 395
Taylor Bros. 261, 395
Ta Shing 162
TBS Marine 291, 294
Telecom 173
Telstra 177, 197, 368
Thatcher, Margaret 202
Thorpe, Mabel 403
Tisdell, John 408
Tokyo Boat Show 116, 170-171
Trevassa 51, 54, 56- 61, 89, 98-99, 106, 108, 364, 376, 386, 403
Trickey, Michael 227, 324-325, 328, 342, 377
Trident 314, 332
Trilby 2 60
Trinity Yachts 248-249, 251, 285, 310
Triple Seven 200, 201, 203
Triton 99, 248
Trump Princess 182
TT Line 259, 262

Tully 257
Turner, David 210
Unibrass Brython 123
United States Army 36
University of Tasmania 125, 408
US Superyacht Association 329
USS Carl Vinson 340,
Van der Staat 346
Van Diemen 106
Van Diemen III 274
Van Diemen (Police Vessel) 159
Van Diemen's Land Bank 34
Vanish 332
van Ketel, Ilja 252
Van Niewenhuisen, Andy 60
Vaughan, Robert 226, 273- 276, 395
Vaughan, Joe 409
Veenman, Gert 285-286,
Venom 82, 84, 346
Venter, Johan 196,
Wake 36-37
Walter, Athol 60
Waltzing Matilda 63, 106, 402
Walsh, David 339
Wardrop, Dave 57, 59, 67, 409
Watson, Bill 406,
Watson, Mr 40, 41, 44
Waubs Bay 103, 346, 368, 370-371, 408-410
Webb, Dave 128, 241, 267-270, 379-380
Websters, A. G., and Woolgrowers 35, 74-76, 78, 82-83, 86, 377, 382
Weindorfer, Gustav 33
Wells, Chris 220
Wells, Nick 226, 275
Wellington Steelworks 396
Wertheimer, Dr. Michael 166
Westward 28, 29, 34, 37, 38, 39, 63, 396, 398
Westward II 59, 94, 166, 216, 251, 347, 350, 359, 372, 387
Westwind 36, 39
White, Arnold 346, 370, 407- 410
White, Michael 407, 410
White, Geoffrey 410
White, Ted 44-45, 57
Whitlam, Gough 137
Whitlock Steering 123
Whitworth, Craig 119-120
Wilce, Hillary 280
Wiekens, Henk 237, 287
Wild Wave 63, 69, 80
Williams, Cedric 224, 225
Williams, Greg 360, 362-364,
Williams, Keith 357
Wilson, Mike 210, 364
Windward Passage 276
Winston Churchill 401
Wisby, Cyril 404-405
Wood, Fiona 31
Worshipful Company of Shipwrights 94
Wyatt, Paul 356-357
XXXX 218
Yacht Distributors 33, 261, 263, 352, 353, 379
Yas 277, 313, 388, 389
Yalla 284
Yersin 319-320, 324
YD Water Sports 352-353
Yonca-Onuk 159
Zak, Nikolaus 39-40, 44

MIKE SWINSON
Writing

GEORGIE PAJAK
Compilation & Design

NICOLE MAYS
Historical Research & Writing

PHIL MUIR
Content, Organisation & Cataloguing

Acknowledgements

Bringing an enormous project like this to fruition is no easy task, and it wouldn't have been possible to wade through such an enormous body of material without the hard-working and talented team of people involved.

Mike handled this enormous task with grace and patience at every turn – and there were plenty of turns. Writing, re-writing, and re-writing again, all with the same enthusiasm he had at the outset. The enormous volume of rough material Mike was presented with would make a lesser man weak at the knees. Wrapping your head around so much information, on an unfamiliar and very technical topic, really takes a special kind of brain. His ability to capture the spirit of John's stories and the colourful characters within such a captivating industry really deserves special commendation.

Nicole Mays must be the world's best time-manager – juggling a full time job, young children, and researching and writing historical maritime books in her 'spare time.' She still managed to find time to promptly review chapters of this book at every stage, and generously shared her own research material with us.

A very special thanks must go to Phil Muir for his unwavering assistance with systemising the thousands of photographs collected during this project. His patience and organisational skills have been inspirational and I truly could not have completed the book layout in so short a time frame without his help.

Bill Foster's beautifully kept photos, and long memories of Jock, Max and all the Muir family, were a huge help in piecing together the story.

Lyndon Potter and Brett Ross were incredibly helpful in naming employees in older photos. We haven't been able to name every single person but if you recognise yourself in any of these, please understand we tried our best to find out who you are.

Joanne Bull promptly provided the greatly appreciated transcription work for some of the longer interviews undertaken. Such a wonderful time saver!

We cannot thank the contributors of photos, stories, anecdotes and technical information enough. Close to 100 shipyards, boat designer, builders, suppliers, customers, distributors, sales representatives, and former and current employees contributed their own time to this story. They generously provided photos from their own collections, sat down with us for interviews, spent time on the phone with me, and took the time to write down their thoughts and feelings about John and Muir products. Many from the 'old school' of wooden boat building were keen to have their stories heard and recorded for posterity. I wish we could have included all of them, but perhaps that's another book.

There are, of course, always things in any story you cannot bring to the public eye. We had a great time hearing about them but some things must remain as 'locker room conversations.'

Lastly, a very big thank you to John Muir and his family for giving us all the opportunity to work on such a fascinating and challenging project. It truly has been a 'once in a lifetime' experience.

GEORGIE PAJAK
October 2016

Written by Mike Swinson
Assisted by Nicole Mays
Book design by Georgie Pajak at SAMBATIKI Design

Published by Forty South Publishing
www.fortysouth.com.au

Printed by Choice Printing Group
www.choiceprintgroup.com

Maps on pages 8 and 9 based on information by Geoscience Australia

COVER IMAGE

John on the foredeck of MY **Ilona**, *2005, following installation and commissioning of the Muir VRC22000 anchor winches.*

BLOOD, SWEAT & THE SEA

"It's not how much money we make that ultimately makes us happy between nine and five. It's whether or not our work fulfills us."

– Malcolm Gladwell,
Outliers: The Story of Success

He flattened fear, built an international business and succeeded against the odds.

This book is about the life of John Muir who winched the world from down under. From humble beginnings in a simple shed at his father's boatyard in Battery Point, Tasmania, to international recognition amongst the builders and owners of an amazing array of sea-going vessels around the world.

His winches are renowned for their quality and he for his inspirational work ethic. This book details the family, friends, employees and colleagues that formed the basis of his success.